T0385133

THE
INDIAN
COOKERY
COURSE

MONISHA BHARADWAJ is a qualified chef and an award-winning author. She was Guild of Food Writers' Cookery Writer of the Year in 2003, *Stylish Indian in Minutes* won the Guild of Food Writers' Cookery Book of the Year and *The Indian Pantry* won a prestigious silver medal at Germany's Deutschland Akademie ausgezeichnet. She runs a successful Indian cookery school in London called Cooking With Monisha (www.cookingwithmonisha.com) and teaches at some of the UK's top cookery schools. Monisha has been Guest Chef at Benares, a Michelin star restaurant in London and at the Intercontinental Hotel, Park Lane. She is often invited to judge food events such as the Great Taste Awards and has lectured at SOAS, University of London, about 'The History and Culture of India through its Food'.

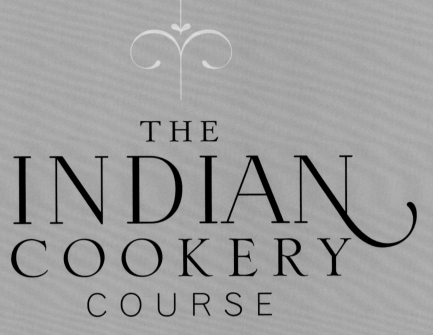

THE
INDIAN
COOKERY
COURSE

TECHNIQUES + MASTERCLASSES + INGREDIENTS + 300 RECIPES

Monisha Bharadwaj

PHOTOGRAPHY BY GARETH MORGANS

KYLE BOOKS

DEDICATION

※

For Arrush and India, with all my love, always

An Hachette UK Company
www.hachette.co.uk

First published in Great Britain in 2016 by Kyle Books, an imprint of Octopus Publishing Group Ltd
Carmelite House, 50 Victoria Embankment, London, EC4Y 0DZ
www.kylebooks.co.uk

11

ISBN: 978 0 85783 328 0

A CIP catalogue record for this title is available from the British Library

Monisha Bharadwaj is hereby identified as the author of this work in accordance with Section 77 of the Copyright, Designs and Patents Act 1988.

Text © Monisha Bharadwaj 2016   Photographs © Gareth Morgans 2016 except those listed on page 496   Design © Kyle Books 2016
Map illustration (page 15) © Jamie Whyte 2016

Editor: Vicky Orchard Editorial assistant: Amberley Lowis Design: Jane Humphrey Photography: Gareth Morgans Food styling: Sunil Vijayakar
Props styling: Polly Webb-Wilson Production: Nic Jones and Gemma John

Printed and bound in China

CONTENTS

FOOD IS CENTRAL TO AN INDIAN PERSON'S LIFE.
IT IS SPOKEN ABOUT ALL THE TIME, IS A GREAT ICEBREAKER AND IS COOKED AND EATEN THROUGHOUT THE DAY.
THE HIGHEST DEMONSTRATION OF LOVE IN INDIA IS TO FEED SOMEONE.

INTRODUCTION

Indian food needs no introduction. Its rich, delicious flavours and enticing aroma of herbs and spices have tempted the most conservative palates and restaurants started by people from the Asian sub-continent have taken Indian food across the seas and made it available to a wide audience. Attention to detail, excellent chefs, clever packaging and marketing have ensured that people know more about it now than ever before.

I grew up in Mumbai when it was still called Bombay, amongst great lovers of food, then went on to train as a chef at the Institute of Hotel Management, Catering Technology and Applied Nutrition, commonly known as IHM, Mumbai. Every evening, I'd be in the family kitchen trying out recipes by blending spices and practising techniques such as grating a coconut to make milk. Those were an intensely food-related three years and I loved the chance to be creative and learn about the diversity of a cuisine that had such a rich history and so much variety. Mumbai was and still is India's commercial capital and therefore attracts people from all over the country. It was wonderful to taste a wide variety of regional Indian cuisines such as Sindhi, Gujarati, south Indian and Kashmiri, through friends, neighbours and speciality restaurants. I also tried a range of regional dishes on family holidays to almost every state of India. I remember eating Kerala 'fish molee' as an eight-year-old and Rajasthani 'dal bati', a rich dough bread served with ghee and lentils, at ten. I still visit India a few times a year and go on food trips – driving off the tourist track to visit market towns and villages that hold the secrets to good, wholesome, regional fare.

As a newly trained chef I came to England in the 1980s to study journalism. I had completed a degree in Indian History in India and wanted to find a way to combine my interests through writing about Indian food. I arrived from the warm sunshine of Bombay to a foggy February day in London. I knew that I'd have to cook a spiced Indian meal to warm up and set off in search of the right ingredients. In those days, grocery shops still had very seasonal vegetables and all I could see were parsnips, swedes and Brussels sprouts. Not what I was used to at all! Thankfully, I could buy a cauliflower and made my first curry with a few spices that I had brought from India. I learnt that in order to buy a variety of Indian ingredients, I'd have to go to an 'ethnic' area and so made my way to Southall. Imagine my delight upon seeing coriander leaves, coconut and turmeric – all ingredients that now, almost 30 years later, are seen in many supermarkets all over the UK.

There was an interest in Indian food in the UK at the time, but the recipes I found in books and magazines seemed complex, with long lists of ingredients and many steps to achieve an 'authentic' Indian meal. My cooking was simpler, quicker and fuss-free. I started my cookery school in London – Cooking With Monisha – where I taught members of the public, chefs and students of hospitality management an easy, manageable style of Indian cooking. Cooking With Monisha is a vibrant school now and I also teach the Indian courses at several top cookery schools around the UK.

The Indian food that is available in the UK is only a small part of a very vast and diverse cuisine. This has to do with migration: people from northern India, mainly Punjab, Gujarat and Bangladesh (which was a part of India until 1947) brought their food to the West and adapted it to suit local tastes. Dishes were classified by heat – 'hot vindaloo' and 'mild korma' – and were named after cities that were important strongholds of the British Raj – 'Bombay Aloo' and 'Chicken Madras'. Neither of these dishes can be found in India! Today, as more people travel to India from the West, there is an appreciation of what lies beyond the samosa and the jalfrezi.

In this book, I have recreated a cookery masterclass at my school. I'd like you to consider this a personal one-to-one lesson with me standing in your kitchen, guiding you with tips and hints as we create the perfect Indian meal. The step-by-step photographs will give you an idea of technique and texture as well as the different stages of the dishes. Please bear in mind that you can personalise the recipes by adding more or less chilli, seasoning or oil.

An increasing number of people are now cooking Indian food at home. Although jarred curry sauces are available in supermarkets, home cooks have realised that they are often too greasy, overly spiced and full of salt; nowhere close to the real thing. Cookery schools all over the world now offer Indian courses and the interest in learning not just how to use spices, but also regional Indian cooking,

is increasing. People who come to my cookery school now talk about Keralan curries or a Bengali pineapple chutney that they have eaten on visits to India. Many tourists have been to Rajasthan and had a 'thali', where lots of dishes are served all together in small bowls, or to Delhi where they've discovered the joys of richly spiced, Mughal curries such as Butter Chicken.

Food is central to an Indian person's life. It is spoken about all the time, is a great icebreaker and is cooked and eaten throughout the day. The highest demonstration of love in India is to feed someone and one of the first questions older members of an Indian family ask the younger ones who are away from home is 'have you eaten?' Recipes are traditionally passed down from mother to daughter. However, more and more Indian men are now seen in the kitchen, especially outside of India. As people travel and TV shows bring India to living rooms the world over, Indian cookery is receiving attention from newer and evermore curious audiences.

EVERYTHING ABOUT INDIA CAN BE BETTER UNDERSTOOD
IF WE ACCEPT THAT THERE ARE NO GENERALISATIONS ABOUT THE COUNTRY.
EVERY FEW MILES, THE LANGUAGE, FOOD, DRESS AND WAYS OF LIFE CHANGE
AND IT IS A LAND OF BOTH SIMILARITIES AND GREAT CONTRASTS
HELD TOGETHER BY A GEOGRAPHICAL BOUNDARY.

LOCAL FOODS ARE AT THE HEART OF REGIONAL COOKING.
IN INDIA'S TOWNS AND VILLAGES, FRESH FOOD IS BOUGHT DAILY FROM FARMERS' MARKETS
AND EVERYTHING THAT IS COOKED IS CONSUMED ON THE SAME DAY.

DIVERSITY IN INDIAN COOKING

I have addressed regional variations by loosely dividing the country into north, north-east, south, west and east, although no such division can cover the entirety of Indian cooking, as that may take a lifetime of travel, research and experimentation!

This diversity can be better understood by exploring four aspects.

Climate → In the hotter regions of India such as in the south, which is close to the Equator, or in Rajasthan, part of which is desert, foods need to be cooling. Within the repertoire of spices, chillies are considered cooling as the capsaicin in them makes you sweat. This cools the body down, and therefore foods from these regions are very hot and spicy, unlike in the north, which can be cold and therefore uses a lot of garam masala, a warming spice blend.

Geography → Local foods are at the heart of regional cooking. People living along India's 4,000-mile coastline eat seafood combined with foods such as coconut, which commonly grow there. A Goan fish curry most often has pomfret, a sea fish, gently simmered in a tangy, spicy coconut curry. In the fiery heat of the Rajasthan desert, water is scarce and foods are therefore often cooked in milk.

Religion → Almost 35 per cent of Indians are vegetarian (see page 32), mainly for religious reasons. Hindus do not generally eat beef and the Muslim population does not eat pork. In an Indian home, non-vegetarian meals are served only a couple of times a week and these usually include chicken, fish or mutton, which in India is goat meat and not lamb. When Indian dishes are adapted for the Western world, lamb replaces goat. The cost of these non-vegetarian foods and the tropical heat mean that family meals are usually lighter and lean towards vegetarian dishes. Vegetarianism in India has its roots in two religions – Jainism and Buddhism – although many Buddhists in India do eat meat. Their religion allows them to eat whatever is offered to them as long as they have not witnessed the slaughter of the animal. The Jains follow non-violence further by not even consuming root vegetables such as onions and garlic that may lead to the destruction of life during harvesting.

Foreign influences → These have had a large part to play in shaping the modern cuisine of India. The Greeks, Chinese, Mughals, Portuguese, Dutch, French and the British brought their own cuisines, ingredients and cooking techniques to India and took deliciously spicy recipes alongside spices when they returned home. Today black pepper is used to flavour not just Indian food but many cuisines all over the world. Many ingredients that Indian cooking is based on – chillies, tomatoes and potatoes – were introduced to India by the Portuguese only about 500 years ago. According to T.R. Gopalakrishnan's book *Vegetable Crops*, the British introduced cauliflowers and cabbages to India in 1822. British varieties were grown in May/June when India enjoys summer and thus these cauliflowers adapted to the hot and humid conditions of their new environment.

THE REGIONS

I have always found it quite hard to divide India up into regions. There is a political division that's followed by the government but I tend to look at the country from a culinary perspective. I, therefore, almost draw a cross through the centre and address each quarter as a region, with the addition of the north-east which is unique in itself.

The North

PUNJAB A large number of Indians who live outside of India are Punjabi in origin. In many families, ancestors several generations ago left India in search of better economic prospects and a new way of life. They carried with them the culture of India so much so that today in many parts of the world when one talks of Indian cooking, it is Punjabi food that is being referred to. Rich onion- and tomato-flavoured curries, or the delicious tandoori foods that are cooked slowly in a clay oven called the tandoor (see page 370), originate in Punjab. The Punjabis, both the Hindus and the Sikhs, love to celebrate with food, drink and dancing and their feasts are legendary. It is sometimes said that because much of Punjab is agricultural, the cooking here is rather unsophisticated. In fact, most Indians love Punjabi cooking and restaurants in this style do great business in every Indian town and city. Most non-Punjabis think of this hearty cuisine as being an occasional treat and look forward to a meal laced with ghee and accompanied by fried treats such as samosas and pakoras. Ingredients that you would commonly find in a Punjabi kitchen are meat and chicken, beans such as chickpeas and red kidney beans, black lentils, vegetables such as cauliflower, potatoes, peas and turnips and wholewheat flour to make many kinds of breads.

UTTAR PRADESH Two of India's most sacred Hindu cities lie in this state. Varanasi and Allahabad are thronged with pilgrims each year and it is not surprising that Uttar Pradesh has a rich and varied vegetarian cuisine. All religious food in India must include only those ingredients which are considered acceptable or 'sattvik'. These include grains, spices, naturally ripened fruit and vegetables and milk. An awareness of what is and what is not acceptable is inculcated in each generation through upbringing. However, Uttar Pradesh does have a non-vegetarian repertoire of food as well. Coriander and cumin are favoured spices, while legumes and pulses form the base of many curries.

One of the most famous styles of cooking that originates from this state is the 'Awadhi' style from Lucknow (or Awadh, as it was earlier known). Until nearly the middle of the twentieth century it was a princely state with Nawabs as rulers. Their feasts were renowned and even today the 'Dum Pukht' technique, which literally means 'to choke off the steam' is considered an important skill in any Awadhi chef's repertoire. This is a technique, used to make biryanis and rich curries such as a korma, where a pot is sealed with dough made from chapatti flour (atta) and water. A tight-fitting lid ensures that no steam can escape and that all the flavour is retained in the food. Often, this dish would be placed on coals and slow-cooked for a few hours. Live coals would also be placed on the lid so that heat was provided from above as well as from below. One story says that 200 years ago Nawab Asaf-ud-Daulah began the construction of a huge edifice, the Bara Imambara (which is the most important attraction in Lucknow today and is said to have the biggest vaulted hall in the world). He would destroy a part of the day's building work at night so that his workers would be in continuous

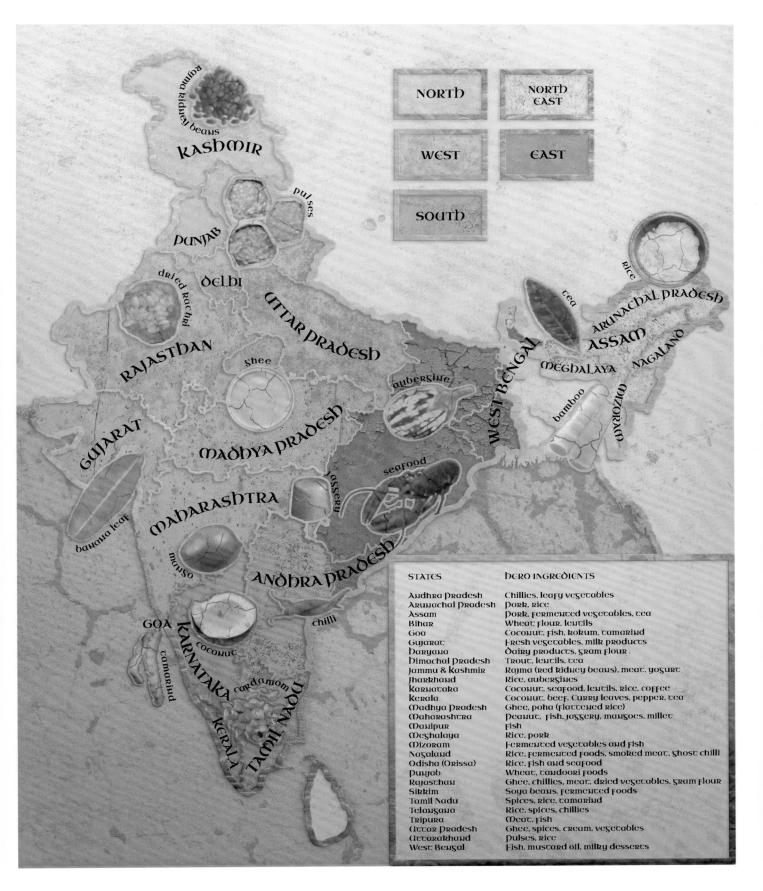

NORTH

NORTH EAST

WEST

EAST

SOUTH

rajma red kidney beans

KASHMIR

pulses

PUNJAB

DELHI

dried rachri

UTTAR PRADESH

RAJASTHAN

RICE

ARUNACHAL PRADESH

tea

ASSAM

ghee

WEST BENGAL

MEGHALAYA

NAGALAND

MIZORAM

GUJARAT

MADHYA PRADESH

aubergine

bamboo

jaggery

seafood

MAHARASHTRA

banana leaf

mango

ANDHRA PRADESH

chilli

GOA

KARNATAKA

coconut

tamarind

cardamom

KERALA

TAMIL NADU

STATES	HERO INGREDIENTS
Andhra Pradesh	Chillies, leafy vegetables
Arunachal Pradesh	Pork, rice
Assam	Pork, fermented vegetables, tea
Bihar	Wheat flour, lentils
Goa	Coconut, fish, kokum, tamarind
Gujarat	Fresh vegetables, milk products
Haryana	Dairy products, gram flour
Himachal Pradesh	Trout, lentils, tea
Jammu & Kashmir	Rajma (red kidney beans), meat, yogurt
Jharkhand	Rice, aubergines
Karnataka	Coconut, seafood, lentils, rice, coffee
Kerala	Coconut, beef, curry leaves, pepper, tea
Madhya Pradesh	Ghee, poha (flattened rice)
Maharashtra	Peanut, fish, jaggery, mangoes, millet
Manipur	Fish
Meghalaya	Rice, pork
Mizoram	Fermented vegetables and fish
Nagaland	Rice, fermented foods, smoked meat, ghost chilli
Odisha (Orissa)	Rice, fish and seafood
Punjab	Wheat, tandoori foods
Rajasthan	Ghee, chillies, meat, dried vegetables, gram flour
Sikkim	Soya beans, fermented foods
Tamil Nadu	Spices, rice, tamarind
Telangana	Rice, spices, chillies
Tripura	Meat, fish
Uttar Pradesh	Ghee, spices, cream, vegetables
Uttarakhand	Pulses, rice
West Bengal	Fish, mustard oil, milky desserts

employment. Food for the workers consisted of rice, meat and vegetables and as this was required day and night, it was put in a pot and sealed with dough to be slow cooked all the time. One day, the Nawab tasted this meal, found it truly delicious and had it adopted into the royal kitchens. Awadh's most famous ruler, the artistic Wajid Ali Shah (1847–56) is said to have refined the technique further by asking his cooks to invent new and exciting dishes to tempt the royal palate. All sorts of fine dishes, such as succulent biryanis and lamb curries called 'nihari', are made in the dum pukht style and speciality restaurants in many five-star hotels around the country specialise in this cuisine. In 1999, some districts were separated into a new state, Uttarakhand.

KASHMIR Due to its proximity to the Himalayas, Kashmir was the natural passage to India for many invaders. Its cuisine is therefore a mix of Indian, Persian and Afghan styles. There are two distinct communities who live in Kashmir – the Muslims and the Hindu Brahmins who are known as 'Kashmiri Pundits'. The Pundits are one of the few meat-eating Brahmin communities in India although beef is strictly taboo. Their cooking is based on ingredients such as yogurt and asafoetida whereas the Muslims use garlic and Kashmiri shallots called 'praan'. The cuisine of Kashmir also makes the most of the local produce such as walnuts, dried apricots and pistachios. Spices such as dried ginger powder, fennel powder and Kashmiri saffron are used. Yogurt forms the base for many curries. The true cooking of Kashmir can be seen in the Wazawan style, which is fragrant with spices including cardamom, cloves and cinnamon. Even today, the master chefs of Kashmir are the descendants of the traditional chefs from Samarkand, the Wazas. The original Wazas came to India with the ruler Timur when he entered India in the fifteenth century. The royal Wazawan, comprising of 36 courses, is a feast that few can get through and is therefore served only at special occasions like weddings. The meal begins with the ritual of washing the hands, then the dishes ('tramis') filled with food begin to arrive. The entrées are eaten with a sticky, dense variety of rice which is prized. Much of the Wazawan is meat-based as this is a sign of affluence, but vegetarian dishes with lotus root or potatoes are also served. The meal is washed down with Kahwa tea which is flavoured with saffron, cinnamon and almonds.

DELHI New Delhi is the capital of India and has a cosmopolitan population of politicians, diplomats and business officials. The cuisine reflects the diversity of its people and a variety of styles from the rich Punjabi to the vegetarian Bania and the non-vegetarian Kayastha coexist. Speciality food quarters are lined with stalls selling tandoori foods, crisp samosas and syrupy sweets but, as evening turns to dusk, the city's rich and famous dress up in their best silks to attend countless cocktail and dinner parties. Alcohol is served freely at these parties and the food is a mix of styles from around the world, each tempting the gourmet with newer and fancier creations.

Delhi is famous for its 'Mughlai' cooking, a legacy of the Mughal rulers who reigned over a large part of India from Delhi, their capital, before the British took over. The official language of the Muslim rulers of this dynasty was Persian as were the names of dishes such as biryani, kebabs and koftas, which are still in use. Dishes prepared in the imperial kitchens – meats in buttery sauces, a medley of seasonal vegetables flavoured with exotic ingredients such as white cumin, dried plums and pomegranate seeds, and fruit and rose-flavoured sweets – have influenced a rich and festive cuisine that is still much loved today.

The West

RAJASTHAN Rajasthan, which lies in the Thar Desert of India, is also called the 'Land of Princes' because of the many princely kingdoms that existed here before India became independent from British rule in 1947. In all the royal kitchens of Rajasthan, the preparation of food was raised to the levels of an art form. The 'Khansamas' or royal cooks were artists who guarded their recipes with a vengeance and passed them down only to a worthy successor.

Everyday Rajasthani cooking was designed for the war-like lifestyle of medieval Rajasthan when warlords spent many days away from home, in battle. Also being an arid desert, the availability of ingredients of the region was limited. Food that could remain unspoilt for several days and could be eaten without heating was preferred, more out of necessity than choice. The scarcity of water, fresh vegetables and delicate spices has had its effect on the cooking of this state. Most foods in this hot region are still cooked in ghee as it is considered cooling in Ayurveda.

In the desert belt of Jaisalmer, Barmer and Bikaner, chefs use less water and more milk, buttermilk and ghee. A special feature of Rajasthani cooking is the use of amchoor (mango powder) that makes up for the scarcity of tomatoes in the desert, and asafoetida, that flavours curries that do not have onions and garlic.

Generally, most bright red Rajasthani curries look spicier than they actually are – Mathania chillies from near Jodhpur were traditionally used for colour and a unique flavour that was earthy rather than simply hot. The production of these chillies has decreased in the past few years and cooks now substitute these with the more readily available Kashmiri dried red chillies.

GUJARAT Gujarat is the mango-shaped state to the west of India. Its northern region is famous for its delicate, vegetarian cuisine and most especially for the 'thali' – a metal plate with several small bowls filled with an array of tempting dishes. The thali has rice, breads, fried accompaniments called 'farsans', vegetables, lentils and sweets all served at once.

Even within Gujarat, the cuisine is varied within the different areas. Some areas are drier than others, with less rainfall. Kathiawari and Kachchi food both use red chilli powder to create heat. In the southern part of the state, green chillies are used, most often with fresh ginger. In Surat, sugar is added to most dishes, even lentils and vegetables, and much of the cuisine has a sweet, tangy flavour.

Gujarat was also home to the Bohri Muslim community who migrated to Mumbai in large numbers. Their cooking is a mix of the local Gujarati with Islamic overtones such as the inclusion of meat and dates and some of the delicacies such as 'lamba pau', a smoky, wood-baked bread that can now be eaten only in exclusive eateries.

MAHARASHTRA Maharashtra lies to the west of India and has a long coastline along the Arabian Sea. Many communities live here – different sects of Maharashtrians and the settlers who came from other states.

Native Maharashtrian cooking has many styles – the Pune Brahmin style with its sweet, simple flavourings and use of peanuts, the fiery curries of the Deccan Plateau and the coconut and tamarind flavourings of the coastal areas. The state grows a large variety of crops such as peanuts, coconut, rice and mangoes. The most sought-after mango in India, the 'Alphonso', is grown here in Ratnagiri.

The biggest city in the state is Mumbai, where I was born. This is a cosmopolitan city dotted with restaurants serving up every type of regional cuisine. Half of my family is Maharashtrian and I grew up eating curries with coconut and pepper. The Parsis who came from Persia and settled in Gujarat later moved to Mumbai. Their cooking is a mix of Iranian and Hindu and out of respect to the local community, they do not eat beef. Their cooking is exemplified by the sweet and sour dhansak, a thick curry made with lentils and vegetables flavoured with spices and vinegar, stews and dessert custards.

The Sindhi community migrated from Pakistan and many of them set up homes in Mumbai. They are known for their love of food and their cooking is fresh and flavourful. Leafy vegetables flavoured with cumin, fried breads and spiced lentils with garlic are specialities.

MADHYA PRADESH This state lies at the centre of India and therefore the cooking is influenced by all the surrounding states, most importantly, by Gujarat and Maharashtra. MP, as it is known, has a great culture of hospitality and I have never

been to any other place in the world where the people eat and offer others so much food. There seem to be six meals a day – breakfast, elevenses, lunch, tea, dinner and supper with many 'munchings' in between!

Much of MP has Hindu cooking. Indore is famous for its pickle shops that sell preserved fruit and vegetables. In Indore, the local high street turns into a food lane called the 'sarafa' after the shops close and every night people stroll along this road to eat fresh samosas and hot sweet jalebis and to drink warm nut-flavoured milk. Bhopal, the capital, is an exception. Ruled for many years by a Muslim ruler, the cuisine is a mix of Islamic and Hindu styles. Kebabs and biryanis sit next to simple stir-fries and fresh breads.

The South

TAMIL NADU Tamil Nadu is situated on the eastern coast of India by the Bay of Bengal. This state has some of the oldest and most famous of all Hindu temples, such as the Nataraja temple in Chidambaram and the Brihadeeshwara temple at Tanjore. Tamil culture is resplendent with classical literature and dance, fascinating bronze sculpture and awe-inspiring architecture. Chennai is the capital and is home to some of the finest artists and artisans in the country. A meal here is mainly made up of rice served in three different courses. First with sambhar, a thick lentil dish that is flavoured with fresh vegetables, then with rasam, a thinner version of the sambhar and one that is slurped up along with the rice (a great experience!) and finally with yogurt and rice to cool one in the strong southern heat. Other rice preparations include coconut rice, tamarind rice, lemon rice and countless other flavourings that provide variety and taste. Black pepper, red chillies, cumin, turmeric, coriander, fenugreek and mustard seeds are used in cooking vegetables such as plantains, yams, gourds and greens.

ANDHRA PRADESH Situated in the central south, Andhra Pradesh is a combination of Hindu and Muslim cookery. Before the partition of India and Pakistan in 1947, the city of Hyderabad was ruled by the Nizam, a man reputed to be the wealthiest person in the world at the time.

LEFT: *Mecca Masjid mosque (Charminar), Hyderabad, Andhra Pradesh.*

His kitchens produced some of the richest and tastiest fare and many of his favourite dishes have become trademark recipes of the region such as the rich dessert 'Khubani ka meetha', where stewed Indian apricots are served with nuts, cream and spices. Hyderabadi cookery is characterised by slow-cooking methods.

An Andhra meal is also served in courses. In Hyderabad, it is the Mughlai set of courses, replete with kebabs and biryanis. In other parts of the state, the food is mainly vegetarian and again, rice forms a staple part of the diet. Andhra Pradesh is most famous for its pickles and many chutneys that are made from just about anything – from mangoes, aubergines and tomatoes to ginger and 'gongura', an aromatic, local reddish-green leafy vegetable. The food of Andhra Pradesh is known for its chilli heat! In February 2014, the Andhra Pradesh Reorganisation Act divided this state in two – Andhra Pradesh and Telangana.

KARNATAKA Karnataka has given India a classic restaurant style. Udipi, a small temple town, is famous for its Brahmin cooks. The town has a beautiful, ancient Krishna temple and the Brahmins will first offer all cooked food to the gods before serving it to devotees. Pancakes called 'dosas', rice cakes called 'idlis' and luscious chutneys are made in Udipi and tiny cafés that serve such food (called Udipi restaurants) are popular. They serve vegetarian food. Coconuts, tamarind, beans and kokum, a sour purple fruit are used in the cooking. In these parts, coconut (called 'Shriphal') is considered the fruit of the gods. Every part of the coconut tree is useful – the fruit is eaten, the water within is drunk, the leaves are used for roofing and the husk on the outside of the fruit is made into scouring tools. In Hinduism, the coconut is a complete, special fruit – one that can be used in its entirety, in many different ways and is therefore used in ritual worship. The hard outer shell and the soft interior symbolise a Hindu way of life where one must be impervious to the difficulties of daily life while still maintaining an inner calm and balance.

Many of my ancestors, who are Saraswat Brahmins, come from Karnataka and as a child I would spend my summers in the little village of Gokarn just off the coast. I remember eating fresh curries flavoured with coriander

and cumin, roomfuls of mangoes and many unusual dishes made with jackfruit and breadfruit. We would wait for the breadfruit to fall off the trees and then my aunt would peel and slice it, rub it with chilli and salt and deep-fry the slices. Pure jaggery or a slice of star fruit was often handed out after dinner and some of my best childhood memories are of stoning tamarind trees to get at the sour-sweet fruit!

KERALA The serving of a meal is an art form in this state. Traditionally, a banana leaf is used as a plate and all courses are served at once. Rice, lentils, vegetables, chutneys, crisp accompaniments and sweets, flavoured with coconut, form a fragrant feast. Curry leaves and mustard seeds are used to temper many dishes. Preparations such as thorans (vegetable stir-fries), sambhar (lentils with tamarind) and dishes cooked with plantains, yams and cabbages are popular. Cabbages are grown all over India due to their neutral taste, which can be combined with a variety of spices.

Kerala has many communities and therefore has a great mix of cuisines. Syrian Christians, Malabar Muslims, Jews from Cochin and Hindus all live and work peacefully and share a culture that is vibrant and yet gentle. This is the state where Ayurveda (see pages 26–27) has been preserved for centuries, away from foreign conquests and interference, and is still practised through food and lifestyle.

GOA Goan food is a blend of the various influences that have been a part of the region's history. The main communities that live here are the Christians and the Hindus. For both the main food is fish, which is natural because Goa is on the coast. Fishing boats go out into the Arabian Sea in the early hours and are back, laden with seafood, by dawn.

Goa was a Portuguese colony for many years and the food of that land has mainly influenced the Christian food of Goa. The Portuguese introduced pork and beef to the Catholic converts of the region, who came to love dishes such as sorpotel, a spicy pork curry, whereas the Hindus, a fish-eating community, did not adopt this new cuisine due to religious restrictions.

Hindu cookery is mainly from the Saraswat community who use local produce, such as coconuts, cashew nuts and mangoes. Spices such as asafoetida, mustard seeds and 'tirphal' or Szechuan pepper, are used to flavour many vegetables such as bitter gourds, pumpkins and plantain.

RIGHT: *Chinese fishing nets, believed to have been introduced to India by Portuguese settlers from Macau in the sixteenth century, on the bay of Fort Cochin. These nets have been in use in Fort Cochin for centuries, although these days are more used as tourist attractions.*

REFERRED TO AS *Kettuvallams*, HOUSEBOATS WERE INTRODUCED TO
INDIA BY THE CHINESE. FIRST BUILT IN SOUTHWESTERN INDIA, THEY WERE
USED TO TRANSPORT MERCHANDISE, SUCH AS RICE AND SPICES, ALONGSIDE
PASSENGERS, AROUND THE BACKWATERS AND LAGOONS OF KERALA.

The East

As in other parts of the country, availability of local ingredients has determined the flavours of this region. The many rivers and the fertile soil allows rice, mangoes and coconuts to grow in plenty. Fresh ginger and mustard seeds, both whole and crushed to a paste, are used to flavour curries.

Rice is eaten with all curries and the Bengalis grow one crop a year, leaving time to pursue what they love only second to eating – appreciation of the fine arts –music, painting and literature. Due to its proximity to the Mughal-influenced north, the Bengali Muslim cuisine adopts the best of the kebabs and biryanis, which are the pride of Mughlai cooking.

West Bengal has a great vegetarian repertoire, although fish dishes such as 'Macher Jhol', a thin soupy fish curry (page 205) and 'Shorshe Bata Macch', fish is cooked in mustard paste, are most famous. The use of spices here is unique and a special five-spice blend called 'panch phoron' is used extensively. This is a mixture of cumin, fennel, fenugreek, kalonji (also called onion seeds) and black mustard seeds. This is fried in a little oil and added to most dishes.

The most characteristic feature of Bengali food is the repertoire of sweets. There is a speciality 'mishti' or sweet shop on every street corner in Kolkatta and they are even prized in other Indian cities. Syrupy rasmalai, where soft dumplings of clotted milk are steeped in sweet, spiced milk; sandesh, a fudge-like sweet made of thickened milk, and a sweet yogurt called 'mishti dhoi' that is sweetened with date palm jaggery, all come originate from the east.

The North-East

This region is made up of the Seven Sister States: Arunachal Pradesh, Assam, Manipur, Meghalaya, Mizoram, Nagaland and Tripura as well as the Himalayan state of Sikkim.

The north-east is home to a vast number of tribes who have their own unique cuisine. The Adi tribe of Arunachal Pradesh cultivate rice and rear their own pigs and chickens. The Angami of Nagaland and Manipur love pork with bamboo shoots and the Bhutia of Sikkim eat dishes such as 'phagshapa' – strips of pork fat cooked with radish and chilli. The food here is mostly non-vegetarian, with influences from nearby China and Myanmar. Being close to the Bay of Bengal,

fish is popular in Assam and is cooked in mustard oil and eaten with rice.

The north-east is famous for arguably the hottest chilli in the world (pictured below). Aptly called 'Bhut Jolokia' (Ghost Chilli) in Assam, 'Naga Jolokia' in Nagaland and 'Umorok' in Manipur, it is highly regarded for its medicinal properties such as its use in pain-relief treatment.

The food of Nagaland is quite different from that of the rest of India due to the Chinese influence – ingredients such as pork, beef, bamboo shoots and soya bean feature in many dishes. Manipuri tribes are divided into those that live in the hills and those of the plains. They exchange their produce, sharing meat and grains, and each tribe has a slightly different cuisine depending on what they grow or rear.

In Mizoram, the cooking can be rather bland but includes lentils, chicken, wild game, pork, bamboo shoots, local grape wine and a drink called 'zu' or 'zu tea' which is locally brewed rice beer. Arunachal Pradesh also has a bland cuisine eaten with the local rice beer called 'apang', whereas in Meghalaya rice and pork are often eaten with a spiced mix called 'tungrymbai' which has, amongst other ingredients, fermented soya beans, black sesame seeds and garlic.

AYURVEDA

The basis of all Indian cookery is the ancient science of Ayurveda, the system of holistic healing which is the oldest known form of medicine. It was transcribed about 5,000 years ago by Himalayan sages who understood the value and health effects of the various herbs that grew around them.

Ayurveda believes that we can achieve optimum health by nourishing the 'dhatus' or the seven major kinds of tissues, both liquid and solid, including the blood, plasma, muscles, fat, bone, bone marrow and reproductive fluids, and by cleansing the body of 'ama' or the toxic waste that accumulates in the body due to poor digestion.

The Indian kitchen is therefore an apothecary which tends to the everyday health and wellbeing of a family. Daily food must be fresh, use healing spices and herbs such as turmeric and coriander and include a host of food groups. A traditional Indian meal is balanced so that there is always a carbohydrate, a protein-rich curry, fruit and vegetables and dairy in the form of yogurt, cheese or milk.

Ayurvedic wisdom is passed down the generations and children are often told to eat certain seasonal foods or food combinations that work well together. My grandmother would always make sure I had a cooling glass of milk or some yogurt if I'd eaten a mango, considered 'heating' in Ayurveda as it overstimulates the digestion, especially in the tropical summer heat. My children, although brought up in the West, know the benefit of ginger, honey and turmeric tea when nursing a cold. Indian recipes ensure healing ingredients are cooked in the best way to retain all of their goodness. Thus vegetables are lightly cooked to improve their digestibility (over raw vegetables) and basmati rice is sometimes dry-roasted for a few minutes before being boiled to make it lighter and easier to digest.

Ayurveda addresses individual nutritional needs and suggests eating foods that suit your own constitution or 'dosha'. Each 'dosha' is created by the proportion and balance of the five elements – earth, fire, water, air and ether – in your body and therefore everyone will respond to foods in a unique way. The three doshas are Vata (governed by air and ether), Pitta (governed by fire and water) and Kapha (governed by water and earth). The core of a good Indian diet is one where you are aware of how your body reacts to various foods at different times, and you eat accordingly. Often two doshas can be present in a person at the same time or they can change according to the seasons. At times all the doshas combine in an individual making the constitution a balanced or 'tridoshic' one. It's not always easy to follow an Ayurvedic diet but cooking simple meals with fresh, seasonal, varied ingredients that give you a sense of wellbeing is quite achievable.

SOME HEALING SPICES

Cinnamon – Lowers blood sugar, antioxidant

Garlic – Lowers cholesterol, anti-clotting

Ginger – Alleviates motion sickness and indigestion

Turmeric – Anti-inflammatory and antioxidant properties

Chilli – Aids digestion

Asafoetida – Helps digestion and prevention of flatulence

Cumin – Aids digestion

Fennel – Eases colic

Coriander – Aids digestion; high in fibre and vitamin C

THE SIX TASTES

Ayurveda recognises six tastes: sweet, sour, salty, pungent, bitter and astringent. All foods and herbs are classified by taste. The taste of a food gives us the key to its actions upon the digestion, the body and ultimately our emotions and our sentiments. In Sanskrit, the word for taste and emotion is the same – 'rasa'.

SWEET → *Grains, lentils, fruit, vegetables, dairy.* Sweet taste is also called neutral taste. This is to distinguish it from the idea of simple sugar or desserts. It includes proteins, carbs and fats, as well as most fruits and vegetables. About 90 per cent of food is of the sweet/neutral taste.

SOUR → *Cheese, sour fruit, citrus fruit, yogurt, fermented foods, wine.* Sour taste includes all foods that are aged, ripened, fermented or naturally acidic. They are considered to be partially pre-digested foods or digestive aids. Thus they help stimulate appetite. Too much sour can lead to blood toxicity, heartburn, acidity or itching.

SALTY → *Sea plants, salt.* Salty tastes stimulate the flow of saliva and the creation of hydrochloric acid in the stomach, thus aiding digestion. Too much salt disturbs the blood, leads to inflammation or fluid retention and overwhelms all the other senses.

PUNGENT → *Cloves, chillies, garlic, onion.* Pungent taste includes all foods and spices that are spicy, hot and sharp. The warming quality stimulates the digestive fire known as 'agni'. It reduces fluids and has a cleansing action. Too much pungent food can lead to excessive heat, burning, dehydration, restlessness and irritability.

BITTER → *Aubergine, spinach, leafy vegetables, turmeric.* Bitter taste is considered balancing and healing and is an essential part of Indian cookery.

ASTRINGENT → *Broccoli, pomegranate, quinoa, cranberry.* This is the dry taste left in the mouth after a sip of black tea or dry white wine.

Balance Indian cookery aims to combine foods and herbs of all six tastes into a balanced whole. A well-rounded meal uses all six tastes in proportion.

Home Cooking vs Restaurant Food

Eating out was not the norm for most Indians until a few years ago. With an extended family living under one roof, it was cheaper and more practical to eat at home than to go out to a restaurant. Today, nuclear families with less time find it easy to eat out but most people are aware that they will never be able to get 'ghar ka khana' or a taste of home, when they eat in a restaurant.

The biggest difference between home and restaurant food is that all home cooking is based on the principles of good health, with attention being paid not just to ingredients and their sourcing but also to their preparation (see Ayurveda on page 26). You hardly ever see the wonderful range of vegetables used in an Indian home on a restaurant menu. Eateries will often over-spice, over-salt and over-grease their dishes to make them taste good but this is not healthy in the long run. Home food is generally fresher and lighter in taste.

An Indian home-cooked meal is suitable for the entire family, including children and older relatives. Therefore most of it, except in some regions that rely heavily on the use of chillies, is moderately spiced. On the table you will find a small selection of pickles and chutneys – some hot, others sweet – that are used to personalise the meal and make it hotter or sweeter. Plain, cooling yogurt also features in most regional meals. It is a complete myth that all Indian food is searing hot.

Indian food is not generally divided into courses. Everything is served at the same time so that the meal is an exciting kaleidoscope of colour, texture, temperature and taste. Poppadums, so typically produced at the start of a meal in most restaurants around the world, provide an interesting contrast of texture and taste in an Indian home-cooked meal. Most restaurants will agree that they become a 'first course' to keep the guest busy while the meal is being prepared!

When you eat in an Indian home, you will be told that there is, for example, chicken curry or dal for dinner. No one says 'we are having chicken tikka masala for dinner'. General names are enough to give the family an idea of what to expect at the table because recipes that have been used for years will be familiar. Restaurants, on the other hand, have names for dishes that are quite spectacular in their richness ('Shahi Malai Paneer' – Royal Creamy Paneer Cheese) and at so many restaurants and takeaways in the West, the classification of curries is based on the level of heat. A 'Korma' is supposedly mild, a 'Madras' is moderate and a 'Vindaloo' is fiery hot. This distinction neither takes into account regional influences nor core ingredients. This is a fusion British Raj cuisine where ingredients and cooking styles combine in a haphazard manner to create a style that has, thankfully, not permeated into Indian homes or indeed into restaurants in India.

MEALS IN AN INDIAN HOME

The kitchen in an Indian home is a busy one. Various meals or ingredients such as spice blends are prepared throughout the day. In the interest of hygiene in the blazing tropical heat, Indians prefer piping hot food over cold and don't like eating leftovers, so fresh food is cooked on a daily basis.

Breakfast → The kitchen opens with the making of tea, popular in central or northern India, or coffee, usually in south India. In larger cities, people may rush off to work after a breakfast of toast and eggs but in most places, the main cook, who is often the lady of the house, will make a fresh, hot regional breakfast. In the south, this could be lentil and rice pancakes called 'dosa' (see page 126), in Maharashtra it could be savoury flaked rice called 'Poha' (see page 358) and in Punjab it could be a paratha (see page 120).

Lunch → Many people in India, including school-going children and office workers, carry a packed lunch with them. This is often roti, a vegetable or meat curry, a vegetable side dish and yogurt, all of which have been freshly cooked that morning and can last in the tropical heat of India. In Mumbai, a unique lunchbox delivery system developed in 1890 has grown to become a godsend for those who prefer their daytime meal sent from home, for taste and hygiene reasons. Thousands of lunchboxes are collected from homes each morning and delivered to workplaces by midday using a coding system understood only by the delivery men. Growing up, I had a hot, fresh meal brought to my school every day by our home cook. I didn't really think much of it then but what wouldn't I give to have that luxury in London today!

Dinner → This is when the family eats together and the meal consists of rice or some form of Indian bread such as roti or paratha, curries and side dishes, always accompanied by yogurt. Desserts are not eaten every day, instead a piece of fruit such as a seasonal mango or the more readily available and cheaper banana will be served. Dinner in an Indian home is served later than in the West. As days are longer for most months of the year, families tend to eat at about 8pm, after members have returned from work and school.

SAMPLE MENUS

South Indian breakfast
Dosa (fermented lentil and rice pancakes)
Sambhar (spiced lentils with vegetables)
Coconut Chutney
Coffee

Gujarati lunch
Rice
Dal with tamarind and coriander
Kobi Vatana Nu Shak (spiced cabbage and peas stir-fry)
Khandvi (soft gram flour rolls)
Yogurt

Punjabi dinner
Roti
Chicken Curry
Rajma (red kidney bean curry)
Aloo Gobi (potatoes with cauliflower)
Cucumber Raita (yogurt with cucumber)

COOKING FOR CHILDREN

People often ask me about how to introduce Indian foods (cooking) to children. It's worth bearing in mind that children in India are brought up eating Indian food, and spices are introduced quite early. A light tea made with fennel seeds is fed to babies as young as a few months old. Soft-cooked rice is a popular weaning food and yogurt is mixed into this from when the baby is 8–9 months old. Children always indicate when they are ready to move on to the next stage of diet or skill. I fed my daughter, amongst other bland foods, a gentle mix of rice and yogurt until one day when she was just over a year old, I tried a little mildly spiced chicken curry. She loved it and has eaten spiced food ever since.

In every Indian home, children are offered mild dishes from whatever has been cooked for the family. As it is, home cooking in most parts of India is not very hot. There are no special 'children's meals'. For example, if the family is eating rice, a spicy fish curry, a mild dal and a mild cauliflower side dish, the child will be fed everything except the fish curry and may even be introduced to a bit of fish without the spicy sauce.

In my experience, it is a good idea to introduce young children early to a variety of foods as part of a natural way of family eating. Children as young as two enjoy rotis and as they get older will be happy to help cook them. Dosas or rice and lentil pancakes, idlis (steamed rice cakes), breads, rice, mild curries and vegetables are all suitable for children. Cumin, coriander and turmeric are mild spices and can be added to children's meals for flavour rather than for heat.

VEGETARIANISM

Almost 85 per cent of Indians are Hindu and many are vegetarian all or some of the time due to religious reasons. Religious abstinence from non-vegetarian foods such as meat, poultry, fish and even eggs is common all over the country. However, not all Hindus are vegetarian, as caste and community also affects this choice. Most non-vegetarians will eat meat or fish a few times a week or just once a week, firstly because it is expensive and secondly because the choice of vegetables, lentils, beans and dairy products is so vast that there is a seemingly endless variety. Vegetarian food is also considered healthier than meat because it is easier to digest. Few people today believe that a vegetarian diet is lacking in protein; in fact, the yogurt and beans that are an essential part of this diet are an extremely good source of protein.

India is well-known for its tradition of vegetarianism, which has a history going back almost two millennia. During the Vedic period, almost 5,000 years ago, animals were hunted for food and meat was eaten regularly by the warrior community of Kshatriyas. The anti-meat-eating sentiment began to be felt at the end of the Vedic period. This period coincided with the rise of Buddhism and Jainism, whose founders the Buddha and Lord Mahavira respectively, taught their followers the doctrines of non-violence. As more and more people began to convert to these newer beliefs, Hindu priests, fearing that a great number of their people would convert, also began preaching against the killing of animals. They adopted the practice of 'ahimsa' or non-violence and followed a vegetarian diet, regarding it, as well as advertising it, as superior to the older Brahminical ideas of animal sacrifice. Today, almost a third of India is vegetarian and most of these people are Hindu and Jain. Most Buddhists in India eat meat in the belief that this is allowed as long as they have not participated in the killing of the animal.

The availability of ingredients as well as Indians migrating and taking their food with them around the world has meant that Indian vegetarian food is more popular now than ever before.

Quantities, Ingredients and Standardisation

It is often amusing to chefs not of Indian origin that at the heart of this cuisine there is no concept of standardisation! Ask an Indian cook for a recipe and you will hear the word 'andaaz' – which roughly means intuitive approximation. Most Indian cooks rely on their sense of sight, smell and hearing to decide what to put in the pan or when the dish is perfectly cooked. Having said that, quantities and proportion are vital when learning to cook and it can take years to perfect this intuitive 'andaaz'!

The names of recipes are also vague enough that a cook can interpret them in whichever way he or she likes – keeping true, of course, to the ingredients and techniques of the region. 'Saag Aloo' literally means a leafy vegetable and potatoes. We know that it is a north Indian dish because the name is in Hindi and therefore the style of cooking (starting with the frying of onions) and ingredients used (a combination of onions, ginger, tomatoes and chillies) will be in the northern style. The same combination of vegetables may be called 'Palak Batata nu Shak' in Gujarat, in western India, and have mustard seeds, green chillies, ginger and even a bit of sugar. This shows the different possibilities of interpreting the same dish.

Due to the fact that not only regional diversity but also personal variations influence the cooking in an Indian home, there is no single 'correct' recipe for a particular dish. My friends from the Sindhi community make a tantalising curry using gram flour as the base for a selection of vegetables. I have been given at least six different recipes for the same dish and have come to realise that my own version is based on arriving at the taste that I prefer of all the ones I have eaten. This means, again, that many Indian cooks will use a recipe created in order to achieve a particular result, knowing full well that several interpretations, all probably correct, will exist.

It is also important to bear in mind that ingredients have changed over the last few decades. In some Western countries where the cold weather does not permit the adequate ripening of vegetables throughout the year, traditionally used Indian ingredients have to be adapted. I use tomato purée in many of my recipes as it is readily available in the West and can provide an instant depth of flavour. I find that it provides the intensity of colour and flavour that I'm trying to achieve, especially in the UK where tomatoes tend to be too watery.

Time constraints, the lack of the right equipment and the availability of prepared ingredients also influence how we cook. For example, in many homes in southern India, fresh coconuts are cracked open and shredded on a coconut scraper every single day to use in curries or as a garnish. In the West, if a curry calls for coconut this would be tedious without a scraper (a long sharp blade with a serrated disc attached to one end) and lack of practice. I have therefore substituted fresh coconut with readily available desiccated coconut wherever possible, used in the dry form or reconstituted by soaking it in warm water for 20 minutes or so.

In this book, I have written recipes for four people. If you need to double the recipe, please double the spices.

Culinary Terms and Techniques

Good ingredients and spices are at the heart of Indian cooking but the right techniques are required to make them come alive in a flash of taste and texture. Considering that India has hundreds of languages, this list of culinary terms could be endless! I have used Hindi terms for the most part, as it is the most widely spoken Indian language in India.

DUM

Dum literally means steam. It is a technique where a pot is sealed with dough made from chapatti flour (atta) and water. A tight-fitting lid ensures that no steam can escape and all the flavour is retained in the dish. Often, this dish would be placed on coals and slow-cooked for a few hours. Hot coals would also be placed on the lid so that heat was provided from above as well as from below. The ingredients would be partially cooked then sealed so that they became tender and the fat rose to the top. This was considered appetising by cooks of bygone years but modern tastes are moving towards lighter, less oily food.

In modern kitchens, this technique can be achieved in the oven, which provides even heat, whereby a dish is sealed with dough or with several layers of foil. Recipes for Dum Biryanis and some curries are cooked this way.

BAGHAR/ TADKA/ CHOWNK

There are several Indian words for this essential procedure of tempering foods. Spices or ingredients such as onions, garlic, ginger or chillies are cooked in hot oil to extract and develop their flavour. Tempering can be done at the beginning of cooking, where for example, spices and onions are cooked before adding cooked lentils to make Tarka Dal (page 279), or at the end when, for example, cumin seeds may be fried in oil and poured over a curry. The oil contains the aromatic oils extracted from the spices and becomes 'flavoured' itself.

BHUNA

This is a process of sautéing or stir-frying, usually in some fat, over a high heat that is reduced to medium when the ingredient has started to soften or brown. It is done at several stages of the cooking process and sometimes a little liquid – water, yogurt or tomato, for instance – is added to prevent ingredients such as spices from sticking. To start, the onions, ginger, garlic, etc., are stir-fried until they are well done. Next, the main ingredient such as meat or vegetables is stir-fried until it is sealed or partially cooked. Meat for a curry is not browned in batches as this can create a layer that prevents the spice flavours fully permeating it. Sealing it by bhuna ensures that the juices get locked in but the spices thoroughly flavour the meat.

After the stir-frying stage, liquid is added to finish off the cooking and create a sauce. In the West, many Indian takeaways sell a 'bhuna' which has come to mean a meat dish with little sauce that is medium-hot to spicy, although its cooking does begin with this 'bhuna' method.

Tips for Tadka

1 Although many cooks claim that the oil has to be smoking hot for a tadka to work, I encourage people to simply warm the oil over a high heat before adding spice seeds. This gives you control as you watch them pop or sizzle, change colour and develop an aroma. It also reduces the likelihood of them burning but if they do, you will have to discard them and start again.

2 Make sure that you have all your ingredients prepared. Oil can come up to temperature quite quickly, depending on the source, so keep spices, chopped onions, garlic and ginger next to the hob.

3 Ingredients are added in succession, depending on the time they take to cook. Spice seeds go in first, then onions and lastly tomatoes.

4 Pour the tempering along with the oil or ghee over finished dishes for extra flavour or where the main dish is not cooked (sometimes salads are finished with a warm tempering of spice seeds).

DHUNGAR

This is a stovetop smoking method that is popular in north Indian Awadhi cookery.

YOU WILL NEED:
a small metal bowl
a small piece of coal
1 teaspoon ghee or oil

1 Place a small metal bowl in the centre of the pan which holds your cooked food, for example a curry, dal or kebabs.

2 Light the coal and when the initial thick smoke has died away and the coal has turned grey, place it in the bowl.

3 Pour the ghee over the coal. Cover the pan with a tight-fitting lid and seal for 2–3 minutes. The longer you leave it, the smokier your food will be, but I'd suggest a maximum of 10 minutes.

4 Lift the lid, remove the bowl of coal and serve the curry, dal or kebabs immediately.

TALNA

This is a deep- or shallow-frying technique, usually done in a karahi, a heavy, wok-shaped metallic pan.

To fry evenly, heat the oil until a piece of what is to be fried (perhaps a slice of onion or a drop of batter) can be added to the oil and it cooks quickly. A drop of batter will rise to the top in a few seconds. Heat regulation is critical during frying, as foods need to cook evenly, especially in the middle, without burning on the surface. For this, start off at a high heat then, when the food has sealed and started to colour, reduce the heat to medium until the right colour has been achieved.

CONDENSATION

When cooking dry dishes, especially vegetables, a clever but simple condensation technique is used in Indian home kitchens. This eliminates the need for adding cooking liquid to the pan which can dilute flavour and change the consistency of the dish.

Place a convex lid on the pan and fill the lid with a few tablespoons of cold water. As the vegetables heat up, the salt in the recipe draws out their juices which rise up as steam. This steam hits the inside of the lid, condenses and falls back into the pan providing a bit of moisture.

BOTI AND TIKKA

Both of these terms are used for cuts of meat or poultry. Boti generally refers to diced leg meat, which is the darker in colour in birds, and tikka is diced breast. You will find that tikka is usually associated with chicken and boti with lamb or mutton. Sometimes restaurants will use these terms loosely, variously calling diced, spiced, grilled meat, poultry or paneer cheese, boti, tikka or kebab.

MASALA

This is a general term to mean spice, a spice blend or a spiced curry paste. When a curry paste is made from fresh ingredients, such as coriander leaves or onions blended with water, vinegar, coconut milk etc., it is called a wet masala.

An example of a dry masala is the ever popular spice blend garam masala. The 'curry powder' sold in the West is not used by Indian cooks – it was a British Raj creation to loosely replicate Indian flavours. Each region of India, indeed every community, has its own spice blend and as such there are hundreds of 'curry powders', each distinct and unique, with specific names such as the southern 'sambhar powder' (see page 65) made from spices such as chilli and fenugreek or 'goda masala' (see page 65) made from cinnamon, poppy seeds and coconut in Maharashtra. Recipes are passed down the generations, with each cook making slight changes according to their own taste.

MUGHLAI COOKERY

This is a style of cooking developed in the imperial kitchens of India's Muslim rulers of the Mughal dynasty. They ruled from Delhi and have influenced the cookery of north India. Recipes are rich with nuts, cream, dried fruit and spices. Meat and poultry are the stars here, as well as milky sweets flavoured with saffron and nuts.

CURRY

The word curry comes from the Tamil word 'kari' which means sauce or vegetable dish. To an Indian, curry is a dish that has gravy but to those not too familiar with the cuisine, any savoury dish that is cooked with spices or curry powder, whether it has a sauce or not, is curry. I have heard people refer to samosas as curry!

CONSISTENCY → A good curry should have the right consistency. Is it too thick or too watery? Some curries are meant to be thicker than others but they must always be moist enough to act as a sauce for the carbohydrate dishes such as rice or bread. Some foods, such as lentils, thicken upon keeping. Loosen them up with a splash of water before serving. If your curry is too thin, you can thicken it with a paste of fried onions or ground nuts, such as cashews or almonds, or with tomato purée.

COLOUR → Turmeric, chillies, tamarind and fresh coriander are some of the ingredients that add colour to a curry. These add flavour and aroma as well. Generally curries can be white (as in a Kashmiri yogurt-based yakhni), red (as in a makhani), yellow (as in many kormas) and green (as in a south Indian nilgiri).

OILS → The oil used also varies from region to region, giving each curry a unique fragrance. Many parts of the south use peanut oil or coconut oil. In Bengal, it is mustard oil. Over most of the country middle-class households use vegetable or sunflower oil. Ghee is also used but is increasingly reserved for festive dishes and desserts. Ghee is considered nutritious if eaten in moderation but it is best made at home from milk that comes from grass-fed cows.

Most recipes can be cooked in sunflower, vegetable, corn or rapeseed oil, all of which can be heated up to the high temperature required by most Indian cooking.

Curries are made in steps, almost like building blocks. The blocks can be moved around and re-arranged in countless ways to give personalised recipes.

HOW TO MAKE A BASIC CURRY

Many Indian curries begin with onions. Some recipes need sliced ones and others require them to be finely diced. Indian onions are white, pink or purple and range from small to the size of a tennis ball. There are also the small pearl onions that are used in south Indian 'sambhar' or lentils. Most north Indian curries begin with the frying of onions. The onions used in most Indian recipes can be substituted with Spanish onions in the West. These are mild and juicy and add bulk as well as moisture.

ONIONS

The first step is to cut all your ingredients evenly – this will ensure even cooking. Peeling or chopping onions is never easy. In my cookery classes, this is the task that draws the most moans from participants because Indian cookery seems to need so many onions! I have found that the best way to lessen the crying is to put onions in the fridge for a little while before chopping them. This seems to stabilise the sulphur oils. Also, not disturbing the root too much helps – while slicing onions, cut off the root and while dicing, cut around it, discarding some of the flesh around it. When slicing onions, work along the grain or the fine lines that you see on the onion. This helps the slices to cook evenly.

The secret of many curries is to cook the onions well at the beginning. Some curries need the onions to be blended into a paste – I have found that cooking the onions first helps to bring out their flavour better than blending them and then cooking the paste. If you want colour in your curry, the onions will have to be shallow-fried. Start them over a high heat, sprinkling in a pinch of salt to hasten the cooking. When they begin to brown, reduce the heat to medium and continue cooking for 7–8 minutes until they are very soft and you can insert a knife into a piece of onion easily. In recipes where you do not want colour, the sliced onions can be boiled in just enough water to cover them.

When the onions are not to be puréed, cook them until soft but not as long as above because they will continue cooking with the rest of the ingredients.

For a deep brown colour, fry the onions in a little extra oil for about 15 minutes, stirring frequently.

GINGER

Ginger is one of the most healing ingredients in the Indian kitchen. It is widely available in the West but depending on where the ginger has been grown, the taste will differ from the one grown in India, which is quite intense. Chinese ginger is more watery and therefore weaker in flavour. Ginger tea is said to soothe colds and coughs, is anti-inflammatory and stops motion sickness. The most healing part of ginger lies just beneath its skin. Choose pale, smooth, shiny ginger that can be scraped easily. Rather than peeling ginger, which will almost certainly take away that healing layer, scrape the top skin off with a small knife or a teaspoon.

GARLIC

The garlic one sees in the West is an oriental variety called elephant garlic, which is larger and milder than the small variety sold in India. This is why curries in the West are sometimes not as intense as the ones in India. However, this is not a bad thing – foods in the tropics need to be much higher in flavour to counteract the heat. This is also addressed by adding more salt to food in hot countries. Garlic has an unmistakable and pungent aroma. It has a flavour that is much stronger than that of onion. The scent has an undertone of sulphur, which is either loved or hated, as some people find its lingering smell distasteful. The taste can be quite sharp and biting and can increase the heat of a dish, so do take this into account when adding the other spices.

In India garlic is used in curries, marinades, chutneys, vegetable dishes, barbecued meats, pickles and countless other preparations. Each garlic clove is first peeled, and then the flesh can be chopped, grated or made into paste. Garlic can be eaten raw or cooked; when frying make sure that the oil is not too hot or the garlic will burn and taste acrid. A few garlic cloves, roughly bruised, fried in a little hot oil and poured into a curry can give it a real lift.

GINGER-GARLIC PASTE

The next step may well be adding the ginger and garlic. You can add chopped ginger and garlic if the mixture is going to be blitzed, or use paste if you already have some in the fridge. Garlic and ginger complement each other and are often used together.

1 part ginger, scraped and chopped
2 parts garlic, chopped (by volume)

1 Combine the ginger and garlic. If making a small amount, you can grate both or crush them in a mortar and pestle. You don't need to discard the green 'soul' from the centre of the garlic; it is edible and any bitterness it has will add to the balance of flavours in the entire dish.

2 If making a larger amount, blitz the peeled and chopped ginger and garlic in a blender along with a little water to turn the blades and make a smooth purée.

3 You can store this paste in the fridge or freezer. Put it into a clean jar, top it up with oil (any cooking oil) and put it in the fridge. You can use this for up to 3 weeks. You will find that the oil layer may decrease with each scoop of paste used – just top up as necessary.

4 To freeze the paste, either put it into ice-cube trays, cover it with clingfilm and store for 3 months or put it into a freezer bag, lay this on a metal tray and freeze it flat. It becomes quite brittle and you can break off as much as you need for each recipe. While ginger-garlic cubes need thawing, the bits broken off from a flat sheet can be added directly to the pan.

TOMATOES

Often, a north Indian curry will have tomatoes. In season you can use fresh ones but in many recipes where I require depth and colour, I use tomato purée or canned tomatoes. Indian tomatoes are brighter red and more intense in taste so in many of my recipes, I have used tomato purée to recreate this depth of colour and flavour.

BLENDING

The mixture can then be blitzed in a blender to make a curry paste. You will need to add water to help turn the blades – begin by adding just enough to cover the mixture. Pour in more water, a little at a time, until you get a smooth purée.

SALT

My recipes don't give the amount of salt needed as individual tastes vary. You will need to salt your food as it is essential to create a balance of the six tastes (see page 27). If you find that something is missing in the final dish, and it does not taste quite finished, it is probably salt and not more spices. Use good-quality sea salt and you'll find that it is not easy to exceed recommended daily allowances if you cook your food from scratch. It is the salt in processed foods that is the real hidden danger.

Planning a meal

Given that the repertoire of Indian cooking is so vast and that regional differences make choosing very difficult, keeping the meal simple is vital. In many Indian homes an everyday meal has 3–4 dishes including rice and/or chapattis, a meat or vegetable curry and lentils that are served with yogurt, salad and pickle. In Indian homes outside of India, meals tend to be simpler as families are smaller and there is no household help.

An easy way to plan a meal is to think of the food groups, taste, colour, texture and temperature.

FOOD GROUPS

Begin by choosing a rice and/or a bread. Indians will commonly have plain boiled rice as it acts as a neutral backdrop for the flavour in all the other dishes. Add a protein such as a chicken, fish or meat curry or choose a vegetarian lentil, bean, pulse or dairy one.

A salad or vegetable side dish will add fibre.

Taste → A balanced meal should have all the six tastes (see page 27). An Indian home meal is not always spicy hot – this depends on the region – but is generally suitable for the children and elders of the house. A range of pickles and relishes is served with the meal so that diners can personalise their meal.

Colour → An attractive plate should be colourful and healthy. Bring in colour with fresh vegetables and spices. It is easy to add a golden hue to rice by adding a pinch of turmeric or to add a fresh green salad to a curry and rice meal.

Texture → Bring in contrasts such as grainy, smooth, chewy or crisp. An Indian meal does not have courses and each component adds a different texture to create interest with each mouthful. Poppadums are served as part of the main meal to add a crisp element.

Temperature → Most Indian meals are served hot. However, yogurt in some form is also served in every part of the country. This adds a temperature variation, cools the palate and aids digestion. In the south, a meal ends with some yogurt and rice whereas in the north, yogurt flavoured with spices adds a cool contrast. Indians prefer homemade yogurt and set a pot of it daily using the live cultures from the previous pot.

WHAT TO DRINK WITH A MEAL

Almost every Indian home will serve water with a meal. Alcohol is not widely consumed and if it is, it will be drunk before the meal rather than with it. India has a wide variety of beverages made of yogurt, milk, herbs, spices, fruit and vegetables but these are drunk through the day to quench thirst and to stave off the tropical heat rather than with a meal.

Sometimes a meal may end with a digestive drink such as buttermilk. Tea or coffee to finish is more of a restaurant concept than something you wouldd see in an Indian home.

Some restaurants in India, and outside, serve a variety of beers and wines, both Indian and international.

MENUS FOR ENTERTAINING

Festive and party menus will often demonstrate how much time the cook has spent in the kitchen by presenting a spread of up to 20 different dishes. Special ingredients such as nuts, saffron, meat, poultry, fish or cream will also feature but the sheer variety that is cooked makes the meal special. The food at weddings is second only in importance to the bridal couple and each family vies with the other to offer an increasing number of exotic dishes.

Festivals are associated with certain foods and each Hindu god has their own favourite, which is cooked on their special day. The Hindu god Ganesh loves coconut and jaggery sweets called 'modak' and these are made each year only during the Ganesh festival.

Religious 'fasts' are equally important, although this does not always mean a complete abstinence from food. A special 'fasting' cuisine has developed with dishes that can include ingredients such as potatoes, sago, nuts, fruit and dairy, all considered 'sattvik' or calming to the body and mind.

Equipment

If you have been cooking for some time, you will probably have all the equipment needed to make an Indian meal. Most Indian cooks swear by cooking on gas and all over India, food is cooked this way or on wood or coal fires, so kitchen equipment is designed to suit these forms of cooking.

Knives A sharp chef's knife that can mince garlic, finely slice onions or chop fresh coriander to fine shreds is invaluable. Make sure to keep it sharpened. A sharp knife is much safer than a blunt one as you'll use far less pressure to chop ingredients and therefore there is less risk of the knife slipping and injuring you.

Chopping boards I use polyethylene plastic as it can go into the dishwasher, is non-porous and therefore does not hold on to smells such as onion or garlic. Wooden boards are long-lasting but will need regular sanitising with a kitchen-safe cleaner and proper drying so that they do not become mouldy. I know that some cooks regularly oil their wooden boards. Glass or marble chopping boards will dull the blade of your knife. It's a good idea to have a small selection of coloured boards. My kitchen has green and brown for vegetarian food preparation, red for raw meat and blue for raw fish.

Utensils You'll need a peeler, grater, a spatula and a reasonable number of wooden or silicone spoons, some slotted and others plain. Ladles are used to scoop up curries and lentil dishes.

Most Indian breads are rolled out, so you will need a rolling pin. A traditional Indian rolling pin is slimmer than a Western one and comes with a round rolling board which acts as a guide to get the chapattis round as you roll them. The pin itself is tapered and light which allows you to put just enough pressure and not too much, dusting flour to roll the chapatti into an even shape without making it stick to the surface.

Pans The pan you use will affect the final consistency of your dish. If you cook a curry in a frying pan, there will be more evaporation than in a saucepan and therefore you will have a thicker sauce and may need to add a bit of water during cooking to prevent the food from sticking to the bottom of the

pan. I tend to use a frying pan for recipes with shorter cooking times – up to 30 minutes – or for 'drier' dishes such as stir-fries, and a saucepan for recipes with meat or lentils that take longer or those that are cooked in liquid, such as curries.

A few good frying pans will be enough – I use a 30cm one for a curry for four people and you'll find that a 25cm one can be used for smaller portions. A little 15cm pan can be used for that all-important technique called 'tadka', where spice seeds are fried in hot oil and poured over the main dish. Indian kitchens have a baby karahi, a small round bowl that sits safely on a gas hob.

Good non-stick pans work well for quick cooking and for 'dry' dishes such as vegetable stir-fried 'subji' and iron skillets can help seal and brown foods like fish or onions. Lids reduce the cooking times of foods by sealing in the heat and also avoid evaporation of liquid.

Heavy stainless-steel or non-stick 3-litre saucepans can be used for curries, rice dishes and lentils. Choose one with a lid as this can increase pressure within the pan, seal in juices otherwise lost by evaporation and reduce cooking times.

Blender/mortar and pestle In the days before blenders, people used grinding stones. These are flat stone slabs with a heavy, rounded grinding stone that are still used in some parts of India. Stoneground curry pastes are more concentrated as they use less water to achieve a very fine purée than do electric blenders. Most modern kitchens will have a powerful electric blender and these have various attachments for dry and wet grinding and can pulverise the hardest spices to a fine, soft powder or make smooth curry pastes. If buying a blender, choose one that's over 500W as you'll get a finer product as the wattage goes higher. Indian restaurants usually have 1000W professional blenders.

I firmly believe that you do not need to grind up spices every time you cook an Indian meal. It is fine to use ready-bought spices although some, such as ground coriander or garam masala, certainly lose their vigour very quickly and are best ground at home.

Some spices such as garam masala can be easily made in a small electric spice grinder. I have a little one with a push-down top that blitzes whole spices in a few seconds. Alternatively, use a mortar and pestle. When buying one, bear in mind that it must be heavy and hard enough to crush tough spice seeds. I find that a ceramic one is too delicate for robust spice crushing. My kitchen has three pestle and mortars: a small, antique brass one that I use for small quantities of 'sweet' ingredients such as cardamom and pistachios; a shallow, rough wooden one to pound dry spices, and a large, deep granite one for 'wet' grinding, such as making ginger-garlic or green chilli paste or for pulverising herbs and fried spice mixes. Bashing away with a pestle and mortar is one of the most therapeutic tasks in a kitchen! Many Indian cooks truly believe that hand-crushed spices and curry pastes taste far better than those made in electric machines and I think that a happy blend of both techniques will achieve a good flavour with an efficient use of time and energy!

Some people use a coffee grinder to grind small quantities of spices very effectively. However, remember to wash it well after use or you might end up with spice-flavoured coffee the next time you use your machine. Another way to crush toasted spice seeds is to put them between sheets of greaseproof paper to stop them from flying about and roll over them with a rolling pin. I always have a peppermill of toasted garam masala spices that I can freshly crush over curries.

Even if your kitchen is well stocked with most of the above, it's useful to know about, and exciting to own, some specialised or traditional Indian equipment.

Spice tin In all my years of teaching cookery, I have come across so many ways in which people store their spices. I have a three-way system at my cookery school (I buy large bags, then decant into jars and then into my spice tin) but most Indian homes can get by very well with a two-tier process if they buy small quantities.

Firstly, one buys the pack of spices (for more on spices, see page 54). These are decanted into a spice box, which typically has seven compartments. Every Indian home has this spice box or 'masala dabba' – it's most often round, made of stainless steel and has small bowls that fit snugly inside. Some boxes have a double lid to seal in the freshness. In my school, bulk buying of spices means that I store larger packs in my spice cupboard. These are decanted into small containers which are stored in my handy kitchen cupboard and from where I decant them into my 'masala dabba' a couple of times each week.

I like to believe that as an everyday spice box has seven compartments, one surely must not need to use more than seven spices for one's daily cooking! Interestingly, the seven spices in the tin may vary from one region of India to another but a few key spices such as turmeric, chilli, cumin and coriander remain the same throughout the country.

Kadhai/karahi This looks somewhat similar to a wok but is made of a thicker material, has a round bottom and comes with two small handles or none. It is also heavier, making it more stable on the hob. It is typically sold with a pair of tongs called 'chimta' or 'pakkad'. The tongs, held in one hand, help to steady the karahi as one stirs with the other hand. One can then lift the karahi with the tongs, but this needs a tight grip and lots of practice! A karahi will often come as a set with a lid.

Karahis are usually made of stainless steel, aluminium or an alloy of mixed metals and come in varying sizes. It is also possible to find non-stick ones but these need to be used with care as they can get scratched with abrasive utensils. I use a 35cm (diameter) karahi for a curry for four although I have a huge set of karahis in varying sizes all stacked up in my kitchen drawer. The best thing about my pans is that they get 'seasoned' with every use, making them virtually non-stick, and they are dishwasher safe. Many restaurants serve dishes like Karahi Paneer or Balti Chicken which have been cooked in such a dish. The largest karahis I have seen are at Amber Fort in Rajasthan and each one can safely hold 5–6 people! You would need a ladder to climb into it though…

Karahis are used for frying as the convex shape allows the oil to pool at the bottom, thus using much less oil than one would need in a frying pan. In India, karahis used for cooking may sometimes double up as serving dishes but the opposite never happens. Often made of burnished copper, brass or silver, tableware karahis are too light for hob use. Smaller in size or for family-style service, they may have flattened bottoms to sit securely on a table.

Pressure cooker I cannot vouch for these enough. They cut down on cooking times and are very fuel efficient, too. Best of all, they seal in nutrients and retain the juices in the food. Many Western cooks have said to me that they are frightened of pressure cookers blowing up but honestly speaking, modern ones are much safer than the ones that were used 40–50 years ago. There are two types of pressure cooker: the whistling one and steam-release type. Indian cooks use the whistling pressure cooker and it's not uncommon to find recipes that ask you to cook a curry for 3–4 whistles.

Pressure cookers come in various sizes and I have about five in my kitchen – small ones for everyday cooking and the largest one for entertaining. There is no real substitute for a pressure cooker. Most Indian homes have at least one and it is used for cooking meats, lentils, potatoes and even rice. Without a pressure cooker, the same curry can take two or three times the amount of time to cook.

Coconut scraper In India, where coconut inspires the cuisine of many states, and especially in southern India, a coconut scraper is found in the majority of homes. This is a flat, wooden base to which a sickle-shaped blade is attached (see photo below). This has a serrated fan at the end, which is used to scrape out the white flesh from the coconut shell. The blade is used to chop meat and vegetables. The whole device is placed on the floor and one has to sit on the plinth to use it. Modern coconut scrapers can be fixed to the kitchen counter, locked into place and stored away after use. Coconut can also be effectively grated in a food processor after breaking open the shell and prising away the flesh with a small, sharp knife.

Tava A tava or tawa is a flat or slightly curved griddle for cooking chapattis/rotis or other breads on. Sometimes vegetables or meats are also cooked on a tava and are called 'tava fry' – these are popular at Indian weddings where tavas as large as 3–4 feet in diameter are set up to serve over 1,000 guests!

Indian kitchens often have an iron tava, which when seasoned and used correctly can last a lifetime. In India, this 'seasoning' happens through regular use. In the West where the tava may not be used a few times a day as it is in India, it may need to be 'seasoned' to make it almost non-stick and rust free. Apply a thin coating of sunflower oil and put the pan in an oven at the highest temperature possible for 1 hour. Remove and leave it to cool. If you do not use your pan once every couple of weeks, you will have to repeat this process.

A Western substitute for a tava is a 25cm non-stick frying pan that can comfortably hold a roti.

Degchi This is a round, tall, thick-bottomed pan mostly made of aluminium, stainless steel or brass that is used for making dishes with a liquid base such as curries, dals and milk-based puddings. A degchi often has a lip for ease of holding and moving from the hob to the kitchen counter after cooking has finished. A 'pakkad' is used to clasp the degchi around the lip. A saucepan can easily replace a degchi.

Handi A handi is a circular pan or pot made of metal or clay that has a curved, saucer-like lid. It is fairly thick to allow long, slow cooking. A clay handi is used for one-pot cooking where all the ingredients are placed in it and gently sautéed to seal the food and blend flavours. Enough liquid is added, the lid is then sealed with a thick dough of flour and water and the entire pot is placed on a wood or coal fire. The lid can be used to place hot coals on. This is called 'dum pukht', cooking made popular by the Nawabs of Awadh in northern India and is still used in some parts of India. Restaurants serving dum pukht dishes in big cities, such as Mumbai and New Delhi, are sought after and attract diners who are not able to make this kind of smoky food in their urban kitchens.

Idli steamer This piece of equipment is found in all south Indian homes but you will need it only if you plan to make idlis – small, spongy rice and lentil cakes – at least a few times a month. An idli steamer is made of metal (more traditional and used on the hob) or plastic (more recent, for use in a microwave) and has a set of indented layers inside. Both work well enough. The batter is poured into the indents and steamed. An egg poacher or little individual bowls placed in a steamer can be used instead.

Sequence of Cooking

Indian cookery is a set of orchestrated processes that will result in the right flavour, colour, texture and aroma. This is the sequence. It is influenced by how long each ingredient takes to cook to perfection in that particular recipe. For example, a curry recipe where browned onions are to be ground to a paste will need those onions to be stir-fried slowly at the right temperature until they are soft and cooked through. If the onions are not cooked all the way through, there will be an unpleasant taste of raw onions in the final dish.

The sequence is also determined by how each ingredient influences the other. Adding an acid such as tomatoes while cooking lentils increases the cooking time and cooks the dal unevenly.

It is best not to take shortcuts while cooking because recipes have been written with this sequence in mind. Of course, each cook may vary this slightly – some fry ginger and garlic before adding onions to the pan, which can result in a deeper, smokier taste. I add them after the onions are almost cooked to prevent them from burning (typically onions take 8–10 minutes to cook, whereas garlic and ginger take just 3–4) and for a more balanced flavour.

Spices are especially important in this sequence. Seed spices and powders take different times to cook and are therefore added to the pan at varying times (see page 54). Raw spices will bring an unappetising bitterness to the dish.

Colour is an important consideration and each ingredient must be allowed to develop the right colour or be cooked in such a way that it does not colour at all. Rich, golden meat curries get their lovely colour from the browning of onions and spices.

DRYING RED CHILLIES, KISHANGARH FORT, KISHANGARH, RAJASTHAN.
DRIED RED CHILLIES ADD COLOUR AS WELL AS A DEEP, SMOKY
INTENSITY OF FLAVOUR TO MANY INDIAN DISHES.

THE SPICE CUPBOARD IN AN INDIAN KITCHEN ALWAYS HOLDS PRIDE OF PLACE.
PROPERLY STORED SPICES, USED JUDICIOUSLY, CAN MAKE ALL THE DIFFERENCE TO A BALANCED, DELICIOUS MEAL.

SPICES

Using spices for health → We use spices for several reasons – first and foremost for their health-giving properties. All spices are good for one's health if eaten in moderation. Turmeric, which is my favourite spice, is used both fresh as a root and in powder form. It contains the antioxidant curcumin, thought to help conditions such as a sore throat and possibly prevent cancer.

Chilli, in moderation, can activate the saliva and gastric juices and help us to digest food better. Black pepper, which is native to southern India, contains an essential oil called piperine which can aid the absorption of nutrients such as selenium and beta carotene from our food. Pepper is added to many curries either on its own or as part of garam masala, a fragrant, warm spice blend.

Using spices for flavour → The aromatic oils in spices are used to impart flavour to cooking. These oils are released in two ways – by heating and by crushing or splitting. This is why spice seeds and spice powders behave differently in the cooking process. The seeds require a higher cooking temperature to split them whereas the powders need moderate heat to release their oils.

Using spices for colour → Indian recipes are created keeping in mind not just flavour but also colour, texture and temperature. Turmeric adds a bright golden colour to many savoury dishes and as it does not change the flavour greatly, Indian cooks will add a tiny touch more if they think that the dish looks too pale after they have finished cooking it. Frying spice powders in oil at the start can add to the final dark colour of the dish.

Using spices to increase shelf life → Some spices are known to have antimicrobial properties and can help to preserve foods for longer. Mustard, cinnamon and cloves are particularly effective and many pickles in India contain split mustard seeds for this reason.

Spice Seeds

If the recipe has oil and seeds, the seeds will always go into the oil first, with the rest of the ingredients added on top in a sequence that depends on the time taken for each of them to cook. Seeds are also fried in oil and poured on top of a dish as tempering or 'tadka' (see page 36). I simply warm the oil over a high heat rather than allowing it to become blazing hot before adding the seeds to the pan. This gives me control as I watch the spice seeds slowly pop or sizzle rather than fly out of the pan or possibly burn if the oil is too hot.

TOASTING SPICE SEEDS

Spice seeds are sometimes dry-toasted and crushed for freshness of flavour. Not all spices need to be crushed every single time you make a meal. The ones that I would recommend be crushed at home are coriander seeds, cumin seeds and garam masala. Simply toast the spice seeds in a dry frying pan to release their aromatic oils and dry out any residual moisture, making them brittle and easier to crush. As soon as the pan is hot, in a matter of seconds, they will darken and develop an aroma. Tip them into a mortar and pestle or a spice mill and crush them to a powder. For the freshest flavour of all, you can put toasted garam masala spices in a peppermill and, with a few turns each time, sprinkle them onto curries just before serving.

Tip: When making a powdered blend, make sure that the toasted spices are completely cool before crushing or blitzing them otherwise they will become cakey and form lumps.

POWDERED OR GROUND SPICES

Powdered or ground spices, on the other hand, can go in at three different stages of the cooking. If you want depth of flavour, they go into the warm oil at the beginning. As the oil heats up, you will see three distinct stages. This is true of seeds and powders.

1 The spices will pop, crackle or sizzle.
2 They will change colour (except for black or brown mustard seeds).
3 They will develop a cooked aroma.

When cooking spice powders in oil, it is sometimes difficult to estimate exactly when they are 'done'. You can add a couple of tablespoons of water to the pan and let it cook for a few minutes until the water has evaporated, leaving the spices sizzling in the oil. The aroma will have changed from being quite strong to becoming mellow. Indian recipes also ask for spice powders to be mixed into a little water and then added to the pan. This allows them to cook without scorching.

These stages progress within seconds when the oil has reached the correct temperature, so be sure to have your next ingredient close at hand. If you have seeds in the pan, you can add any ingredient, such as onions, tomatoes, chillies, meat or vegetables next. However, if you are cooking spice powders, you will have to add a liquid ingredient as soon as the spices are cooked. This could be tomatoes, tamarind pulp, cooked lentils or curry pastes.

Most of my recipes ask you to sprinkle in the ground spices on top of ingredients that have reduced the temperature of the pan. For example, the onions go into the oil at the beginning. When they soften enough, the ginger, garlic and fresh chillies are added. Tomatoes may be next, followed by the spice powders. This way, the temperature in the pan is not high enough to burn the spices unless, of course, it is left on the heat unattended for too long.

Some spice powders are used as 'finishing spices'. The usual ones are red chilli powder and toasted cumin powder, which are often seen sprinkled on salads, street food called 'chaat' and yogurt-based curries. Garam masala is also dusted onto curries for a top note of aroma and warmth.

My Five Basic Spices

TURMERIC → One of the most traditional and versatile spices used in Indian cooking, turmeric is the heart and soul of any curry. This key ingredient is used daily in every part of India as its unique colour, due to the presence of the pigment curcumin, and flavour enriches all regional cuisine.

As for the root, only cured turmeric has the aroma and colour (chiefly due to the presence of curcumin) necessary for cooking. Turmeric has an earthy, sensual fragrance and a musky, dry taste, but it is used wholeheartedly in Indian cooking for its wonderful quality of enhancing and balancing the flavours of all the other ingredients. However, be careful not to use turmeric when cooking green vegetables as they will turn dull and taste bitter. Be wary when storing and using turmeric as it will stain hands and clothes quite quickly.

CHILLI POWDER → Chilli powder is used not only for its heat but also for its colour. Many varieties of chillies, such as Kashmiri red chillies, are bright red but only moderately hot. They are sometimes soaked in water or vinegar and ground to a paste to add a certain colour and smokiness to curries. Byadagi chillies, grown in Karnataka, are deceptively deep red in colour but have minimal heat. Commercially available chilli powder is usually a blend of several varieties and is sold in extra hot, hot, medium and mild versions. I think it's best to buy the moderate version. Interestingly, in India, the Bhut Jolokia, which has acquired celebrity as one of the world's hottest chillies, is rarely seen outside of the north-eastern region where it is grown.

In the West, chillies from all over the world, including Thailand and India, are imported and can be seen next to each other in supermarkets. I use bird's-eye chillies, variously called 'long thin' or 'thin green' chillies.

CUMIN → Cumin seeds are elongated, oval and long. They range from sage-green to tobacco-brown in colour and have longitudinal ridges. Another variety of cumin is black cumin ('kala jeera', 'shahi jeera' or 'siya jeera'): the seeds are dark brown to black and are smaller and finer than cumin. The smell of cumin is distinctive; it can be described as strong and bitter and is usually loved or hated. Cumin has a warm, somewhat bitter taste.

It is available whole as seeds, or crushed to a powder, which is often blended with ground coriander to form a widely used mixture called 'dhana-jeera'. This combination is one of the essential spice blends used in Indian cookery. Toasted cumin powder (see page 56) gives a lift to many curries and yogurt-based raitas.

CORIANDER → This pretty herb is the most commonly used garnish in northern and western India, and adds a dewy-green touch to red or brown curries. Seeds of the coriander plant are the spice. Coriander is perhaps one of the first spices known to man and has been around for over 3,000 years.

Coriander leaves and seeds are completely different with regards to aroma and flavour. The leaves taste and smell fresh and fruity with a hint of ginger. The seeds, on the other hand, have a sweet aroma with a subtle whiff of pine and pepper. Little bunches of fresh coriander are commonly available at greengrocers and supermarkets. It looks quite like parsley but the test lies in the aroma – parsley has a more delicate smell than coriander.

MUSTARD SEEDS → There are three main varieties of mustard seeds: yellow, and the ones used in Indian cooking – brown and black – which are interchangeable. Raw mustard seeds have almost no smell, but on cooking they acquire a distinctive, acrid, baked-earth aroma that dominates any dish. The seeds are sharp, nutty, slightly bitter and aromatic in taste. Their heat is often misjudged, so be careful when adding them to recipes. Mustard paste has a unique flavour that hits you in the nose.

Indian cooking does not use commercially blended mustards but they can make a reasonable substitute for homemade mustard paste. In south India and along the coast, mustard is used primarily as tempering (see page 36). In Bengal, mustard seeds are crushed to a paste for use in fiery marinades and curries.

OTHER SPICES THAT I COMMONLY USE ARE:

Cinnamon → Cinnamon *(7)* is an evergreen tree of the laurel family. The dried inner bark of the cinnamon tree is the spice used in cooking. I use cinnamon sticks for biryanis and curry pastes as they have a more powerful flavour than shop-bought ground cinnamon. Not all recipes call for cinnamon and it's not one of the everyday spices in Indian cooking. When used, it is often added whole into curries or rice, so it's best to crush the sticks in a mortar and pestle as and when needed. It is also an essential part of the standard blend of garam masala.

Cardamom → Cardamom *(1)* is one of the most expensive spices in the world. The fat, green pods grown in Kerala, south India, are considered the best. Cardamom pods are oval capsules containing hard, dark brown seeds that are sticky and cling together. The two main varieties are green and black. The green ones have a 'sweet' aroma and are used in desserts or savoury dishes, whereas the black ones are smoky and are only used in rich savoury dishes.

Asafoetida (Hing) → Although not native to India, asafoetida *(5)* has for centuries been an essential part of Indian cookery and medicine. Asafoetida is the dried latex from the rhizomes of several species of ferula or giant fennel. It is grown chiefly in Iran and Afghanistan from where it is exported to the rest of the world. Asafoetida has a pungent, unpleasant smell quite like that of pickled eggs, due to the presence of sulphur compounds. This pungency reduces when the spice is cooked and it acquires an aroma like that of cooked onions and garlic. Its powerful smell complements lentils, vegetables and pickles. It is often used as a digestive spice in vegetarian cookery and in place of garlic in the cookery of some religions such as Jainism that forbid the use of garlic or any ingredient grown underground as it could lead to the destruction of life when these are uprooted. It is always used in small quantities – a pinch added to hot oil before the other ingredients is enough to flavour a dish for four.

Mango Powder (Amchoor) → Mango powder *(3)* is made from raw, sour, green mangoes, especially windfalls or wild mangoes. The unripe fruits are peeled, cut into thin slices, dried and powdered to make a fruity, sour spice that is used as a souring agent, especially in dry recipes that would change by the addition of a wet ingredient. Amchoor is available in speciality supermarkets in the West and can be substituted with lemon juice.

Pepper → In India, pepper *(4)* is used in every type of regional cookery, often as part of a garam masala blend. It can be cooked with the main ingredients or sprinkled on top as a finishing spice.

Ajowan (Ajwain) → Ajowan *(2)* is a close relative of dill, caraway and cumin. The fragrance of the spice is very similar to that of oregano. Ajowan goes particularly well with green beans, root vegetables and in dishes that are flour-based, all of which form an important part of India's vast vegetarian cuisine. Snacks like Bombay mix and onion bhajias depend on spices like ajowan for their unique flavour.

Saffron → At one time, saffron *(6)* grew wild in Persia and Asia Minor but today India and Spain are the only major producers. In India it only grows in the valley of Kashmir. Saffron is the dried stigmas of the *Crocus sativus*, a perennial bulb, which flowers for just two weeks in late October. In India the lavender-blue blossoms are plucked at dawn before the hot sun wilts them. Then the delicate stigmas are prised out from within each flower and dried artificially or in the sun.

Saffron is made up of fine, orange-gold threads that are so light that 750,000 handpicked flowers yield only about 450g. When fresh, saffron is bright and glossy, but exposure to light and air makes it dull and brittle. Pure saffron is believed to be able to colour and flavour 70,000 times its weight in liquid. Its intense, musky aroma suffuses the dish to which it has been added and the taste is delicate and only very slightly bitter. It is the most expensive spice in the world due to its scarcity, fragility and flavour. That is why the temptation to adulterate it is considerable. The usual adulterant is safflower, aptly called 'bastard saffron'. Cheaper and with thicker strands than saffron, it will turn food golden but will not flavour it.

Saffron enhances savoury food as well as sweet. A few strands soaked in a little warm water or milk and added to the dish along with the liquid add a fragrant richness. It especially complements milk desserts, rice pulaos and biryanis and white meats such as fish and chicken.

SPICE BLENDS AND CURRY POWDERS

There is no one blend called 'curry powder' in India. Each region and every community of people has a unique recipe special to that group. Here are some basic recipes that will make a batch of a few tablespoons.

How to store spices If stored properly, in a dark cupboard and away from air and moisture, spice seeds will last up to a year. Powders and powdered spice blends should ideally be used up in 6 months.

Garam Masala

Some of the most expensive spices go into the making of garam masala (literally 'warming spices') and there are as many recipes for it as there are households in India. Depending on individual taste, the proportions of the various ingredients can be adjusted to make this an aromatic rather than hot blend. I have created my blend as below using spices for aroma (cardamom, cinnamon, fennel) as well as for bulking and thickening curries (coriander, cumin). I also keep away from recipes that have a long list of ingredients as some garam masala mixes do, and find that this recipe is sufficiently aromatic.

Garam masala is used whole or ground depending on what's cooking. The basic blend includes cloves, cinnamon, cardamom, peppercorns, bay leaf, mace, cumin and coriander seeds. Commercially-bought garam masala is quite good if used within a couple of months. The blend is easy to grind at home, so it is best to buy whole, plump spices and crush them in an electric grinder, coffee mill or using a mortar and pestle. This mixture can then be stored in an airtight container for up to 6 months.

Indian cooks use garam masala in small amounts. It can be added at different stages of cooking for different degrees of flavour. It is also used as a finishing spice.

1 teaspoon black peppercorns
2 teaspoons cumin seeds
2cm piece of cinnamon stick
10 green cardamom pods, deseeded and husks discarded
5 black cardamom pods, deseeded and husks discarded
10 cloves
3 bay leaves
2 blades of mace
1 teaspoon fennel seeds
2 teaspoons coriander seeds

1 Heat a dry frying pan over a medium heat, add the spices and dry-toast until they start to darken and become aromatic. Remove from the heat and leave to cool completely before grinding to a fine powder in a spice mill or using a mortar and pestle. Store in an airtight container in a cool, dark place and consume within 6 months. You can also put the whole toasted spices into a peppermill to use as and when required.

Sambhar Powder

This spice blend is found in every south Indian home. Ready-made sambhar powder is available in India but you can make your own quite easily as it is not as readily available in the West. It goes mainly into sambhar (see page 282) or south Indian dal, or into vegetable dishes.

1 teaspoon black mustard seeds
1 teaspoon fenugreek seeds
2 teaspoons cumin seeds
1 teaspoon black peppercorns
1 teaspoon coriander seeds
1 teaspoon toor dal
1 teaspoon split black lentils (urad dal)
1 teaspoon ground turmeric
¼ teaspoon asafoetida

1   Heat a heavy-based pan over a medium heat, add the whole spices one by one and dry-toast. Keep the heat low and stir constantly to stop them from burning. The seeds will crackle and fly out so beware! When they have darkened and begin to smoke, tip each spice into a bowl.
2   In the same pan, dry-toast the toor dal for 5–6 minutes until it starts to change colour, then tip this into the toasted spice mix. Dry-toast the urad dal for 4–5 minutes and add this in as well.
3   Leave the mixture to cool completely, then add the turmeric and asafoetida and grind in a spice mill or mortar and pestle until fine. Store in an airtight container in a cool, dark place and consume within 6 months.

Goda Masala

This Maharashtrian spice blend is a dark, aromatic powder with a burnt sweetness which comes from the coconut in the mixture.

1 teaspoon sunflower oil
1cm piece of cinnamon stick
5 cloves
5 green cardamom pods, deseeded and husks discarded
2 bay leaves
2 teaspoons white sesame seeds
2 teaspoons coriander seeds
4 tablespoons desiccated coconut
10 black peppercorns
2 tablespoons white poppy seeds

1   Heat the oil in a frying pan over a medium heat, then add the cinnamon, cloves, cardamom seeds and bay leaves and fry for 2–3 minutes until the cloves swell. Remove from the pan, wipe it dry and use the same pan for dry-toasting.
2   Dry-toast the remaining ingredients one by one over a low heat until they darken. The coconut should be toasted until dark brown. Remove from the heat and leave to cool, then grind with the fried spices in a spice mill until fine. Store in an airtight container in a cool, dark place and consume within 6 months.

Kolhapuri Masala

This is a fiery spice blend from Kolhapur in Maharashtra. It is used in both vegetable as well as meat or chicken curries.

10 dried red chillies
2 tablespoons sesame seeds
1 tablespoon coriander seeds
1 tablespoon cumin seeds
1 tablespoon freshly ground black pepper
1 teaspoon fenugreek seeds
6 cloves
1 tablespoon black or brown mustard seeds
50g desiccated coconut
½ teaspoon ground nutmeg
1 teaspoon medium hot red chilli powder

1 Heat a frying pan over a medium heat and dry-toast the spices (except the nutmeg and chilli powders) and coconut one by one for a few minutes. The spices will begin to sizzle and pop and the colour of the chillies and the coconut will darken. Remove from the heat, as overcooking them will make the spices bitter. Tip into a bowl.

2 Leave to cool completely, then blitz to a fine powder in a coffee mill. Store in an airtight container in a cool, dark place and consume within 6 months.

Panch Phoron

This Bengali spice blend is used whole or in powder form. I tend to keep my blend in the seed form. In Bengal, the mix would contain 'radhuni' (wild celery seeds). As these are not so widely available in the West, cooks substitute them with mustard seeds.

Mix equal quantities of:
Cumin seeds
Fennel seeds
Fenugreek seeds
Black mustard seeds or radhuni
Nigella seeds

1 Store the mix in seed form or dry-toast the spices and crush them to a fine powder in a spice mill or using a mortar and pestle. Store in an airtight container in a cool, dark place and consume within 6 months if powdered, or within a year if stored in seed form.

RIGHT: *1 Panch Phoron; 2 Goda Masala; 3 Kolhapuri Masala; 4 Sambhar Powder; 5 Garam Masala.*

RICE

RICE ORIGINATED AS A WILD GRASS IN THE REGION OF WHAT WE NOW CALL CHINA.
Oryza sativa HAS TWO MAJOR SUBSPECIES THAT WE USE TODAY – THE SHORT-GRAINED, STICKY JAPONICA
USED IN THAI AND OTHER EAST ASIAN CUISINES AND
THE FLUFFY, LONG-GRAINED INDICA USED IN INDIAN COOKERY.

The *Yajurveda* (c.1200–1,000 BCE), one of the four key Sanskrit texts of Hinduism, describes the making of rice cakes as a ritual offering to Agni, the God of Fire. The *Shunya Purana*, written by Ramai the Wise in the 10th–11th century AD, states that 50 varieties of rice, such as Nagra, Jhinga-sal and Panloi, were grown in Bengal even then. Many of those varieties are now extinct but these three varieties are still being conserved on special farms by rice conservationists.

Early European visitors to India were not familiar with rice. Aristobulus, who came with Alexander the Great around 326 BCE, described it as a strange plant standing in water, and the Greek explorer Megasthenes described it as being a staple in the Indian diet.

Indians have a unique relationship with rice. Besides being at the heart of many regional cuisines such as Tamilian and Bengali, it is also associated with religious and social rituals and sacraments. Traditional Hindu cookery differentiates between 'kaccha' and 'pukka' foods; kaccha are those that are cooked in water and are consumed in the kitchen. Pukka foods are cooked in ghee and can be taken out of the kitchen for public consumption. These rules were made for reasons of health and hygiene but became religious practices of purity. Even today temple foods are pukka foods and often include fried delicacies sweetened with jaggery or sugar. Rice was a kaccha food and could only be eaten fresh.

The 'annaprashana' Hindu sacrament is when a child is given their first solid food and this is almost always some soft rice mixed with creamy homemade ghee. Funerals are marked with rice balls being offered to the ancestors as a symbolic meal in their honour.

The Hindu goddess Parvati is also called 'Annapurna' (provider of a bounty of rice). In a Hindu wedding, rice coloured with turmeric and vermilion is scattered over the couple to signify sustenance and fertility. A bride enters her husband's house by overturning a small pot of raw rice with her toe, inviting good luck and prosperity into her new home.

Even today, the rice-growing culture of rural India is influenced by this belief in Parvati. In the top rice-cultivating regions such as West Bengal, Uttar Pradesh and Andhra Pradesh, where the cuisine centres around this staple, each stage of production, such as ploughing, transplantation, harvesting and storing the rice is done on an auspicious day and various rituals called 'pujas' are performed.

Apart from the vast array of rituals, rice is an important part of Indian cookery. Every region produces its own variety and although outside of India basmati rice is popular, within the country people will eat their local rice on a daily basis. In Andhra Pradesh, a medium-grain aromatic rice called 'sona masuri' is favoured. In the south, an inexpensive short-grained red rice called 'matta' is prized, whereas in Maharashtra in the West it is the short-grained 'ambemohar', which smells like mango flowers when cooked. In wealthier families, basmati rice is cooked on special occasions or for certain dishes like biryanis.

Each region of India has unique rice preparations. It is cooked in its grain form, beaten to make flat rice 'poha' (see page 358) or crushed into flour for batters and poppadums. In Maharashtra and southern India it is served in courses, accompanied by a different curry or lentil dish each time. In a southern home, you will be served rice first with spicy lentil 'sambhar', then with a thinner 'rasam' and finally with plain yogurt. In the north-east, various communities such as the Khamtis grow their own rice, and in Assam, rice is cooked with fragrant Shewali flowers to make a slightly bitter preparation called 'teeta bhaat' that is served at the beginning of the meal.

Rice provides a major proportion of calories in the Indian diet. It is always eaten in combination with dal or beans to make a complete protein. Rice contains the cysteine and methionine that lentils lack and lentils provide the lysine that rice does not have enough of.

Rice Classifications

SIZE OF GRAIN

Long-grain rice The grains are slim and four to five times longer than they are wide. They are known to cook fluffier than the other varieties and are therefore usually more expensive. Long-grain rice is used in biryanis and pulaos, such as Murgh Dum Biryani (page 86) and Pudina Pulao (page 91), as the rice needs to be fluffy and separate.

Medium-grain rice The grains are almost twice as long as they are wide and cook softer and moister than long-grain rice. This is used in everyday meals as it helps to hold together wet curries and dals. Typical recipes include Mung Dal Khichdi (page 88) and Mosaranna (page 93).

Short-grain rice This looks slightly oval or round in shape. It is quite starchy and may be used for rice pudding-style dishes such as Rice Kheer (page 451) and Phirni (page 459).

PROCESSING

When rice is harvested, it is first called 'rough rice' and is still covered by a non-edible husk. At the mill, rough rice is processed through sorting machines that clean the kernels and remove foreign matter.

The husk is then removed, leaving brown rice with the bran layers still surrounding the rice kernel. Grains of brown rice are polished by removing the bran layers, revealing white rice. As the most nutritious layers of the rice grain have been removed in the milling process, white rice is often enriched with thiamin, niacin and iron to restore it back to its original levels and help prevent conditions such as cardiovascular disease and anaemia.

Some of the rice is separated to go through an extra initial processing step that will turn it into parboiled rice. Parboiled rice is brown rice that is steamed or parboiled so that nutrients from the outer husk move into the grain itself.

Basmati

HOW TO BUY BASMATI RICE

This is the most widely available Indian rice all over the world. It is sold under various brand names, and bags of rice sometimes mention that the rice has been aged. Basmati rice, like wine, gets better with age. Top-quality basmati is stored for 1–2 years in highly-controlled conditions. Optimum temperature and low moisture levels help to dry the rice and harden the outer shell. This enhances and intensifies its taste, bouquet and cooking characteristics: old rice cooks up fluffy, with separate grains, while new rice can become sticky.

In India, one can ask the grocer for aged rice and it will be more expensive than new rice. There is a wide price range for basmati rice, and buyers in the West often think that they are being asked to pay for fancy brand names whereas in fact, it is the ageing process they are paying for.

How much to make As a general rule, allow 50g raw rice per person. Do bear in mind what else is being served – if you also have a bread or lots of different dishes, you will need a bit less.

HOW TO COOK BASMATI RICE

Cleaning In India, rice always has to be cleaned as it is sold loose from burlap sacks. Traditionally it is sifted and cleaned in a 'supdi', a small, flat cane basket where the rice is tossed up and down gently to separate it from tiny stones or foreign particles. It can also be spread on a white dinner plate and small quantities worked to the opposite side of the plate, picking out any foreign objects. Outside of India, where rice is almost always sold bagged, this process is not necessary.

Washing Indians will put rice into a bowl and pour in cold water from the tap. Then the fingers are swirled through to loosen the starch from the grains and the water is carefully poured off. Without experience, this may seem tricky so it is best to wash the rice in a sieve under cold running water for a couple of minutes until the water runs clear.

Soaking After washing, some cooks suggest soaking the rice for anywhere between 15 minutes to 1 hour to allow the grains to absorb moisture, relax and expand. Basmati rice cooks well, depending on the recipe, even if it isn't soaked.

Rice Cooking Tips

How to get separate grains Buy the right brand of rice – one that has been aged and is therefore a bit pricier. Lightly frying the grains in a few drops of cooking oil before adding water may help the grains to cook up fluffy and light.

The two main methods You can cook rice by the draining or the absorption method (see pages 78–79).

How much water? This will depend on various factors, including the variety and age of the rice, the depth of the pan and the source and strength of heat. In a deep pan, there is less evaporation and you will need slightly less water than if you use a wide pan. Similarly, when cooking over gas or electric heat you may need different amounts of water as well as different cooking times.

Which pan to use? A heavy-based saucepan with a tight-fitting lid is essential. This will distribute the heat evenly, ensure that a minimum amount of steam escapes and that the water is absorbed by the grains. If your lid does not seal the pan, use a tea towel or foil to cover the pan, then place the lid on top. The towel will absorb the steam and prevent it from escaping, whereas the foil will act as a tight seal.

To stir or not? When you've combined the rice and water or any other liquid, stir once very gently then resist the temptation to stir again. Rice grains are delicate and susceptible to breaking if handled too much, and over-stirring will make the rice starchy. Also, once you've put the lid on, don't remove it, even to check the rice or amount of water. This cooks the rice unevenly and the recipe may not work. Once you've removed the pan from the heat, leave the cooked rice covered for 5 minutes or so to rest and fluff up. Remove the lid and run a fork through it to loosen the grains.

To salt or not? Various Indian recipes suggest using salt or not, depending on the cook. I don't add salt to plain rice or any rice dish that is to be eaten with a dal or curry because those accompaniments will always have salt in them. If a rice dish can be eaten on its own, for example a biryani or lemon rice, I do add a bit of salt.

Electric rice cooker Many Indians and cooks from Far Eastern countries use this simply because of the quantities of rice they cook on a daily basis. Follow the manufacturer's instructions and put rice and the exact amount of water into the cooker. Do not add salt. Switch it on and leave it to turn itself off. It will turn itself on from time to time to keep the rice hot.

HOW TO STORE COOKED RICE SAFELY

Below are the recommendations of the NHS in the UK. It is possible to get food poisoning from improperly stored cooked rice that has been reheated.

Uncooked rice contains spores of *Bacillus cereus*, bacteria that can cause food poisoning. The spores survive even after cooking and, at room temperature, these can grow into bacteria and produce toxins that cause the symptoms of food poisoning. The longer the rice is left at room temperature, the higher the chances of bacteria growing, making the rice unsafe to eat.

Rice should ideally be eaten as soon as it is cooked. Leftovers should be cooled quickly before storing; this can be done by spreading the rice out on a tray to cool then chilling it. You can store rice in the fridge for a day then reheat it until it is steaming hot, either in a microwave or in a steamer. It's best not to reheat rice more than once.

VARIETIES OF RICE

Although India has hundreds of varieties of rice, these are some of the most common that are found around the world:

Basmati→ True to its name 'Queen of Fragrance', this rice has a nutty aroma and a smooth, buttery flavour. The grains elongate and plump up as they cook and the end result is a dry, fluffy, separate rice. Basmati rice grows in snow-fed paddy fields at the foothills of the Himalayas, is more expensive than other Indian rice, and is available as brown or white.

Patna→ This is a long-grain, slender rice that comes from the Gangetic plains of Bihar in north India. It resembles basmati rice but has less fragrance and is opaque rather than translucent. Nevertheless, in areas where it is grown, it is also referred to as 'Parimal' or perfumed. It is used to make everyday boiled rice that is eaten with curries.

Matta→ The grains of this rice are short, coarse and pink in colour. It is grown in Kerala and Karnataka and is used in south India as well as Sri Lanka. Of the various types of matta rice, 'Palakkadan Matta' and 'Navara' are both regional, organically grown varieties and are registered under the Geographical Indications of Goods Act 1999, which means that they are associated with a specific location and origin. The unique, earthy taste of matta makes it a popular accompaniment to meat. It is sold parboiled, which ensures that the nutrients are locked into each grain.

Sona Masuri→ This medium-grain, white, aromatic rice is lightweight and low in starch. It grows mainly in Andhra Pradesh and Karnataka and is used in southern biryanis and a jaggery-sweetened rice dish called 'pongal'.

Sella→ This rice is golden in colour as the paddy is first steamed, then dried and milled. This seals in the nutrients. Long-grain rice grown in Punjab is often used to make this type of rice which is used in biryanis and pulaos.

Surti Kloam→ A medium-grain variety, it is most popular in the Gujarat region of India where it is used as an everyday rice. It has a milder flavour and aroma than basmati rice.

RIGHT: *1 Sella; 2 Patna; 3 Sona Masuri; 4 Matta; 5 Basmati.*

CHAVAL – Plain Boiled Rice – absorption method

Plain rice is the most popular rice in India as it acts as the perfect backdrop to flavourful curries and dals.

Serves 4 PREPARATION → *5 minutes*
COOKING *20 minutes*

YOU WILL NEED:
200g basmati rice

1 Measure the rice in a measuring jug, then wash in a sieve, drain and put into a heavy-based saucepan with double the amount of water to rice (measured in the same jug). Bring to the boil without stirring.

2 Reduce the heat to low, stir once gently and cover the pan. Simmer for 10 minutes, then remove from the heat and leave the rice to rest for 5 minutes, covered.

3 Remove the lid, gently run a fork through the rice to loosen it, and serve hot.

CHAVAL – Plain Boiled Rice – draining method

This is a good way of cooking rice when you have many dishes on the go. Once you've done it a few times, you'll be able to judge how long it takes to cook perfect rice in your pan, on your hob and with the rice you normally buy. You can use this method with brown or wholegrain basmati rice but the cooking time will be longer – allow 30–45 minutes of simmering time. *Serves 4* PREPARATION → *5 minutes* COOKING *25 minutes*

YOU WILL NEED:

200g basmati rice

1 Measure the rice in a measuring jug, then wash in a sieve, drain and set aside. Put six times the volume of water (measured in the same jug) to rice in a large saucepan and bring to the boil. You can also use boiling water from the kettle.

2 Add the rice and stir once, gently. Bring back to the boil, reduce the heat to a simmer and cook until the rice is done. This can take 10–15 minutes, depending on your pan and heat source. Partially covering your pan will cook the rice faster. You can test the rice by squashing a grain between your thumb and forefinger or simply by tasting it!

3 Drain the rice through a sieve, allowing all the water to drain away. Serve hot.

Thengai Sadam

| COCONUT RICE |

The juiciness of fresh coconut is vital to this dish and therefore it cannot be substituted with desiccated coconut. For instructions on how to grate a coconut, see page 310.

Serves 4 PREPARATION → *15 minutes* COOKING *30 minutes*

200g basmati rice, washed and drained
2 tablespoons vegetable oil
1 teaspoon black mustard seeds
2 tablespoons cashew nuts
1 teaspoon chopped fresh green chillies
1 teaspoon split, skinless black lentils (urad dal),
    soaked in water for 15 minutes and drained
large pinch of asafoetida
7 fresh or 10 dried curry leaves
50g fresh coconut, grated
salt

1 Put the rice and double the amount of water by volume in a heavy-based saucepan and bring to the boil. Reduce the heat to low, stir, cover and cook for 10 minutes until the water has been absorbed and the rice is cooked. Remove from the heat and set to one side, covered.

2 Heat the oil in a large frying pan over a high heat and add the mustard seeds. Fry until they start to pop, then add the cashew nuts, chillies, lentils, asafoetida and curry leaves (standing back from the pan if using fresh leaves, as they will splutter). Fry for 1 minute, then add the grated coconut and stir until the mixture starts to turn golden. Season to taste with salt.

3 Remove from the heat and fold into the cooked rice. Serve hot with Sambhar (page 282) or Vellarikka Kootu (page 293).

Chettinad Mutton Biryani

| LAMB BIRYANI WITH SOUTHERN SPICES |

A few years ago, I did a food trip around the southern state of Tamil Nadu and stopped at a small highway café serving only biryani. Here I had one of the tastiest rice dishes I have ever sampled. So I made my way to the kitchen only to be told that the chef 'had left for the day'! Leaving without a recipe but armed with spices from a local shop, I tried out several versions in my own kitchen and this one comes closest to what I ate in Karaikudi in Chettinad. Mountain moss (dagad phool) is a papery spice that smells of aniseed. If you can't find it, use aniseed or fennel seeds instead. *Serves 4* PREPARATION → *15 minutes* COOKING *1½ hours*

400g lamb or mutton shoulder on the bone,
    cut into bite-sized pieces
2 tablespoons ginger-garlic paste *(page 45)*
1 large onion, diced
2 star anise
4 cloves
large pinch of mountain moss (dagad phool) or 1 teaspoon
    aniseed or fennel seeds
4 green cardamom pods, husks removed and seeds crushed
4 black cardamom pods, husks removed and seeds crushed
2.5cm piece of cinnamon stick
10 fresh or 15 dried curry leaves
2 fresh green chillies, diced
4 dried red chillies, halved and seeds shaken out
1 teaspoon ground turmeric
1 teaspoon garam masala *(page 64)*
200g basmati rice, washed and drained
a handful of fresh coriander leaves, chopped, to garnish
salt

1 Put the lamb, ginger-garlic paste and enough salt to season in a pan with 400ml water. Bring to the boil, cover, reduce the heat and simmer for 40 minutes until the lamb is cooked.

2 Put the remaining ingredients, except the coriander, in a heavy-based saucepan and pour in the lamb stock along with the cooked lamb. Season to taste.

3 Bring to the boil, reduce the heat to the lowest setting and cook, covered, for 15 minutes until all the stock has been absorbed. Remove from the heat and fluff with a fork. Sprinkle with the coriander to serve.

Pulao Rice

| RICE WITH CUMIN AND FRIED ONIONS |

Pulao often features spice and vegetables, meat, chicken or seafood combined with rice. It is quite a simple but fragrant dish, where a few whole spices such as cardamom and cloves are used rather than complex blends as in a biryani. *Serves 4* PREPARATION → *5 minutes* COOKING *25 minutes*

1 tablespoon vegetable oil
2 onions, thinly sliced
½ teaspoon cumin seeds
200g basmati rice, washed and drained
salt (optional)

1 Heat the oil in a heavy-based saucepan, add the onions and fry for 8–10 minutes until golden brown. Adding a small pinch of salt will help to cook the onions faster and prevent them from burning. Remove from the pan and set to one side. Add the cumin seeds to the same pan with and fry in the remaining oil until they darken slightly.

2 Tip in the rice, and let it fry for 1 minute or so until it becomes shiny.

3 Pour in double the amount of water to rice by volume (measured in the same jug), stir once and bring to the boil. Reduce the heat to low, cover and cook for 10 minutes, until the water has been absorbed and the rice is cooked. Remove from the heat, leave the rice to rest for 5 minutes, covered, then remove the lid, fluff the rice with a fork and serve hot, topped with the fried onions.

Elumichai Sadam

| LEMON RICE |

South India has a vast number of rice recipes and this one is my favourite because it is a complete meal in itself, but is so simple to prepare. Fragrant, festive and beautiful to look at, it can be served with a bowl of plain yogurt and some hot pickle, with a spicy curry, or simply on its own. *Serves 4* PREPARATION → *10 minutes, plus soaking time* COOKING *25 minutes*

200g basmati rice, washed and drained
2 tablespoons vegetable oil
1 teaspoon black mustard seeds
6 fresh curry leaves
1 teaspoon split yellow gram lentils (chana dal), washed
    and soaked in hot water for 15 minutes and drained
10 unsalted cashew nuts
2 tablespoons unsalted peanuts
1 teaspoon ground turmeric
3 tablespoons lemon juice
salt

1 Put the rice and double the amount of water by volume in a heavy-based saucepan and bring to the boil. Reduce the heat to low, stir, cover and cook for 10 minutes until the water has been absorbed and the rice is cooked. Set aside.

2 In a separate pan, heat the oil over a high heat, add the mustard seeds and fry until they start to pop. Add the curry leaves (standing back from the pan, as they will splutter), lentils, cashew nuts and peanuts, reduce the heat and fry for a minute or so.

3 When the cashews are slightly brown, add the turmeric. Immediately remove from the heat and add the lemon juice. Season to taste with salt.

4 Gently fold the cooked rice into the mixture and serve hot.

Vangi Bhaath

| SPICED AUBERGINE RICE |

This dish is from Maharashtra, where it is served at weddings and feasts. Spiced, flavoured rice is considered festive as it takes longer to prepare than plain rice, and is colourful and fragrant. You can make it as spicy as you wish but I prefer a medium heat, served with yogurt, hot mango pickle and crisp poppadums. *Serves 4*

PREPARATION → *10 minutes* COOKING *30 minutes*

2 tablespoons vegetable oil
1 medium onion, thinly sliced
large pinch of asafoetida
8–10 fresh or 15 dried curry leaves
1 medium aubergine, cut into 2.5cm cubes
10 cashew nuts
1 teaspoon ground turmeric
1 teaspoon medium-hot red chilli powder
1 tablespoon goda masala *(page 65)*
200g basmati rice, washed and drained
2 teaspoons lemon juice
salt
yogurt, shop-bought hot mango pickle and poppadums,
    to serve (optional)

1 Heat the oil in a heavy-based saucepan over a high heat and add the onion. Stir for 5–6 minutes until it turns golden, then add the asafoetida and curry leaves. Fry for 30 seconds, then add the aubergine and stir-fry until it starts to soften, then add the cashew nuts and cook for a minute until golden. Add the turmeric, chilli powder, goda masala and season to taste with salt. Stir a couple of times, then add the rice and stir for a couple of minutes until it becomes opaque.

2 Pour in double the amount of water by volume to the rice. Stir, bring to the boil, then reduce the heat to low, cover and cook for 10 minutes until the water has been absorbed and the rice is cooked. Remove from the heat and set aside, covered, for 5 minutes, before removing the lid. Add the lemon juice, fluff the rice with a fork and serve hot.

Tamater Pulao

| TOMATO PULAO |

This simple north Indian rice dish is pretty and tangy, and can be eaten simply with some yogurt for a light meal.

Serves 4 PREPARATION → *5 minutes* COOKING *25 minutes*

1 tablespoon vegetable oil
3 bay leaves
1 tablespoon tomato purée or 2 grated fresh tomatoes
200g basmati rice, washed and drained

1 Heat the oil in a heavy-based saucepan over a high heat, add the bay leaves and fry for a minute or so until they begin to darken. Add the tomato purée or grated tomatoes. Cook for 1–2 minutes then tip in the rice. Stir once, to blend it with the tomatoes, then pour in double the amount of water by volume to the rice, stir and bring to the boil.

2 Reduce the heat to low, cover and cook for about 10 minutes until the water has been absorbed and the rice is cooked. Remove from the heat, leave the rice to rest for 5 minutes, covered, then remove the lid, fluff the rice with a fork and serve hot.

Kofta Pulao

| VEGETABLE PULAO WITH MEATBALLS |

2 tablespoons vegetable oil

3 cloves

4 green cardamom pods, husks removed
   and seeds crushed

2 black cardamom pods, husks removed
   and seeds crushed

2.5cm piece of cinnamon stick

2 star anise

1 medium onion, thinly sliced

2 teaspoons ginger-garlic paste *(page 45)*

2 teaspoons tomato purée

100g mixed diced vegetables, such as carrots,
   peas and green beans

1 teaspoon ground turmeric

1 teaspoon garam masala *(page 64)*

200g basmati rice, washed and drained

a handful of chopped fresh coriander leaves

For the meatballs

150g lean lamb mince

1 teaspoon ginger-garlic paste *(page 45)*

1 fresh green chilli, finely chopped

salt

An easy yet festive dish, you can stir the meatballs into the rice just before serving or simply place them on top. When the Mughal emperor Humayun was ousted from power by Sher Shah Suri in 1539, he went to Persia to seek help to regain his throne. He returned greatly influenced by Persian culture and food. The pulao, a spiced rice dish, was one of the delicacies introduced to the imperial kitchens at this time. *Serves 5*

PREPARATION ⟶ *15 minutes* COOKING *25 minutes*

1 Preheat the oven to 220°C/gas mark 7 and line a baking tray with foil. Mix all the ingredients for the meatballs together in a large bowl, then form into cherry-sized balls. Place the meatballs on the lined tray and bake for 10 minutes, then remove from the oven and set aside.

2 Meanwhile, heat the oil in a heavy-based saucepan over a high heat, add the cloves, both cardamom seeds, cinnamon stick and star anise and fry until they sizzle. Add the onion and cook until soft, then stir in the ginger-garlic paste and tomato purée.

3 Add the vegetables and the spice powders and stir for a couple of minutes, then tip in the rice and fry for a further minute until it turns opaque. Add most of the chopped coriander leaves, reserving some for the garnish.

4 Pour in double the amount of water to rice by volume, plus 4 extra tablespoons, into the rice and bring to the boil. Reduce the heat, stir once, cover and leave to cook for 10 minutes until the water has been absorbed and the rice is cooked. Remove from the heat and set aside, covered, for 5 minutes.

5 To serve, remove the lid, gently fluff the rice with a fork, fold in the meatballs and sprinkle with the remaining coriander.

MURGH DUM BIRYANI – North Indian Chicken Biryani

YOU WILL NEED:

3 tablespoons whole milk

large pinch of saffron

4 tablespoons rose water

3 tablespoons ghee

3 large onions, thinly sliced

2 tablespoons ginger-garlic paste *(page 45)*

3 fresh green chillies, chopped

2 tablespoons tomato purée

600g skinless chicken breast, diced

1 teaspoon ground turmeric

1 teaspoon garam masala *(page 64)*

300g basmati rice, washed and drained

a handful of fresh mint leaves, chopped

a handful of fresh coriander leaves, chopped

3 tablespoons flaked almonds

salt

6–8 hard-boiled eggs, to serve

For the bouquet garni

10 green cardamom pods

5 black cardamom pods

12 black peppercorns

small cinnamon stick

10 cloves

a few shavings of nutmeg

1 teaspoon fennel seeds

3 bay leaves

The word biryani is derived from the Farsi word 'birian', which means 'fried before cooking'. It is thought to have originated in Persia or Arabia and could have come into north India via Afghanistan. As the Mughals spread their empire, the biryani travelled to various parts of the country. Today many Muslim communities in India have their own versions, each slightly different from the other. The Hyderabadi biryani, where lamb, spices and rice are cooked together, became popular during the rule of Asaf Jah I, who was Emperor Aurangzeb's deputy to the region. In the Lucknowi biryani, the rice and meat are cooked separately then layered and finished by the dum pukht method (see page 14). When the ruler of Awadh, Wajid Ali Shah, was exiled by the British, he moved to Calcutta and a new version of the biryani was created, using more potatoes and less meat for the poorer residents of the city. *Serves 6–8* PREPARATION ➞ *40 minutes* COOKING *1½ hours*

1 Crush the seeds of 5 of the green cardamom pods and all the black cardamom pods in a pestle and mortar and discard the husks.

2 Put the bouquet garni spices (except the 5 whole green cardamom pods) in a pan with 500ml hot water and bring to the boil. Remove from the heat, cover the pan and leave to steep. This is the savoury aroma liquid.

3 Finely crush the reserved cardamom pods in a pestle and mortar (discarding the husk) and mix with the milk, saffron and rose water. Set aside. This is the sweet aroma liquid.

4 Preheat the oven to 220°C/gas mark 7.

5 Heat 1 tablespoon of the ghee in a heavy-based frying pan, add the onions and fry for 8–10 minutes until brown and crisp. Remove half the onions and reserve for the garnish. Add the ginger-garlic paste and chillies and stir for 2 minutes, then add the tomato purée and cook for a further 2 minutes. Transfer the mixture to a blender, add enough cold water to cover and blitz until smooth.

6 Heat another tablespoon of the ghee in the pan and fry the chicken for 5–6 minutes. (If making a vegetable biryani, add 300g mixed, cooked vegetables, such as carrots, peas and potatoes, to the pan here.)

7 Add the powdered spices and season with salt. Cook for 2 minutes until the spices have turned dark, then add the purée from the blender and stir. Mix well, add 100ml water and simmer for a few minutes until the chicken is cooked. Remove from heat and set aside.

8 Heat the remaining ghee in a heavy-based saucepan over a high heat. Add the rice and fry for a few minutes, until shiny, then strain three-quarters of the savoury aroma liquid into the pan. Season with salt, stir once, bring to the boil, then reduce the heat, cover and cook for about 10 minutes until the liquid has been absorbed.

9 It's time to assemble the dish. The bottom and top layers are always rice. Put a layer of rice at the bottom of a 25–30cm deep ovenproof dish. Sprinkle over some of the remaining savoury liquid and some sweet aroma liquid, then cover the rice with a layer of the curry. Sprinkle some of the fried onions, mint leaves and coriander leaves over the curry then top with another layer of rice. Repeat until everything is used up and the top layer is rice. Sprinkle with the almonds and fresh coriander. Seal the dish with foil.

10 Put the biryani in the oven for 40 minutes, reducing the oven temperature to 190°C/gas mark 5 after 20 minutes. Remove from the oven, uncover, decorate with halved hard-boiled eggs and serve.

Mung Dal Khichdi

| SOFT RICE AND LENTILS WITH SPICES |

A khichdi is considered a warming comfort food or, if more vigorously spiced as in West Bengal, it is offered as blessed food in temples or at religious feasts. The British fish and egg kedgeree is a derivative, although an Indian khichdi is always vegetarian. *Serves 4* PREPARATION → *10 minutes* COOKING *35 minutes*

1 tablespoon vegetable oil or ghee
5 cloves
10 black peppercorns
1 bay leaf
½ teaspoon cumin seeds
4 tablespoons split mung dal, washed and drained
½ teaspoon ground turmeric
200g short-/medium-grain rice, washed and drained
salt
natural yogurt, to serve

1 Heat the vegetable oil or ghee in a large heavy-based saucepan over a high heat, add the cloves, peppercorns, bay leaf and cumin seeds and fry for about 1 minute until the aroma fills the kitchen. Reduce the heat to medium, add the mung dal and fry for a couple of minutes until the grains look shiny.
2 Add the turmeric, rice and 600ml boiling water. Season with salt and bring back to the boil. Reduce the heat and simmer for about 30 minutes, stirring and adding more hot water as necessary, until the rice is creamy and very soft. This dish will be quite moist, like a risotto, which only increases its digestibility. Serve with natural yogurt on the side.

Subziyon Ki Tahiri

| SPICED NORTH INDIAN RICE AND VEGETABLE MEDLEY |

A traditional tahiri or tahari is similar to a pulao, though it is vegetarian and slightly more spiced. It was created in Mughal times for Hindu courtiers by substituting the meat in a biryani with potatoes. With time, more vegetables were added, but even today, a tahiri is incomplete without potatoes. *Serves 4* PREPARATION → *25 minutes* COOKING *45 minutes*

vegetable oil, for deep-frying
100g mixed diced vegetables, such as potatoes, cauliflower and aubergine
1 large onion, thinly sliced
2 teaspoons ginger-garlic paste *(page 45)*
2 fresh green chillies, minced
½ teaspoon ground turmeric
1 teaspoon garam masala *(page 64)*
200g basmati rice, washed and drained
a handful of fresh coriander leaves, chopped
salt

1 Heat enough oil to accommodate a single layer of vegetables in a deep frying pan over a high heat. Deep-fry the vegetables: first, the cauliflower and potatoes, for 6–7 minutes, then transfer these to drain on kitchen paper and fry the aubergine in the same oil for 3–4 minutes until golden. Remove with a slotted spoon and drain on kitchen paper, season with salt and set aside.
2 Carefully scoop 1 tablespoon of the hot oil into a saucepan over a high heat, add the onion and fry for 5–6 minutes until browned. Add the ginger-garlic paste, chillies, turmeric and garam masala and fry for 1 minute before adding the rice. Add the rice, fry for 1 minute until it turns opaque, then pour in double the volume of water to the rice. Bring to the boil, then reduce the heat to low, stir once, cover and cook for 10 minutes until the water has been absorbed and the rice is cooked. Remove from the heat, set aside for 5 minutes, covered, then remove the lid and fluff the rice.
3 Gently fold in the fried vegetables, sprinkle with the coriander and serve hot.

Hyderabadi Kucchi Biryani

| SLOW-COOKED BIRYANI |

2 tablespoons vegetable oil or ghee
3 large onions, thinly sliced
1 tablespoon ginger-garlic paste *(page 45)*
1 teaspoon medium-hot red chilli powder
1 teaspoon ground turmeric
2 teaspoons garam masala *(page 64)*
5cm piece of raw papaya, crushed to a paste
150g natural yogurt
400g lamb on the bone, cut into small dice
200g basmati rice, washed and drained
small cinnamon stick
2 green cardamom pods, bruised
3 cloves
1 tablespoon ghee, melted
a handful of fresh coriander leaves, chopped
2 pinches of saffron, dissolved in
    1 tablespoon warm milk
3 tablespoons wholemeal flour, mixed
    with enough water to make a stiff dough
salt

In this dish, marinated raw meat (goat is the meat that's predominantly used all over India) is cooked with the rice in layers. The sealing of the pot makes the dish moist and fragrant. *Serves 4* PREPARATION → *20 minutes, plus 3 hours marinating time* COOKING *1 hour*

1 Heat the oil or ghee in a heavy-based saucepan or pot over a high heat, add the onions and fry for about 8 minutes until they are crisp and brown. Drain and set aside.

2 To make the marinade, combine the ginger-garlic paste, chilli powder, turmeric, garam masala, raw papaya paste and yogurt in a bowl and season with a little salt. Add the lamb, mix to coat it in the marinade and set aside for 3 hours.

3 Put the rice in a pan with the cinnamon stick, cardamom pods and cloves and add 800ml water. Season with salt and bring to the boil. Reduce the heat and simmer, uncovered, for 5 minutes (the rice will just be partially cooked). Drain in a colander.

4 Start assembling the dish. Put the marinated meat in the heavy-based saucepan along with all the marinade and half of the melted ghee. Sprinkle over some of the chopped coriander and some of the fried onions. Spread the rice over this. Drizzle over the remaining ghee and saffron along with the milk.

5 Roll the dough into a cylinder and place it around the edge of the saucepan. Place a lid on top to seal it tightly so that no steam escapes. Cook over a high heat for 6–8 minutes until you can hear a sizzle from the pan, then reduce the heat to low (as low as it will go) and cook for 45 minutes.

6 Once you have removed the pan from the heat, leave the biryani to rest, then remove the lid, discard the pastry and mix gently with a fork to combine the rice, meat and spices. Serve hot, garnished with the remaining fried onions and coriander.

Kolmi Bhaat

| PRAWN PULAO |

One of my favourite dishes, this pulao gets cooked on a regular basis in my home. It's a simple one-pot meal and the sweetness of the prawns is perfectly complemented by the chillies and the tang of tomato. Buy the best prawns you can afford and you will have the taste of Mumbai's beaches on your plate. *Serves 4* PREPARATION→ *15 minutes* COOKING *25 minutes*

2 tablespoons vegetable oil
1 teaspoon cumin seeds
1 large onion, finely chopped
1 teaspoon ginger-garlic paste *(page 45)*
2 fresh green chillies, finely chopped
2 tablespoons tomato purée
150g raw prawns, shelled and deveined
200g basmati rice, washed and drained
1 teaspoon ground turmeric
1 teaspoon ground coriander
a handful of fresh coriander leaves, chopped
salt

1 Warm the oil in a heavy-based saucepan over a high heat and add the cumin seeds. When they start to darken, add the onion and cook for 5–6 minutes until soft. Add the ginger-garlic paste and the chillies. Fry for 1 minute then add the tomato purée. Cook for a further minute, add the prawns and stir again.

2 Tip in the rice, ground turmeric and coriander. Stir once, season with salt and stir in half the coriander leaves. Cook for 2 minutes.

3 Pour in double the amount of water by volume to the rice and bring to the boil. Reduce the heat to low, cover and cook for 10 minutes until the water has been absorbed and the rice is cooked. Remove from the heat and set aside for 5 minutes, covered, before removing the lid.

4 Remove the lid and fluff the rice with a fork, before serving with the remaining coriander leaves sprinkled on top.

Pudina Pulao

| MINT AND CUMIN-FLAVOURED RICE |

This is an easy but stunning entertaining centrepiece, with all the flavour of fresh mint. You can omit the green chillies if you want a mild dish, or you can serve it with a creamy raita (page 397). *Serves 4* PREPARATION→ *10 minutes* COOKING *25 minutes*

a large handful of fresh mint leaves
1 tablespoon ginger-garlic paste *(page 45)*
2 fresh green chillies
1 tablespoon vegetable oil or ghee
1 teaspoon cumin seeds
200g basmati rice, washed and drained
salt
creamy raita, to serve (optional)

1 Put the mint, ginger-garlic paste and chillies in a blender with a little water and blitz to form a smooth purée. Transfer the purée to the jug used for measuring the rice and top it up with enough water to make double the volume of rice.

2 Warm the oil or ghee in a saucepan over a high heat and add the cumin seeds. Fry for a few seconds until they start to turn dark, then add the rice, season with salt and fry for a minute until it turns opaque. Add the puréed mint mixture, stir once, bring to the boil, then reduce the heat to low, cover and cook for 10 minutes, until the water has been absorbed and the rice is cooked. Remove from the heat, cover and set aside for 5 minutes.

3 Remove the lid, fluff the rice with a fork and serve hot with a creamy raita alongside, if you like.

Mosaranna

| SOFT RICE WITH YOGURT, CUCUMBER, CARROT AND SPICES |

This dish is found all over south India where a meal always ends with a serving of 'curd rice'. In Karnataka it is called Mosaranna, whereas in nearby Tamil Nadu it is called Tayir Sadam. *Serves 4* PREPARATION → *5 minutes* COOKING *25 minutes*

200g short-grain rice, washed and drained
100ml semi-skimmed milk
100g natural yogurt
1 tablespoon vegetable oil
1 teaspoon black mustard seeds
1 teaspoon cumin seeds
pinch of asafoetida
8 fresh or 12 dried curry leaves
¼ cucumber, peeled and finely diced
1 small carrot, peeled and grated
pinch of caster sugar
½ teaspoon finely grated fresh root ginger
salt
shop-bought spicy mango pickle or Aubergine Chutney
    (page 427), to serve (optional)

1 Put the rice and double the amount of water by volume in a heavy-based saucepan and bring to the boil. Reduce the heat to low, stir once, cover and cook for 10 minutes until the water has been absorbed and the rice is cooked. Remove from the heat, cover and leave to rest for 5 minutes.
2 Remove the lid and gently fluff the rice with a fork to loosen it. Lightly mash the rice with a potato masher and mix in the milk. Transfer to the fridge to cool. When the rice is cold, stir in the yogurt.
3 Warm the oil in a small pan over a high heat and fry the mustard seeds for a few minutes until they begin to pop. Add the cumin seeds, asafoetida and curry leaves (standing back from the pan if using fresh leaves, as they will splutter), fry for a few seconds, then stir the mixture into the rice.
4 Stir the cucumber, carrot, sugar and ginger into the rice and season to taste with salt. Serve cold with spicy mango pickle or Aubergine Chutney, if you like.

Mushroom Pulao

| RICE WITH MUSHROOMS AND CUMIN |

We never had mushrooms in my childhood home as my grandmother said they were Ayurvedically 'tamasic' or 'lacking in positive energy', because they grew in dark, dank places. I love them now and have used chestnut mushrooms in this recipe. They have a nuttier flavour and shrink less, as they contain less water than white mushrooms, but you can use whichever kind you have to hand. *Serves 4* PREPARATION → *5 minutes* COOKING *25 minutes*

2 tablespoons vegetable oil
2 tablespoons unsalted cashew nuts
½ teaspoon cumin seeds
6–7 chestnut mushrooms, cleaned and thickly sliced
½ teaspoon ground turmeric
200g basmati rice, washed and drained
salt

1 Heat the oil in a heavy-based saucepan over a high heat, add the cashew nuts and fry for a couple of minutes until golden. Remove the nuts from the oil and set aside.
2 Add the cumin seeds to the oil and fry until they begin to darken, then add the mushrooms and turmeric. Tip in the rice and season with salt. Stir gently for 1 minute until the rice turns opaque.
3 Pour in double the volume of water to rice, stir once and bring to the boil. Reduce the heat to low, cover and cook for about 10 minutes until the water has been absorbed and the rice is cooked. Remove from the heat, leave the rice to rest for 5 minutes, covered, then remove the lid, fluff the rice with a fork and serve sprinkled with the fried cashew nuts.

Kovil Pulihodarai

| TAMARIND RICE |

There are several versions of this dish in south India but
this is the most popular and closest to that served as
'prasadam' or blessed food in temples. *Serves 4* PREPARATION →
30 minutes, plus 20 minutes soaking time COOKING *30 minutes*

200g basmati rice, washed and drained
2 tablespoons vegetable oil
½ teaspoon black mustard seeds
large pinch of asafoetida
4 dried red chillies, deseeded and crumbled
1 teaspoon gram lentils (chana dal), soaked in water
    for 20 minutes and drained
2 teaspoons cashew nuts
10 fresh or 15 dried curry leaves
1 teaspoon ground turmeric
lime-sized block of tamarind, diluted in 6 tablespoons of
    water, squashed, then passed through a sieve to extract
    the pulp (discard the seeds) or 5 tablespoons tamarind pulp
    (page 418) or shop-bought tamarind paste (not concentrate)
salt
For the spice blend
½ teaspoon fenugreek seeds
8 black peppercorns
1 teaspoon coriander seeds
3 dried red chillies, split and seeds shaken out
1 teaspoon white sesame seeds, toasted

1 To make the spice powder, dry-toast the fenugreek seeds,
peppercorns, coriander seeds and red chillies in a small frying
pan until they change colour. Tip into a spice mill or pestle
and mortar, add the sesame seeds and grind to a powder.
2 Put the rice and double the amount of water by volume in a
heavy-based saucepan and bring to the boil. Reduce the heat,
stir once, cover and cook for 10 minutes until the water has
been absorbed. Remove from the heat and set aside, covered.
3 Heat the oil in a heavy-based saucepan over a high heat,
add the mustard seeds, asafoetida, crumbled chillies, drained
lentils, cashew nuts and curry leaves and fry for a couple of
minutes. When the cashew nuts have turned golden, stir in
the turmeric and the spice powder from Step 1. Season with
salt, add the tamarind pulp and cook for a few minutes until it
thickens slightly.
4 Fold the rice into the spice paste and serve hot.

Parsi-style Brown Rice

| RICE WITH FRIED ONIONS AND CARAMEL |

The Parsis came to India from Iran around the eighth
century as they fled from religious persecution. They
arrived on the west coast of India, making their home
in Gujarat and Sind. Their cuisine is a fabulous mix of
Indian, Persian and European styles. This is a signature dish
and is eaten with Dhansak, the famous spiced lentil and
vegetable curry (see page 143) and a fresh onion salad.
Serves 4 PREPARATION → *10 minutes* COOKING *35 minutes*

200g basmati rice, washed and drained
1 teaspoon caster sugar
2 tablespoons vegetable oil
2 small cinnamon sticks
3 cloves
1 large onion, thinly sliced
salt

1 Measure double the volume of water to rice in a jug.
2 Put the sugar and a teaspoon of water in a large saucepan
and set over a high heat until the sugar dissolves. Reduce
the heat to medium and continue cooking until the sugar
caramelises to a rich golden colour. Remove from the heat,
stand back and slowly pour in the water from the jug. It will
bubble furiously so be careful. Mix well so that you get a
warm brown liquid. Set aside.
3 Heat the oil in a saucepan over a high heat and add the
cinnamon sticks and cloves. As the oil heats up, they will
begin to sizzle and develop an aroma. Add the onion and cook
over a high heat for 5–6 minutes, stirring, until it starts to turn
golden. Reduce the heat to medium and continue cooking for
7–8 minutes until it develops a deep brown colour.
4 Tip in the rice and fry for a couple of minutes until it turns
opaque, then pour in the caramel liquid and season with salt.
5 Bring to the boil, stir once, then reduce the heat to low,
cover and cook for 10 minutes until the water has been
absorbed and the rice is cooked. Remove from the heat, leave
the rice to rest for 5 minutes, covered, then remove the lid,
fluff the rice with a fork and serve hot.

FLOURS

Wheat is the most common grain to be crushed into flour. Archaeological surveys have found that it was used in the Indian subcontinent since the Indus Valley civilisation (3300 BC–1700 BC). Ancient Indian scripts including the *Rigveda* (one of the oldest surviving texts known to man) mention the use of wheat flour in various forms, including being mixed with milk, fried in ghee and spiced with cardamom, pepper and ginger. Barley and rice flours were also used.

Regional differences play an important role: the cuisine in some parts of the country, such as the south and the north east, is rice-based, whereas in Punjab it is wheat-based. This is not to say that the south does not eat rotis, but most meals are based around a rice preparation.

Indians love breads that are leavened, such as naan, unleavened such as roti, or Western-style sliced bread. European breads were introduced into India about three centuries ago, mainly by the Portuguese. Their 'pao', a small bun, is still eaten with curries or a crushed vegetable street snack called 'pao-bhaji'. Early Zoroastrians (who came from Iran) set up bakeries using the Iranian technique of using 'khamir' or the fermented yeast that went into making a sourdough bread. Irani cafés, which the Zoroastrians started and which are sadly in decline now, sell a hard, crusty version called 'brun' that is buttered and eaten dipped in sweet tea. These European-style breads are not made at home because most Indian kitchens do not need and therefore do not have Western-style ovens. Bakeries in most cities provide them, and sliced bread is made in large factories on a commercial scale and sold in shops all over the country.

Milling of grain has been carried out in the Indian subcontinent for thousands of years. The earliest mills found in the Indus Valley Civilisation (3300–1700 BC) excavations were of two types – one flat and circular, the other, a large stone with a central shallow depression that could hold grain to be crushed with a rounded stone held in one hand. Versions of these mills are still seen in Indian homes today. Another type of crusher that was common was the giant mortar, which was used standing up with the long, heavy pounding pestle held in both hands. This instrument is described in early Tamil literature of the third century AD. In southern India, too, excavations of sites dating from the second century BCE have uncovered pestles and mortars as well as milling stones.

Home milling: In days gone by, every kitchen in wheat-growing areas had a 'chakki' to mill the wheat. This was made of two heavy round stone plates 7.5–10cm thick. The lower plate was fixed while the top plate could be rotated. Both were held together by a spindle and on top was a receptacle hole to feed the wheat in. As the top plate was rotated, the wheat was crushed between the plates and moved to the outer edges and could then be collected.

Chakki milling: As a child, I was fascinated how every household would buy wheat from the grocer, clean it of minor impurities at home and take it to the nearest 'chakki' or mill to have it crushed into flour. We would help with this sifting and cleaning as it made us feel very grown up! These chakkis also had mills for spices. Today city kitchens buy bags of ready-made flour, but in smaller towns and villages, taking wheat to the chakki is still a regular domestic task.

Commercial milling: From the late 1800s mills powered by oil and then by electricity spread through India and were used to de-husk paddy.

Wheat Flours

Atta → Although wheat has been grown in India for hundreds of years, today two major varieties are used to make wholewheat flour or 'atta'. These are the hard 'durum' and the semi-hard variety called 'aestivum'. Hard wheat has a high gluten content, which gives dough its elasticity and therefore makes it easier to roll out thinly into chapattis. To make atta, the outer husk of the grain is removed, leaving behind three layers – the bran, the endosperm and the germ. Bran is essentially fibre, the endosperm is starch and the germ is protein. These are coarsely ground to make atta, which is primarily used to make rotis or chapattis and similar flatbreads. Bags of atta are often labelled on the basis of their use, as chapatti flour. There are many varieties of atta, such as brown or medium, and these usually indicate the amount of bran or the coarseness of the flour. Many bags mention the word 'chakki', meaning stone-milled.

Maida → The bran is removed and the starchy endosperm of the grain is milled and bleached to make this refined flour that is finer and paler than atta. As it is quite fine, it is mostly used for recipes that require a soft texture. Certain breads like roomali roti, literally 'handkerchief bread' or naan are made of maida, as is the crisp shortened pastry for savoury samosas.

Dalia (Bulgar Wheat) → This is cracked wheat and it resembles grits. It is also known as lapsi, bulghur wheat or fada. Fine and coarse versions are cooked into a sweet porridge called 'kheer' (see page 440) or used to make hot snacks.

Rava/Sooji (Semolina) → When wheat is milled to resemble sand, it is called rava, sooji or semolina. There are several varieties available and they all result in different textures in the final dish. Extra coarse and coarse rava is gritty and delightfully nutty and is used for puddings or a savoury south Indian dish called 'upma' (see page 364). Fine rava is also used for puddings, to create a crust on fried fish and seafood, or added to shortened pastry for extra crispness. They all feature in one of India's best-loved desserts, variously called 'sheera', 'sooji ka halwa' or 'rava kesari' (see page 446).

Rice Flour

This is made from polished, broken rice and is used in everyday cooking mostly in the south and in Gujarat. It is mixed with water or coconut milk to make a gluten-free batter for pancakes called dosas (see page 118), made into a dough or used to thicken milky desserts.

Bajra (Millet) Flour

Bajra, bajri or millet flour is made from a small round grain that resembles mustard seed. It is earthy and nutty in flavour with a slightly sweet aftertaste. Indians consider it healthy as it contains many vital nutrients, such as iron, as well as fibre. Dense bajra rotis called 'bhakris' (see page 117) are eaten by farmers in Maharashtra, often with a wedge of onion and garlic and chilli chutney. Although seen as poor man's food, they are considered a delicacy when eaten with a dollop of homemade butter.

Bajra flour tends to require a binding agent while being made into a dough, so sometimes a little rice flour is added. It is often patted into shape by moistened hands rather like moulding clay. If the dough is dry, it will crack and it is for this reason that it is not rolled like wheat flour rotis.

Makai (Maize) Flour

This is called makai or makki flour in India. Dried corn is soaked in lime solution or slaked, then hulled. The damp corn is then milled into a slightly coarse flour which is used to make breads such as Punjab's famous 'makki ki roti' (see page 117), a flat, unleavened corn bread, or is used as a thickener in curries and vegetable dishes like 'sarson ka saag', a Punjabi delicacy of seasonal mustard greens cooked with spices and eaten with homemade ghee. The very fine cornflour used in other countries has limited use in traditional Indian cookery, although it is an essential ingredient in the spicy hybrid Indo-Chinese food that combines elements of both cuisines.

Lentil Flours

Lentils are found in every Indian kitchen. As flours, they are used to thicken, bind, coat and add crispness to dishes.

Besan (Gram) Flour → Gram flour is made by milling dried chickpeas. It is nutty, protein rich and gluten free. Gluten-free pancakes are made from a thick batter of besan and water.

Besan is used to make sweets like 'laddoos', where it is roasted in ghee, sweetened with sugar and pressed into balls that will keep for days. Sindhi Kadhi, a savoury vegetable curry (page 332), has a base of besan and tomatoes. Pakoras (page 349) are made by dipping vegetables, paneer, fish or chicken into a seasoned besan batter before deep-frying them.

Mung Flour → This is made from mung beans and is also called green bean flour. It is lighter than other pulse flours and is used to make dosas and for poppadums or papads. A dough is made with mung flour and water, spiced and seasoned, then rolled out into thin discs. In an Indian home, these discs are sun-dried for later use. Most urban Indians today have neither the time nor the resources in the form of a sunny roof or courtyard to dry their own poppadums and readily buy commercially made ones instead, in an assortment of flavours.

Urad Flour → Urad or urid beans are black in colour but once peeled, they reveal a creamy white interior. These cream-coloured beans are milled to form the flour which is used to make various kinds of dosas (see page 126).

It is sometimes sold as 'mapte bean flour' or 'papad flour' as it is largely used to make poppadums, or 'papads' as they are called over most of India. Being gluten free, dosas made with urad flour can be a good substitute for wheat rotis.

Flour Mixes → Indian grocers often offer a variety of mixed flours. These are sold blended for ease of use and to save the cook some time. Examples are 'idli flour' to make steamed south Indian rice cakes called idlis, 'dhokla flour' to make savoury rice and lentil cakes, or 'dosa flour' which has the same ingredients as 'idli flour' but in different proportions.

HOW TO STORE FLOURS

It is best to store all flours in a dry, well-ventilated cupboard for no more than 6 months or so. Moisture can make it clumpy and keeping it too long may give rise to insects, such as weevils, which live in dry food.

ROTIS AND CHAPATTIS

Rotis are India's everyday bread. The word comes from the Sanskrit 'rotika' and the word 'chapatti' possibly comes from Hindi word 'chappat' meaning flat. Both roti and chapatti are used interchangeably, with one being in more popular in some parts of the country than the other.

A roti is a flat, unleavened bread made of stoneground wholemeal wheat flour called atta. The word 'chapatti' has been mentioned in the *Ain-i-Akbari*, a sixteenth-century treatise written by Abu'l-Fazl ibn Mubarak on the workings of the Mughal emperor Akbar's court:

'The thin kind is baked on an iron plate. One sér will give fifteen, or even more. There are various ways of making it: one kind is called chapatti, which is sometimes made of khushkah; it tastes very well, when served hot. For the bread used at court, one man of wheat is made to yield ½ m. of fine flour; 2 s. coarsely pounded flour; and the rest bran; if this degree of fineness be not required, the proportions are altered.'

Rotis differ in size and thickness from one region to another, and they also have various names, depending on their thickness or the method of cooking. They are used to mop up curry sauces or to transfer food from the plate to the mouth. Typically, Punjabi rotis are denser and thicker than Gujarati 'rotlees' or Maharashtrian 'polis', which are thin and delicate. Most rotis are cooked on a flat or slightly convex griddle pan called the 'tava' or 'tawa' (see page 51).

From 1833 to 1920, as millions of Indians were taken to different European colonies as indentured labourers to work on sugar plantations or to build railways, the roti travelled to new shores and became popular in various forms – as 'rooti' in South Africa, 'roti canai' in Malaysia, 'sada roti' made with plain flour in Trinidad, and 'dhal poori' made with lentils in Mauritius. Today many forms exist, as wraps or filled with potatoes or meat trimmings (as in the amusing and cheap 'piper roti' served in Trinidad and Tobago where a piper is a drug addict with little money to buy food).

Rotis cooked in a coal-fired clay oven are called 'tandoori roti'. These are usually eaten in Punjab where one finds these ovens and not all over India as many people think. The tandoori roti is made with wholewheat atta and is much thicker and chewier than a griddle-baked roti.

'Phulkas' are rotis cooked directly on an open flame or on coals after being lightly sealed on a tava (see page 51).

The 'roomali roti' is an extremely thin, soft roti made of a mixture of atta and maida that is served folded and is a part of North Indian Mughlai cookery. The word 'roomali' refers to handkerchief (roomal) and the roti is made by tossing the dough high up in the air to stretch it. Specialist chefs at Mughlai restaurants make quite a show of their skill as it is an art to make this restaurant bread. It is cooked on the convex side of an Indian griddle pan or tava.

POORIS

This festive bread (see pages 114–115) is made with a similar dough to rotis but uses a bit more oil to bring it all together. Then oil is used to roll them out, much smaller than rotis, after which they are deep-fried until puffed and golden. Pooris are considered indulgent and are therefore often served at weddings and celebrations. They are sometimes flavoured or stuffed, as in 'dal poori', made with lentils. Small, bite-sized, crisp versions are fried and filled with sweet and sour tamarind water to make one of India's favourite street foods, variously called 'pani-puri', 'gol guppe', 'batasha' or 'phuchka'.

PARATHAS

Popular in Punjab and nearby regions, parathas are made with roti dough but are cooked in ghee or oil and are layered breads. They can be stuffed with potatoes as in 'aloo ke paronthe' (pages 122–123) or with cauliflower, mooli (daikon radish), meat or paneer. They are heavy and are often eaten for breakfast in the north. The south also has its versions. The 'malabar parotta' of Kerala is a layered, fluffy bread that is eaten with luscious coconut curries.

PREVIOUS PAGES: PAGE 102: *Types of flour – 1 Atta; 2 Bajra; 3 Besan; 4 Rice; 5 Dalia;* PAGE 103: *6 Rava/Sooji; 7 Urad; 8 Maize; 9 Mung; 10 Maida.*

MASTERCLASS

MAKING A DOUGH

In spite of roti being India's favourite bread, made daily in many homes, it is quite tricky to get the dough right and roll out circles when you first start. When I made my first roti at the age of around twelve, it looked like a cross between Australia and Sri Lanka and I truly believed that I would never get it right. This made me give up roti-making until I went to catering college a few years later!

1 Use good-quality atta. Ask around for a good brand – this will be slightly more expensive as they have probably used good-quality wheat with enough gluten.

2 Indian cooks use one hand to knead the dough in the bowl while the other is used to pour in water and hold the bowl firmly. European cooks use both hands to knead.

3 Use tepid water. It is difficult to calculate exactly how much water will be needed for a particular dough – factors such as the quality of the flour, the hardness or softness of the water (the mineral salts in mildly hard water reinforce the gluten) and temperature in the kitchen can all make a difference to the amount needed. As a rough guide, for 200g flour you need 100–125ml water.

4 Start by pouring in enough water to create a breadcrumb texture.

5 Bring the dough together firmly but not using too much pressure. If you need to force it, it is still too dry. Keep adding water, a little at a time, until the dough forms a ball when pressed together. It should feel slightly sticky at this point.

6 This step is the secret to making soft rotis. Knead the dough on a lightly floured surface for 5–8 minutes. The more you knead, the better the dough. Make sure to use pressure, using your knuckles and the base of your palm to stretch the dough. Caressing it won't work! You are trying to stretch the gluten strands to create the correct texture, so be firm. The final dough should be springy and not sticky so keep kneading until the dough is as slack as it can be in order to roll it out.

7 If you have added too much water and the dough is sticking to your fingers, add more flour to correct this. A wet dough is difficult to roll and you will end up using too much dusting flour that will burn as a residue in a hot pan.

8 If you have added too little water and the dough feels hard, moisten your hands and keep working the dough, sprinkling over a bit of water to stretch it.

9 Some people add a few drops of oil (vegetable or similar) to the dough when it's being kneaded. This can help to soften it.

10 Rest the dough in the bowl for 10 minutes – a bit longer if you can. Cover it with a clean, damp tea towel or loosely with clingfilm. (Wrapping it tightly in clingfilm may make it sweat and become sticky.)

11 Once made, you can brush the rotis with a little oil or ghee. If making them in advance, wrap them in a tea towel to absorb the steam and stop them from becoming soggy. Reheat when you're ready.

12 Leftover dough can be stored in an airtight container in the fridge for up to 2 days.

ROLLING ROTIS

1 Use the correct rolling pin. Indian pins are tapered so that they don't exert too much pressure and allow you to roll the roti from the centre out to create a neat circle. The thickness should be even so don't be tempted to go over the edges in order to make a perfect circle.

2 An Indian kitchen will have a circular rolling board as a template for the shape.

3 Use a tava, griddle pan or a frying pan but make sure that it is non-stick or have been seasoned by previous use. The pan must be very hot so that the roti seals as soon as it is placed on it.

4 Quick cooking at a high temperature allows the water in the dough to turn to steam and puff the roti, making it soft. Overcooking will result in a crisp or leathery roti!

ROTIS/CHAPATTIS — Unleavened Flatbreads

I tend not to salt my rotis as they are always going to be eaten with something savoury or sweet. Indian children are sometimes given a roti with jam or a fragrant mix of ghee and granulated sugar as a quick snack. They are often cooked fresh as the family is eating, and in this instance they do not need to be brushed with oil. But you can brush them with oil if you are making a batch in advance, to keep them soft. *Makes 10 rotis* PREPARATION → *15 minutes, plus resting time* COOKING *20 minutes*

YOU WILL NEED:
300g stoneground wholewheat flour (atta),
    plus extra for dusting
150–175ml tepid water, as needed
vegetable oil, for brushing (optional)

4 Heat a griddle pan or shallow frying pan over a high heat. Fry the discs one at a time on the griddle until the surface appears bubbly. Flip over and press the edges down with a clean cloth or spatula to cook evenly. As soon as the roti is opaque and flecked with brown spots, it is done. Make sure that the roti is cooked evenly all over.

5 Remove and brush with oil, if using. Cook all the rotis in the same way.

1 Place the flour in a bowl and, using your fingers, gradually mix in the tepid water until you have a pliable dough. Knead on a lightly floured surface for 5–8 minutes (the more you knead the dough, the softer the rotis), then leave the dough to rest for 10 minutes in the bowl under a clean, damp tea towel.

2 Divide the dough into 10 equal-sized portions each the size of a small lime. Coat lightly with flour, shape into a ball in your palm and flatten slightly.

3 Roll each ball out into a flat disc, 12cm in diameter, dusting the surface with flour as necessary.

NAANS — Oven-baked Leavened Breads

Naan, even in India, is a restaurant bread. Firstly, as it is made with refined flour rather than wholewheat, people do not think of it as being too healthy. Secondly, a traditional naan is made in a tandoor oven, which is impractical in a home environment, and thirdly, being a leavened bread, it is more time consuming to make than a roti, which all means that people don't make it at home. This recipe has been adapted to be cooked in the oven, and is a good recipe to make at home in the West where kitchens are fitted with conventional ovens, unlike in India. *Makes 12 mini naans* PREPARATION → *20 minutes, plus 1½ hours rising time* COOKING *20 minutes*

YOU WILL NEED:

100ml tepid water

1 teaspoon active dry yeast

1 teaspoon caster sugar

380g self-raising flour, plus extra for dusting

20ml vegetable oil or ghee

30g natural yogurt

salt

toasted sesame or nigella seeds, to finish

4 Punch the dough down and knead it well. Divide it into 12 balls and roll the balls into small rounds, triangles or oblong shapes.

5 Grease a baking tray and put the naans on it, then place under a hot grill for about 2 minutes on each side until puffy and cooked. You can also bake them in an oven preheated to 200°C/gas mark 6, cooking them for 4–5 minutes on each side.

6 Brush the naans with the remaining oil or ghee and sprinkle with toasted sesame or nigella seeds to serve.

1 Whisk the tepid water, yeast and sugar in a bowl or jug until the yeast has dissolved. Leave it to stand for 10 minutes to activate the yeast.

2 Sift the flour and a pinch of salt into a bowl and add the yeast, half the oil or ghee and all the yogurt. Mix to form a soft dough then transfer to a floured surface and knead for 5 minutes until the dough is smooth and no longer sticky, adding more tepid water if necessary.

3 Place the dough in a greased bowl, cover with a clean, damp tea towel or loosely with clingfilm and set aside in a warm place for 1½ hours until the dough has doubled in size.

Peshwari Naans

| SWEET NAAN VARIATION |

Indian restaurants the world over serve this sweet naan from the north-west frontier region of Pakistan. The true name of this bread is Peshawari naan, in reference to the city Peshawar from where it originates.

To make this version you will need all the ingredients for plain naan, plus the following for the filling. *Makes 12 mini naans* PREPARATION → *35 minutes* COOKING *20 minutes*

100g finely crushed pistachios
30g chopped raisins
30g fine desiccated coconut
1 teaspoon ground fennel seed
1 quantity naan dough *(page 110)*

1 Combine the ingredients for the filling. Make the naan dough as on pages 110–111.
2 After rolling out a naan, place a small spoonful of the sweet nut mixture at the centre and carefully fold in the edges to seal in the filling. Flatten slightly and gently roll back out into a small oblong, circle or triangle. Repeat with the remaining naans. Cook as on page 111. Wrap the cooked naan in foil to keep them warm while cooking the rest.

Garlic Naans

| VARIATION |

Another restaurant favourite, the garlicky flavour of this bread goes well with spicy north Indian curries. Sometimes freshly chopped coriander is also added along with the diced garlic. *Makes 12 mini naans* PREPARATION → *25 minutes* COOKING *20 minutes*

1 quantity naan dough *(page 110)*
3–4 garlic cloves

1 Make the naan dough as on pages 110–111.
2 Finely chop 3–4 garlic cloves and sprinkle a bit on each naan before grilling them. When they are done, brush them with oil or ghee and serve hot.

Rava Uttapam

| SEMOLINA PANCAKES |

Uttapams and dosas are classic foods in the south. I apply the term 'pancake' quite loosely here because the word conjures up images of a mixture of eggs, wheat and milk, which these foods are not. However, they are made with a batter, ladled into a hot pan, spread into a circle and sometimes flipped over to be cooked on both sides. They are often served with White Coconut Chutney (page 424) and Sambhar (page 282). *Makes 8* PREPARATION → *10 minutes, plus standing time* COOKING *25 minutes*

½ medium onion, finely chopped
150g coarse semolina
pinch of ground turmeric
a handful of fresh coriander leaves, finely chopped
1 fresh green chilli, finely diced (seeds and all)
vegetable oil, for shallow-frying
salt

1 Combine the onion, semolina, turmeric, salt to season, coriander and chilli in a bowl. Stir in enough cold water (150–180ml) to make a batter with a pouring consistency, almost like thick custard. Leave to stand for 10 minutes.
2 Heat 1 teaspoon of oil in a large saucepan. Pour a ladleful of the batter into the centre and spread it out with the back of a spoon into a flattish disc about 10cm in diameter. Cover the pan and cook the pancake in its steam for 2–3 minutes.
3 Flip the pancake over when the underside has turned golden and is flecked with brown. Cook the other side for 1–2 minutes, uncovered, dotting the edges with oil. Remove from the pan and wrap in foil to keep warm while you cook the remaining batter.

POORIS — Puffy Fried Breads

The Sanskrit word 'pura', which means being filled or blown up, may have given this deep-fried bread its name. It is eaten for breakfast, as a snack or as part of a feast. Poori-bhaji is a classic combination with spiced potatoes. North Indian temples serve halwa-poori as blessed food, the halwa being a sweet semolina pudding, whereas Maharashtrian wedding feasts often include shrikhand poori, where they are served with saffron- and cardamom-flavoured sweetened hung yogurt (see page 448). *Makes 18–20 small pooris* PREPARATION → *15 minutes* COOKING *20 minutes*

YOU WILL NEED:
300g stoneground
    wholewheat flour (atta),
    plus extra for dusting
vegetable oil, for deep-frying
tepid water, as needed

1   Combine the flour and 1 tablespoon of oil in a bowl. Add a little tepid water at a time, until the flour comes together and you can knead it without it sticking to your fingers. Knead the dough on a lightly floured surface for 5–6 minutes, until smooth. The dough should be stiff but springy.

2   Divide the dough into 18–20 equal-sized balls, the size of a large cherry. Smear your palms with oil and smooth each ball.

3   Heat enough oil in a deep frying pan or karahi to fill it up to 6cm over a high heat. While the oil is heating up, roll each ball out into a flat disc, 2.5cm in diameter, on a sheet of greaseproof paper or worktop, flouring the surface minimally if necessary. Too much flour will settle as a burnt residue in the hot oil and spoil the look of the pooris. Test the temperature of the oil by dropping in a pea-sized ball of dough. It should rise up to the surface in a couple of seconds. If it rises immediately, the oil is too hot so reduce the heat.

4   Gently place a disc in the hot oil, pressing it down with the back of a slotted spoon until puffy and golden. Flip it over and fry for 1 minute. It will puff up only if the oil is hot enough and the disc has been submerged. Lift it out with a slotted spoon and drain on kitchen paper. Keep warm in foil while the rest of the pooris are being fried.

5   Fry the remaining pooris, adjusting the heat so that the pooris do not brown excessively.

Palak Poori
| FRIED SPINACH BREAD |

This is a healthy and delicious poori that goes well with savoury curries or simply with some hot pickle and plain yogurt. The Bengali 'luchi' is a similar fried bread made without the spinach, with plain flour or 'maida'. *Makes 18–20 small pooris* PREPARATION → *15 minutes* COOKING *30 minutes*

2 handfuls of fresh spinach, washed
    and drained
1 fresh green chilli
2.5cm piece of fresh root ginger, scraped
    and chopped
300g stoneground wholewheat flour (atta), plus extra for dusting
vegetable oil, for deep-frying
tepid water, as needed
salt

1   Heat the spinach in a small pan with a couple of tablespoons of water, the chilli and ginger for 5–6 minutes until the spinach has wilted. Transfer the mixture to a blender and blitz until smooth.

2   Combine the flour, 1 tablespoon of oil, the spinach purée and a pinch of salt in a bowl. Depending on how wet your spinach purée is, you will need only a little warm water if at all. Pour this in, a little at a time, until the ingredients come together, then place on a surface and knead to form a stiff dough.

3   Heat enough oil in a deep karahi or pan to fill it up to 6cm over a high heat. While the oil is heating up, shape the dough into 18–20 equal-sized balls, then roll each ball on a floured board into a flat disc 5–6cm wide and a couple of millimetres thick. Shake off any excess flour and fry a poori in the hot oil, submerging it with the back of a slotted spoon so that it puffs up. Flip it over and cook for a further minute. Remove and drain on kitchen paper. Keep warm in foil while you cook the rest of the pooris.

4   Fry the remaining pooris, adjusting the heat so that the pooris do not brown excessively. Serve hot.

Kheeme Ke Paratha

| LAMB MINCE-STUFFED BREAD |

For the stuffing
1 tablespoon vegetable oil
½ teaspoon cumin seeds
1 teaspoon ginger-garlic paste *(page 45)*
2 fresh green chillies, finely chopped
200g lean lamb mince
½ teaspoon ground turmeric
½ teaspoon garam masala *(page 64)*
2 tablespoons finely chopped fresh
    coriander leaves
salt
For the bread
400g stoneground wholewheat flour (atta)
vegetable oil, for frying
200–225ml tepid water, as needed

In the north of India, breads are made with a variety of stuffings, such as spiced potatoes, cauliflower, turnips and mooli. This lamb-mince paratha is a rich bread eaten with plain yogurt. The lamb can be substituted with beef mince, if you prefer. *Makes 8 parathas* PREPARATION → *20 minutes, plus 10 minutes resting time* COOKING *45 minutes*

1 Heat the vegetable oil in a frying pan over a high heat. Add the cumin seeds and fry until slightly dark, then add the ginger-garlic paste, chillies, mince, turmeric and garam masala, and season with salt. Break up the mince with a wooden spoon, cover and cook, reducing the heat when the mixture begins to bubble. Simmer for 15 minutes until the mince is cooked. Remove the lid and increase the heat to allow any liquid in the pan to evaporate, then add the coriander leaves. Transfer the mixture to a food processor or blender and blitz until quite smooth.

2 While the mince is cooking, make the dough. Place the flour (reserving some for dusting) in a bowl with 1 tablespoon of oil and a large pinch of salt, then gradually add the tepid water until you have a smooth and firm dough (see Masterclass on page 120). Transfer to a surface and knead well for 7–8 minutes until smooth and no longer sticky. Rest the dough in the bowl for 10 minutes, covered with a clean, damp tea towel.

3 Divide the dough into 16 equal-sized balls. Roll each ball into a flat disc about 10cm in diameter, dusting the dough with a little flour if sticky.

4 Smear a layer of the lamb mince over one disc then place another disc of dough on top. Seal the edges to make a flat parcel. Repeat with the remaining parathas and place them on greaseproof paper.

5 Heat a frying pan over a high heat and dot it with oil. Cook a paratha for 3–4 minutes on one side until flecked with tiny dark spots on the underside, then flip it over and cook on the other side for 3–4 minutes. Remove and keep warm, wrapped in foil.

6 Cook the rest of the parathas in the same way.

Bajre Ki Bhakri

| PEARL MILLET BREAD |

This is a rough-textured, dry bread that is eaten with butter or ghee. As millet is a gluten-free grain, you need to pat these into shape rather than rolling them, as they tend to break easily. Bhakris can be large or small (I like the small ones as they are easier to handle). *Makes 8 bhakris*

PREPARATION → *10 minutes* COOKING *35 minutes*

300g millet flour
125–150ml tepid water, as needed
melted butter or ghee, for brushing

1 Put the flour in a large bowl, make a well in the centre and gradually pour in the tepid water until you have a soft, smooth dough.
2 Moisten your palms and divide the dough into 8 equal-sized balls. Place a ball of dough on a sheet of greaseproof paper or plastic. Pat the dough into a flat disc, about 10cm wide and 5mm thick, using your moistened palms. You will need to keep wetting your palm so that the disc does not break into bits. Alternatively, flatten the ball of dough, place it on a well-oiled sheet of greaseproof paper or plastic and cover it with another oiled sheet of greaseproof paper or plastic and press down on it gently with a small plate to flatten it. Gently peel away the plastic and remove the bhakri, which should be slightly smaller than the size of the plate. Repeat with the 7 remaining dough balls and place them on a sheet of greaseproof paper.
3 Heat a griddle pan or frying pan over a high heat and brush it with butter or ghee.
4 Place one bhakri on the hot pan. Cook for 2–3 minutes until small bubbles appear on the surface, then carefully flip over to cook the other side. Press it down with the back of a spatula, brush each side with more ghee and cook until opaque and flecked with brown spots on both sides. Repeat with the remaining bhakris.
5 This bread must be eaten immediately as it gets hard and leathery if made in advance.

Makki Ki Roti

| CORN BREAD |

This gold-coloured bread is a Punjabi winter delicacy and is eaten with 'sarson ka saag', seasonal mustard greens cooked with lots of ghee. Most Punjabis would agree that this could be called the signature meal of their state as it's so local, seasonal and delicious! *Makes 8 rotis*

PREPARATION → *10 minutes* COOKING *30 minutes*

300g cornmeal (makki ka atta)
pinch of salt
150–180ml tepid water, as needed
cornflour, for dusting
vegetable oil or ghee, for brushing

1 Place the cornmeal in a bowl with the salt, make a well in the centre and gradually add the tepid water, mixing until you have a stiff dough. Transfer to a surface and knead for 3–4 minutes until smooth, then form into 8 equal-sized balls.
2 Place one dough ball on a floured surface and pat it with your palm to flatten it into a disc 10cm in diameter and 5mm thick. Dust your palm with cornflour if necessary. Repeat with remaining balls. You can also place the ball on a sheet of plastic and pat it with moistened hands to flatten it into a small circle. This will allow you to lift it easily.
3 Heat a griddle pan over a high heat and gently lift a disc onto it. After 2–3 minutes, when the surface appears bubbly, turn it over and cook on the other side. Brush with oil or ghee on both sides and cook for a further 2–3 minutes until the bread has changed colour and is flecked with brown spots. Transfer the cooked roti to a sheet of foil and enclose in the foil to keep it warm, then repeat with the remaining discs.

Pesarattu

| GREEN MUNG BEAN DOSA |

This is a breakfast speciality of Andhra Pradesh, where dosas are called 'attu' and green mung beans are known as 'pesara pappu'. The batter is unfermented and the dosa is usually served with ginger and coconut chutneys. A version sold in restaurants in Hyderabad is MLA pesarattu with savoury semolina called 'upma' (see page 364) as a stuffing. Increasing the amount of rice slightly will give a crisper dosa. *Makes 10 dosas* PREPARATION ⟶ *15 minutes, plus overnight soaking* COOKING *30 minutes*

200g whole green mung beans, soaked in water overnight
100g inexpensive white rice, soaked in water overnight
1 teaspoon cumin seeds
2 fresh green chillies, diced
thumb-sized piece of fresh root ginger, scraped and diced
1 medium onion, diced
a few fresh coriander leaves, finely chopped
vegetable oil, for frying
salt

1 Drain the beans and rice, rinse and transfer to a blender with the cumin seeds, green chillies, ginger, onion and coriander leaves. Blend until smooth with enough water (about 300ml) to make a smooth batter with a pouring consistency. Season with salt.

2 Heat a griddle pan or frying pan over a high heat and pour a ladleful of the batter into the centre. Spread it out with the back of a spoon to make a disc about 10cm in diameter.

3 Dot the edges with oil and cook for 2–3 minutes. When the underside is cooked, turn it over to cook the other side for 1–2 minutes.

4 Remove from the heat, wrap the dosa in foil to keep warm, and repeat with the remaining batter. Sometimes pesarattu is served with a little diced onion and chilli sprinkled on it as well.

Besan Ki Roti

| GRAM FLOUR PANCAKES |

This recipe is cooked in different parts of the country but is variously called 'chilla', 'cheela', 'pudla' or 'poora'. In Rajasthan, these are also made with green beans or mung bean flour and are called 'cheeldo'. It is served with a curry or vegetable side dish or simply with yogurt, as a light meal. *Makes 8 rotis* PREPARATION ⟶ *15 minutes* COOKING *15 minutes*

200g gram flour
100–150ml cold water
1 small onion, finely diced
thumb-sized piece of fresh root ginger, scraped and grated
small sprig of fresh coriander leaves, chopped
1 fresh green chilli, finely diced
¼ teaspoon ground cumin
vegetable oil, for frying
salt

1 Put the flour in a bowl with some salt to season. Add a little of the cold water and whisk to start making a batter. Continue adding the water, a little at a time, until you have a thick batter of pouring consistency, whisking well to remove any lumps.

2 Add the onion, ginger, coriander, chilli and cumin to the batter and mix well.

3 Heat a frying pan over a high heat and dot with oil. Pour a ladleful of batter into the pan and spread it with the back of the spoon into a thin disc. After 2–3 minutes, flip the roti over and cook on the other side with some more oil. Both sides should be golden.

4 Remove from the pan and wrap the roti in foil to keep it warm. Make 7 more rotis with the remaining batter.

5 If making the batter in advance, don't add the onion and ginger until you're ready to cook the roti as the salt will draw out their juices and thin the batter.

RIGHT: *Pesarattu (top left/middle); Besan Ki Roti (top right); Thalipeeth (bottom) – recipe on page 124.*

LACCHA PARATHA – Soft, Layered Bread with Crisp Edges

The best laccha paratha I've eaten was at the gorgeous Bombay Brasserie restaurant in London when I worked there in the early 1990s. It was flaky, soft and crisp and I always had mine with the savoury lamb rogan josh. A Kerala or Malabar parotta is made in a similar way, but with more plain flour than wholewheat flour than here, to make a softer, more elastic bread. *Makes 8 parathas* PREPARATION → *15 minutes, plus 15 minutes resting time* COOKING *30 minutes*

YOU WILL NEED:
250g stoneground wholewheat flour (atta), plus extra for dusting
50g plain flour or maida
pinch of salt
2 tablespoons vegetable oil or melted ghee, plus extra for brushing
    and shallow-frying
150–180ml tepid water, as needed

1 Combine the two flours and salt in a bowl. Rub the oil or ghee into the flour then add the tepid water, a couple of tablespoons at a time, until you have a soft dough. Knead the dough well on a surface until smooth and no longer sticky, then place it back in the bowl, cover the bowl with a clean tea towel and leave it to rest on the kitchen surface for 15 minutes.

2 Remove the dough from the bowl and knead it again, then divide it into 8 equal-sized portions and shape each portion into a ball. Flatten the balls slightly and roll them each out into a circle about 10cm in diameter.

3 Brush the dough circles liberally with oil or melted ghee and dust with a little flour. Starting at one end, fold the roti into small pleats like a fan. Fold the entire roti to the other end until it resembles a long strip of tiny folds.

Now, starting from one end, coil it into a tight spiral, folding the end into the centre. Fold and roll the remaining dough circles into spirals.

4 Without dusting them with flour, flatten the spirals and roll them out again, gently, to about 10cm in diameter.

5 Heat a griddle pan over a high heat. Place one paratha on the hot pan and cook for 2–3 minutes until the surface begins to bubble. Flip it over and cook on the other side for 1–2 minutes. Brush both sides with ghee or oil while cooking, until golden and flecked with brown spots.

6 Transfer the cooked paratha to a plate and crush slightly to loosen the layers. This is essential for them to achieve the right appearance. Wrap the cooked parathas in foil to keep them warm while cooking the rest.

MASTERCLASS

ALOO KE PARONTHE – Potato-stuffed Bread

Two different techniques for stuffing a paratha/paronthe.

This is a popular Punjabi or north Indian breakfast but it is also served at mealtimes with yogurt and hot pickle. There are two ways to stuff the bread, either by rolling out two discs, putting some of the filling in between and sealing the edges or by the method described opposite. Both have the same results. *Makes 8 parathas* PREPARATION → *10 minutes, plus 10 minutes resting time* COOKING *40 minutes*

YOU WILL NEED:

For the stuffing
2 medium potatoes
½ teaspoon cumin seeds
a handful of fresh coriander leaves, finely chopped
juice of 1 lemon
1 fresh green chilli, minced
For the bread
300g stoneground wholewheat flour (atta), plus extra for dusting
150–180ml tepid water, as needed
vegetable oil, for frying and brushing
salt

1 Boil the potatoes whole until very soft, then peel and mash them. I boil them in their skins (rather than cook them peeled and diced) as they tend to absorb less water this way, making for a drier mash.

2 Dry-toast the cumin seeds in a frying pan over a high heat until they change colour and become aromatic. Tip them into a pestle and mortar or spice mill and crush coarsely.

3 Combine the toasted cumin, coriander, mashed potato, lemon juice and chilli, season with salt and mix well. Divide the mixture into 8 equal-sized parts. This is the filling.

4 Put the flour in a large bowl, make a well in the centre and gradually add the tepid water to make a soft dough. Transfer to a surface and knead well for 7–8 minutes until smooth and no longer sticky. Rest the dough in the bowl under a clean, damp tea towel for 10 minutes.

5 Divide the dough into 8 equal-sized balls. Roll out a ball of dough on a floured surface to a small disc, about 10cm in diameter. Place one part of the filling in the centre of the disc and gather up the edges of the disc around it. Flour a surface and lightly roll out the paratha to about 15cm in diameter.

6 Heat a teaspoon of oil in a large frying pan over a high heat. Gently lift the disc and place it in the pan. Cook for 3–4 minutes, brush with oil, then carefully flip over to cook the other side. Press it down with the back of a flat spoon, especially around the edges, so that the paratha cooks evenly.

7 Remove from the heat, brush with oil and keep warm. Repeat with the remaining dough and filling. Wrap the cooked parathas in foil to keep them warm while cooking the rest.

Thalipeeth

| SPICED MULTIGRAIN BREAD |

This is a much-loved Maharashtrian bread (see photo on page 119). The flour mix can contain up to six grains and lentils such as wheat, rice, chickpeas, split black lentils, pearl millet and sorghum or jowar, which are roasted and crushed in a mill. As this may be tedious to make, people buy a ready-made flour mix called 'bhajani'. This recipe is an easy version, using flours readily available in the kitchen cupboard. *Makes 8 thalipeeth* PREPARATION —→ *20 minutes* COOKING *30 minutes*

300g mixed flours, such as gram flour, rice flour, pearl millet flour and stoneground wholewheat flour in equal quantities, plus extra for dusting
½ teaspoon ground cumin
1 onion, finely chopped
2 fresh green chillies, minced
a handful of fresh coriander leaves, finely chopped
150–180ml tepid water, as needed
vegetable oil, for frying

1 Combine the flours, cumin, onion, chillies and coriander in a large bowl. Make a well in the centre and add the water, a little at a time, until the mixture forms a stiff dough, then transfer to a surface and knead until smooth. Divide the dough into 8 equal-sized balls.

2 Place one dough ball on a sheet of floured greaseproof paper and place another sheet on top. Pat the dough into a flat disc 8cm in diameter. Repeat with the 7 remaining dough balls.

3 Heat a griddle pan over a high heat and gently lift one disc onto it. Pierce some small holes in the disc with a skewer or the tip of a small knife (this helps the bread cook evenly) and cook for 2–3 minutes. Dot the thalipeeth with oil. Flip it over and cook on the other side for 2–3 minutes until the bread is flecked with brown spots on both sides. Wrap the cooked thalipeeth in foil to keep it warm and repeat with the remaining discs.

Bhatura

| FLUFFY, SOFT BREAD |

Cholay bhature is a classic Punjabi combination of chickpeas served with fluffy, fried bread. It is as natural to eat this in a gourmet restaurant as it is to eat it at a roadside stall in any northern city of India. Restaurants serve large bhaturas, as they are fried in big commercial karahis. Homemade ones are smaller as they are cooked in domestic frying pans. *Makes 10 bhaturas* PREPARATION —→ *15 minutes, plus 30 minutes resting time* COOKING *30 minutes*

300g plain flour or maida
½ teaspoon baking powder
pinch of salt
100g natural yogurt
150–180ml tepid water, as needed
vegetable oil, for deep-frying
chana masala, to serve (optional)

1 Sift the flour, baking powder and salt into a bowl. Add the yogurt and mix well. Mix in the tepid water, a couple of tablespoons at a time, until you have a soft dough. Add 1 tablespoon of oil at this point and knead the dough for 7–8 minutes until it is very soft but no longer sticky.

2 Place in the bowl, cover with a clean, damp tea towel and set aside for 30 minutes in a warm place.

3 Heat enough vegetable oil in a deep frying pan to deep-fry the bhaturas. Divide the rested dough into 10 small equal-sized balls, each about the size of a lime. Grease your hands and a ball of dough with oil and roll lightly into a small, flat disc or oblong shape about 10cm wide and 5mm thick.

4 When the oil is smoking hot, reduce the heat and fry the bhaturas, one at a time, for about 2 minutes until fluffy. Repeat with the remaining balls, making sure to regulate the heat so that it is hot enough to cook the bhaturas within a couple of minutes without browning them too quickly. Wrap the cooked bhatura in foil to keep it warm while frying the rest. Serve hot with chana masala, if you like.

DOSAS – Lentil and Rice Pancakes

These are south India's favourite pancakes and are mostly eaten for breakfast. They are served plain, as in this recipe, or stuffed with a spiced potato mixture and called 'masala dosa'. Restaurants serve versions called 'paper dosa' that are crisp and so fine you can almost see through them, or 'metre dosa' that is 1-metre long and can feed the whole family. The key to a successful dosa is the fermentation. You'll need to find a warm spot (22°C or above) to leave the batter. There should be small bubbles in the fermented batter.

Makes 16 dosas PREPARATION → *15 minutes, plus 5 hours soaking and overnight fermenting* COOKING *25 minutes*

YOU WILL NEED:
300g inexpensive basmati rice, washed, drained and soaked in water for 5 hours
150g split skinless black lentils (these look white and are called urad dal), soaked in water for 5 hours
vegetable oil, for frying
salt

1 Drain the rice and lentils and blitz them separately in a blender, adding enough cold water to just cover each of them, until you have two smooth, thick batters. Combine these batters, cover with clingfilm and leave to ferment in a warm place for 12 hours.

2 Season the batter with salt and heat a frying pan over a high heat. Stir the batter well and pour a ladleful of it into the centre of the pan. Spread the mixture out quickly from the centre out to the edges with the back of a spoon, to make a neat 10cm circle.

3 Drizzle a few drops of oil around the edges of the dosa if it starts to stick. Reduce the heat, cover the pan and cook for about 30 seconds. Remove the lid, turn the dosa over with a spatula, replace the lid and cook on the other side for about 30 seconds until it is sealed. Repeat with the remaining batter, keeping the cooked pancakes warm on a covered plate, and serve at once with a coconut chutney (see page 424) and sambhar (see page 282).

Neer Dosa
| WATER PANCAKES |

These are served for breakfast in the Udipi region of Karnataka. They are light and lacy and not very filling, so they are served with thick lentil sambhar (see page 282). *Makes 22 dosas*

PREPARATION → *20 minutes, plus overnight soaking*
COOKING *25 minutes*

300g inexpensive basmati rice, washed, drained and soaked in water overnight
100g fresh coconut, grated
vegetable oil, for frying
salt

1 Drain and rinse the rice and place it in a blender with the coconut and enough water to cover the mixture and blitz to make a fine purée. Pour the batter into a bowl. At this stage it will probably coat the back of a spoon. If so, add more water – enough to make a thin runny batter that will not coat the back of a spoon. Season with salt.

2 Heat a frying pan over a high heat and drizzle in a few drops of oil. Wipe the oil around the pan with some kitchen paper.

3 Pour in a ladleful of batter and swirl the pan: the batter should coat the pan in a thin layer. Cover the pan and let the dosa cook over a high heat for a couple of minutes.

4 Lift off the edges with a spatula, fold the dosa into a triangle and serve at once. Repeat with the remaining batter.

Appams

| SAVOURY COCONUT PANCAKES |

This is a south Indian rice and coconut fermented pancake that is eaten for breakfast or with a main meal. Various recipes use fresh coconut or yeast but I use coconut milk and baking powder for ease. There are various kinds of appams – both sweet and savoury – which are eaten with fiery coconut-based stews and curries. They are traditionally made in an 'appam chatti', a convex, rounded pan. You can use a wok or a karahi. *Makes 16 pancakes* PREPARATION → *20 minutes, plus 3 hours soaking time and overnight fermenting* COOKING *25 minutes*

300g inexpensive basmati rice, washed, drained and soaked
    in water for 3 hours
150ml coconut milk
2 teaspoons caster sugar
pinch of salt
½ teaspoon bicarbonate of soda
sunflower or gingelly (til) oil, for greasing

1 Drain the rice and put it in a blender with the coconut milk. Blitz until you have a fine batter with a pouring consistency. Rice can become gritty in a batter so keep the blender going a little bit longer than you think you need to, to get it as fine as possible.
2 Pour the batter into a bowl, cover with clingfilm and leave to ferment overnight in a warm place.
3 The following day, add the sugar, salt and bicarbonate of soda. If the batter is no longer runny, add a little water.
4 Heat a round-bottomed pan, such as a wok or karahi, over a high heat and brush it with the tiniest amount of oil.
5 When the pan is hot, pour a ladleful of the batter into the centre and swirl the pan to coat the sides. Cover the pan and let the appam cook for a minute or so: it will get a honeycomb look and the edges will be thinner than the sides – the thicker centre should become opaque. Lift it out of the pan gently and serve immediately. Repeat with the remaining batter.

Paalaada

| RICE, COCONUT AND EGG PANCAKES |

These are velvety soft pancakes eaten by the Muslim population of Tamil Nadu and Kerala, with spicy chicken, mutton or beef curries. The name probably comes from the fineness of the skin that forms on top of boiled milk ('paal-aada' in Tamil and Malayalam). It is a festive pancake eaten during Eid and – being so fine – several are made per person. *Makes 22 pancakes* PREPARATION → *15 minutes, plus 5 hours soaking time* COOKING *25 minutes*

300g inexpensive white rice, washed, drained and soaked
    for 5 hours
200ml coconut milk
2 medium eggs
salt

1 Drain the rice and put it in a blender with the coconut milk. Blitz to a fine purée to make a smooth batter.
2 Pass most of this batter through a sieve into a bowl, leaving about 4 tablespoons behind in the blender. Add the eggs to the blender and blitz for a minute, then pour this mixture through the sieve. Season with salt. The batter should be very runny and barely coat the back of a spoon. If it isn't runny enough, add a little water to thin it down.
3 Heat a non-stick frying pan over a high heat. Pour in a ladleful of batter and swirl the pan so it coats the sides of the pan. The pancake takes seconds to cook. Once it has become opaque and set, fold it into a triangle and serve at once. Repeat with the remaining batter.

Adai

| RICE AND YELLOW LENTIL PANCAKES |

In many Tamil households, the batter for dosas, adais and various other breakfast and snack foods is made once a week and stored in the fridge. Most of these kitchens have a 'wet grinder' that can successfully pulverise hard grains and pulses with the help of a liquid. These adai are also called 'ada dosa'. *Makes 10 pancakes* PREPARATION→ *15 minutes, plus 4 hours soaking time* COOKING *35 minutes*

1 small onion, finely diced
1 teaspoon ginger-garlic paste *(page 45)*
1 small green chilli, minced
vegetable oil, for frying
For the batter
150g inexpensive white rice, washed, drained and soaked
    in water for 4 hours
50g toor dal or split gram lentils (chana dal),
    soaked in water for 4 hours
50g split skinless black lentils (urad dal),
    soaked in water for 4 hours
salt

1 Drain the rice and lentils and put them in a blender with enough water to just cover them. Blitz to a fine purée. The batter should have a thick pouring consistency, so add a couple more tablespoons of water if necessary. Season with salt.

2 Add the diced onion, ginger-garlic paste and green chilli to the batter and mix them in.

3 Heat a non-stick frying pan over a high heat and pour in a ladleful of batter. Spread it out thinly with the back of the ladle and drizzle a little oil around the edges. Cook for 1–2 minutes, then flip it over and cook on the other side for about 1 minute. Both sides should be golden. Serve at once. Repeat with the remaining batter.

Pakwan

| CRISP SINDHI-STYLE BREAD |

This Sindhi bread is often eaten for breakfast along with Sindhi Dal (page 296), but I could eat it at any time of the day. The bread is pricked with a fork before frying so that it does not puff up: instead it becomes crisp, a texture that complements the creaminess of the accompanying dal. *Makes 8 breads* PREPARATION→ *15 minutes, plus 10 minutes resting time* COOKING *40 minutes*

300g plain flour, plus extra for dusting
1 tablespoon ghee
pinch of salt
150–180ml tepid water, as needed
vegetable oil, for deep-frying

1 Mix the flour, ghee and salt in a bowl. Add the tepid water, a couple of tablespoons at a time, until you have a soft dough. Transfer to a surface and knead the dough well for 5–6 minutes, then leave the dough to rest for 10 minutes in the bowl, covered with a clean, damp tea towel.

2 Divide the dough into 8 equal-sized balls and roll out each ball into thin discs about 8cm in diameter. Flour the board as necessary.

3 Prick the discs all over with a fork.

4 Heat enough oil in a deep frying pan or kadhai to come up to 5cm over a high heat. When nearly smoking, reduce the heat and gently slide in a pakwan. Fry them one at a time for 3–4 minutes until golden and crisp.

5 Drain on kitchen paper and keep warm, wrapped in foil, while you fry the rest of the pakwans.

MEAT

IN INDIA MEAT HAS ALWAYS BEEN COOKED WITH SPICES
AND EVEN IN THE *Ramayana*, ONE OF INDIA'S GREATEST AND OLDEST EPICS, MUTTON AND PORK
ARE COOKED IN FRUIT JUICES WITH CLOVES AND OTHER SPICES.

Meat consumption has a long and varied history in India. Bones of buffalo, sheep, fish and fowl have been found in Indus Valley (3300 BC–1700 BC) excavations and detailed descriptions of animal sacrifice and eating meat are seen in later Vedic texts. The *Vedas* themselves, which are some of the most sacred texts of Hinduism, list domesticated cattle, swine and wild animals among those that could be sacrificed.

Charaka, one of the earliest practitioners of Ayurveda, recommended meat and its broth for convalescents and for those doing hard physical work, meaning men. It was only after the arrival of Buddhism and Jainism, two religions that believe in non-violence, that Hinduism turned towards vegetarianism. Today, almost a third of India is vegetarian and most religious Hindu feasts do not contain meat.

In India, the word 'mutton' loosely refers to meat and this could be sheep, goat or beef. The most common is goat meat, also called 'bakre ka gosht'. Beef, called 'bade ka gosht' (meat of the big one), is sold in some states whereas cow slaughter is illegal in others. These laws are not uniform, so some states allow cows above a certain age to be killed whereas others ban the practice completely. This means that beef is usually buffalo meat, as cows are considered sacred in Hinduism.

Although beef is not commonly seen in shops or on restaurant menus, it is certainly eaten in India. Popular dishes such as the Kalyani Biryani of Hyderabad is a 'poor man's dish' using fewer spices and cheaper cuts of meat but with lots of flavour. In Kerala, the Beef Fry (page 155) or 'ularthiyathu' is savoured by the Syrian Christian community.

Meat has always been cooked with spices and even in the *Ramayana*, one of India's great and old epics, mutton and pork are cooked in fruit juices with cloves and other spices. In south India, meat was cooked with black pepper and

the finished dish was called 'kari'. Much later, the Mughals brought new ways of cooking meat in cream and with nuts and fruit. Volume One of the *Ain-i-Akbari* written by Abu Faz'l (1590 AD) describes dishes such as biryani made by cooking sheep in ghee with saffron, cloves, pepper and cumin seed. 'Yakhni' was meat cooked with onions and a lamb or kid was preferable. Kebabs combined meat with ghee, fresh ginger, onions and spices.

CUTS OF MEAT USED IN INDIAN COOKING

Mutton, beef, lamb or pork curries rely on a stewing technique where the meat is cooked slowly with the rest of the ingredients to absorb flavour as well as soften. Therefore, slightly cheaper cuts of meat such as shoulder can be used. Recipes such as 'boti' kebabs use the diced leg of the animal whereas 'seekh kebabs' that are shaped around skewers use minced meat. Indians often prefer to use meat on the bone as it adds flavour to curries.

All meat is cooked until well done rather than rare or medium. Indians are fussy about the smell of meat and will add spices and herbs to mask the strong aroma and to add flavour.

Indian Muslims eat only halal meat. Halal is the Arabic word for 'permissible' and this food is that which adheres to Islamic law, as defined in the Koran. The Islamic ritual form of slaughtering animals or poultry by cutting the jugular vein in a single swipe is called dhabiha, and all blood is drained away from the dead animal.

I like to use shoulder of lamb for curries, as it has a proportion of fat that helps to soften the meat as it stews, and leg with more muscle for roasting, so it gives you a leaner finished product.

MARINADES

TENDERISERS → Meat is often marinated before being cooked, to allow flavours to penetrate and to soften it. Marinades have three components – spices and herbs for flavour, oil or dairy to carry flavour and to bind ingredients together, and acid to tenderise. Salt adds flavour and helps to soften the meat.

Acidic marinades Acidic liquids such as lemon and lime juice or vinegar denature protein and loosen the muscle fibre as well as adding flavour. They can, however, over-soften the meat and are therefore combined with oil to dilute them slightly.

Enzymatic marinades Some fruit and vegetables, such as ginger, pineapple, figs and kiwis, have enzymes which help to break down protein. The most commonly used one is papain from raw papaya. This is sold as a white powder in Asian food stores, or you can grate a small lime-sized piece of raw papaya. Meat left in papain for too long can get mushy and tenderise unevenly, so don't leave it in for more than a couple of hours if using the powder, or 6 hours if using fresh.

Dairy marinades Yogurt is a mild marinade used in Indian cooking. It is widely available and softens the meat all the way through. The yogurt also helps to hold the rest of the ingredients together and bind them to the meat.

 If you are not using dairy, mix the marinade ingredients (such as spices, salt, ginger and garlic) together and rub them onto the meat. Finish with a coating of oil. If you combine the spices with oil to begin with, it acts as a barrier to the absorption of spices and salt into the meat.

A note about the recipes: Many of the recipes in this chapter would be cooked with goat meat in India – outside of India, one can use lamb.

Dal Gosht

| LAMB WITH LENTILS |

600g lamb on the bone, cubed
2 tablespoons full-fat yogurt
150g split gram lentils (chana dal), soaked
2 tablespoons vegetable oil
2 large onions, finely chopped
2 teaspoons ginger-garlic paste *(page 45)*
2 fresh green chillies, finely chopped
2 tablespoons tomato purée
1½ teaspoons ground turmeric
1 teaspoon ground coriander
1 teaspoon garam masala *(page 64)*
a few turns of a peppermill
3 teaspoons lemon juice
a few sprigs of fresh coriander leaves,
    washed and chopped, to garnish
salt
boiled rice *(pages 78–79)* or Rotis *(pages 108–109)*,
    to serve

The combination of meat with lentils as a sauce is a mix of Mughal and Indian styles. Today, this dish is commonly found in places that have had Islamic rulers in the past, such as Hyderabad, where it is called 'dalcha'. The chana dal adds a grainy texture (some versions of this recipe use toor dal, which makes a smoother sauce). *Serves 4* PREPARATION → *10 minutes, plus marinating time for lamb and soaking time for lentils (about 1 hour)* COOKING *1 hour 15 minutes*

1 Place the lamb in a bowl with the yogurt and season with salt, then set aside to marinate for 1 hour. Soak the lentils in plenty of hot water for 1 hour.
2 Drain the lentils and put them in a heavy-based saucepan with double the volume of water (and no salt) and bring to the boil. Reduce the heat and cook for 45 minutes until soft, adding a few tablespoons of water if the lentils dry out.
3 Meanwhile, heat half the oil in a separate heavy-based saucepan over a high heat, add the onions and fry for 7–8 minutes until soft and brown. Add the ginger-garlic paste and green chillies, then stir in the tomato purée and cook for a minute. Tip this mixture into a blender, add enough water to cover the mixture and blitz to make a smooth curry paste. Set aside.
4 Heat the remaining oil in the same pan over a high heat and add the marinated lamb. Stir to mop up all the flavour from the bottom of the pan and seal well. Sprinkle in the ground spices, cook for 30 seconds then pour in the curry paste and season with salt. Mix well and pour in 250ml water. Bring to the boil, reduce the heat and simmer for 1 hour or until the lamb is tender. You may need to add a bit more water while cooking if the curry gets too dry.
5 Pour in the cooked and drained lentils and mix well. Add the lemon juice and season to taste. Sprinkle with the coriander and serve with rice or rotis.

Kofta Curry

| MEATBALL CURRY |

The word 'kofta' denotes ground meat in Persian. This dish is made all over India with lamb or beef mince, depending on religious preferences. I cook the meatballs in the oven because it's healthier to oven-bake them than fry them, but they can be pan-fried and added to the sauce while it's cooking, if you like. *Serves 4* PREPARATION ➝ *15 minutes* COOKING *35 minutes*

boiled rice *(pages 78–79)*, to serve
a handful of chopped fresh coriander leaves, to garnish
salt
For the meatballs
300g lean lamb mince
2 teaspoons ginger-garlic paste *(page 45)*
2 fresh green chillies, finely diced
For the curry
2 tablespoons vegetable oil
2 bay leaves
2 large onions, very finely chopped
1 tablespoon ginger-garlic paste *(page 45)*
2 fresh green chillies, minced
2 tomatoes, diced or ½ x 400g can of chopped plum tomatoes
1 teaspoon ground turmeric
1 teaspoon garam masala *(page 64)*

1 Preheat the oven to 200°C/gas mark 6. Combine the meatball ingredients in a large bowl with a pinch of salt. Form into 20 large cherry-sized balls. Line a baking tray with foil, place the meatballs on the tray and bake for 10 minutes. Remove from the oven and set aside.

2 Meanwhile, heat the oil in a heavy-based saucepan over a high heat and add the bay leaves. As they darken, add the onions and cook for 7–8 minutes until soft and brown. Add the ginger-garlic paste and chillies and fry for a few seconds, then tip in the tomatoes and stir to soften. Add the spices and season with salt. Cook for 10 minutes over a medium heat until well blended, adding a splash of water if the curry begins to stick to the bottom of the pan.

3 Gently place the meatballs in the curry. Cook for a further 5 minutes, season to taste, sprinkle with the coriander and serve with rice.

Kheema Mutter

| MINCED LAMB WITH PEAS |

This is a popular dish all over India and is eaten with bread called 'pao', rolled into rotis, or simply served with plain rice. It also makes a good filling for samosas. You can substitute the peas with mushrooms or diced potatoes as a variation. *Serves 4* PREPARATION ➝ *15 minutes* COOKING *30 minutes*

2 tablespoons vegetable oil
10 black peppercorns, crushed
2 medium onions, finely chopped
2 teaspoons ginger-garlic paste *(page 45)*
2 tablespoons tomato purée
2 fresh green chillies, finely diced
600g lamb mince
150g green peas, shelled if fresh, or frozen
1 teaspoon ground turmeric
1 teaspoon garam masala *(page 64)*
small sprig of fresh coriander leaves, chopped, to garnish
salt
Rotis *(pages 108–109)*, pao or boiled rice *(pages 78–79)*, to serve

1 Heat the oil in a frying pan over a high heat, add the crushed peppercorns and fry for a minute. Tip in the onions, fry for 7–8 minutes until golden, then add the ginger-garlic paste. Stir a few times then add the tomato purée and chillies. Cook for a couple of minutes.

2 Add the mince, green peas, ground spices and season with salt. Break up the mince and stir to brown evenly, then cover and cook over a low heat for 20 minutes, until the lamb is tender.

3 Season to taste and serve hot, garnished with the chopped coriander, with roti, pao or rice.

Saag Gosht

| LAMB WITH SPINACH |

Saag gosht is also known as palak gosht, as the words 'saag' and 'palak' are used interchangeably for spinach in some parts of India, such as Punjab. You can use lamb chops for this recipe, if you prefer. *Serves 4*

PREPARATION → *15 minutes* COOKING *1 hour 15 minutes*

200g spinach, cleaned, washed and chopped
2 tablespoons vegetable oil
1 tablespoon coriander seeds
2 onions, chopped
2.5cm piece of fresh root ginger, scraped and chopped
4 garlic cloves, chopped
2 fresh green chillies, chopped
1 tablespoon tomato purée
800g lamb shoulder on the bone, cubed
1 teaspoon ground turmeric
1 teaspoon ground coriander
1 teaspoon ground cumin
1 teaspoon garam masala *(page 64)*
salt
Rotis *(pages 108–109)* or boiled rice *(pages 78–79)*, to serve

1 Put the spinach in a pan with a few tablespoons of water and cook for 5 minutes until wilted. Blitz to a purée in a blender with the cooking liquid and set aside.
2 Heat half the oil in a frying pan over a high heat, add the coriander seeds and fry for 40 seconds until slightly dark. Add the onions and fry for 8–9 minutes until brown, then add the ginger, garlic and green chillies. Fry for 1 minute then add the tomato purée. Mix everything together, cook for 1 minute until blended, then transfer to a blender with enough water to cover the mixture, and blitz to make a smooth curry paste.
3 Heat the remaining oil in a pan over a high heat and add the lamb. Fry, stirring, for 4–5 minutes until sealed, then add the ground spices and season with salt.
4 Add the curry paste and enough water to make a thick sauce. Bring to the boil then cook over a low heat for 1 hour until the lamb is tender, adding more water if necessary. Add the puréed spinach and stir to blend. Season to taste and serve hot with rice or rotis.

Lamb Dhansak

| PARSI LAMB AND LENTIL CURRY |

Although this much-loved dish is eaten for Sunday lunch in Parsi homes, it is traditionally cooked on the fourth day after the passing away of a relative. Meat is not cooked for the first three days of mourning and this dhansak is prepared to mark the end of the abstinence. Therefore dhansak is not considered a celebratory dish. *Serves 4*

PREPARATION → *30 minutes* COOKING *1½ hours*

1 large onion, finely chopped
2 tomatoes, chopped
1 small bottle gourd or courgette, finely chopped
80g red pumpkin or butternut squash, chopped and deseeded, skin left on
a small handful of fresh fenugreek leaves, chopped, or 2 tablespoons dried fenugreek leaves
a handful of fresh coriander leaves, chopped
a handful of fresh mint leaves, chopped
300g boneless lamb shoulder, cubed
150g red lentils, washed and drained
1½ teaspoons ground turmeric
1 teaspoon medium-hot red chilli powder
2 teaspoons dhansak masala or garam masala *(page 64)*
4 tablespoons malt vinegar
1 tablespoon vegetable oil
1 teaspoon cumin seeds
salt
Parsi-style Brown Rice *(page 94)*, to serve

1 Put all the ingredients except the vinegar, oil and cumin seeds in a large pan along with enough water to cover them and bring to the boil. Reduce the heat and simmer, covered, for 1 hour or until the lamb and lentils are soft.
2 Lightly whisk the vegetables and lentils to mash them. The meat will not get mashed. (Some recipes cook the meat and lentils separately or scoop the meat out of the curry before puréeing it in a blender – I use a whisk as it is equally efficient and quicker.)
3 Add the vinegar, season with salt and stir.
4 Heat the oil in a small frying pan over a high heat, add the cumin seeds and fry for about 30 seconds until slightly dark. Pour the oil over the dhansak and serve hot with Parsi-style brown rice.

Lamb Vepudu

| ANDHRA MUTTON FRY |

Andhra Pradesh in south India grows almost half of India's entire chilli crop and therefore the style of cooking is quite spicy. Most of the chillies produced there are dried to increase their shelf life and they are found in almost every recipe from the region, including this one. This dish is also found in highway eateries and popular restaurants in Hyderabad. *Serves 4* PREPARATION → *10 minutes* COOKING *1 hour*

800g lamb on the bone, cubed
1 teaspoon ground turmeric
1 tablespoon ginger-garlic paste *(page 45)*
3 tablespoons vegetable oil
1 large onion, finely diced
3–4 dried red chillies, broken in half and seeds shaken out
2 fresh green chillies, finely diced
10 fresh or 15 dried curry leaves
1 teaspoon ground coriander
1 teaspoon garam masala *(page 64)*
10 black peppercorns, coarsely crushed
salt
Parathas *(pages 120–121)* or Dosas *(pages 126–127)*, to serve

1 Put the lamb, turmeric and half the ginger-garlic paste in a pan, season with salt and add enough water to cover the lamb. Bring to the boil, then reduce the heat and simmer for 50 minutes or until the lamb is tender. Drain and set the meat to one side. Keep the broth to use as a stock in another dish such as Lamb Dhansak (page 143).

2 Meanwhile, heat the oil in a large frying pan, add the onion and fry for 7–8 minutes until soft. Add the remaining ginger-garlic paste and cook for 30 seconds. Add the red and green chillies and curry leaves (standing back from the pan if using fresh leaves, as they will splutter) and cook for a further minute.

3 Sprinkle in the ground coriander and garam masala, then add the cooked lamb and season with salt. Cook for 6–7 minutes until the sauce coats the meat. Sprinkle in the pepper, season to taste and serve hot with paratha or dosa.

Laal Maas

| RAJASTHANI MEAT AND CHILLI CURRY |

Many bright red Rajasthani curries look much spicier than they actually are – Mathania chillies from near Jodhpur are used for colour and have a unique flavour that is earthy rather than simply hot. I've used the more readily available Kashmiri dried red chillies, which are also bright red and have a moderate level of heat. *Serves 4* PREPARATION → *15 minutes, plus 1 hour marinating time* COOKING *1 hour 20 minutes*

800g lamb shoulder on the bone, cubed
1 teaspoon ground coriander
1 teaspoon ground cumin
1 teaspoon garam masala *(page 64)*
50g full-fat yogurt
12 dried red Kashmiri chillies, broken in half and seeds shaken out
2 tablespoons vegetable oil
1 tablespoon coriander seeds
2 onions, chopped
6 garlic cloves, minced
salt
Rotis *(pages 108–109)* or boiled rice *(pages 78–79)*, to serve

1 Combine the lamb in a bowl with the ground coriander, cumin and garam masala. Tip in the yogurt, season with salt, mix and leave to marinate for 1 hour.

2 Meanwhile, put the dried chillies in a small saucepan over a high heat, pour in enough water to just cover them, and bring to the boil. Reduce the heat and simmer for 6–7 minutes until the chillies are soft. Remove from the heat and set aside.

3 Heat half the oil in a frying pan over a high heat, add the coriander seeds and fry for about 30 seconds until slightly dark. Add the onions and fry for 7–8 minutes until brown, then add the garlic and cook for a further few minutes. Put this mixture into a blender along with the soft chillies and their cooking liquid. Top up with water so that it just covers the mixture and blitz to form a fine purée.

4 Heat the remaining oil in a pan over a high heat and add the marinated lamb. Fry the lamb for a few minutes, then add the onion and chilli purée. Season to taste and cook over a medium heat for 50 minutes until the lamb is tender. You may need to add some water during cooking if the curry dries out. Season to taste and serve hot with rotis or rice.

Aab Gosht

| LAMB CURRY WITH MILK |

This is a much-loved Kashmiri dish with a soupy gravy and tender pieces of lamb. It is fragrant without being too hot and is often served as part of a festive Kashmiri meal at weddings or for Eid. *Serves 4* PREPARATION → *20 minutes* COOKING *1½ hours*

800g lamb shoulder on the bone, cubed
4 large garlic cloves, peeled
2 teaspoons ground ginger
2 teaspoons ground fennel seeds
1 small cinnamon stick
2 black cardamom pods, seeds crushed and husks discarded
5 green cardamom pods, seeds crushed and husks discarded
8 black peppercorns
3 cloves
2 tablespoons ghee
2 onions, sliced
250ml whole milk
salt
boiled rice *(pages 78–79)*, to serve

1 Put the lamb, garlic, ground ginger and fennel, cinnamon stick, crushed cardamom seeds, peppercorns and cloves in a saucepan. Season with salt, then pour in just enough water to cover the meat and bring to the boil. Reduce the heat and simmer for 1 hour or until the meat is tender. The cooked meat will now be in a meat stock.

2 Meanwhile, heat half the ghee in a frying pan over a high heat, add the onions and fry for 8–9 minutes until they are well browned, reducing the heat as they begin to change colour. Drain them, reserving the ghee for the curry. Put the drained onions in a blender, add enough cold water to just cover them and blitz to a fine purée.

3 Heat the remaining ghee in a saucepan and add the brown onion purée. Cook for a couple of minutes then lift the pieces of cooked lamb out of the stock and add them to the onions.

4 Coat the lamb well and cook for 2–3 minutes. Pour the meat stock through a sieve into the pan with the meat and discard the spices.

5 Pour in the milk and cook for 7–8 minutes until the sauce is well blended. Season to taste and serve hot with rice.

Saoji Mutton

| SPICY LAMB WITH SPICES AND DRIED COCONUT |

The Saoji or Savji are a silk-weaving community who migrated from north India to various parts of the country carrying their cuisine with them. This recipe from Nagpur is eaten with spicy wheat pooris called 'edmi'. It uses a local spice called 'dagad phool' which looks like burnt paper with an aniseed-like flavour. If you can't source it, use aniseed instead. *Serves 4* PREPARATION → *20 minutes* COOKING *1 hour 15 minutes*

3 tablespoons vegetable oil
2 tablespoons coriander seeds
1 small cinnamon stick
3 cloves
8 dried red Kashmiri chillies, broken in half and seeds shaken out
1 tablespoon white poppy seeds
1 tablespoon mountain moss (dagad phool) or 1 tablespoon aniseed or fennel seeds
2 onions, sliced
2 tablespoons ginger-garlic paste *(page 45)*
3 tablespoons desiccated coconut
800g goat or lamb on the bone, cubed
2 black cardamom pods, seeds crushed and husks discarded
4 green cardamom pods, seeds crushed and husks discarded
salt
Pooris *(pages 114–115)*, to serve

1 Heat half the oil in a frying pan over a high heat and add the coriander seeds, cinnamon stick, cloves, Kashmiri chillies, poppy seeds and mountain moss. Fry for 1 minute, then when the seeds darken, add the onions. Cook for 8–9 minutes until the onions are soft and brown.

2 Add the ginger-garlic paste and coconut. Cook until the coconut turns golden brown, then transfer to a blender, add enough cold water to just cover it and blitz to a fine purée.

3 Heat the remaining oil in a heavy-based saucepan over a high heat and fry the meat for 4–5 minutes. Pour in the purée from the blender, add the crushed cardamom seeds and season with salt. Rinse out the blender with 300ml water and pour this into the curry. Bring to the boil, then reduce the heat and cook for 50 minutes or until the meat is tender. Season to taste and serve hot with pooris.

Rogan Josh

| RICH RED KASHMIRI CURRY |

This fragrant Kashmiri dish is sometimes referred to as 'Sabut Salan' because the meat is not minced but cubed. The colour was originally derived from the root of Alkanet or Ratan Jot. These days, cheaper Kashmiri chilli powder is used instead. *Serves 4* PREPARATION —➔ *20 minutes* COOKING *1½ hours*

4 tablespoons vegetable oil
4 cloves
2 small cinnamon sticks
2 large black cardamom pods, seeds crushed and husks discarded
4 green cardamom pods, seeds crushed and husks discarded
1 blade of mace
2 large onions, sliced
2 teaspoons ginger-garlic paste *(page 45)*
2 tablespoons tomato purée
2 bay leaves
600g lamb shoulder on the bone, cubed
1 teaspoon ground fennel seeds
2 teaspoons ground coriander
2 teaspoons Kashmiri chilli powder
1 teaspoon ground turmeric
2 tablespoons ground almonds
50g full-fat yogurt
salt
boiled rice *(pages 78–79)* or Rotis *(page 108–109)*, to serve

1 Heat half the oil in a heavy-based saucepan over a high heat, add the cloves, cinnamon sticks, cardamom seeds and mace. Fry for a couple of minutes until aromatic then add the onions. Fry over a medium heat for 10–12 minutes until the onions are golden brown and soft. Add the ginger-garlic paste, fry for a minute then add the tomato purée. Stir a few times and remove from the heat. Transfer to a blender, add a few tablespoons of water and blitz until smooth. Set aside.
2 Heat the remaining oil in a pan over a high heat, add the bay leaves and fry for 30 seconds. Add the lamb, reduce the heat to medium and fry until brown, then add the ground spices and cook for a couple of minutes. Add the curry paste and enough water to make a thick sauce. Season with salt and bring to the boil. Reduce the heat, cover and simmer for 50 minutes or until the lamb is tender.
3 Fold in the ground almonds and yogurt and remove from the heat. Season to taste and serve hot with rice or rotis.

Railway Mutton Curry

| LAMB CURRY SERVED ON THE INDIAN RAIL NETWORK |

One of the great joys of train travel in India is the endless variety of food that is sold. Long journeys involve entire meals being served to you at your seat. This curry became standard fare on trains during the Raj and was mildly spiced to suit the delicate British palate. The addition of tamarind or vinegar helped to make it last for a few days. Today's railway curries are spicier but still quite delicious! *Serves 4* PREPARATION —➔ *15 minutes* COOKING *1 hour 15 minutes*

800g lamb on the bone, cubed
1 tablespoon ginger-garlic paste *(page 45)*
1 teaspoon medium-hot red chilli powder
1 teaspoon ground coriander
1 teaspoon ground turmeric
2 tablespoons vegetable oil
8 black peppercorns
1 small cinnamon stick
3 green cardamom pods, seeds crushed and husks discarded
3 dried red Kashmiri chillies, broken in half and seeds shaken out
8 fresh or 15 dried curry leaves
2 onions, thinly sliced
2 tablespoons malt vinegar or 4 tablespoons tamarind pulp *(page 418)* or shop-bought tamarind paste
salt
boiled rice *(pages 78–79)*, to serve

1 Place the lamb in a large bowl with the ginger-garlic paste and ground spices, , season with salt and combine. Set aside while you prepare the remaining ingredients.
2 Heat the oil in a heavy-based saucepan over a high heat and add the whole spices, Kashmiri chillies and curry leaves (standing back from the pan if using fresh leaves, as they will splutter). When they sizzle and change colour, add the onions. Fry for 8–9 minutes until soft and brown.
3 Tip in the meat and fry to seal, then pour in the vinegar or tamarind pulp and enough water to just cover the lamb. Bring to the boil, then reduce the heat and cook for 50 minutes, or until the lamb is tender and the curry is thick. Season to taste and serve hot with rice.

Raan

| ROAST LEG OF LAMB |

Raan is associated with Kashmiri cooking or that of the north-west frontier. In Indian restaurants it is cooked in a tandoor but home cooks can use domestic ovens. The meat is marinated to tenderise it and slow, long cooking ensures that it falls off the bone. *Serves 4* PREPARATION ⟶ *15 minutes, plus 1 hour marinating time* COOKING *about 1½ hours (depending on size and quality of the lamb)*

½ leg of lamb (about 1kg)
150g full-fat yogurt
2 teaspoons medium-hot red chilli powder
1 teaspoon ground turmeric
2 teaspoons garam masala *(page 64)*
4 teaspoons ginger-garlic paste *(page 45)*
2 tablespoons grated raw papaya or 1 teaspoon papain powder
2 tablespoons lemon juice
vegetable oil, for greasing
salt
Parathas *(pages 120–121)* or Naans *(pages 110–113)*, to serve

1 Make 6–8 deep incisions in the leg of lamb and rub with salt to season.
2 Mix the yogurt, spices, ginger-garlic paste, papaya and lemon juice with salt to season and rub the mixture onto the meat. Leave the lamb to stand for 1 hour and preheat the oven to 180°C/gas mark 4.
3 Place the meat in a greased roasting tin and pour in 5 tablespoons of water. Seal the tin with foil and cook for 30 minutes per 450g meat. When the meat is cooked, turn off the oven and leave the meat to rest in the oven for 20 minutes.
4 Transfer to a serving dish and serve with parathas or naans.

Nihari

| BREAKFAST MEAT CURRY |

This is a famous Delhi meat curry eaten for breakfast after the first Muslim prayers. In days gone by, rulers and kings could then have a nap until the afternoon prayers. Today, some restaurants that serve Nihari claim that the addition of a portion of the previous day's curry, called 'taar', adds flavour to the fresh one. *Serves 4* PREPARATION ⟶ *20 minutes* COOKING *1 hour 20 minutes*

800g lamb on the bone, including marrow bones, diced
2 tablespoons ginger-garlic paste *(page 45)*
1 teaspoon medium-hot red chilli powder
1 teaspoon ground coriander
1 teaspoon ground turmeric
1 teaspoon ground fennel seeds
2 tablespoons ghee
4 cloves
1 small cinnamon stick
3 black cardamom pods, seeds crushed and husks discarded
½ teaspoon freshly ground black pepper
2 onions, thinly sliced
2 tablespoons stoneground wholewheat flour (atta), mixed with some water to make a paste
juice of ½ lemon
thumb-sized piece of fresh root ginger, scraped and cut in julienne strips, to garnish
a small handful of fresh coriander leaves, chopped, to garnish
salt
boiled rice *(pages 78–79)* or Rotis *(pages 108–109)*, to serve

1 Combine the meat, half the ginger-garlic paste and all the ground spices in a saucepan along with enough water to cover the meat, season with salt and bring to the boil. Reduce the heat and simmer for 1 hour or until the meat is tender.
2 Heat the ghee in a separate pan over a medium heat and add the whole spices, crushed cardamom seeds and pepper. Fry for 30 seconds until they start to sizzle, then tip in the onions and fry for 7–8 minutes until soft. Add the remaining ginger-garlic paste and fry for 1 minute, then add the meat along with the stock it has been cooked in. Stir in the flour paste and cook for 4–5 minutes until the sauce thickens slightly. Add the lemon juice and season to taste.
3 Serve hot, garnished with the julienned ginger and fresh coriander, with rice or rotis alongside.

Lamb Rezala

| LAMB CURRY WITH SCREW PINE WATER |

Wajid Ali Shah, the Nawab of Awadh, near present-day Lucknow, who was exiled in Calcutta, took with him his dancing girls, animals and cooks and added a new way of cooking to the local cuisine. This fragrant curry is now so popular that it is considered a part of Bengali cookery. Screw pine water is available from Indian or Thai grocers as kewra, kewda or pandan water. *Serves 4*

PREPARATION → *15 minutes, plus 30 minutes marinating time*

COOKING *1 hour*

600g boneless shoulder of lamb, trimmed and cubed
150g full-fat yogurt
2 tablespoons ginger-garlic paste *(page 45)*
1 teaspoon medium-hot red chilli powder
1 teaspoon ground turmeric
1 teaspoon ground cinnamon
1 teaspoon garam masala *(page 64)*
1 teaspoon salt, plus extra to season
2 tablespoons vegetable oil
3 large onions, thinly sliced
3 cloves
2 black cardamom pods, seeds crushed and husks discarded
1 teaspoon kewra or screw pine water
Rotis *(pages 108–109)* or Naans *(pages 110–113)*, to serve

1 Place the meat in a bowl with the yogurt, ginger-garlic paste, ground spices and salt and leave to marinate for 30 minutes.
2 Meanwhile, heat half the oil in a heavy-based saucepan over a high heat, add the onions and fry for 7–8 minutes until golden. Drain and set aside.
3 Add the remaining oil to the pan and, once it's warm, add the cloves and crushed cardamom seeds. When they sizzle, add the marinated meat and stir.
4 Add a little water to make a thick sauce and cook over a low heat for 50 minutes until the meat is tender and the oil separates from the gravy. You may need to add a little water if the sauce dries up.
5 Add the onions and cook for a further 5 minutes. Season to taste, drizzle with the kewra or screw pine water and serve hot with rotis or naans.

Bhuna Gosht

| SAUTÉED MEAT CURRY |

As this dish is sautéed and stir-fried, it is semi-dry with the curry clinging onto the pieces of juicy meat. A popular restaurant-style dish, it is a part of Indo-Islamic, north Indian cookery. Bhuna is a technique of cooking (see page 36) rather than referring to ingredients or heat level.

Serves 4 PREPARATION → *15 minutes, plus 2 hours marinating time*

COOKING *1 hour 15 minutes*

800g lamb on the bone, cubed
5 tablespoons full-fat yogurt
2 tablespoons grated raw papaya paste or 1 teaspoon papain powder
2 tablespoons vegetable oil
2 onions, finely diced
2 tablespoons ginger-garlic paste *(page 45)*
3 tomatoes, diced or ½ x 400g can of chopped tomatoes
1 teaspoon ground turmeric
1 teaspoon ground coriander
2 teaspoons garam masala *(page 64)*
1 teaspoon medium-hot red chilli powder
½ teaspoon crushed black pepper
a handful of fresh coriander leaves, to garnish
salt
boiled rice *(pages 78–79)* or Laccha Paratha *(pages 120–121)*, to serve

1 Combine the lamb, yogurt and papaya in a bowl. Season with salt, cover and marinate for 2 hours in the fridge.
2 Heat the oil in a large frying pan over a high heat and add the onions. Sprinkle in a pinch of salt and fry for 7–8 minutes until soft. Add the ginger-garlic paste and fry for 1 minute, then add the tomatoes. Cook over a high heat for 4–5 minutes until a blended paste forms.
3 Add the marinated lamb and marinade and fry over a high heat to seal. Sprinkle in the ground spices, season with salt and add enough water to coat the pan. Bring to the boil, reduce the heat, cover and cook for 1 hour or until the meat is tender. Stir the meat from time to time and if it begins to stick, add a little water.
4 When the meat is done, remove the lid and cook over a high heat to evaporate most of the liquid. The sauce should be concentrated. Season to taste, sprinkle with pepper and fresh coriander, and serve hot with rice or Laccha Paratha.

Nilgiri Kurma

| LAMB IN A SPICED HERB CURRY |

The Nilgiri (Blue Mountain) in Tamil Nadu, south India, is a range of mountains that is probably named after the carpet of blue flowers that grow there. Its lush evergreen rainforests have inspired the name of this green curry, which is thickened with poppy seeds and coconut, giving it a creamy flavour. *Serves 4* PREPARATION →
15 minutes COOKING *1 hour 15 minutes*

2 tablespoons vegetable oil
1 teaspoon black mustard seeds
1 teaspoon fennel seeds
1 medium onion, finely chopped
2 teaspoons ginger-garlic paste *(page 45)*
1 teaspoon garam masala *(page 64)*
1 teaspoon ground turmeric
800g lamb shoulder on the bone, cubed
good squeeze of lime
salt
boiled rice *(pages 78–79)* or Appams *(page 129)*,
    to serve
For the first curry/green herb paste
2 handfuls of fresh coriander leaves,
    washed and chopped
2 handfuls of fresh mint leaves,
    washed and chopped
2 fresh green chillies
8 fresh or 15 dried curry leaves
For the second curry/coconut paste
1 tablespoon white poppy seeds
2 tablespoons freshly grated or
    desiccated coconut

1 Put the ingredients for the first curry paste in a blender with enough water to cover them and blitz until smooth. Set aside.

2 Dry-toast the poppy seeds for the second curry paste in a hot frying pan until they begin to change colour. Transfer to a blender and add the coconut and enough water to cover the mixture. Blitz until smooth.

3 Heat the oil in a heavy-based saucepan over a high heat, add the mustard seeds and fry until they begin to pop. Tip in the fennel seeds and wait until they darken, then add the onion. Sprinkle in a pinch of salt to help the onion soften faster.

4 When the onion is soft and golden, add the ginger-garlic paste and fry for a couple of minutes. Stir in the garam masala and turmeric, cook for a minute then pour in the second curry paste. Cook for a couple of minutes. You may need to add a bit of water if the mixture begins to stick to the bottom of the pan.

5 Add the lamb and fry to seal, then pour in the first curry paste and season with salt. Add a little water to the pan then cover and cook over a high heat until the curry bubbles. Reduce the heat and simmer for 1 hour, covered, or until the lamb is tender. Season to taste, add a squeeze of lime, and serve hot with rice or appams.

Kosha Mangsho

| BENGALI LAMB CURRY |

'Kosha' is to 'sauté' in Bengali and is known as 'bhuna' in north India. My Bengali friends swear by the spicy Kosha made by the famous 'Golbari' restaurant in Kolkatta.

Serves 4 PREPARATION → *20 minutes, plus 2 hours marinating time or overnight if possible* COOKING *1½ hours*

4 medium onions, sliced
2 fresh green chillies, roughly chopped
2.5cm piece of fresh root ginger, scraped and chopped
7 garlic cloves, chopped
800g lamb shoulder on the bone, cubed
1 teaspoon ground turmeric
1 teaspoon ground coriander
4 tablespoons full-fat yogurt
1 teaspoon caster sugar
2 tablespoons mustard oil
3 bay leaves
4 green cardamom pods, seeds crushed and husks discarded
5 cloves
1 small cinnamon stick
1 teaspoon garam masala *(page 64)*, to garnish
salt
boiled rice *(pages 78–79)*, to serve

1 Put the onions, chillies, ginger and garlic in a blender with a little water and blitz to a purée. Combine the lamb, half the purée, turmeric, ground coriander and yogurt in a bowl, season with salt, cover and marinate in the fridge for 2 hours or overnight if possible. Transfer the remaining purée from the blender into a container, then add a few tablespoons of water to the blender to collect all the flavour and pour this in too. Chill while the lamb is marinating.

2 When the marinating time is up, heat the sugar in a heavy-based saucepan over a high heat until it begins to caramelise. Pour in the mustard oil, heat to smoking point, then reduce the heat and add the whole spices. When they begin to darken, add the marinated lamb and fry to seal.

3 Add the remaining chilled purée. Season with salt and cook over a medium heat for 1 hour 25 minutes or until the meat is tender. The sauce should be thick and the oil separated. Season to taste and serve hot, sprinkled with the garam masala and with rice alongside.

Kolhapuri Tambda Rassa

| RICH RED MAHARASHTRIAN CURRY |

Kolhapur in Maharashtra is known for its spicy, rich meat and chicken curries flavoured with small, hot 'lavangi' chillies and Kolhapuri masala, a bright red spice blend (see page 66). Sankeshwar also provides chillies for Kolhapuri curries and these are fiery red, too! *Serves 4*

PREPARATION → *15 minutes* COOKING *1 hour 20 minutes*

800g lamb on the bone, diced
1 teaspoon ground turmeric
1 teaspoon cumin seeds
1 tablespoon white sesame seeds
3 tablespoons desiccated coconut
2 tablespoons ginger-garlic paste *(page 45)*
a small handful of fresh coriander leaves
2 tablespoons vegetable oil
2 onions, thinly sliced
3 tablespoons kolhapuri masala *(page 66)*, or a mix of
     1 tablespoon garam masala *(page 64)*, 1 teaspoon medium-hot
     red chilli powder and 1 teaspoon crushed black pepper
juice of 1 lemon
salt
boiled rice *(pages 78–79)*, to serve

1 Put the lamb and turmeric in a pan, pour in enough water to cover, season with salt and bring to the boil. Reduce the heat and simmer, covered, for 1 hour or until the lamb is tender.

2 Meanwhile, heat a frying pan over a high heat, add the cumin seeds and dry-toast them until they start to darken. Add the sesame seeds and coconut, then when they start to turn golden, tip the toasted spices into a blender along with the ginger-garlic paste and fresh coriander. Pour in enough cold water to just cover the mixture and blitz to form a paste.

3 Heat the oil in a heavy-based saucepan over a high heat, add the onions and fry for 7–8 minutes until soft. Add the Kolhapuri masala and the contents of the blender, then add 1 tablespoon of water – this will cook the spices without scorching them and encourage the oil to separate at the edges.

4 Add the cooked meat and stock, bring to the boil and simmer for 4–5 minutes to blend the flavours. Squeeze in the lemon juice and season to taste. The curry should be thin, with the oil ('kat') floating on top. Serve hot with rice.

Nadan Beef Fry

| SPICY BEEF WITH ONIONS |

boiled rice *(pages 78–79)*, Rotis *(pages 108–109)*
    or Paalaada *(page 129)*, to serve
For the spice mix
1 teaspoon fennel seeds
1 small cinnamon stick
4 cloves
2 star anise
10 black peppercorns
For the curry
800g boneless beef, cubed
2 tablespoons ginger-garlic paste
    (page 45)
8 shallots or 3 onions, finely sliced
3 tablespoons dried coconut slices
1 teaspoon medium-hot red chilli powder
1 tablespoon ground coriander
1 teaspoon ground turmeric
2 tablespoons malt vinegar
2 tablespoons coconut oil
10–12 fresh or 20 dried curry leaves
1 teaspoon garam masala *(page 64)*
1 teaspoon ground black pepper
salt

This famous Christian dish from Kerala uses sweet shallots called 'chuvanulli'. If you cannot find shallots, you can use onions. Many Hindus in Kerala eat beef, and such delicacies are served in small bars called 'toddy shops' all around the state. *Serves 4* PREPARATION —➔ *15 minutes* COOKING *1 hour 15 minutes*

1 Heat a small frying pan over a high heat, add the spices for the spice mix and dry-toast for about 1 minute until slightly dark and fragrant. Crush to a powder in a spice mill or pestle and mortar.

2 Mix the beef, crushed spice mix, ginger-garlic paste, half the sliced shallots or onions, the coconut slices, ground spices and vinegar in a bowl and season with salt.

3 Put the beef in a saucepan and pour in enough water to come halfway up the mixture. Stir and bring to the boil. Reduce the heat, cover and simmer for 1 hour, or until the beef is tender. If the mixture begins to stick to the bottom of the pan, add a couple of tablespoons of water, taking care not to add too much as the final dish should be dry.

4 Remove the lid and cook over a high heat until all the liquid has evaporated.

5 Heat another pan over a high heat and add the coconut oil. Fry the curry leaves (standing back from the pan if using fresh leaves, as they will splutter) and tip in the remaining shallots or onions. Cook for 7–8 minutes until soft, then add the cooked beef.

6 Season to taste, sprinkle in the garam masala and pepper, cook for a further few minutes to blend and serve hot with rice, rotis or paalaada.

Pork With Gaanj Tenga
| CHILLI PORK WITH BAMBOO SHOOTS |

Assam in the north-east eats various meats such as pork or 'gahori'. It is eaten on festive days, as meat can be expensive and is considered special. It is sometimes combined with exotic ingredients such as bamboo shoots or fiddlehead fern shoots called 'dhekia'. These are the unfurled fronds of a young fern and look like tight green coils. If left on the plant, they eventually open into a frond. Fiddleheads are a good source of omega 3 and 6 fatty acids and are high in fibre. *Serves 4* PREPARATION → *15 minutes* COOKING *1 hour*

6 dried red chillies
5 garlic cloves, chopped
2.5cm piece of fresh root ginger, scraped and chopped
2 tablespoons lard
2 onions, thinly sliced
800g pork shoulder on the bone, cubed
150g fresh bamboo shoot, grated, or a 225g can
    of bamboo shoots in water, drained
a handful of fresh coriander leaves, chopped, to garnish
salt

1 Soak the red chillies in boiling water for 15 minutes. Transfer the softened chillies to a pestle and mortar and add the garlic and ginger. Sprinkle in some salt and a couple of tablespoons of the chilli soaking liquid. Crush to a paste.
2 Heat the lard in a large frying pan over a high heat, add the onions and cook for 7–8 minutes until brown and soft.
3 Add the pork and cook over a high heat for 3–4 minutes to seal and brown it, then add the paste from the mortar and season with salt. If using fresh bamboo shoots, add them now. If using tinned ones, add them after the pork has cooked. Pour in enough water to just cover the pork, bring to the boil, then reduce the heat and cook for 50 minutes, covered, or until the meat is tender. Season to taste and serve hot, sprinkled with the coriander.

Pork Vindaloo
| GOAN PORK CURRY |

This is one of the most popular curries on Indian restaurant menus the world over. However, not all Indians know a vindaloo as it is a regional Goan curry influenced by the Portuguese, who made it with 'vinho' or wine and 'alho' or garlic. The wine was replaced with coconut vinegar, making this a spicy, tangy curry that is eaten with rice or savoury cakes called 'sannas'. In the West, where Indian takeaway curries are classified only by heat, a vindaloo signifies a spicy hot dish suitable for the brave. But in fact a traditional Goan vindaloo needs to be only as hot as the cook thinks it should be. *Serves 4* PREPARATION → *15 minutes, plus 20 minutes soaking time* COOKING *1 hour*

15 dried red Kashmiri chillies (or 6–7 for a milder curry),
    broken in half and seeds shaken out
5 garlic cloves, chopped
2.5cm piece of fresh root ginger, scraped and chopped
3 tablespoons coconut or white vinegar
3 cloves
2 teaspoons cumin seeds
1 small cinnamon stick
½ teaspoon freshly ground black pepper
2 onions, sliced
2 tablespoons vegetable oil
800g boneless pork, cubed
salt
boiled rice *(pages 78–79)* or Appams *(page 129)*, to serve

1 Soak the chillies, garlic and ginger in the vinegar with ½ teaspoon of salt for 20 minutes. Heat a frying pan over a high heat, add the cloves, cumin seeds, cinnamon and pepper and dry-toast for 40 seconds, then add these to the soaking chillies. Tip the onions and the chilli mixture into a blender and blitz to a purée, adding a little water to help turn the blades. This is the vindaloo masala.
2 Heat the oil in a heavy-based saucepan over a high heat, add the pork and fry for 3–4 minutes to seal, then tip in the vindaloo masala from the blender. Stir to blend and coat the pork. Rinse out the blender with a little water and add this to the pork. Bring to the boil then reduce the heat to medium, cover and cook for 40 minutes, until the pork is tender. Season to taste and serve hot with plain rice or appams.

POULTRY

THE DOMESTICATED CHICKEN THAT WE EAT TODAY IS A DESCENDANT OF THE INDIAN JUNGLE FOWL.
TODAY, INDIANS EAT MORE CHICKEN THAN EVER BEFORE.

Religious food taboos in India mean that beef and pork are not widely eaten. Goat and lamb are expensive and considered heavy and unhealthy for regular consumption, and Ayurvedic nutrition considers red meat 'heating' and acid-forming in the digestive system. Chicken is the most popular 'non-vegetarian' food enjoyed by Indians, who cook it in many ways – in creamy curries, smoked and grilled, in soups or in rich spiced biryanis.

The domesticated chicken that we eat today is a descendant of the Indian jungle fowl. Today, Indians eat more chicken than ever before – young people travel to new places, world cuisines are offered in restaurants and chicken is considered healthy as it has less saturated fat than most red meat. There are two popular varieties of chicken – the 'free-run' ones on small holdings and the 'broilers' reared on commercial poultry farms.

Free-run chickens are bred in village backyards and fed on kitchen scraps. They are most often killed for household use. Broilers are cut into pieces and frozen or sold bagged in city shops. Indian cooks prefer the meatier, more flavourful free-run chicken, but the fattier broilers are considered more hygienic. Non-vegetarian families living in villages often have a few chickens running around and sometimes people living on the outskirts of big cities rear them to sell at poultry markets in the city.

The most common method of buying chicken in India is to go to the chicken shop, which will have many birds in a coop. You choose the one you want and it is weighed and killed there and then. The dead bird is de-feathered and cut into pieces for you. You pay for the whole, live bird. This process does not allow for buying just the breast or the legs, so cooks will sometimes make two dishes out of one bird, although curry is the most popular way of eating all cuts of

chicken. Indian cooks don't typically buy specific cuts of chicken, as the whole bird is used in curries. If they do – for specific dishes such as pan-fried kebabs – they use chicken legs, wings or breast.

Although duck meat is not popular all over India, the south Indian native Kuttanad duck is reared for its tasty meat and eaten in Kerala, Tamil Nadu and Andhra Pradesh. Duck rearing and farming is encouraged by some state governments, and south Indian varieties were introduced into Assam when the low production of eggs by the local duck 'Pati' could not match demand.

Game birds such as pheasant and quail are hunted in Indian forests but rarely seen on restaurant menus or in city kitchens. The erstwhile Maharajas of India were known for their shoots and their recipes include roasts of peacock, black partridge and jungle fowl. Today, peacock, which is the national bird, is a protected species under the Wildlife Protection Act of 1972 and its hunting is punishable by law. However, jungles tribes and villagers who live on the outskirts of forests still hunt this beautiful bird as the meat commands a good price.

TIPS FOR PREPARING AND COOKING CHICKEN

1 Remove the skin. Most Indian recipes are for skinless chicken as Indians prefer lean meat and poultry and dislike the texture of animal fat.

2 Seal the meat rather than brown it when cooking. This helps to lock in the juices but does not create a thick barrier that prevents spices from flavouring the flesh.

3 Cook the chicken until it is white throughout. Any pink flesh means that it needs more cooking time and is unsafe to eat. Chicken on the bone will take longer to cook than boneless chicken.

Murgh Makhani

| BUTTERY CHICKEN CURRY |

800g skinless chicken breast,
    cut into 2.5cm cubes
boiled rice *(pages 78–79)* or Laccha Paratha
    (pages 120–121), to serve
For the marinade
50g natural yogurt
1 teaspoon red Kashmiri chilli powder
1 tablespoon ginger-garlic paste *(page 45)*
2 tablespoons lemon juice
½ teaspoon garam masala *(page 64)*
salt
For the makhani sauce
2 tablespoons salted butter
1 tablespoon vegetable oil
½ teaspoon dried fenugreek leaves
    (kasoori methi), plus extra to serve
1 fresh green chilli, finely chopped
1 tablespoon ginger-garlic paste *(page 45)*
150g tomato purée
½ teaspoon Kashmiri red chilli powder
½ teaspoon garam masala *(page 64)*
2 tablespoons honey
100ml single cream, plus extra to serve

This is a very popular north Indian restaurant dish. The original recipe was created by the Moti Mahal restaurant in New Delhi and it is still a top-seller. Marinated chicken is usually cooked in the tandoor, then folded into a buttery or 'makhani' sauce. I use a mixture of oil and butter so that the butter does not burn when heated. You can use paneer instead of chicken for a vegetarian version. The sauce should be spicy, sweet and tangy, with the fragrance of butter and herbs. *Serves 4* PREPARATION —➔ *20 minutes, plus 1 hour marinating time or overnight if possible* COOKING *30 minutes*

1 Combine the marinade ingredients in a bowl and add the cubed chicken. Cover and leave to marinate in the fridge for at least for 1 hour or overnight if possible.

2 Preheat the oven to 200°C/gas mark 6. Transfer the chicken and marinade to an ovenproof dish and bake for 10–15 minutes until tender and cooked through.

3 For the makhani sauce, heat the butter and oil in a saucepan over a high heat and add the kasoori methi and green chilli. Stir in the ginger-garlic paste, cook for a minute or so, then add the tomato purée and stir to blend for a couple of minutes.

4 Mix in the chilli powder, garam masala and honey, and season with salt. Finish with the cream, then add enough water to give the sauce a pouring consistency.

5 Add the cooked chicken to the sauce. Serve with rice or laccha paratha, with a swirl of single cream and a sprinkling of kasoori methi.

Murgh Ka Korma
| CREAMY CHICKEN CURRY |

The word 'korma' comes from the Turkish 'kavurma', which means 'braised meat'. The word is variously spelt as 'quorma' or 'qorma' and is often thickened with nuts and cream. In the south, a kurma is similar but has coconut in the curry sauce. In Indian takeaways in the West, a korma is a popular dish amongst those who do not enjoy chillies, as it has come to mean a pale, sweet curry that is classified as mild. However, some kormas in India, such as the Kashmiri 'Marchwangan Korma', made with mutton and lots of chilli, can be searingly hot. *Serves 4*
PREPARATION → *10 minutes* COOKING *35 minutes*

1 large onion, sliced
1 fresh green chilli, chopped
50g unsalted cashew nuts
3 tablespoons vegetable oil
2 teaspoons ginger-garlic paste *(page 45)*
800g skinless chicken breast, cubed
1 teaspoon ground coriander
1 teaspoon ground cumin
½ teaspoon garam masala *(page 64)*, plus extra to serve
½ teaspoon ground turmeric
2 tablespoons single cream (optional)
salt
boiled rice *(pages 78–79)*, Rotis *(pages 108–109)* or Parathas
    (page 120–121), to serve

1 Put the onion, chilli and cashew nuts in a pan with a little water and bring to the boil. Simmer for about 10 minutes, until the onion is very soft, then transfer to a blender and blitz to a paste, adding water as necessary to turn the blades. Set aside.

2 Heat the oil in a heavy-based saucepan over a high heat, then add the ginger-garlic paste, followed by the chicken, and fry until sealed.

3 Season with salt and stir in the ground spices, then add the onion purée. Rinse out the blender with a few tablespoons of water and add this to the pan. Cook for 12–15 minutes until the chicken is tender and cooked through.

4 Stir in the cream, if using, and heat through. Season to taste, sprinkle with a pinch of garam masala and serve hot with rice, rotis or parathas.

Murgh Jalfrezi
| CHICKEN CURRY WITH PEPPERS |

Another restaurant curry, this has distinct chunks of onion, pepper and tomatoes in it. Restaurant curries have specific names like 'jalfrezi'. At home this would simply be called a chicken curry, and peppers would be added as a variation. It is said to be a creation of the Raj, where leftover meat was stirred into a spiced hot sauce, such as the one here, called 'jhal' in Bengali. *Serves 4* PREPARATION → *15 minutes*
COOKING *45 minutes*

3 tablespoons vegetable oil
2 large onions, one thinly sliced, the other cut into large chunks
1 tablespoon ginger-garlic paste *(page 45)*
2 teaspoons tomato purée
1 teaspoon cumin seeds
600g skinless chicken breast, cubed
1 large green pepper, deseeded and thinly sliced
½ teaspoon ground turmeric
½ teaspoon medium-hot red chilli powder
½ teaspoon ground coriander
1 ripe tomato, sliced
a small handful of fresh coriander leaves, chopped, to garnish
salt
boiled rice *(pages 78–79)* or Rotis *(pages 108–109)*, to serve

1 Heat 2 tablespoons of the oil in a heavy-based frying pan over a high heat and fry the sliced onion for 7–8 minutes until soft. Add the ginger-garlic paste and the tomato purée and fry for a further 3–4 minutes until well blended. Remove from the heat, leave to cool slightly, then transfer to a blender and blitz until smooth, adding enough water to turn the blades and make a thick curry paste. Set aside.

2 Heat the remaining oil in a heavy-based saucepan over a high heat and fry the cumin seeds until they darken slightly, then add the chicken and fry until sealed. Add the green pepper and chunks of onion, sprinkle in the ground spices, stir in the curry paste and season with salt. Pour in about 100ml water to make a thick sauce consistency and cook over a medium heat for 12–15 minutes, until the chicken is cooked through.

3 Add the tomato and cook for a couple of minutes until soft but not mushy, then remove from the heat. Season to taste, garnish with the coriander and serve hot with rice or rotis.

Murghi Na Farcha

| PARSI-STYLE FRIED CHICKEN |

I remember eating this crisp, delicious chicken at Parsi weddings as a child. It is served at Parsi celebrations, as being deep-fried, it is not cooked very often at home. Also, it is interesting that in India many fried foods such as this one are served with tomato ketchup, a legacy of the Raj. Indians love the sweet, tangy flavour of ketchup and several varieties are available with added spices such as cumin or chilli. *Serves 4* PREPARATION→ *10 minutes, plus 1 hour marinating time or overnight if possible* COOKING *35 minutes*

1 teaspoon garam masala *(page 64)*
2 teaspoons ginger-garlic paste *(page 45)*
1 teaspoon medium-hot red chilli powder
1 teaspoon ground cumin
1 teaspoon ground coriander
1 teaspoon ground turmeric
2 tablespoons lemon juice
4 chicken legs, skinned and halved at the joint
vegetable oil, for deep-frying
plain flour, for dusting
3 large eggs, beaten
salt and freshly ground black pepper
tomato ketchup, to serve

1 Combine the garam masala, ginger-garlic paste, chilli powder, cumin, coriander, turmeric, lemon juice and salt and pepper to season in a large bowl.
2 Pierce the chicken legs, add them to the bowl and coat them in the marinade, cover and leave to marinate in the fridge for at least 1 hour or overnight if possible.
3 Heat enough oil in a wok or karahi to deep-fry the chicken in a single layer. When very hot, reduce the heat slightly. Place some flour in a shallow bowl and the beaten eggs in another shallow bowl, then dip each piece of marinated chicken into the flour then the beaten egg and lower carefully into the hot oil. (You may have to do this in batches.) Cook over a medium heat for 8–9 minutes until golden brown, spooning the hot oil over the chicken to cook it evenly. Lift out with a slotted spoon and check if it is cooked through by cutting into the meat near the bone – the meat should be white. Drain on kitchen paper. Cook the remaining chicken in the same way and serve hot with tomato ketchup.

Chicken Chettinad

| SPICY SOUTH INDIAN CHICKEN CURRY |

The very spicy food of Chettinad, a region in Tamil Nadu, is suited to the dry, hot land and ingredients are often cooked in sesame oil, which adds a unique flavour. It is a cuisine of rich meat and chicken curries flavoured with aromatic spices such as star anise and cinnamon. *Serves 4* PREPARATION→ *10 minutes* COOKING *25 minutes*

4 dried red chillies, broken in half
½ teaspoon black peppercorns, crushed
1 teaspoon aniseed
4 cloves
3 green cardamom pods, seeds removed and husks discarded
½ teaspoon ground cinnamon
2 tablespoons sunflower or sesame oil
8–10 fresh or 15 dried curry leaves
3 star anise
2 green chillies, finely diced
2 onions, chopped
1 teaspoon ginger-garlic paste *(page 45)*
1 tomato, chopped
½ teaspoon ground turmeric
800g boneless, skinless chicken thighs, cut into 2.5cm pieces
a handful of fresh coriander leaves, chopped, to garnish
salt
boiled rice *(pages 78–79)*, Rotis *(pages 108–109)* or
    Dosas *(pages 126–127)*, to serve

1 Heat a frying pan over a high heat, add the chillies, crushed peppercorns, aniseed, cloves and cardamom seeds and dry-toast until they begin to darken and develop an aroma. Remove from the heat and crush to a powder in a pestle and mortar or spice mill then mix in the cinnamon. Set aside.
2 Heat the oil in the frying pan over a high heat and drop in the curry leaves (standing back from the pan if using fresh leaves, as they will splutter), star anise, chillies and onions. Stir-fry for 7–8 minutes until the onions are soft, then tip in the ginger-garlic paste and stir, add the tomato and season with salt. Cook for 3–4 minutes until well blended.
3 Add the ground spices and turmeric, then stir in the chicken and cook until sealed on all sides.
4 Add a few tablespoons of water and cook for 15–20 minutes until the chicken is cooked. Season to taste, sprinkle with the coriander and serve hot with rice, rotis or dosas.

Kosha Murgir Mangsho
| BENGALI CHICKEN CURRY |

When I was young, my mother employed a Bengali cook who made this curry on his first day in our kitchen. I was quite excited about this 'new' recipe and loved it at first bite for its rich tomato sauce. Food linked to memories is always special and it remains one of my favourite curries. It is cooked without water making it quite rich and oily, but that's why it is so delicious! *Serves 4*

PREPARATION → *15 minutes* COOKING *45 minutes*

3 tablespoons mustard or vegetable oil
2 bay leaves
4 cloves
4 green cardamom pods, seeds crushed and husks discarded
3 large onions, finely diced
2 teaspoons ginger-garlic paste *(page 45)*
2 fresh green chillies, slit lengthways
3 tomatoes, finely chopped
1 teaspoon ground turmeric
1 teaspoon ground cumin
1 teaspoon ground coriander
½ teaspoon medium-hot red chilli powder
800g chicken thighs on the bone, skinned and flesh
    cut into 4cm pieces
salt
a handful of fresh coriander leaves, chopped, to garnish
boiled rice *(pages 78–79)* or Pooris *(pages 114–115)*, to serve

1 Heat the oil in a frying pan to smoking point then reduce the heat. Add the whole spices and the crushed cardamom seeds. When they sizzle and darken, add the onions and fry for 8–10 minutes until they are very soft.
2 Stir the ginger-garlic paste and chillies into the onions and cook for 1 minute, then tip in the tomatoes and cook for 3–4 minutes until they soften.
3 Add the ground spices, stir a few times, then add the chicken and salt to season. Cook over a high heat for 3–4 minutes to seal, then reduce the heat and simmer for 20 minutes until the chicken is tender and cooked through. Keep spooning the sauce over the chicken from time to time, to ensure it cooks evenly. Season to taste, sprinkle with coriander and serve hot with rice or pooris.

Murgh Achari
| CHICKEN IN PICKLING SPICES |

'Achaar' in Hindi means 'pickle' and this north Indian curry uses traditional pickling spices such as fennel and mustard for flavour and heat. Many versions exist but you can use as many or as few chillies as you like. I prefer this curry to be fragrant rather than hot and it's best enjoyed with a roti or naan to mop up the tangy sauce. *Serves 4*

PREPARATION → *15 minutes* COOKING *45 minutes*

2 tablespoons sunflower or mustard oil
1 teaspoon black mustard seeds
1 teaspoon cumin seeds
1 teaspoon nigella seeds
1 teaspoon fennel seeds
½ teaspoon fenugreek seeds
2 large onions, finely diced
2 teaspoon ginger-garlic paste *(page 45)*
2 tablespoons tomato purée
800g boneless, skinless chicken thighs
1 teaspoon ground turmeric
½ teaspoon medium-hot red chilli powder
1 teaspoon garam masala *(page 64)*
3 tablespoons full-fat yogurt
good squeeze of lemon juice
salt
boiled rice *(pages 78–79)*, Rotis *(pages 108–109)*,
    Pooris *(pages 114–115)* or Naans *(pages 110–113)*, to serve

1 Heat the oil in a frying pan over a high heat and add the whole spices. When they pop, sizzle and darken, add the onions. Fry for 8–10 minutes until very soft, then stir in the ginger-garlic paste and tomato purée. Cook for a couple of minutes.
2 Add the chicken and fry to seal, then reduce the heat to prevent the mixture from sticking to the bottom of the pan. Sprinkle in the ground spices, stir a few times to coat the chicken and pour in 100ml water. Season with salt, cover and cook for 20–25 minutes until the chicken is cooked through, adding more water if necessary to stop the curry from drying out.
3 Fold in the yogurt and lemon juice, season to taste, simmer for a couple of minutes then serve hot with rice, rotis, pooris or naans.

Seyal Murgh
| SINDHI-STYLE CHICKEN CURRY |

I grew up in Mumbai amongst Sindhi family friends. Food would be exchanged on Sundays – their kids loved the coconut-based curries of Maharashtrian cooking – and I became familiar with classics such Sindhi Kadhi, a vegetable curry with gram flour, and 'Saibhaji', a mixed green vegetable side dish and, many years later, still cook them for my children. The Sindhis, originally from Pakistan, are Hindus or Sikhs who moved to India during the Partition of 1947. 'Seyal' refers to a dish cooked with very little water. *Serves 4* PREPARATION → *15 minutes* COOKING *45 minutes*

2 tablespoons vegetable oil
2 onions, finely diced
2 teaspoons ginger-garlic paste *(page 45)*
2 fresh green chillies, diced
a small handful of fresh coriander leaves, finely chopped
3 tomatoes, halved and cut sides grated (skin discarded)
1 teaspoon ground turmeric
1 teaspoon ground coriander
1 teaspoon garam masala *(page 64)*
800g boneless, skinless chicken thighs
3 tablespoons full-fat yogurt
3 green cardamom pods, seeds crushed and husks discarded, to garnish
salt
Rotis *(pages 108–109)* or boiled rice *(pages 78–79)*, to serve

1 Heat the oil in a frying pan over a high heat, add the onions and fry for 8–10 minutes until very soft, golden and caramelised. Stir in the ginger-garlic paste, green chillies and fresh coriander and cook for 2 minutes, then tip in the grated tomatoes and cook for 2–3 minutes until soft and well blended.

2 Add the ground spices and cook for 5–6 minutes until the oil separates. This will happen faster if you cover the pan.

3 Add the chicken thighs and season with salt. Cook over a high heat to seal, then reduce the heat to medium. Pour in the yogurt, cover and cook for 15–20 minutes until the chicken is cooked through. Season to taste and serve hot, sprinkled with the crushed cardamom, alongside rotis or rice.

Chicken Cafreal
| GOAN GREEN CHICKEN |

Introduced to Goa by the Portuguese, who had their stronghold there from 1510 AD, this is always made with chicken legs, is semi-dry to dry and can be eaten with rice or bread. *Serves 4* PREPARATION → *10 minutes, plus 1 hour marinating time or overnight if possible* COOKING *35 minutes*

1 teaspoon cumin seeds
1 small cinnamon stick
1 teaspoon coriander seeds
10 black peppercorns
1 large bunch of fresh coriander leaves
2.5cm piece of fresh root ginger, scraped and chopped
5 garlic cloves, chopped
2 fresh green chillies, chopped
2 tablespoons white wine vinegar
1 teaspoon ground turmeric
4 chicken legs, skinned and halved at the joint
2 tablespoons vegetable oil
1 onion, thinly sliced
salt
lime wedges, to serve
boiled rice *(pages 78–79)* or breads, to serve (optional)

1 Heat a small frying pan over a high heat, add the cumin seeds, cinnamon stick, coriander seeds and peppercorns and dry-toast until they start to darken and become fragrant. Remove from the heat and crush to a powder in a pestle and mortar or spice mill.

2 Put the coriander leaves, ginger, garlic, chillies and vinegar in a blender with enough water to turn the blades. Blitz to a purée, season with salt and add the turmeric. Mix in the crushed spices. This is the cafreal masala.

3 Pierce the chicken legs and place them in a container with the cafreal masala, turning them to coat, and marinate in the fridge for at least 1 hour or overnight if possible.

4 Heat the oil in a pan over a high heat and fry the onion for 6–7 minutes until soft, then add the chicken and fry to seal.

5 Add enough water to coat the base of the pan, cover and cook over a medium heat for 30 minutes, adding water as necessary. By the time the chicken is cooked through, the water should have evaporated. Season to taste, and serve hot with the lime wedges, and rice or bread, if you like.

MASTERCLASS

METHI MURGH – Chicken Curry with Fenugreek

The warm, earthy taste of fenugreek complements the creaminess of chicken in this recipe, which is made all over north India. I have used both fresh and dried fenugreek leaves for depth and intensity. Fenugreek leaves can taste quite bitter if they are not cooked for long enough, which is why in most recipes, such as this one, they are added towards the beginning. *Serves 4* PREPARATION → *15 minutes*

COOKING *45 minutes*

YOU WILL NEED:

3 tablespoons vegetable oil

2 large onions, sliced

2 teaspoons ginger-garlic paste *(page 45)*

2 fresh green chillies, minced

1 teaspoon dried fenugreek leaves (kasoori methi – *page 393)*

4 chicken legs, skinned and halved at the joint

1 teaspoon ground turmeric

1 teaspoon ground coriander

1 teaspoon ground cumin

1 teaspoon garam masala *(page 64)*

1 tablespoon tomato purée

1 bunch of fresh fenugreek leaves, cleaned and chopped (discard large stems, retain the fine ones)

2 tablespoons full-fat yogurt

salt

Rotis *(pages 108–109)* or Parathas *(pages 120–121)*, to serve

1 Heat half the oil in a heavy-based frying pan over a high heat, add the onions and fry for 8–10 minutes until very soft and golden, then tip in the ginger-garlic paste and green chillies and fry for a minute. Remove from the heat, transfer to a blender and blitz to a paste with enough water to turn the blades. This is the curry paste.

2 Heat the remaining oil in a heavy-based pan over a high heat. Add the dried fenugreek, cook for a few seconds then add the chicken and fry until sealed.

3 Tip in the ground spices and tomato purée, then add the fresh fenugreek and fry for 5–6 minutes until wilted. Pour in the curry paste. Rinse out the blender with a little water and add the water to the pan. Add the yogurt and season with salt. Cook for 12–15 minutes, until the chicken is tender and cooked through and the fenugreek has completely softened. Season to taste and serve hot with rotis or parathas.

Karahi Murgh Kofte

| CHICKEN MEATBALLS IN A TOMATO CURRY |

Meatballs are traditionally served with a dip as a cocktail snack, or stirred into curries as they are here. You can bake them in an oven at 200°C/gas mark 6 for 10 minutes if serving them as a snack. A 'karahi' literally just means that the dish has been cooked in a 'karahi' dish (see page 50)!

Serves 4 PREPARATION → *15 minutes* COOKING *30 minutes*

600g chicken mince
1 fresh green chilli, very finely diced
2 teaspoons ginger-garlic paste *(page 45)*
2 tablespoons vegetable oil
2 onions, finely diced
1 teaspoon ground turmeric
1 teaspoon ground coriander
1 teaspoon ground cumin
1 teaspoon garam masala *(page 64)*
½ teaspoon medium-hot red chilli powder
2 tablespoons tomato purée, ½ can of tinned chopped
    tomatoes or 4 fresh tomatoes, chopped
½ teaspoon caster sugar
a small handful of fresh coriander leaves, chopped, to garnish
1.5cm piece of fresh root ginger, scraped and julienned
salt
Rotis *(pages 108–109)* or boiled rice *(pages 78–79)*, to serve

1 Combine the chicken mince in a bowl with the green chilli, half the ginger-garlic paste and season with salt. Form into small balls or koftas each the size of a large cherry. Set aside.

2 Heat the oil in a frying pan over a high heat, add the onions and fry for 8–10 minutes until very soft and golden. Stir in the remaining ginger-garlic paste and the ground spices. Cook for a few minutes, adding a splash of water to help the spices cook without burning, then add the tomato purée, tinned tomatoes or fresh tomatoes and sugar. Pour in 200ml water, season with salt and bring to the boil. Slip in the koftas and bring the curry back to the boil. Reduce the heat and simmer for 10–15 minutes until the meatballs are cooked through and the sauce has thickened slightly.

3 Season to taste and serve hot, sprinkled with the coriander and julienned ginger, alongside rice or rotis.

Xacuti

| GOAN COCONUT CHICKEN CURRY |

Pronounced 'shakooti', this Portuguese-inspired curry is also called 'sagoti', and can be made with prawns or meat. It is a thick curry made as hot or mild as the cook likes it, and is a part of the local Christian cuisine all over Goa.

Serves 4 PREPARATION → *15 minutes* COOKING *1 hour*

2 tablespoons vegetable oil
1 small cinnamon stick
10 black peppercorns
5 dried red Kashmiri chillies, broken in half and seeds shaken out
1 tablespoon coriander seeds
1 teaspoon fennel seeds
1 teaspoon white poppy seeds
2 onions, sliced
2.5cm piece of fresh root ginger, scraped and chopped
7 garlic cloves, chopped
4 tablespoons fresh grated coconut, or desiccated coconut
    soaked for 20 minutes in warm water
800g chicken legs, skinned and halved at the joint
1 teaspoon ground turmeric
3 tomatoes, finely chopped
salt
few shavings of nutmeg, to serve

1 Heat half the oil in a frying pan over a high heat and add all the ingredients from the cinnamon to the poppy seeds. As soon as they start to sizzle, tip in the onions and fry for 7–8 minutes until very soft and golden, then add the ginger and garlic and fry for a minute or so.

2 Stir in the coconut and fry until toasted and brown, stirring continuously to prevent it from scorching. Tip this mixture into a blender and add enough water to just cover it. Blitz to a fine purée and set aside.

3 Heat the remaining oil in the same frying pan (after giving it a wipe) over a high heat, add the chicken pieces and fry until sealed and light brown. Sprinkle in salt to season and the turmeric and cook for a minute or so, then pour in the purée from the blender and rinse the blender out with a little water. Pour this in as well. Add the tomatoes, bring to the boil then reduce the heat and simmer for 15–20 minutes or until the chicken is cooked through. Season to taste and serve hot with a few shavings of nutmeg.

Kozhi Kuzhambu

| MADURAI CHICKEN CURRY |

1 teaspoon coriander seeds

4 dried red Kashmiri chillies, broken in half
and seeds shaken out

10 black peppercorns

1 teaspoon uncooked rice

1 teaspoon fennel seeds

1 tablespoon white poppy seeds

1 tablespoon split gram lentils (chana dal)

2 tablespoons desiccated coconut

2 tablespoons sesame or vegetable oil

1 teaspoon black or brown mustard seeds

2 onions, finely diced

7–8 fresh or 10 dried curry leaves

2 teaspoons ginger-garlic paste *(page 45)*

2 tomatoes, chopped

800g chicken legs, skinned and halved
at the joint

1 teaspoon ground turmeric

1 teaspoon garam masala *(page 64)*

a small handful of fresh coriander leaves,
chopped, to garnish

salt

boiled rice *(pages 78–79)*, to serve

This curry comes from the Madurai region of Tamil Nadu and is cooked by the Naidus and Reddiyars who live there. Their spicy, fragrant cuisine is so famous that it has given rise to speciality restaurants that are renowned for their meat and chicken curries and biryani. These are highly spiced with pepper and garam masala yet are quite light and not oily, unlike many of the curries found in Indian restaurants all over the world. *Serves 4*

PREPARATION —→ *15 minutes* COOKING *1 hour*

1 Heat a small frying pan over a high heat, add the coriander seeds, chillies, peppercorns, rice, fennel seeds, poppy seeds, chana dal and coconut and dry-toast for 4–5 minutes until golden and fragrant, stirring to avoid them scorching. Remove from the heat, tip into a pestle and mortar or spice mill and crush to a powder. Set aside.

2 Heat the oil in a heavy-based pan over a high heat and add the mustard seeds. When they start to pop, add the onions and fry for 7–8 minutes until very soft.

3 Add the curry leaves and ginger-garlic paste. (Stand back from the pan if using fresh leaves, as they will splutter.)

4 Stir in the chopped tomatoes and cook for a couple of minutes until soft, then add the chicken legs to the pan and cook for 3–4 minutes until sealed. Sprinkle in the ground spices, including the ground spice mix, and season with salt.

5 Pour in 200ml water and bring to the boil. Reduce the heat, cover and simmer for 25–30 minutes until the chicken is cooked through. Season to taste, sprinkle with the coriander and serve hot with rice.

Pathare Prabhu Chicken Masala

| CHICKEN CURRY WITH CREAM AND SPICES |

2 teaspoons ground turmeric

2 teaspoons ginger-garlic paste *(page 45)*

3 tablespoons full-fat yogurt

800g chicken legs, skinned and halved
    at the joint

2 tablespoons vegetable oil

2 onions, sliced

2 tomatoes, chopped

½ teaspoon medium-hot chilli powder

1 teaspoon ground coriander

2 teaspoons parbhi sambhar powder
    (page 65) or garam masala *(page 64)*

1 teaspoon caster sugar

2 tablespoons single cream

a small handful of fresh coriander leaves,
chopped, to garnish

salt

Rotis *(pages 108–109)* or boiled rice *(pages 78–79)*,
    to serve

The Pathare Prabhu community of Mumbai are great philanthropists and highly educated. They worked closely with the British during the Raj and adopted many of their customs, such as dress and speech. The women started wearing saree blouses, influenced by the European 'bon bon' sleeves, and the men wore waistcoats. Many were educated in English and took up law and administration. Their cuisine is a delicate mix of styles, rich and varied and with subtle foreign influences, such as the use of broths and stocks rather than the heavy curry bases found over most of India. They make a special curry powder called 'parbhi sambhar' (see page 65) which is added to many curries for a delicate yet fragrant effect. *Serves 4*

PREPARATION → *15 minutes, plus 2 hours marinating time or overnight if possible*

COOKING *45 minutes*

1 Combine half the turmeric, half the ginger-garlic paste, yogurt and salt to season in a bowl. Add the chicken, coat it in this mixture, cover and marinate in the fridge for 2 hours or overnight if possible.

2 Heat half the oil in a pan over a high heat, add the onions and fry for 8–10 minutes until very soft and golden. Add the remaining ginger-garlic paste and the tomatoes. Fry until soft, then remove from the heat, tip the mixture into a blender, add enough water to cover and blitz to a purée. This is the masala paste.

3 Heat the remaining oil in a heavy-based saucepan over a high heat. Lift the chicken out of the marinade and add it to the pan. (The marinade will go in a bit later.) Fry for 4–5 minutes to seal.

4 Sprinkle in the ground spices and the remaining turmeric and stir a few times, then pour in the masala paste. Rinse the blender with a few tablespoons of water and pour this in. Add the remaining marinade to the pan, season with salt (not too much as the chicken has already been seasoned), sprinkle in the sugar and bring to the boil. Reduce the heat and simmer for 25–30 minutes until the chicken is tender and cooked through. Season to taste, stir in the cream and serve hot, sprinkled with the coriander, alongside rotis or rice.

Kuttanadan Tharavu Roast

| PEPPERY KERALA DUCK |

Duck meat is eaten in some southern and eastern states, such as Kerala and Assam, where government initiatives have encouraged the rearing of these birds. *Serves 4* PREPARATION → *Preparation time: 15 minutes, plus 30 minutes marinating time* COOKING *1 hour 15 minutes*

4 shallots, chopped
2 teaspoons ginger-garlic paste *(page 45)*
1 teaspoon medium-hot red chilli powder
3 teaspoons ground coriander
1 teaspoon ground turmeric
1 teaspoon garam masala *(page 64)*
1 teaspoon freshly ground black pepper
3 green cardamom pods, seeds crushed and husks discarded
1 teaspoon ground cinnamon
2 tablespoons malt vinegar
800g duck legs, halved at the joint (leave the skin on or off as per your preference)
2 tablespoons sunflower or coconut oil
2 onions, thinly sliced
6–7 fresh or 10 dried curry leaves
salt
Appams or Paalaada *(page 129)*, to serve

1 Put all the ingredients from the shallots to the vinegar in a blender and blitz to a purée, adding enough water to turn the blades. Season with salt and transfer to a bowl. Rinse out the blender with 100ml water and set this aside separately.
2 Rub half of the curry paste onto the duck legs and set them aside to marinate for 30 minutes.
3 Heat the oil in a saucepan over a high heat, add the onions and fry for 8–10 minutes until very soft. Add the curry leaves and fry for 1 minute, then add the marinated duck legs to the pan and cook over a high heat for 5–6 minutes to seal and brown the meat.
4 Stir in the remaining curry paste and pour in the reserved water from the blender. Bring the curry to the boil, cover, reduce the heat and simmer for 40–50 minutes until the duck is tender and the sauce is thick, adding a splash of water from time to time if the curry dries up. The final dish should have a thick sauce coating the duck rather than a curry sauce. Season to taste and serve hot with appams or paalaada.

Kodi Kurma

| ANDHRA-STYLE CURRY WITH POPPY SEEDS |

Andhra cooking is typically hot, especially in the region near Guntur which grows most of the chillies that India exports around the world. *Serves 4* PREPARATION → *15 minutes* COOKING *45 minutes*

2 tablespoons white poppy seeds
3 tablespoons grated fresh coconut, or desiccated coconut soaked in hot water for 20 minutes
1 tablespoon halved cashew nuts
2 tablespoons vegetable oil
2 star anise
2 bay leaves
3 cloves
1 small cinnamon stick
7–8 fresh or 10 dried curry leaves
2 large onions, finely diced
2 teaspoons ginger-garlic paste *(page 45)*
800g boneless, skinless chicken thighs, cut into 4cm pieces
1 teaspoon ground turmeric
1 teaspoon medium-hot red chilli powder
1 teaspoon garam masala *(page 64)*
2 tomatoes, chopped
a small handful of fresh coriander leaves, chopped, to garnish
salt
boiled rice *(pages 78–79)*, to serve

1 Heat a small frying pan over a high heat, add the poppy seeds, coconut and cashews and dry-toast until they turn golden, stirring frequently. Transfer to a blender with enough water to just cover and blitz to a fine purée. Set aside.
2 Heat the oil in a heavy-based pan over a high heat, add the whole spices and fry for a minute or so until they sizzle, then tip in the curry leaves and onions. Fry for 8–10 minutes until the onions are very soft and golden.
3 Stir in the ginger-garlic paste then add the chicken. Cook over a high heat for 4–5 minutes to seal.
4 Mix in the ground spices. After 1 minute, add the tomatoes. When the tomatoes have softened, pour in the purée from the blender. Rinse the blender with about 100ml water and pour this in as well. Season with salt. Bring to the boil then reduce the heat and simmer for 25 minutes or so until the chicken is cooked through and tender. Sprinkle with coriander and serve hot with rice.

Kori Gassi

| SPICY CHICKEN AND COCONUT CURRY |

This is a speciality of the Tulu-speaking Bunt community of Mangalore in Karnataka. Their cuisine is based on spices such as pepper and garam masala, and coconut – fresh, desiccated or as milk. Many south Indian restaurants across India are owned by people originating from this region and this curry has become famous by featuring on so many of their restaurant menus. It is a spicy curry that is eaten with light pancakes called Neer Dosa (page 127) or with rice. I sometimes make a vegetarian version with cauliflower.

Serves 4 PREPARATION → *10 minutes*

COOKING *40 minutes*

4 tablespoons vegetable oil
1 tablespoon coriander seeds
½ teaspoon fenugreek seeds
2 onions, sliced
3 tablespoons desiccated coconut
1 teaspoon garam masala *(page 64)*
2 teaspoons ginger-garlic paste *(page 45)*
7–8 fresh or 10 dried curry leaves
800g chicken thighs on the bone, skin removed
1 teaspoon medium-hot chilli powder
1 teaspoon ground turmeric
1 teaspoon freshly ground black pepper
2 tomatoes, chopped
2 tablespoons tamarind pulp *(page 418)* or
    shop-bought tamarind paste
300ml coconut milk
salt
Neer Dosa *(page 127)* or boiled rice *(pages 78–79)*,
    to serve

1 Heat half the oil in a heavy-based frying pan over a high heat and add the coriander and fenugreek seeds. Fry for a minute until they start to darken then add the onions. Stir for 8–10 minutes until soft and brown.

2 Add the coconut, garam masala and ginger-garlic paste and stir for 3–4 minutes until the mixture turns golden, then remove from the heat, cool and transfer to a blender. Blitz until smooth, with enough water to turn the blades. Set aside.

3 Heat the remaining oil in a frying pan over a high heat and add the curry leaves and chicken (standing back from the pan if using fresh leaves, as they will splutter). Stir to seal, then add the chilli powder, ground turmeric and pepper and season with salt. Add the tomatoes and tamarind paste. Cook over a high heat for 3–4 minutes to soften the tomatoes, then tip in the onion and coconut mixture from the blender. Rinse out the blender with a little water and pour this into the curry. Bring to the boil then reduce the heat, cover and simmer for 20 minutes until the chicken is tender and cooked through.

4 Stir in the coconut milk, season to taste, heat through and serve hot with rice or Neer Dosa.

Palak Murgh

| CHICKEN AND SPINACH CURRY |

1 bunch of spinach, washed

a handful of fresh dill, chopped

a large handful of fresh coriander leaves, chopped

2 tablespoons, plus 1 teaspoon vegetable oil (for frying the chillies, optional)

2 medium onions, thinly sliced

1 teaspoon dried fenugreek leaves (kasoori methi – *page 393* – optional)

2 fresh green chillies, chopped

2 tablespoons ginger-garlic paste (*page 45*)

2 tablespoons tomato purée

800g chicken legs, skinned and halved at the joint

1 teaspoon ground turmeric

1 teaspoon medium-hot chilli powder

1 teaspoon ground coriander

1 teaspoon garam masala (*page 64*)

1 tablespoon lemon juice

2 fresh green chillies, slit lengthways (optional)

salt

Rotis (*pages 108–109*), Parathas (*pages 120–121*) or boiled rice (*pages 78–79*), to serve

I love the creamy combination of spinach and chicken, and often add whatever green vegetables I can find in my fridge, including broccoli and beans, to the sauce. The fried green chillies added at the end add a fresh herby flavour, but you can leave them out if you prefer a milder dish. This recipe is from north India, where meat and chicken is often combined with vegetables such as spinach, fenugreek, okra or corn. *Serves 4*

PREPARATION ⟶ *15 minutes* COOKING *45 minutes*

1 Put the spinach in a saucepan and cook over a medium heat for 3–4 minutes until just wilted. Remove from the heat and transfer to a blender with the dill and coriander and a few tablespoons of water. Blitz to a fine purée, then set aside.

2 Heat 2 tablespoons of the oil in a heavy-based pan over a high heat, add the onions and fry for 7–8 minutes until very soft.

3 Add the kasoori methi or dried fenugreek leaves (if using), chillies, ginger-garlic paste and the tomato purée and fry for a few minutes. Add a couple of tablespoons of water and cook for a further 1–2 minutes until the oil separates.

4 Add the chicken legs, fry for 2–3 minutes to seal, then stir in the ground spices. Season with salt, drizzle in the lemon juice and mix well. Pour in about 150ml water and bring to the boil. Reduce the heat, cover and cook for 20–25 minutes until the chicken is tender and cooked through.

5 Stir in the puréed greens, season to taste, and remove from the heat.

6 If you want to serve the curry with fried green chillies, heat a teaspoon of oil in a small frying pan over a high heat, add the green chillies and fry for 40 seconds or so until they start to change colour. Pour the oil and chillies over the curry and serve hot with rotis, parathas or boiled rice.

Kolhapuri Pandhra Rassa

| MAHARASHTRIAN WHITE CHICKEN CURRY |

This Kolhapuri curry is famous for its unusual white
(pandhra) colour and can be made with mutton or lamb.

Serves 5 PREPARATION → *15 minutes, plus soaking time*
COOKING *45 minutes*

800g chicken thighs on the bone
2 teaspoons ginger-garlic paste *(page 45)*
1 tablespoon white sesame seeds, soaked in a little
    warm water for 30 minutes
1 tablespoon white poppy seeds, soaked in a little
    warm water for 30 minutes
2 tablespoons unsalted cashew nuts, soaked in a little
    warm water for 30 minutes
2 fresh green chillies, diced
200ml coconut milk
2 tablespoons vegetable oil
4 cloves
1 small cinnamon stick
4 green cardamom pods, seeds crushed and husks discarded
2 bay leaves
1 onion, finely diced
salt
boiled rice *(pages 78–79)*, to serve

1 Put the chicken, salt to season and half the ginger-garlic
paste in a saucepan and pour in enough water to just cover.
Bring to the boil then reduce the heat and simmer for
15–20 minutes until the chicken is tender and cooked through.
Lift the chicken out with a slotted spoon and reserve both
the chicken and the stock in which it has been cooked.

2 Meanwhile, put the sesame and poppy seeds along with
the cashew nuts in a blender. Add the chillies and blitz for a
few minutes, adding a little water if necessary, to make a fine
purée. Transfer the purée to a bowl and add the coconut milk.

3 Heat the oil in a heavy-based frying pan over a high heat
and add the cloves, cinnamon, cardamom and bay leaves.
When they begin to sizzle and darken, add the onion and
cook for 8–10 minutes until very soft. Stir in the remaining
ginger-garlic paste, cook for a few seconds, then pour in
the stock from Step 1 and bring to the boil. Add the cooked
chicken and stir in the white paste. Heat the curry without
allowing it to boil, as it is quite delicate and can split if cooked
to a high temperature. Season to taste and serve hot with rice.

Nadan Kozhi Ishtu

| KERALA CHICKEN STEW |

This curry is often eaten for breakfast on Christmas day or
on Sundays in Syrian Christian homes in Kerala because
people believe in cooking a little of many meats on festive
days. A Christmas menu may have a chicken stew, duck
roast (see page 179) and a beef dish and there are always
lots of family and friends around the table to finish it all.

Serves 4 PREPARATION → *15 minutes* COOKING *50 minutes*

400ml coconut milk
2 onions, sliced
2 teaspoons ginger-garlic paste *(page 45)*
2 carrots, peeled and cut into thick chunks
1 large potato, peeled and quartered
800g boneless, skinless chicken thighs (or skin left on
    for a fattier stew)
1 teaspoon freshly ground black pepper
1 tablespoon white wine vinegar or distilled vinegar
1 tablespoon coconut or vegetable oil
4 cloves
2 star anise
1 small cinnamon stick
7–8 fresh or 10 dried curry leaves
1 teaspoon cornflour, mixed with a little water to make a paste
salt
boiled rice *(pages 78–79)*, bread rolls or Appams *(page 129)*, to serve

1 Shake the can of coconut milk, then open it and divide the
contents of the can between two separate bowls. Add half a
can of water to one bowl to make a thin coconut milk. The
other bowl contains the thick milk.

2 Put the onions, ginger-garlic paste, carrots, potato, chicken
and pepper in a saucepan and season with salt. Pour in the
vinegar and the thin coconut milk. Bring to the boil then
reduce the heat and simmer for 25–30 minutes until the
vegetables are tender and the chicken is cooked through.

3 Heat the oil in a small saucepan over a high heat and add
the whole spices. When they start to sizzle add the curry
leaves (standing back from the pan if using fresh leaves, as
they will splutter). Pour this into the stew, then stir in the
cornflour paste and thick coconut milk. Bring to almost
boiling point then remove from the heat. Season to taste and
serve hot with boiled rice, bread rolls or appams.

FISH & SEAFOOD

With over 4,000 miles of coastline and hundreds of rivers, such as the Ganga and the Narmada, India is rich with fish and seafood. Coastal regions have fishing communities – in Mumbai it is the 'Kolis', who are considered to be original inhabitants of the area. Their patron goddess Mumbadevi gave the city Mumbai its name. At dawn each day, the fish market fills with vendors who have designated stalls and loyal customers who almost always buy from the same seller. These are typically women who look after the sales while the men go out fishing.

The freshwater fish of India are also quite famous. People in Kerala swear by the karimeen (pearl spot) which is found in the brackish backwaters of the state. It is considered such a delicacy that it has been declared the state's official fish!

Bengalis go dewy-eyed about the oily, bony fish 'hilsa' or 'ilish' and buy them in pairs to mark festive and auspicious days. The hilsa is actually a sea fish but lays its eggs in Bengal's rivers. The young fish are caught as they swim out to sea and these are considered the most delicious.

Fish has been eaten in India since ancient times. Cave paintings in Bhimbetka in central India, considered to be 30,000 years old, include images of fish, and at other nearby sites there is evidence of fishing with nets and stones. Travellers to India, including the Greeks, Chinese and French, noted that fish was eaten in profusion. The Mughal emperor Babur's (1483–1530 AD) historical record, the *Baburnama*, describes unique methods of catching fish practised by the locals:

'At some convenient place lower down the river, in a hole below a fall, they will have fixed beforehand a wattle of finger-thick willow-withes, making it firm by piling stones on its sides. The water goes rushing and dashing through the wattle, but leaves on it any fish that may have come floating down. This way of catching fish is practised in Gul-bahar, Parwan and Istalif.'

Crustaceans such as prawns, crabs and lobsters are also popular, and several varieties, such as the giant tiger prawn and the spiny lobster, are found in the wild as well as farmed. India exports vast quantities of prawns, both frozen and dried.

Many Indians follow the Ayurvedic rule of not mixing fish with milk or dairy, as these are considered incompatible foods. Milk is considered 'cooling' whereas fish is believed to be 'heating'. Combining the two is said to hamper the effectiveness of the gastro-intestinal tract, however some Indian recipes do exist that combine these two foods, such as the fish and yogurt Bengali curry, Doi Mach (page 208). The Ayurvedic concept of 'sathmya' suggests that eating a food or combination of foods over a long time makes us immune to its negative effects.

In the recipes in this chapter, I have used raw prawns as they are always so much more delicious than the cooked ones. Also, cooked ones need to be cooked again in a curry to absorb the flavours of the spices, which makes them rubbery. If you have to use cooked prawns, add them at the last minute and simmer for a minute or so.

I have also suggested substitutes for traditional fish if you cannot find them. In my experience, except for a few frozen fish or shellfish, such as kingfish or prawns, it's best to use fresh local fish. Many fish lose their texture and taste when frozen and I have been especially disappointed with frozen pomfret bought in the UK, which is such a delicacy in India when fresh.

Fish Markets In India

When my children were little on our visits to Mumbai, we'd go to the Sassoon Dock fish market in Colaba early on Sunday mornings. We would wear flip flops to negotiate the wet floors of the market as we looked for the best bargains and waited for the boats to come in.

At around 7am, the boats would come into the dock and amidst much excitement and shouting, the catch would be offloaded into baskets on shore. Fishmongers and restaurants would quickly buy what they wanted and the rest was sold to buyers like us. Some fish in Mumbai is still expensive, especially the silver, delicate pomfret and huge tiger prawns. At home, the kitchen would come alive with the toasting of spices, blending of coconut curry masala and the sizzle of fried prawns that would make a fine Sunday lunch!

Another favourite fish market of mine, even today, is the one at Grant Road, where my regular saleslady Sandhya gives me the best deals as she knows I visit only a few times a year. A savvy saleswoman, she has sold me fish for the past 15 years. She knows what I always buy, will give me a few extra plump prawns for my loyalty and cleans my fish and prawns for me. I have seen the price of fish treble in the last few years and yet the fish market, especially at weekends, is full.

Many cities and towns in India have such fish markets – bustling busy places with fresh fish, prawns, crabs and other seafood. It's a treat I look forward to on every trip I make back to Mumbai.

HOW TO CHOOSE YOUR FISH

1 It should have very little odour, if any. Fish should have a clean, briny smell. Any strong fishy odour will not go away completely on cooking. Many Indians do not like the overpowering smell of fish and will wash it with tamarind or lemon before using it, or marinate it in salt and turmeric before cooking it.

2 Bright, clear eyes. If the eyes are glazed and sunken, the fish has been kept for a while. Although not unsafe to eat, it will not taste fresh.

3 Shiny scales. Fresh fish does not look dull or faded.

4 Red gills. Lift up a gill and look for a deep bloody colour as opposed to a dull brown hue.

5 Buy whole, frozen, raw prawns if you can't get fresh. The shell keeps the moisture in and raw ones absorb flavours better than cooked ones.

HOW TO TELL IF FISH IS COOKED

Indians like their fish well done and do not appreciate a slightly translucent look. Generally fish and prawns are cooked when they turn opaque and will carry on cooking a little when they are removed from the heat.

The easiest way to check is by cutting a small slit into a piece of fish to check if it is opaque and flaky. Typically, fish is added to curries as one of the last ingredients as it cooks so quickly. Marinades for fish should not include lemon if used overnight or over any length of time as the acid can begin to cook the fish. Add the lemon just before cooking.

Kerala Fish Molee

| CREAMY FISH CURRY |

This unique south Indian fish curry is not a fiery dish, in fact it is quite creamy with the thick coconut milk that is used. Traditional fish used would be seer, kingfish, pomfret or pearl spot but you can use salmon, halibut or similar firm-fleshed fish if you can't get one of these. *Serves 4*

PREPARATION → *10 minutes* COOKING *40 minutes*

2 tablespoons coconut or vegetable oil
1 teaspoon black or brown mustard seeds
1 medium onion, finely diced
2 teaspoons ginger-garlic paste *(page 45)*
2 fresh green chillies, chopped
1 teaspoon ground turmeric
600g firm-fleshed fish fillets, such as salmon, halibut or red mullet
300ml coconut milk
5 fresh or 10 dried curry leaves
2 tomatoes, chopped
2 teaspoons lemon juice
salt
boiled rice *(pages 78–79)*, to serve

1 Heat the oil in a medium saucepan over a high heat, add the mustard seeds and wait until they pop. Add the onion and fry for 7–8 minutes until soft, then stir in the ginger-garlic paste and the chillies.
2 Stir in the turmeric and place the fish in the pan. Fry on both sides for 3–4 minutes on each side until partially cooked.
3 Pour in the coconut milk, then add the curry leaves and the tomatoes.
4 Season with salt and cook over a low heat for 7–8 minutes, until the fish is tender.
5 Remove from the heat, stir in the lemon juice, season to taste and serve at once with rice.

Goenchi Kodi

| GOAN FISH CURRY |

There are several versions of this classic dish, depending on which community is cooking it but all of them have bright red chillies and a sour ingredient like tamarind. The curry is often flavoured with a local spice called tirphal (a variety of Szechuan pepper). If you can't find it, leave it out, or use the same quantity of Szechuan pepper. *Serves 4*

PREPARATION → *15 minutes* COOKING *30 minutes*

4 x 180g steaks of a firm-fleshed white fish, such as pomfret or pollock
1 teaspoon ground turmeric
2 tablespoons vegetable oil
1 small onion, finely diced
3 tablespoons tamarind pulp *(page 418)* or shop-bought tamarind paste
3–4 tirphal (optional)
200ml coconut milk
salt
boiled rice *(pages 78–79)*, to serve
For the purée
10 black peppercorns
1 teaspoon cumin seeds
1 large onion, sliced
4 garlic cloves
7 dried red Kashmiri chillies, soaked in a little hot water for 10 minutes

1 Rub the fish fillets with the turmeric and salt to season and set aside while you prepare the remaining ingredients.
2 Put the ingredients for the purée into a blender, including the water the chillies were soaking in, along with enough water to cover them and blitz to a fine purée.
3 Heat the oil in a pan over a high heat and add the diced onion. Fry for 6–7 minutes until soft, then pour the contents of the blender into the pan. Rinse out the blender with a little water and pour this in as well. Add the tamarind and tirphal (if using) and season with salt.
4 When the curry comes to a bubble, reduce the heat and simmer for a couple of minutes then increase the heat and slip in the fish, pour in the coconut milk and simmer for 7–8 minutes or until tender.
5 Season to taste and serve hot with rice.

PATRA NI MACCHI – Fish cooked in Coriander Chutney

The first time I had this Parsi delicacy was at a wedding in Mumbai when I was about 8 years old. Having being brought up with Hindu rituals, the thought of a 'non-vegetarian' wedding feast was both intriguing and exciting. The traditional fish used is pomfret, steamed in banana leaves, both these ingredients being local to Gujarat and Mumbai, where many Parsis live. *Serves 4* PREPARATION →
15 minutes, plus 20 minutes soaking time COOKING *20 minutes*

YOU WILL NEED:

4 x 150g firm-fleshed fish fillets, such as pomfret,
    cod or hake
½ teaspoon ground turmeric
For the coriander chutney
a large handful of fresh mint leaves
a large handful of fresh coriander leaves
2 fresh green chillies
1 tablespoon ginger-garlic paste *(page 45)*
½ teaspoon cumin seeds
3 tablespoons lime juice
1 teaspoon caster sugar
6 tablespoons freshly grated coconut or desiccated
    coconut (soaked in a little warm water
    for 20 minutes to soften)
salt
4 squares of banana leaves or foil

1 Blitz the chutney ingredients in a food processor or blender until they form a fine paste, adding a tiny bit of water if necessary.

2 Season each fillet of fish with salt and rub with the turmeric.

3 Coat each fillet with a quarter of the chutney and wrap them individually in banana leaf or foil. Secure with cocktail sticks or tie with a piece of string to hold the parcel together. Steam the fish for 20 minutes in a steamer or bake for 20 minutes in an oven preheated to 200°C/gas mark 6.

4 Remove from the steamer or oven and serve immediately.

Malvani Rus-Golichi Amti

| MAHARASHTRIAN FISH CURRY |

The term 'rus-golichi' refers to coconut milk and the spice paste that is cooked with it. Mackerel or any firm fish such as sea bass or swordfish can be used for this fiery curry. Kokum, a sour purple fruit, is used for tang – if you can't get hold of it, you can use tamarind pulp instead. *Serves 4*

PREPARATION → *15 minutes* COOKING *30 minutes*

4 x 180g steaks of firm-fleshed fish, such as mackerel,
    sea bass or swordfish
1 teaspoon ground turmeric
2 tablespoons vegetable oil
6 kokum, rinsed and soaked in 2 tablespoons warm water
    or 4 teaspoons tamarind paste
salt
boiled rice *(pages 78–79)*, to serve
For the curry paste
8 dried red Kashmiri chillies, soaked in a little hot water
    for 10 minutes to soften
3 onions, finely diced
½ freshly grated coconut or 5 tablespoons desiccated coconut
    (soaked in hot water for 20 minutes to soften)
1 teaspoon coriander seeds
3 garlic cloves, chopped

1 Rub the fish with the turmeric and salt to season.
2 Put the curry paste ingredients (reserving one-third of the diced onion), including the soaking liquid from the chillies, in a blender with enough water to cover and blitz to a very fine purée.
3 Heat the oil in a saucepan over a high heat and add the reserved onion. Fry for 7–8 minutes until soft, then add the paste from the blender. Rinse the blender out with a little water and add this to the pan, then add the kokum along with the soaking water (or the tamarind) and bring to the boil. Season with salt.
4 Slip in the fish and simmer for 8–10 minutes until done. Season to taste and serve hot with rice.

Bhujane

| SWEET AND SOUR FISH CURRY |

The Pathare Prabhus are considered to be one of Mumbai's earliest Hindu settlers, having lived there since the thirteenth century. They are known for their unique traditions, such as celebrating the festival of Diwali over 8 days instead of 5 days like the rest of India, and their stylish living, as well as boasting a luxurious, delicious cuisine. Unlike many parts of India where meat and fish, being expensive, is just eaten occasionally, the Pathare Prabhus consume them regularly, often combined with vegetables. Western techniques such as baking came to be a part of the Pathare Prabhu kitchen, where foods such as 'pies' with spices and herbs were made as family meals.

Serves 4 PREPARATION → *15 minutes* COOKING *30 minutes*

4 x 200g fillets of firm-fleshed fish, such as kingfish, tuna or hake
1 teaspoon ground turmeric
2 teaspoons minced garlic
4 large onions, finely chopped
2 fresh green chillies, finely diced
a large handful of fresh coriander leaves, chopped
3 tablespoons vegetable oil
2 tablespoons tamarind pulp *(page 418)* or shop-bought
    tamarind paste, mixed with 2 tablespoons water
salt
boiled rice *(pages 78–79)*, to serve

1 Rub the fish fillets with half of the turmeric, the minced garlic and salt to season.
2 Mix the onions, chillies and coriander in a large bowl and crush with your hands to bruise them together. The more you crush this mixture, the smoother the sauce will be.
3 Heat the oil in a flat frying pan over a high heat and add the fish. Gently fry on both sides until sealed and just partially cooked, then transfer to a plate and set aside.
4 Add the onion mixture to the pan and fry for 8–9 minutes, until the onions are very soft, then pour in the tamarind paste and remaining turmeric. Cook for a couple of minutes.
5 Put the fish into this mixture and continue cooking for 8–9 minutes, turning the fish a few times, until it is tender. Season to taste and serve hot with rice.

Chingri Maccher Malaikari

| CREAMY BENGALI PRAWN CURRY |

My Bengali friend Nima says that some people believe
that an early version of this recipe was brought via the Bay
of Bengal by Malaysian sailors, which is why it's called a
'Malai' (meaning Malay) kari (curry). 'Malai' in some Indian
languages translates as milk cream, which this recipe does
not contain. Instead, coconut, which is commonly used in
Far Eastern cuisines, is the base for this delicious dish.

Serves 4 PREPARATION → *15 minutes* COOKING *25 minutes*

600g raw jumbo prawns, shelled and deveined
½ teaspoon ground turmeric
2 tablespoons mustard or vegetable oil
2 bay leaves
1 small cinnamon stick
1 large onion, finely chopped
2.5cm piece of fresh root ginger, scraped and finely grated
1 teaspoon ground coriander
1 teaspoon medium-hot red chilli powder
3 tablespoons freshly grated coconut, or desiccated coconut
    (soaked in hot water for 20 minutes to soften)
100ml coconut milk
2 tablespoons lemon juice
salt
boiled rice *(pages 78–79)*, to serve

1 Mix the prawns and turmeric together, season with salt
and set aside.

2 Heat half the oil in a saucepan over a high heat, add the
prawns and fry them briefly. When they start to change
colour, drain on kitchen paper and set aside.

3 Heat the remaining oil in a saucepan over a high heat and
add the bay leaves and cinnamon stick. When they start to
darken, add the onion and fry for 7–8 minutes until soft, then
add the grated ginger. Stir in the ground spices and grated or
desiccated coconut. Cook for a couple of minutes, then pour
in the coconut milk and lemon juice. Bring almost to
boiling point.

4 Add the prawns and season to taste. Simmer for a minute
or so then remove from the heat. Serve hot with plain rice.

Vanjaram Meen Varuval

| SOUTH INDIAN FRIED KINGFISH |

Kingfish is the popular Indian name for the Indo-Pacific
king mackerel. It has firm flesh that holds its shape and
is therefore eaten fried or in pickles. You can use any
firm-fleshed fish such as salmon in this recipe, but avoid
flipping it over too many times as this can dry out the flesh.
Kingfish can be bought frozen in many Indian or Sri Lankan
shops around the world. *Serves 4* PREPARATION → *10 minutes, plus
2 hours marinating time or overnight if possible* COOKING *20 minutes*

4 x 200g steaks of kingfish, salmon, bream or hake
coconut or vegetable oil, for shallow-frying
salt
onion rings and wedges of lime, to serve
For the marinade
1 teaspoon ground turmeric
2 teaspoons medium-hot red chilli powder
2 teaspoons ground coriander
1 tablespoon ginger-garlic paste *(page 45)*
1 teaspoon freshly ground black pepper
2 tablespoons tamarind pulp *(page 418)*
    or shop-bought tamarind paste

1 Combine the ingredients for the marinade in a bowl and
season with salt. Put the fish in the bowl and rub the marinade
onto it with your fingers to coat it evenly. Cover and refrigerate
for a couple of hours or overnight.

2 Bring the fish to room temperature. Heat enough oil to
cover the base of a frying pan and shallow-fry the fish for
5 minutes on each side. Drain on kitchen paper then serve
with onion rings and wedges of lime.

Kolmi Fry

| CRISP GARLIC PRAWNS |

This is not just a favourite recipe in my home but also at many of my classes. Simple to make, stunning to look at and a perfect blend of sweet, hot, salty and tangy flavours in a crisp coating, these are made for Sunday lunch in Maharashtrian homes. *Serves 4* PREPARATION→ *5 minutes, plus 1 hour marinating time or overnight if possible* COOKING *15 minutes*

600g large raw prawns, shelled and deveined
vegetable oil, for shallow-frying
squeeze of lemon juice
3 tablespoons fine semolina or rice flour
salt
boiled rice *(pages 78–79)* and Aamti *(page 279)*, to serve
For the marinade
½ teaspoon ground turmeric
1 teaspoon medium-hot red chilli powder
½ teaspoon ginger-garlic paste *(page 45)*

1 Combine the ingredients for the marinade in a bowl, season with salt, and mix the prawns into it. Make sure you season the prawns well as they will later be coated with unseasoned semolina or rice flour. Transfer to the fridge to marinate for 1 hour or overnight if possible.

2 Heat enough oil to cover the bottom of a large frying pan, and squeeze the lemon juice into the bowl with the prawns. Toss to mix.

3 Roll a few of the prawns in the semolina or rice flour and place gently into the oil when it is hot. Place them in a clockwise direction so that you can flip them over in the same order to ensure even cooking. Reduce the heat and fry the prawns for a couple of minutes on each side until done.

4 Drain and transfer to kitchen paper. Repeat until all the prawns are cooked. Serve hot with rice and Aamti.

Khekda Masala

| CRAB STUFFED WITH MUSTARD AND COCONUT |

4 x large (450g) fresh or cooked, dressed crab,
    or 8 small ones
2 tablespoons vegetable oil
½ teaspoon black mustard seeds
8 fresh or 12 dried curry leaves
3 green chillies, finely chopped
2 onions, finely diced
1½ teaspoons ginger-garlic paste *(page 45)*
1 teaspoon ground turmeric
4 tablespoons of freshly grated coconut,
    or desiccated coconut (soaked in hot water
    for 20 minutes to soften)
a small handful of fresh coriander leaves,
    chopped
salt
boiled rice *(pages 78–79)* and dal, to serve
    (optional)

The Maharashtrian coastline offers a variety of large sea crabs but the inland rivers also host their own smaller freshwater ones. Either can be used for this recipe. It makes a good main course served with rice and dal.

Serves 4 PREPARATION —➔ *20 minutes, plus 30 minutes to cook the crab if using fresh* COOKING *20 minutes*

1 If you are using fresh crabs, bring a large saucepan of water to the boil and gently lower in the crabs. Bring back up to the boil, cover and simmer for 30 minutes. Remove from the heat and leave the crabs in the water to cool.

2 To prepare the crab, place it on its back on a board, with its eyes towards you, and prise off the claws, which contain most of the white meat. Set the claws aside. Break off and discard the six legs. Insert a knife under the large triangular 'purse' between the eyes and lift it up. Remove and discard it. Inside, you will see grey wispy gills. Remove and discard these as they should not be eaten. Remove the flesh (white meat only) from the crabs and shred it. Crack open the claws by wrapping them in a tea towel and smashing them with a hammer. Peel away the claw shells to extract the meat, taking care to discard the sharp central blade bone. Reserve the body shells, cleaning out the brown meat from the shells, as they are to be used as a vessel in Step 6, and repeat with the remaining three crabs.

3 If you are using dressed crab, scrape out the white meat into a bowl and save the shells.

4 Heat the oil in a saucepan over a high heat, add the mustard seeds and wait until they pop, then add the curry leaves (standing back from the pan if using fresh leaves, as they will splutter) and the chillies. Add the onions and fry for 7–8 minutes until very soft, then stir in the ginger-garlic paste and sprinkle in the turmeric. Cook for a further minute or so, then add the shredded crab meat and mix well.

5 Remove the crab mixture from the heat, stir in half the coconut and season with salt.

6 Stuff the spiced crab meat back into the shells and garnish with the remaining coconut and the coriander. Serve warm with rice and dal, if you like.

Royalla Vepudu

| ANDHRA-STYLE PRAWN FRY |

This semi-dry dish is fragrant with curry leaves and fennel seeds. Run your knife down the backs of the prawns after deveining them to butterfly them and keep them juicy during cooking. *Serves 4* PREPARATION → *15 minutes* COOKING *25 minutes*

2 tablespoons vegetable oil
1 teaspoon black mustard seeds
1 teaspoon fennel seeds
5–6 fresh or 7–8 dried curry leaves
2 onions, finely diced
1 tablespoon ginger-garlic paste *(page 45)*
1 large tomato, chopped
1 teaspoon ground turmeric
600g large raw prawns, shelled, deveined and butterflied
a large handful of fresh coriander leaves, finely chopped,
    to garnish
salt
Rotis *(pages 108–109)* or boiled rice *(pages 78–79)*, to serve

1 Heat the oil in a frying pan over a high heat, then add the black mustard seeds and, as soon as the seeds start to pop, add the fennel seeds and curry leaves (standing back from the pan if using fresh leaves, as they will splutter). They will cook within seconds. Add the onions and fry for 7–8 minutes until soft and brown, then tip in the ginger-garlic paste and stir for a minute or so.

2 Stir in the chopped tomato and turmeric and cook for 3–4 minutes until soft. The mixture should look well blended, almost like a paste.

3 Add the prawns, season with salt and mix well. Cover the pan and cook for 7–8 minutes. Season to taste, stir in the coriander and serve hot with rotis or rice.

Shorshe Chingri Bhapa

| BENGALI PRAWNS IN MUSTARD AND POPPY SEED SAUCE |

This classic dish is typical of Bengali cookery, where fish is often cooked in 'sorshe bata' or mustard paste. The hit at the back of the nose is cherished but if you prefer a milder dish, reduce the amount of mustard seeds. The prawns can be substituted with a firm-fleshed fish such as hake or bream to make 'Sorshebata Maach', which means 'fish in mustard paste'. *Serves 4* PREPARATION → *10 minutes, plus 30 minutes soaking time* COOKING *40 minutes*

600g large raw prawns, shelled and deveined
1 teaspoon ground turmeric
3 teaspoons black or brown mustard seeds
2 teaspoons white poppy seeds
1 fresh green chilli, diced
2 tablespoons freshly grated coconut or desiccated coconut
    (soaked in hot water for 20 minutes to soften)
½ teaspoon caster sugar
100ml coconut milk
2 tablespoons mustard or vegetable oil
salt
boiled rice *(pages 78–79)*, to serve

1 Place the prawns in a bowl with the turmeric and salt to season. While they marinate, soak the mustard and poppy seeds in enough warm water to cover for 30 minutes.

2 Put the soaked, drained seeds and chilli in a small blender or pestle and mortar and blitz or crush to a fine paste.

3 Put the prawns, spice paste, grated or desiccated coconut, sugar, coconut milk and oil into a heatproof bowl which can be placed in a steamer. Season with salt. This can be done in a pressure cooker, if you have one, without adding the whistle/weight on top.

4 Once the steam has built up in the steamer, cook the curry for 25 minutes or until the prawns are tender and the oil is floating on top. Leave the curry to rest for 5 minutes before opening the steamer. Cooking times may vary slightly, depending on the steamer you use. Serve hot with rice.

Fish Recheado

| FISH STUFFED WITH CHILLI AND SPICE |

7–8 dried red Kashmiri chillies

2.5cm piece of fresh root ginger,
scraped and chopped

5 garlic cloves, chopped

1 teaspoon black peppercorns

1 teaspoon cumin seeds

1 tablespoon caster sugar

3 tablespoons tamarind pulp (page 418)
or shop-bought tamarind paste

3 tablespoons coconut or cider vinegar

2 large fresh mackerel (about 400g each),
gutted, scaled and cleaned, with diagonal
slits cut along the bodies

2 teaspoons ground turmeric

1 teaspoon garam masala (page 64)

vegetable oil, for shallow-frying

salt

lemon or lime wedges and fresh onion rings,
to serve

Like many Goan dishes, this one also has its roots in Portuguese cooking. The word 'recheado' is variously spelt and means 'stuffed' in Portuguese. In Goa, you would most likely eat pomfret or mackerel recheado. *Serves 4*

PREPARATION—➔ *10 minutes, plus 30 minutes soaking time* COOKING *25 minutes*

1 Place the chillies in a bowl with the ginger, garlic, peppercorns, cumin seeds, sugar, tamarind pulp and vinegar, adding salt to season. Add enough water, if required, to just cover the mixture. Set aside to soak for 30 minutes.

2 Rub the fish with half the turmeric and salt to season and set aside.

3 Blitz the mixture made in step 1 in a blender to make a purée, then stir in the remaining turmeric and the garam masala. This recheado masala should be bright red in colour. Stuff the fish and the slits on the body with the masala mix, coating it evenly.

4 Heat enough oil to coat the base of a frying pan over a medium heat and shallow-fry the fish for 7–8 minutes on each side until it is crisp on the outside and cooked through. Test whether the fish is done by lifting one of the slits, the flesh should be white and opaque. Serve hot with wedges of lemon or lime and fresh onion rings.

Doi Mach

| BENGALI FISH IN YOGURT |

4 x 200g steaks of firm-fleshed fish, such as
    salmon or kingfish
1 teaspoon ground turmeric
1 teaspoon medium-hot red chilli powder
3 garlic cloves, chopped
2.5cm piece of fresh root ginger, scraped and
    chopped
1 large onion, diced
2 tablespoons mustard oil
2 bay leaves
3 cloves
1 small cinnamon stick
4 green cardamom pods, seeds crushed and
    husks discarded
½ teaspoon cumin seeds
500g full-fat yogurt
2 fresh green chillies, slit lengthways
salt
boiled rice *(pages 78–79)*, to serve

Although many Indians believe the Ayurvedic suggestion that dairy and fish must not be combined as it can lead to poor digestion, the Bengalis have proved that this is not always the case. Their cuisine has many examples of this combination, either cooked together, as in this recipe, or eaten in quick succession, as in a fish curry followed by a milky dessert. Full-fat yogurt is best used for cooking as it does not tend to split on heating, whereas lower-fat varieties do. You can vary the level of heat by reducing the amount of chilli powder. *Serves 4* PREPARATION → *15 minutes* COOKING *30 minutes*

1 Rub the fish steaks with half the turmeric, half the chilli powder and salt to season. Refrigerate for 15 minutes while you prepare the remaining ingredients.
2 Put the garlic, ginger and onion in a blender and blitz to a purée with a little water.
3 Heat the oil in a frying pan until it reaches smoking point, to take away some of the pungency, then reduce the heat and fry the fish two at a time for about 8 minutes, turning them over a couple of times to seal both sides, until almost done. Lift the fish out of the pan with a slotted spoon, drain on kitchen paper and set aside.
4 Add the bay leaves, cloves, cinnamon stick, cardamom and cumin seeds to the same fishy oil. Fry for a few seconds until they sizzle, then add the onion paste. Fry for 5–6 minutes until the mixture begins to stick, then rinse out the blender with a little water and pour the water into the pan. Add the remaining turmeric and chilli powder. Bring to the boil, reduce the heat and simmer for 8–10 minutes until the mixture is thick.
5 Season the yogurt with salt and stir it into the curry a little at a time. Add the green chillies, then bring up to almost boiling point. Slip in the fish and cover the pan. Cook for a further 4–5 minutes over a medium heat until the fish is cooked through, then remove from the heat, season to taste and serve hot with rice.

Sura Puttu

| SHARK FISH CRUMBLE |

This spicy recipe is made with shark or 'sura' in Tamil Nadu but I have also eaten a Bengali version that uses a bony local fish called 'ilish'. If you cannot find shark, use a firm-fleshed fish such as tuna, snapper, kingfish or swordfish.

Serves 4 PREPARATION → *10 minutes* COOKING *35 minutes*

4 x 200g shark steaks or tuna, snapper, kingfish, swordfish or hake
1 teaspoon ground turmeric
2 tablespoons coconut or vegetable oil
2 onions, finely diced
2 fresh green chillies, finely diced
6–7 fresh or 10 dried curry leaves
2 teaspoons ginger-garlic paste *(page 45)*
1 teaspoon freshly ground black pepper
2 tablespoons lemon or lime juice
salt
a large handful of fresh coriander leaves, finely chopped, to serve
Rotis *(pages 108–109)* or boiled rice *(pages 78–79)*, to serve

1   Rub the fish steaks with half the turmeric and salt to season then set aside while you prepare the remaining ingredients.
2   Heat half the oil in a frying pan and fry the fish in batches for 4–5 minutes on each side until opaque. Cover and let the fish cook in its own steam for 6–7 minutes until cooked through. Remove from the heat, leave to cool slightly then shred the flesh with your fingers, discarding any bones.
3   Heat the remaining oil in a pan over a high heat and fry the onions for 7–8 minutes until very soft. Add the chillies and curry leaves (standing back from the pan if using fresh leaves, as they will splutter) and continue cooking for a minute, then stir in the ginger-garlic paste, remaining turmeric and pepper, cook for a couple of minutes, then add the shredded fish.
4   Remove from the heat, stir in the lemon or lime juice and coriander, season to taste and serve hot with rotis or rice.

Mashyachi Amti

| FISH AND GREEN MANGO CURRY |

I grew up eating this fabulous tangy curry from Maharashtra. As children, we would pick out the sour mango slices as a treat to be eaten at the end of the meal. It is usually made with pomfret, but if this is not available you can use a firm white fish like coley. Raw mangoes are available in India from February to June but I sometimes see them in Indian shops in the UK all year round if they've been flown in from various countries around the world.

Serves 4 PREPARATION → *15 minutes* COOKING *40 minutes*

4 x 200g skinless fillets of firm-fleshed fish, such as pomfret, coley, cod, haddock, bream
1 teaspoon ground turmeric
1 tablespoon ginger-garlic paste *(page 45)*
2 tablespoons vegetable oil
2 onions, finely diced
6–7 fresh or 10 dried curry leaves
2 fresh green chillies, diced
1 green raw mango, peeled and thickly sliced
½ teaspoon medium-hot red chilli powder
1 teaspoon ground coriander
400ml coconut milk
salt
boiled rice *(pages 78–79)*, to serve

1   Rub the fish with half the turmeric, half the ginger-garlic paste and salt to season, then set aside.
2   Heat the oil in a frying pan over a high heat, add the onions and fry for 8–10 minutes until very soft. Add the curry leaves (standing back from the pan if using fresh leaves, as they will splutter), remaining ginger-garlic paste and chillies. Drop in the raw mango. Fry for a couple of minutes over a medium heat.
3   Tip in the ground spices, including the remaining turmeric, and cook for 1 minute, then add the fish and cook for 2–3 minutes on each side to seal. Pour in the coconut milk and bring almost to boiling point.
4   Reduce the heat to medium and cook for 8–9 minutes until the fish is tender. Season to taste and serve hot with rice.

Maccher Jhol

| LIGHT FISH STEW |

2 large (800g) whole mackerel, gutted, cleaned
    and cut into thick steaks
1 teaspoon ground turmeric
2 tomatoes
2 tablespoons mustard oil
1 teaspoon panch phoron spice seed mix
    (or a mix of equal quantities of black
    mustard seeds, cumin, fennel,
    nigella and fenugreek)
1 onion, finely diced
2.5cm piece of fresh root ginger,
    peeled and shredded
2 garlic cloves, minced
2 fresh green chillies, slit lengthways
2 medium potatoes, peeled and cubed
1 small aubergine, cubed
1 teaspoon ground cumin
a handful of fresh coriander leaves,
    finely chopped, to garnish
salt
boiled rice *(pages 78–79)*, to serve

There are many versions of this classic Bengali and Oriya lunchtime curry but the best I've had was late one night at a friend's restaurant in London when, after service, the Bengali chef made a pot of Jhol for the staff. Bengalis insist that rohu, a non-oily fish of the carp family, is best for this curry but I've made this jhol with mackerel and it's equally delicious. Panch phoron is a spice mix, available in seed as well as powder form, which contains black mustard seeds, cumin, fennel, nigella and fenugreek. If you cannot find it, use equal quantities of whichever of these seeds you can find. *Serves 4* PREPARATION —➔ *15 minutes* COOKING *30 minutes*

1 Rub the fish with half the turmeric and salt to season, and set aside.

2 Cut the tomatoes in half and grate the cut sides on the coarsest side of the grater over a bowl. Discard the skin.

3 Heat the oil in a frying pan until it reaches smoking point, then reduce the heat and add the fish to the pan. Fry for 2–3 minutes on each side, to seal and partially cook. Lift the fish out with a slotted spoon and set aside.

4 Add the panch phoron seed mix to the same pan. When it crackles, add the onion and fry for 7–8 minutes until soft, then tip in the ginger, garlic and chillies and fry for 2–3 minutes until golden.

5 Add the potatoes and fry to seal, then stir in the aubergine. Sprinkle in the remaining turmeric and the ground cumin. Season with salt and fry for 6–7 minutes until the potatoes look half done. Add the grated tomatoes, cook for a few minutes to blend, then pour in 300ml water and bring to the boil.

6 Slip in the fish and cook for a further 8–10 minutes until the vegetables are tender. Add a splash of water if the curry dries up, as it is meant to be quite thin and soupy. Season to taste, stir in the coriander leaves and serve hot with rice.

Kolmi No Patio

| PRAWNS IN HOT TAMARIND SAUCE |

The red, cloyingly sweet dish that is known as a 'patia' in many Indian restaurants around the world is nowhere near the beautifully balanced sweet and sour 'patio' one will eat in a Parsi home. As a teenager growing up in Mumbai, I was lucky to be invited by my Parsi friends to eat 'patio' served with rice, topped with golden fried onions.

Serves 4 PREPARATION —➤ *15 minutes* COOKING *40 minutes*

600g large raw prawns, shelled and deveined
1 teaspoon ground turmeric
2 tablespoons vegetable oil
1 large onion, finely diced
2 fresh green chillies, slit lengthways
7–8 fresh or 10 dried curry leaves
1 tablespoon ginger-garlic paste *(page 45)*
2 tomatoes, diced (seeds and all)
3 tablespoons tamarind pulp *(page 418)* or shop-bought
　　tamarind paste
2 tablespoons grated jaggery or soft brown sugar
½ teaspoon medium-hot red chilli powder
1 teaspoon ground coriander
1 teaspoon ground cumin
a small handful of fresh coriander leaves, chopped, to garnish
salt
Parsi-style Brown Rice *(page 94)*, to serve

1　Toss the prawns in half the turmeric and salt to season.
2　Heat the oil in a frying pan over a high heat, add the onion and fry for 7–8 minutes until very soft and golden.
3　Tip in the chillies and curry leaves, then stir in the ginger-garlic paste and fry for a couple of minutes to release all the flavours.
4　Add the diced tomatoes with a pinch of salt and cook for 5–6 minutes until a thick paste is formed. Mix in the tamarind and jaggery or sugar. Sprinkle in all the ground spices, including the remaining turmeric. Cook over a medium heat for a few minutes until everything is well blended, then add a splash of water and bring to the boil.
This will help the oil to separate and the spices to cook.
5　Add the prawns and cook for 7–8 minutes, until they are opaque. Season to taste, sprinkle with the coriander, and serve hot with Parsi-style brown rice.

Kanava Thoran

| SPICY SQUID WITH COCONUT |

This dish from Kerala can be as hot or mild as you want to make it. For a hotter dish, increase the green chillies to four and the pepper to two teaspoons. Indian seafood recipes are typically hot and sour, tempered with the sweetness of onions, coconut or the fish itself. You can buy ready-cleaned squid for this recipe. *Serves 4* PREPARATION —➤ *15 minutes* COOKING *40 minutes*

2 tablespoons coconut or vegetable oil
2 medium onions, thinly sliced
1 tablespoon ginger-garlic paste *(page 45)*
2 fresh green chillies, slit lengthways
600g fresh squid, cut into 1cm-thick rings
10 fresh or 15 dried curry leaves
1 teaspoon ground turmeric
½ teaspoon medium-hot red chilli powder
1 teaspoon freshly ground black pepper
1 teaspoon ground coriander
3 tablespoons tamarind pulp *(page 418)* or shop-bought
　　tamarind paste
3 tablespoons freshly grated coconut (preferable) or desiccated
　　coconut (soaked in hot water for 20 minutes to soften)
salt
boiled rice *(pages 78–79)*, to serve

1　Heat the oil in a heavy-based frying pan over a high heat then add the onions. Fry for 6–7 minutes until translucent, stirring from time to time, then add the ginger-garlic paste and chillies. Fry for a couple of minutes.
2　Tip in the squid rings and fry for a few minutes, then mix in the curry leaves (standing back from the pan if using fresh leaves, as they will splutter), ground spices and season with salt. Cover the pan and cook for 5 minutes. The juices from the squid will be released by now.
3　Stir in the tamarind and coconut, pour in 100ml water and bring to the boil. Cover and simmer for 5 minutes, then remove the lid and cook over a high heat to dry up any liquid. Season to taste and serve hot with rice.

Konkani Chimbori Masala

| CRAB CURRY WITH ROASTED COCONUT |

4 fresh crabs (about 200g each)

4 tablespoons vegetable oil

10 black peppercorns

6 cloves

2 teaspoons coriander seeds

1 large onion, thinly sliced

6 tablespoons freshly grated coconut
    or desiccated coconut (soaked in hot water
    for 20 minutes to soften)

a handful of fresh coriander leaves

3 fresh green chillies

2.5cm piece of fresh root ginger,
    scraped and chopped

4 garlic cloves, chopped

1 teaspoon ground turmeric

2 tablespoons tamarind pulp *(page 418)*
    or shop-bought tamarind paste

salt

boiled rice *(pages 78–79)*, to serve

This is my grandmother's recipe and it reminds me of lazy Sunday lunches in Mumbai. She said that the oil carried the flavours and therefore you need to put in a bit more than you'd expect. *Serves 4* PREPARATION → *15 minutes* COOKING *40 minutes*

1 Clean the crabs. Break off the legs and put them in a blender with enough water to just cover them. Blitz for a couple of minutes, then strain through a sieve into a bowl and discard the contents of the sieve. Reserve the liquid to use as stock in the curry.

2 Heat half of the oil in a deep, heavy-based frying pan and add the peppercorns, cloves and coriander seeds. Stir for 1 minute, then add the onion and fry for 8–10 minutes until brown. (The colour of the curry depends on this browning.) Add the coconut and stir-fry for 4–5 minutes until brown, taking care not to let the mixture burn. Cool the mixture slightly then transfer it to a blender, add enough water to cover the mixture and blitz to a purée. Tip into a bowl. This is the brown masala.

3 Combine the coriander leaves, chillies, ginger and garlic and blitz to a purée along with a little water to turn the blades. This is the green masala.

4 Heat the remaining oil in a large heavy-based pan over a high heat and add the crabs. Fry for 4–5 minutes until they turn red. Add the turmeric and season with salt.

5 Add the green masala and fry for 5 minutes. Pour in the brown masala and the stock from Step 1 and bring to the boil, then stir in the tamarind pulp. Add a splash of water if the curry is too thick, reduce the heat and simmer for about 10 minutes or until the crabs are cooked and the curry is fragrant. Remove from the heat, season to taste and serve hot with rice.

Macchi Masala

| NORTH INDIAN FISH CURRY |

In the north, many curries have warming spices such as cardamom and cloves whereas tamarind and coconut are more popular in the south. The south also uses more chilli and mustard seeds than the north to make diners perspire and help them cool down in the scorching southern heat.

Serves 4 PREPARATION ⟶ *15 minutes* COOKING *30 minutes*

2 tablespoons vegetable oil
1 onion, finely chopped
1 teaspoon ginger-garlic paste *(page 45)*
1 teaspoon tomato purée
2 tomatoes, chopped
2 bay leaves
3 cloves
3 green cardamom pods, seeds crushed and husks discarded
1 teaspoon ground coriander
1 teaspoon ground turmeric
½ teaspoon medium-hot red chilli powder
½ teaspoon crushed black peppercorns
600g firm-fleshed skinless fish fillets such as salmon,
    bream or hake
2 teaspoons lemon juice
a small handful of fresh coriander leaves, chopped, to serve
salt
boiled rice *(pages 78–79)*, to serve

1 Heat half the oil in a saucepan over a medium heat, add the onion and fry for 7–8 minutes until very soft. Add the ginger-garlic paste then the tomato purée and tomatoes. Fry for 5 minutes until mushy, then transfer the mixture to a blender with enough water to cover and blitz to a fine purée.

2 Heat the remaining oil in a frying pan over a high heat and add the bay leaves, cloves and cardamom seeds. When they sizzle, add the ground spices and a splash of water. When the water evaporates, the spices will have turned dark and the oil will have separated.

3 Pour in the purée and bring to the boil. Rinse out the blender with a little water and add this to the pan. Season with salt and add the fish. Bring to the boil, reduce the heat and simmer for 7–8 minutes until the fish is tender.

4 Season to taste, drizzle over the lemon juice, sprinkle with the coriander and serve hot with rice.

Masor Tenga

| TANGY FISH CURRY |

This signature fish curry from Assam is simple and flavourful. It is traditionally made with a spiny, white-fleshed river fish called 'rohu' or 'rui maach', which is available frozen in some Bangladeshi food shops around the world. If you can't get hold of it then you can use coley or bream instead. *Serves 4* PREPARATION ⟶ *15 minutes* COOKING *30 minutes*

4 steaks of firm-fleshed fish, such as rohu, coley or bream
1 teaspoon ground turmeric
4 large tomatoes
2 tablespoons mustard oil
½ teaspoon fenugreek seeds
2 fresh green chillies, slit lengthways
2 tablespoons lemon juice
a handful of chopped fresh coriander leaves, to garnish
salt
boiled rice *(pages 78–79)*, to serve

1 Rub the fish with half the turmeric and salt to season, then set aside while you prepare the remaining ingredients.

2 Cut each tomato in half and grate the cut sides on the coarsest side of a grater over a bowl. Discard the skin.

3 Heat the mustard oil in a heavy-based frying pan to smoking point, then reduce the heat and fry the fish for 2–3 minutes on both sides to seal and partially cook. Remove with a slotted spoon and set aside to drain on kitchen paper.

4 Add the fenugreek seeds to the same oil. When they change colour, add the chillies and the grated tomatoes.

5 Mix in the remaining turmeric and cook for 5 minutes until the curry thickens and the tomatoes are cooked. Pour in 200ml water and the lemon juice and season with salt.

6 When the curry bubbles, slip the fish in and cook for 8–10 minutes (depending on which fish you are using) over a medium heat until the fish is tender. Season to taste and serve hot, sprinkled with coriander leaves and with rice alongside.

EGGS

Eggs, variously called 'anda', 'baida', 'muttai', 'deem' or 'guddu' in India, are considered to be non-vegetarian and are therefore not eaten by some people, such as the Jains or vegetarian Hindus, for religious reasons. Classic vegetarian recipes would never even use eggs as binding agents, as it would put some people off eating these foods. There is a big market for eggless cakes in India!

Eggs have been eaten in India for many centuries. There are references to their use in texts such as the *Ain-i-Akbari* (1590 AD), the memoirs of the Mughal emperor Akbar, where a recipe for 'Mussaman' contains fowl, minced meat, ghee, eggs and spices.

The *Charaka Samhita* (c.900–600 BCE), an ancient text about Ayurveda, says in its Foods and Drinks chapter, 'eggs of swans, chakora, hens, peacocks and sparrows are useful in diminished semen, cough, heart disease and injuries. They are sweet, not causing burning sensation and immediately strength-promoting.' Eggs are still considered energy-giving and a cheap source of protein.

Today, eggs are seen everywhere: in curries, scrambled with spices or simply boiled, sliced and eaten with salt and chilli. I was told some time ago that when driving through Indian towns and villages, if you see a street stall selling boiled eggs with spices, there is every possibility that there is a bar serving local liquor close by! These are basic establishments that serve cheap alcohol and quick snacks and are often hidden away from main streets. In some restaurants the term 'pure veg' is used – this means that there are no alcohol or eggs on the premises.

In India, eggs are most commonly associated with Irani cafés and the Parsi community. Irani cafés were set up by migrants from Iran who came to Bombay in the nineteenth century for economic reasons, much later than the Parsis who fled religious persecution in Iran. The cafés, with their distinctive décor, were opened on street corners, as Hindu shopkeepers believed them to be inauspicious. The ancient Hindu system of Vastu Shastra (possibly developed around 3000 BCE) describes the 'science of architecture' and suggests how to build living or working spaces in keeping with nature. The shape of a plot of land was crucial to the success of the owner – a square plot was considered lucky, whereas a triangular one, as on a street corner, would bring obstructions in one's business and life. These principles are still followed by traditionalists today. However, the Iranians held no such views and felt that these locations would be good for business as customers from two streets could see these cafés and start to frequent them. They were open-fronted, welcoming places, suited to the common man, typically furnished with bentwood chairs (supposedly too uncomfortable to allow one to linger over one's chai) and marble-topped wooden tables. The owner sat behind a counter near the entrance and at the back was the kitchen that created a menu that has lasted to this day, and is the mainstay of many students' diets in the city. One of the most popular items on the menu still remains the omelette or 'amlate'. Made by adding finely diced onions and chillies to eggs, it's oily, frilly and intense and served with crusty bread called 'pav'. Although not a gourmet dish by any chef's standards, it is a delicacy etched into the memory of almost everyone who spends their teenage years in Mumbai.

The Parsis use eggs in wedding rituals as food as well as ritual objects. An egg is waved over the groom and smashed to the floor, signifying the destruction of evil forces that may surround him. Their cuisine has many dishes based on eggs or 'eedu'. On the Parsi New Year day ('Navroze'), Indian Parsis serve a traditional sweet called 'sev' (see page 346), which is vermicelli cooked in ghee with lots of nuts and served with a boiled egg. My Parsi friends say that every home has 'kanda, papeta and eedu'– onion, potato and eggs – to cook up into a quick tasty meal for unexpected guests.

ತನ್ ಚಿಕನ್ ಸೆ

CHOOSING EGGS

Most Indian recipes use chicken eggs but duck and quail eggs are both eaten in states such as
Kerala, Tamil Nadu and Maharashtra.

Barn eggs come from hens that are housed in buildings with a couple of storeys, with enough
space to move around freely. Free-range eggs are from hens that are let out into the open during
daylight hours. Organic eggs are produced by hens raised on an organic diet and allowed to roam
on organically farmed land. I use any of these but don't tend to buy eggs from caged hens for ethical
reasons. In India, some people in villages or small townships keep chickens for eggs as well as for
their meat. Often, in small villages, strictly vegetarian communities such as some Hindus, live a
distance away from non-vegetarian communities.

Once bought, make sure to use eggs before their
'best before' date. Use these methods to test if they
are fresh:

- Immerse the egg into a bowl of cold water. If the egg
sinks to the bottom of the bowl and lies on its side,
it is very fresh. If it sinks but stands on one end, it is
still fresh enough to eat. If the egg floats, it is not a
good idea to eat it.

- When you crack open an egg, a firm, bright yolk
indicates freshness whereas a flabby pale one means
the egg is stale.

Muttai Poriyal

| SOUTH INDIAN SCRAMBLED EGGS |

This makes a quick and easy dinner served with roti or toast. Indian recipes often have a 'tempering', where spices, herbs or lentils are fried in hot oil and poured over a finished dish or start the cooking of a dish. The addition of lentils to the tempering here gives texture to this dish. It is eaten for breakfast, with a main meal or as a snack between meals in Tamil Nadu. *Serves 4*

PREPARATION → *10 minutes* COOKING *15 minutes*

4 large free-range eggs
½ teaspoon medium-hot red chilli powder
½ teaspoon ground turmeric
½ teaspoon freshly ground black pepper
1 tablespoon vegetable oil
1 teaspoon brown or black mustard seeds
1 teaspoon split, skinless black lentils (urad dal),
    washed and drained
1 onion, finely diced
1 fresh green chilli, diced
1 tomato, diced
salt
Rotis *(pages 108–109)* or toast, to serve

1 Crack the eggs into a mixing bowl and add the chilli powder and ground turmeric. Add the pepper, season with salt and beat until fluffy.

2 Heat the oil in a frying pan over a high heat and add the mustard seeds. When they start to pop, stir in the urad dal. When the dal begins to turn brown, add the onion and fry for 7–8 minutes until soft. Stir in the diced chilli and tomato and cook for 3–4 minutes until very soft.

3 Pour in the eggs and quickly scramble them with a ladle. You can cook them as soft or hard as you like, but make sure that they set so that the spices get cooked. Serve hot with rotis or toast.

Ande Ki Bhurji

| SPICY SCRAMBLED EGGS |

This dish has various names in India. The Parsis call it 'akoori', some Muslim communities call it 'khagina', and others call it 'egg bhurji'. It is a popular breakfast or street food eaten with Western-style bread or Indian ones such as rotis, parathas or pooris. Indians generally prefer their food well done as they are not fond of a slimy texture – scrambled eggs will always be well cooked and even a bit hard. *Serves 4* PREPARATION → *10 minutes* COOKING *10 minutes*

6 large free-range eggs
1 tablespoon vegetable oil
1 large onion, finely chopped
1 teaspoon ginger-garlic paste *(page 45)*
1–2 fresh green chillies, finely chopped
    (depending on how hot you want it)
2 tomatoes, finely chopped
a handful of fresh coriander leaves, finely chopped
salt and freshly ground black pepper
bread, to serve

1 Season the eggs with salt and pepper and beat until fluffy.

2 Heat the oil in a frying pan over a high heat, add the onion and fry for 5–6 minutes until soft, then add the ginger-garlic paste, chillies and tomatoes. Cook for a few minutes until well blended.

3 Add the beaten eggs and coriander and cook over a low–medium heat, stirring them as they cook, for about 3 minutes. Indian cooks prefer their eggs very well done but you can stop cooking them as soon as you achieve the texture you prefer. Season to taste and serve at once with bread.

TAMOTA PAR EEDU – Baked Eggs with Tomato

My friend Prochy says that when the non-vegetarian Parsis fled from Persia to the west coast of Gujarat, they found a land where meat was not widely available and chickens were reared only for household kitchens. Eggs were plentiful so they combined vegetables with eggs to make a large number of new dishes such as this. *Serves 4* PREPARATION → *15 minutes* COOKING *45 minutes*

YOU WILL NEED:

8 ripe, red tomatoes, washed and scored on one end with an 'X'
2 tablespoons vegetable oil
2 onions, finely diced
1 teaspoon ginger-garlic paste (page 45)
1 teaspoon ground turmeric
½ teaspoon medium-hot red chilli powder
1 tablespoon finely chopped fresh coriander leaves
1 tablespoon malt vinegar
1 teaspoon caster sugar
4 large free-range eggs
salt and freshly ground black pepper
Rotis (pages 108–109) or boiled rice (pages 78–79), to serve

1 Preheat the oven to 200°C/gas mark 6.

2 Bring a saucepan of water to the boil and blanch the tomatoes for a couple of minutes until the skin begins to peel away, then plunge the tomatoes into cold water and peel off the skins. Roughly chop the flesh, retaining the seeds.

3 Heat the oil in a frying pan over a high heat, add the onions and fry for 7–8 minutes until very soft. Stir in the ginger-garlic paste and cook for a couple of minutes, then add the turmeric, chilli powder and coriander leaves. Cook for 1 minute, add the chopped tomatoes and season with salt and pepper. Cook for 5–6 minutes until thick and well blended.

4 Add the vinegar and sugar and continue cooking until the dish is almost dry. Transfer to an ovenproof flan dish and make four evenly spaced dips in the mixture with the back of a ladle. Break an egg into each hollow and bake in the oven for 20 minutes or until the eggs have set. Remove from the oven and serve hot with rotis or rice.

Kodi Guddu Beerakaya Kura

| EGG AND RIDGE GOURD CURRY |

This curry from Andhra Pradesh makes clever use of eggs and vegetables – ridge gourd or 'beerakaya' – in one recipe. You can use a watery vegetable such as courgette if you cannot find ridge gourd. The ridges are sliced off and can be made into a delicious chutney to serve on the side.

Serves 4 PREPARATION → *15 minutes* COOKING *25 minutes*

2 tablespoons vegetable oil
1 teaspoon black or brown mustard seeds
½ teaspoon cumin seeds
8–10 fresh or 10 dried curry leaves
1 teaspoon white urad dal, washed and drained
1 large onion, finely diced
3 garlic cloves, finely diced
2 fresh green chillies, slit lengthways
2 ridge gourd or courgettes, peeled and cut into 3cm pieces
1 teaspoon ground turmeric
1 teaspoon garam masala *(page 64)*
4 large free-range eggs, hard-boiled and shelled
100ml full-fat milk
salt
boiled rice *(pages 78–79)* or Rotis *(pages 108–109)*, to serve

1 Heat the oil in a frying pan over a high heat and add the mustard seeds. When they begin to pop, add the cumin seeds, curry leaves (standing back from the pan if using fresh leaves, as they will splutter) and urad dal.

2 When they begin to darken, tip in the onion and fry for 7–8 minutes until very soft. Stir in the garlic and chillies.

3 Add the ridge gourd or courgettes, turmeric and garam masala. Season with salt. The gourd or courgette will release its juices as the curry comes to the boil. Reduce the heat, cover and simmer for 10–12 minutes, until the gourd or courgette is tender.

4 Make shallow slits along the sides of the eggs and stir them into the curry. Pour in the milk, bring to the boil, season to taste and serve hot with rice or rotis.

Baida Masala

| SIMPLE INDIAN EGG CURRY |

This is often a simple Sunday night dinner in my home. It is real comfort food when the family is still a bit full from a heavy lunch! We eat it with rotis but it also goes well with rice or other breads. I'm always surprised that Indian restaurants don't serve this very popular family-style dish – it just goes to show how different home and restaurant cooking styles are! *Serves 4* PREPARATION → *15 minutes* COOKING *25 minutes*

2 tablespoons vegetable oil
½ teaspoon cumin seeds
2 large onions, finely diced
1 teaspoon ginger-garlic paste *(page 45)*
2 fresh ripe red tomatoes, chopped, or ½ x 400g can of chopped tomatoes
1 tablespoons tomato purée
½ teaspoon ground turmeric
½ teaspoon medium-hot red chilli powder
1 teaspoon garam masala *(page 64)*
4 large free-range eggs, hard-boiled, shelled and halved
a small handful of fresh coriander leaves, chopped, to garnish
salt
Rotis *(pages 108–109)*, boiled rice *(pages 78–79)* or other bread, to serve

1 Heat the oil in a frying pan over a high heat and add the cumin seeds. When they start to darken, tip in the onions and fry for 8–10 minutes until very soft.

2 Stir in the ginger-garlic paste, tomatoes and tomato purée. Cook for a couple of minutes then add the ground spices. Mix well and pour in a couple of tablespoons of water (not needed if using tinned tomatoes). Bring to the boil then reduce the heat and simmer for 4–5 minutes until the oil separates.

3 Gently place the halved eggs in the curry. Heat through, season to taste, sprinkle with the coriander and serve hot with rotis, rice or bread.

Tamater Ka Kut

| EGGS IN TOMATO CURRY |

2 tablespoons gram flour
6 large ripe, red tomatoes, washed and scored
    on one end with an 'X', or 1 x 400g can
    of chopped tomatoes
2 tablespoons vegetable oil
1 teaspoon cumin seeds
7–8 fresh or 10 dried curry leaves
2 garlic cloves, minced
1 tablespoon tomato purée
1 teaspoon ground turmeric
1 teaspoon ground coriander
½ teaspoon medium-hot red chilli powder
4 large free-range eggs, hard-boiled, shelled
    and slit along the sides
1 tablespoon chopped fresh coriander leaves,
    to garnish
salt
boiled rice *(pages 78–79)*, biryani or bread,
    to serve

This famous Hyderabadi dish is also known as 'Anday ka salan' and is a rich tomato and egg curry flavoured with spices. It is eaten with rice, biryani or bread. I add tomato purée along with blanched fresh tomatoes for a deeper colour and flavour, as in India the tomatoes would be sun-ripened and more intense in flavour. *Serves 4* PREPARATION ⟶ *15 minutes* COOKING *30 minutes*

1 Heat a frying pan over a medium heat, add the gram flour and toast it for 8–10 minutes until it changes colour, stirring to prevent it from scorching.

2 Meanwhile, bring a saucepan of water to the boil and blanch the scored tomatoes for a couple of minutes until the skin begins to peel away. Plunge the tomatoes into cold water and peel off the skins. Chop the tomatoes roughly, discarding the seeds, then put them (or the canned tomatoes, if using instead of fresh) in a blender along with the toasted gram flour and enough water to just cover the mixture. Blitz to a fine purée.

3 Heat the oil in a frying pan over a high heat and add the cumin seeds. When they start to darken add the curry leaves (standing back from the pan if using fresh leaves, as they will splutter). Tip in the garlic and fry for 30 seconds until golden.

4 Add the tomato purée and fry for a few seconds, then pour in the purée from the blender. Rinse out the blender with a couple of tablespoons of water and add this to the curry.

5 Sprinkle in the ground spices and season with salt. Bring to the boil, stirring frequently to prevent the flour in the sauce from sticking to the bottom of the pan, and cook for 5–6 minutes.

6 When the sauce has thickened, taste the curry. You shouldn't be able to taste raw flour, and the curry should have a nutty aroma. Add the eggs and continue cooking for a couple of minutes, then remove from the heat, season to taste, sprinkle with the coriander and serve hot with rice, biryani or bread.

Dimer Jhol

| LIGHT BENGALI EGG CURRY |

There are so many versions of this curry – thinner ones are called 'jhol' and the slightly thicker ones are 'dalna'. Bengalis, unlike many other Indian cooks, fry hard-boiled eggs with a little turmeric and salt before adding them to a curry. This gives them a golden skin which is slightly chewy.

Serves 4 PREPARATION → *15 minutes* COOKING *45 minutes*

4 large free-range eggs, hard-boiled, shelled and each slit
    4 times down the sides
2 potatoes, peeled and quartered
1 teaspoon ground turmeric
2 tablespoons mustard or vegetable oil
2 fresh green chillies, slit lengthways
2 large ripe tomatoes, halved and grated on the cut sides
    (discard the skins)
1 teaspoon grated fresh root ginger
a small handful of fresh coriander leaves, chopped, to garnish
salt
boiled rice *(pages 78–79)*, to serve

1 Rub the eggs and potatoes with half the turmeric and salt to season.
2 If using mustard oil, heat it to smoking point in a frying pan or heat the vegetable oil. Reduce the heat, add the potatoes and fry for 7–8 minutes until they start to turn golden, then drain and set aside on a plate lined with kitchen paper.
3 Fry the eggs in the same pan for 4–5 minutes until they crisp up slightly. Drain on kitchen paper and set aside.
4 Fry the chillies in the oil for 30 seconds until they change colour, then add the grated tomatoes and ginger. Season with salt, bring to the boil over a high heat, then add the remaining turmeric. When the mixture has almost dried up, pour in 100ml water and return to the boil. The oil will begin to separate.
5 Return the potatoes to the pan and cook for 20–25 minutes until done. Test this by inserting a skewer or small knife into the thickest part of a potato. Keep adding water as necessary until the curry has a pouring consistency.
6 Add the eggs to the pan, heat through, season to taste and sprinkle with the coriander. Serve with rice.

Baide Ka Kheema

| SPICED MINCED EGGS |

This street food snack can be eaten as a main meal with some crusty bread. You can make the curry as thin or thick as you want – a thin one is delicious to dunk your bread into! A thick one can be rolled into a roti with some salad.

Serves 4 PREPARATION → *15 minutes* COOKING *25 minutes*

1 tablespoon vegetable oil
1 bay leaf
¼ teaspoon freshly ground black pepper
2 onions, finely diced
1 teaspoon ginger-garlic paste
    (page 45)
1 fresh green chilli, diced
1 tablespoon tomato purée
1 tomato, diced
½ teaspoon ground turmeric
1 teaspoon ground coriander
4 large free-range eggs, hard-boiled and shelled
a small handful of fresh coriander leaves, chopped, to garnish
salt
crusty bread or Rotis *(pages 108–109)*, to serve

1 Heat the oil in a frying pan over a high heat and add the bay leaf and pepper. When they start to sizzle, add the onions. Cook for 7–8 minutes until very soft, adding a pinch of salt to hasten the process. Tip in the ginger-garlic paste and chilli and cook for 1 minute, then stir in the tomato purée and diced tomato and cook for 2–3 minutes until mushy.
2 Sprinkle in the ground spices and cook for a couple of minutes, adding a couple of tablespoons of water to prevent the mixture from sticking to the bottom of the pan. If you want a thinner curry, add more water.
3 While the curry is simmering, grate the hard-boiled eggs, chop them very finely or mash them with a potato masher. Add the eggs to the pan and season with salt.
4 Sprinkle with the fresh coriander and serve hot with bread or rotis.

Muttai Kuzhumbu

| EGG DROP CURRY |

2 tablespoons vegetable oil

1 teaspoon fennel seeds

2 dried red chillies, broken in half and seeds
　　shaken out

1 onion, sliced

1 tomato, chopped

1 teaspoon ginger-garlic paste *(page 45)*

1 teaspoon split gram lentils (chana dal),
　　washed and soaked in hot water
　　for 30 minutes

4 tablespoons freshly grated coconut

1 teaspoon black or brown mustard seeds

7–8 fresh or 10 dried curry leaves

1 tablespoon tamarind pulp *(page 418)*
　　or shop-bought tamarind paste

1 teaspoon ground turmeric

4 large free-range eggs

a small handful of fresh coriander leaves,
　　chopped, to garnish

salt and freshly ground black pepper

boiled rice *(pages 78–79)*, to serve

This south Indian recipe uses split gram lentils (chana dal) for thickening. You can add vegetables such as courgettes, carrots or peas just after adding the tamarind and cook them for 8–10 minutes until tender to make the dish more substantial. *Serves 4* PREPARATION —➔ *15 minutes, plus 30 minutes soaking time* COOKING *40 minutes*

1 Heat half the oil in a frying pan over a high heat, add the fennel seeds and red chillies and fry for 30–40 seconds. When they start to change colour, add the onion and cook for 7–8 minutes. When the onion becomes translucent, add the tomato and ginger-garlic paste.

2 Drain the chana dal and add it to the pan. Cook for 7–8 minutes until the tomatoes have completely disintegrated and the lentils have softened.

3 Tip the mixture into a blender along with the coconut and enough water to cover the mixture, and blitz to a smooth purée.

4 Heat the remaining oil in a frying pan over a high heat and add the mustard seeds. When they begin to pop, add the curry leaves (taking care if they are fresh as they will splutter) and tamarind pulp. Sprinkle in the turmeric and a couple of tablespoons of water. Cook over a high heat for 2–3 minutes until the oil separates.

5 Pour in the purée from the blender then rinse out the blender with a little water and pour this in as well. Season with salt and pepper.

6 Gently break the eggs into the curry one at a time and let them poach. Do not stir. Cover the pan and cook for 3–4 minutes. As soon as the eggs have set, remove from the heat. Sprinkle with the coriander and serve hot with rice.

Baida Rashida

| POTATO AND EGG CURRY |

This is a dish we had as a special treat from a nearby restaurant when I was growing up in Bombay, when going to a restaurant or getting a takeaway was not as common as it is today. This is my version of it, made here with potatoes, rather than chicken, which is what the restaurant had on their menu. I love the texture of fluffy potatoes combined with the chewy bits of egg. *Serves 4*

PREPARATION → *15 minutes* COOKING *40 minutes*

2 potatoes, peeled and quartered
1 teaspoon ground turmeric
2 tablespoons vegetable oil
2.5cm piece of cinnamon stick
2 onions, finely diced
2 teaspoons ginger-garlic paste *(page 45)*
2 tablespoons tomato purée
1 teaspoon ground coriander
½ teaspoon medium-hot red chilli powder
1 teaspoon garam masala *(page 64)*
2 tablespoons single cream
3 large free-range eggs, hard-boiled, shelled and finely diced
a few sprigs of fresh coriander leaves, chopped, to garnish
salt
Parathas *(pages 120–121)*, Rotis *(pages 108–109)* or
    Naans *(pages 110–113)*, to serve

1 Rub the potatoes with half the turmeric and salt to season.
2 Heat the oil in a frying pan over a high heat, add the cinnamon stick and fry until it darkens, then add the onions and fry for 7–8 minutes until very soft. Stir in the ginger-garlic paste, add the potatoes and fry for a few minutes until golden, reducing the heat to medium if they stick to the bottom of the pan.
3 Stir in the tomato purée and ground spices, season with salt, pour in 200ml water and bring to the boil. Cover, reduce the heat and simmer for 15–20 minutes until the potatoes are cooked, adding a little water if the curry becomes too dry.
4 Fold in the cream and boiled eggs and season to taste. Bring to the boil, sprinkle with the coriander and serve hot with parathas, rotis or naans.

Bheeda Par Eeda

| OKRA WITH EGGS |

This is another classic Parsi dish that combines vegetables with eggs. Indians don't like their okra slimy and the way to avoid this is to make sure that the okra is completely dry before cooking it. Some cooks break the eggs over the okra, leaving the yolks whole, some separate the yolks and whites, beat the whites, then add them with the yolks, and others make this version, that resembles a frittata. I like this version as it makes quite a hearty meal, especially when served with a couple of bread rolls. *Serves 4*

PREPARATION → *15 minutes* COOKING *40 minutes*

300g okra, washed and dried overnight
    so they are completely dry
1 tablespoon vegetable oil
1 onion, finely diced
1 teaspoon ginger-garlic paste *(page 45)*
½ teaspoon ground turmeric
½ teaspoon medium-hot red chilli powder
1 teaspoon ground coriander
4 large free-range eggs, beaten and seasoned
    with salt and pepper
salt and freshly ground black pepper
bread rolls, to serve (optional)

1 Top and tail the okra then cut them into 2.5cm pieces.
2 Heat the oil in a frying pan over a high heat, add the onion and fry for 7–8 minutes until soft. Add the ginger-garlic paste and cook for a further minute, then stir in the okra, season with salt and pepper and cook over a medium heat for 8–10 minutes until it starts to soften and change colour. Look for a slight give when you press a piece of okra with the back of a ladle.
3 Sprinkle in the ground spices, mix gently and cook for a couple of minutes over a medium heat.
4 Transfer the okra to a clean frying pan and pour over the beaten eggs. Cook over a medium heat, without stirring, until the eggs are set. Slice the frittata and serve hot with bread rolls, if you like.

Nargisi Kofta Curry

| CURRIED EGGS ENCASED IN LAMB MINCE |

For the koftas

500g lamb mince

5 large free-range eggs, 4 hard-boiled and
    shelled, 1 beaten

1 onion, finely diced

1 teaspoon ginger-garlic paste *(page 45)*

1 fresh green chilli, minced

2 teaspoons garam masala *(page 64)*

3 tablespoons gram flour

vegetable oil, for deep-frying

salt

For the curry

2 onions, finely diced

1 teaspoon ginger-garlic paste *(page 45)*

3 ripe tomatoes blitzed to a purée in the
    blender or ½ x 400g can of
    chopped tomatoes

1 teaspoon ground turmeric

½ teaspoon medium-hot red chilli powder

1 teaspoon ground coriander

1 teaspoon ground cumin

3 tablespoons full-fat yogurt

a few sprigs of fresh coriander leaves,
    chopped, to garnish

Pulao Rice *(page 82)* or Naans *(pages 110–113)*,
    to serve

This Muslim party dish has a layer of meat neatly wrapped around an egg which is then deep-fried. As it can be a little tricky to make, it is reserved for festive occasions, like most fried foods. Nargis is the narcissus flower and this kofta is likened to the beautiful white and yellow bloom against dark brown soil. This can be served with a pulao rice or naan. *Serves 4*

PREPARATION→ *20 minutes* COOKING *1 hour*

1 Combine the mince, beaten egg, onion, ginger-garlic paste, chilli, garam masala, gram flour and salt to season in a mixing bowl. Divide the mixture into four equal portions. Take one portion of mince and wrap it evenly around one of the cooled, hard-boiled eggs. Repeat with the remaining mince and eggs.

2 Heat the oil in a deep frying pan over a high heat. Deep-fry the koftas for 5–6 minutes each until golden brown. Remove with a slotted spoon and place on a tray lined with kitchen paper to drain.

3 Ladle 2 tablespoons of oil from the frying pan into a separate pan over a high heat. Add the onions and fry for 7–8 minutes until soft, then tip in the ginger-garlic paste and the puréed or tinned tomatoes and cook for 3–4 minutes. Sprinkle in the ground spices and a couple of tablespoons of water. Season with salt and cook over a medium heat for 4–5 minutes until the oil begins to separate.

4 Fold in the yogurt. Cut each kofta in half lengthways and place them in the curry. Season to taste, bring to the boil and serve hot, garnished with the coriander, alongside pulao rice or naan.

DAIRY

LASSI IS MADE BY BLENDING YOGURT WITH WATER, MILK AND SPICES
AND IS POPULAR ACROSS SOUTH ASIA AND WITH SOUTH ASIAN COMMUNITIES ACROSS THE WORLD.

Milk is eaten in some form in every part of India. Milk is drunk on its own or flavoured with spices, flowers and herbs. It is also made into products that are curdled, as in paneer or chhena, non-curdled, such as ghee and khoya (made by cooking milk until it solidifies), or fermented, as in yogurt.

There is evidence that people of the Indus Valley civilisation bred cattle – their famous seal of a humped bull has been studied by scholars all over the world who have come to the conclusion that these ancient people owned cattle for milk and meat.

Vedic literature is full of references to milk. The *Rigveda* (c.1500–1200 BC) says 'who steals the milch-cow's milk away, O Agni, – tear off the heads of such with fierce fury.' The *Sushruta Samhita*, a sixth-century text about Ayurveda, lists the milk of several animals as being good for health. These include cow, camel and elephant, but cow's milk is considered the best 'rasayana-dravya' – substance that heals, rejuvenates and prolongs life.

Dairy products have a special place in Hindu religious ritual. The cow, as a giver of milk, is considered sacred. In a ritual called 'Abhisheka', images or idols of gods and goddesses are bathed with water, yogurt, milk, honey, rose water and perfume. Milk becomes a part of the blessed food 'panchamrit' or five nectars: milk, yogurt, honey, ghee and sugar syrup.

Regional food practices in India vary depending on many factors, including the climate. In south India, which is close to the Equator, yogurt is eaten with every meal, whereas in north India, which has cooler weather, people believe that yogurt should not be eaten during cold evenings. Much of the southern peninsula drinks a light, digestive drink called 'chaas', 'mor' or 'taak', which is made with yogurt and water. The north drinks a heavier version of this called 'lassi'. Rajasthan, a desert state, has camel dairy farms and the milk as well as milk products such as ice cream are consumed.

Ayurveda suggests incompatible combinations – milk should not be eaten with fish, for example, as they require different rates of digestion. Much of India's milk comes from buffalos. Buffalo milk has a higher fat and protein content but less cholesterol than cow's milk. It is heavier and therefore keeps you feeling full for longer.

MILK IS EATEN IN SOME FORM IN EVERY PART OF INDIA. IT IS MADE INTO PRODUCTS THAT
ARE CURDLED, AS IN PANEER OR CHHENA, NON-CURDLED, SUCH AS GHEE AND KHOYA,
OR FERMENTED, AS IN YOGURT.

CREAM

Cream is considered a luxurious ingredient in Indian cooking.
It is reserved for festive or party dishes and restaurant fare.
Contrary to the belief in the West that many Indian curries
contain cream, it is used very little in everyday home cooking.
A special treat may be cream mixed with sugar and spread on
toast, called 'malai toast', but this is not a regular breakfast.

In restaurant curries, the word 'shahi' or royal, often
denotes the presence of cream. Shahi Paneer (page 264), Shahi
Kofta and Shahi Tukde (page 451), a bread-based dessert, are
all rich and creamy dishes.

Most milk in India is delivered each morning to your
door. As it is a hot country, it has to be boiled before being
cooled and refrigerated. The cooling milk develops a skin of
cream called 'malai' or 'saay' and the fattier the milk is, the
denser this layer will be. Buffalo milk produces a thick layer
of cream. When this milk is refrigerated, the layer of cream
becomes even denser.

BUTTER

Homemade butter, called 'makhhan' or 'loni', is a delicacy
in India. It is soft and white and is traditionally eaten with
breads like 'Makke ki roti' (Punjabi corn bread) or 'Bhakri'
(Maharashtrian millet bread) – see Bajre Ki Bhakri on
page 117.

It is mentioned in many folk stories and is believed
to be the favourite food of India's most-loved Hindu god,
Krishna. Stories of him stealing butter from his mother's
kitchen delight devotees although there is a deeper spiritual
significance. Butter is the essence of milk and symbolises the
core of our beings. In relishing it, Krishna says we should
go deep into ourselves and understand the purity that
lies therein.

Although packs of commercial yellow butter are
available in India, many homes also make their own. This is
because homemade butter is further cooked into ghee.

Cream or 'malai' is collected over a few days and a
starter culture of yogurt is added to it. When the full-fat
yogurt has set, it is churned with a wooden instrument

called a 'ravi', 'mathani' or 'ghotni'. This is a slim stick with
a wooden star-shaped churning bit on one end. The stick
is held between the palms and rolled in small semi-circular
movements. Where the quantity of cream is large, the stick is
coiled into a rope that is pulled one end at a time to create the
same movement.

This movement separates the butter and in India, the
liquid left behind is buttermilk called 'chhaas' or 'mattha'.
This is sometimes used to make a yogurt curry called 'kadhi'
(see pages 256 and 258) or drunk on its own, seasoned with
salt or flavoured with fresh coriander and chilli.

GHEE

Ghee is clarified butter that is made by cooking butter to
evaporate any moisture and caramelise the milk solids that
can be strained off. In India, ghee ('ghrita' in Sanskrit) has
been regarded, since Vedic times, as an unparalleled cooking
fat. Hindus consider fire to be the purest element and ghee
by the very nature of it being cooked over fire makes it
ritually pure.

Traditional Hindu cookery differentiates between
'kaccha' and 'pukka' foods, kaccha being those that were
cooked in water and were to be consumed in the kitchen.
Pukka foods were cooked in ghee and could be taken out of
the kitchen for public consumption. These rules were based
more on health, hygiene and practicality but, in time, became
religious practices of purity. This is why temple foods that
are distributed to devotees or sweets that can be bought from
shops are cooked in ghee and are often very sweet.

Ayurvedic healing considers ghee to be strengthening
and digestive. Some western research shows that eating a little
bit of ghee, typically less than a couple of tablespoons a day,
can reduce the risk of cardiovascular disease, but increasing
this amount can lead to elevated cholesterol levels. At any
rate, eating ghee in a hot tropical climate and a cold one must
make a difference as it is, after all, a saturated fat. I make ghee
with butter from grass-fed cows as this provides good levels of
omega 3.

Many people outside India believe that all good Indian cooking must begin with ghee but this is a myth. Most Indian cooks use plant oils for everyday cooking and use small amounts of ghee as a drizzling fat over rice and bread or for special sweets and desserts.

One of my best food memories is of coming home from school in Bombay to a house that smelled of heaven. My grandmother would be making ghee, the scent of which was pure, buttery and rich. She would sometimes add a fresh turmeric leaf or a betel nut leaf for flavour. Fresh turmeric leaves have a floral fragrance while betel nut ones smell grassy. Today, the best thing about making ghee is that wonderful aroma that takes me straight back to my childhood.

YOGURT

Yogurt, 'dahi' or 'tayir' as it is called in India, is integral to Indian food. Most Indians eat it several times a week if not every day. North Indians make lassi or raita or eat it with breads called paratha, whereas in the south they finish each meal with tayir and rice. In India, yogurt is also called curd. Unlike in the West, where milk is curdled with acid to form curd in the first step towards making cheese, curd in India refers to homemade yogurt.

The taste and texture of yogurt is important. The most preferred one is mildly tart but with a sweetness that 'quenches the thirst'. It should be thick and not watery. The microflora in yogurt help digestion and in many parts of India, a meal is concluded with a thin drink called 'chaas' made by mixing a little yogurt with water. 'Chaas' is also the name given to the buttermilk left behind when butter is churned out of yogurt or cream.

Yogurt has been eaten in India since prehistoric times. The *Rigveda* mentions it as mixed with ground meal: 'The other (Pusan the Nourisher) longs for curd and meal'. The *Arthashastra* (c.350–283 BCE), a treatise on statecraft, advises how to deal with spies who offer you poisoned curd, and marinating meat with curd is mentioned in the *Ain-i-Akbari*, the Mughal emperor Akbar's memoirs.

PANEER/CHHENA

Paneer is the most commonly used cheese in Indian cooking. It is an unaged, non-melting, salt-free cheese that is made both at home as well as commercially.

The exact origin of paneer in India is unclear. It was possibly the Portuguese who introduced the art of cheesemaking into Bengal, although references to curdled milk preparations can be found in the twelfth-century text *Manasollasa* by King Someshwara, who ruled parts of south India. The Portuguese stronghold was along the west coast of India, where their influence can be seen even today in places like Goa, but they also had settlements in Bengal which never became really important.

The *Manasollasa* mentions recipes adding buttermilk to slightly warmed milk and then pouring all the separated milk into a cloth, tying and hanging the parcel so that all the water drips down. The method in which milk was curdled varied through the ages.

The Bandel cheese, introduced by the Portuguese, was made in their settlement of the same name, about 30 miles north of Kolkatta in Bengal. This unripened cow's milk cheese was made by separating the curd with the help of lemon juice, then draining it in perforated pots. It was sometimes smoked but always had lots of salt added to it to increase its shelf life. Bandel cheese is still made, but production has moved to Tarkeshwar and Bishnupur, both a distance away from Kolkatta.

Surti paneer is made in the western state of Gujarat – this is coagulated with rennet and matured in its whey. It is mostly sold locally.

Fresh cheese is called 'chhena' or 'chhana', not to be confused with chana or chickpea. The Bengalis found that the unsalted curd could be kneaded and made into various sweets by adding sugar and spices and, today, Bengali milk sweets are some of the best-known desserts in the country.

When 'chhena', which is crumbly, is pressed under heavy weights, it loses most of its moisture to become a firm, dense cheese called paneer.

Today, cooks in many parts of north India make 'chhena' at home and use it in dishes such as Bhurji (scrambled) – see page 224 – or sweets such as 'rasmalai', or buy ready-made paneer to use in dishes such as Saag Paneer (page 260) where spinach is combined with a firmer cheese. The term 'paneer' is applied loosely to homemade chhena as well, and this is made by splitting milk with an acidic liquid such as lemon juice, vinegar or citric acid. Paneer is a mostly north Indian food, used in home cooking. Over most of India, commercial paneer is expensive and is largely used in festive feasts as a vegetarian option. It can be stored in the fridge for 3–4 days or frozen for up to 1 month.

KHOYA

Variously known as 'khoya', 'khava', 'khoa', 'mava' or 'khuvaa', this is made by cooking full-fat milk, either cow's or buffalo's, until the moisture evaporates and concentrated milk solids are left behind. It is used to thicken some rich, festive curries and more importantly for making homemade and commercial sweets called 'mithai' and 'burfi'. The technique of boiling the milk over a well-regulated heat is important so that the milk does not caramelise or burn. Pure khoya is white or pale yellow in colour. Equally important is the stirring and scraping the solids from the sides of the pan back into the mixture.

Traditionally khoya can be made in three forms – 'batti khoya' is the hardest, 'daan-e-daar' ('granular') is medium soft and chewy, and 'chikna' ('sticky') has the highest moisture content. Quick, modern versions include the combination of condensed milk with cream or milk powder.

The milk is cooked into these various forms depending on the final product it will be used for.

Batti Khoya → Also called pindi khoya, this is formed when the milk is reduced until it is very dry. It is then rolled into a dough, or blocks that can be grated. The dense texture makes it perfect for sweets such as Gulab Jamun (page 466), where it is mixed with wheat flour or semolina, fried as small balls, then steeped in sweetened rose water.

Daan-e-daar khoya → This form is moister than batti and is made by stopping the cooking before the mixture reaches the 'batti' stage. Sweets such as 'kalakand' are made by combining this khoya with sugar, spices and nuts, making the most of the granular texture.

Chikna khoya → This is the most moist, sticky form of khoya, also known as 'dhap'. It is made by stopping cooking earlier than for batti or daan-e-daar khoya. Its smooth consistency is used in recipes for 'halwa' or fudge and milky desserts.

MASTERCLASS
HOW TO MAKE BUTTER

FROM MILK SKIN

1 Pour 2 litres of full-fat milk into a heavy-based saucepan and bring to the boil. Remove from the heat, leave to cool completely and refrigerate for a few hours until well chilled. This will help to create a denser 'skin' on top of the milk.

2 Remove the milk from the fridge and gently skim off the skin or 'malai' into another bowl. You will need to do this every day for 3–4 days until you get enough 'malai'. The amount of skin you get will of course depend on the fat content in the milk you are using.

3 Beat or whisk the 'malai' until you see it separating into solid butter and a milky liquid. The butter will float to the top in little cloudy bits. Strain the mixture through a sieve to collect the butter and rinse this under a gently running cold tap. Squeeze the butter with your fingers or the back of spoon to get rid of the moisture. The less wet the butter, the better it will keep. Refrigerate and consume within a couple of days.

FROM YOGURT

1 Refrigerate the 'malai' (cream). Keep going for a few days until you have enough. Bring the cream to room temperature and add a couple of teaspoons of yogurt culture. Keep the bowl in a warm place overnight to set the cream into yogurt.

2 Using a churning stick or whisk, churn the yogurt until the butter floats to the top. Strain this out, reserving the liquid which is cultured buttermilk. Wash the butter under cold running water and refrigerate. Washing out the buttermilk will prevent early spoilage. You can dunk the butter into a bowl of cold water with some ice cubes to firm it up and make washing easier. In India, some of this butter is kept to eat with breads while the rest is turned into ghee.

FROM CREAM

1 Put a carton of double or whipping cream into a large bowl and beat with a hand-held electric whisk or regular whisk until it thickens and butter begins to form. Refrigerate.

ᗰMASTERCLASS

HOW TO MAKE GHEE

YOU WILL NEED:
250g unsalted butter (get the best
    grass-fed or organic butter),
    cut into small squares
– a heavy-based saucepan
– a large spoon, for stirring
– muslin cloth
– sieve
– a 250ml clean, sterilised glass jar

Cutting the butter into cubes when making ghee ensures that it
melts quickly and evenly. COOKING *30–40 minutes*

1 Melt the butter in the saucepan over a medium heat, stirring it from time to time. You should see thick white foam developing on top of the yellow, opaque butter beneath. Keep stirring until the butter begins to simmer, then reduce the heat.

2 Simmer for 4–5 minutes without stirring. The bubbles will increase in size and number and become clearer. The milk solids will start to stick to the sides and bottom of the pan. Scrape these back into the pan to prevent them from burning and turning the ghee a dark colour.

3 The butter will begin to become clear and the solids will sit at the bottom, then the bubbles will become clearer and there will be little or no white foam left.

4 The butter will start to turn a clear golden yellow while the milk solids at the bottom begin to darken. Stir a few times to stop the solids from burning and keep a close watch. The butter will foam up a second time which indicates that it is ready to be strained.

5 Place a muslin-lined sieve over a heatproof jug and strain the ghee into the jug. Leave it to cool slightly then decant into the sterilised glass jar. Squeeze the milk solids in the muslin gently as there will still be a lot of ghee in them. These solids are sometimes mixed with sugar and eaten with rotis, but I just discard them.

6 Transfer the ghee to the fridge. It will keep well for a few months.

MASTERCLASS
HOW TO MAKE YOGURT

Almost every Indian home makes yogurt on a daily basis. Commercial pot yogurts are available only in some places and they are expensive. In a tropical climate, setting yogurt does not take more than a few hours. In colder countries, this will take longer and be successful only if the milk is placed in a warm place. People believe that the over-processing that takes place in the production of commercial products can kill the vital bacteria present in yogurt that makes it so important for good digestion.

YOU WILL NEED:
200ml full-fat milk
2 tablespoons live bio yogurt,
    at room temperature

1 Pour the milk into a saucepan and warm it only until it is hand hot.

2 Put the yogurt in a bowl and add a couple of tablespoons of the warmed milk to it. Mix well, then pour in the remaining milk and stir.

3 Cover the bowl and put it in a warm place – this is crucial – for a few hours, undisturbed, until the yogurt has set. The time it takes to set will depend mainly on the quality of the yogurt culture and the temperature.

MASTERCLASS

HOW TO MAKE CHHENA – Paneer

YOU WILL NEED:
about 1 litre full-fat milk
a few tablespoons of lemon juice
    (about 2 lemons)
– a heavy-based saucepan
– a large piece of muslin
– a deep bowl or bucket
– ladle or wooden spoon

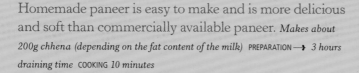

Homemade paneer is easy to make and is more delicious
and soft than commercially available paneer. *Makes about
200g chhena (depending on the fat content of the milk)* PREPARATION → *3 hours
draining time* COOKING *10 minutes*

1 Pour the milk into the saucepan and bring it to the boil. Turn the heat off and add the lemon juice. You will need to add as much lemon juice as required to separate out the solids, which will rise to the top, leaving behind a translucent, milky liquid. I usually need 1½ lemons.

2 Line the bowl or bucket with the muslin and gently pour in the contents of the saucepan. Lift up the muslin and tie the edges to make a tight parcel of cheese. Discard the liquid collected in the bowl.

3 Push the wooden spoon or ladle through the knot in the muslin and hang the parcel over the bowl or bucket, making sure that the parcel does not touch the bottom.

4 Allow the whey to drain off for about 3 hours, then unwrap and store in an airtight container. This 'chhena' will keep in the fridge for a couple of days.

5 You can cut this into soft chunks or for a denser texture, press the chhena under the heaviest object in your kitchen – mine is a large, granite pestle and mortar – for a couple of hours.

HOW TO MAKE KHOYA

Khoya is used as a base for many Indian 'burfies' or fudge-like sweets and can be flavoured with nuts, such as pistachios or almonds, or dried fruit, such as figs and dates. *Makes about 250g khoya* COOKING *about 2 hours, depending on pan and heat source used*

YOU WILL NEED:

1.25 litres full-fat milk
– a heavy-based, preferably non-stick, frying pan
– a silicone or wooden spatula or spoon

1 Pour the milk into the frying pan and bring to the boil. The width of the pan will allow faster evaporation of the milk. When it comes to the boil, reduce the heat and simmer, stirring frequently to prevent it from boiling over.

2 As the milk begins to thicken (after about 40 minutes), scrape the solids from the sides back into the pan with a spatula and stir, to prevent the milk from burning at the bottom.

3 Within about 1 hour, the milk will appear to have bits in it – this is the milk solidifying. Continue cooking over a low–medium heat, stirring frequently.

4 As the mixture dries up, you will see small bubbles on the surface – this is the remaining moisture drying up. Stir continuously. As soon as the bubbles have subsided, remove the pan from the heat. Scrape the contents of the pan into a heatproof bowl and leave to cool.

5 Refrigerate and use within 2 days. It will thicken slightly on cooling.

Sweet Khoya
| VARIATION |

A quick way to make sweet khoya for desserts.

250g milk powder
7 tablespoons condensed milk

1 Combine the ingredients in a heavy-based saucepan and cook over a medium heat for 5–6 minutes until the mixture blends to form a ball. Cool and use within two days.

Pakodewali Kadhi

| YOGURT CURRY WITH FRIED DUMPLINGS |

300g natural yogurt

1 fresh green chilli, finely chopped

½ teaspoon ground turmeric

2 teaspoons caster sugar

250g gram flour

vegetable oil, for deep-frying

1 teaspoon cumin seeds, plus extra
   for the dumplings

10 black peppercorns

6 cloves

1 medium onion, finely chopped

1 teaspoon dried fenugreek leaves
   (kasoori methi – page 393)

1 tablespoon ghee or oil

½ teaspoon medium-hot red chilli powder

salt

boiled rice (pages 78–79) and hot mango pickle,
   to serve

This dish is from the north of India, and is especially loved in Punjab and Uttar Pradesh, although other parts of India also make yogurt-based curries such as the Besan Ni Kadhi (page 258) made in Gujarat. 'Kadhis' are quick to prepare and can be made with ingredients such as gram flour, yogurt and spices that most Indian kitchens have readily available. This is why they are so popular. It is served with rice and hot mango pickle. The 'pakode' or dumplings that go into the curry can be made with a variety of vegetables such as spinach, grated carrots, fenugreek leaves or cauliflower florets.

Serves 4 PREPARATION —➤ *10 minutes* COOKING *40 minutes*

1 Whisk the yogurt with the green chilli, turmeric, sugar, salt to season and 300ml cold water.

2 Heat a frying pan over a medium heat, add 100g of the gram flour and dry-toast it for 8–10 minutes, stirring to stop it scorching, until it is slightly dark in colour. Whisk this into the yogurt mixture, making sure there are no lumps.

3 Heat 2 tablespoons of oil in a heavy-based pan over a high heat and add the cumin seeds, peppercorns and cloves. Fry the spices for a few seconds then give the yogurt mixture a good stir and pour it into the pan. Bring to the boil, reduce the heat and cook for 12–15 minutes, stirring frequently, until it reaches the consistency of a thick batter and the raw flour aroma has gone. Remove from the heat and set aside.

4 For the dumplings, combine the remaining gram flour, onion, fenugreek, a pinch of cumin seeds and add 70–80ml cold water to make a thick batter. The batter should just about drop off a spoon.

5 Heat enough vegetable oil for deep-frying in a heavy-based pan over a high heat. When it starts smoking, reduce the heat and drop in 2–3 separate teaspoons of batter at a time. Fry for 3–4 minutes until golden, remove with a slotted spoon and dip into a bowl of tepid water for 1 minute to soften them a bit. Squeeze out the water and add the dumplings to the yogurt curry. Repeat until you have used up all the batter.

6 Heat the ghee or use a tablespoon of the oil used for deep-frying the dumplings in a small pan and add the chilli powder. As soon as the spice sizzles, pour this mixture over the curry and serve without stirring with rice and hot mango pickle.

Besan Ni Kadhi

| GUJARATI-STYLE SWEET AND SOUR
YOGURT CURRY |

Gujarati-style Kadhi is made with yogurt and gram flour but usually it is lighter, whiter and sweeter than the north Indian version. Gujarat lies on the coast in western India and has very hot summers. Foods need to be rather heavily salted to replace the salt lost in perspiration and spiced to counter the heat as spices promote perspiration and help to cool the body down. In order to balance these strong flavours, Gujarati cooks add sugar or jaggery to much of their food. *Serves 4* PREPARATION → *15 minutes* COOKING *25 minutes*

2 heaped tablespoons gram flour
300g natural yogurt
2 tablespoons caster sugar
1 teaspoon chilli-ginger paste (1 fresh green chilli and
    1.5cm piece of fresh root ginger pounded together
    in a pestle and mortar or very finely chopped)
1 tablespoon vegetable oil
1 teaspoon fenugreek seeds
3 cloves
½ teaspoon crushed black peppercorns
10 fresh curry leaves
3 dried red chillies
salt

1 Heat a frying pan over a medium heat, add the gram flour and dry-toast it for 8–10 minutes, stirring to stop it scorching, until it is slightly dark in colour. Whisk this into the yogurt, making sure that there are no lumps (strain it through a sieve if necessary). Add the sugar and the chilli-ginger paste along with enough water to make a pouring consistency, and season with salt.

2 Transfer the yogurt mixture to a saucepan and cook over a low–medium heat, stirring constantly, for 10–15 minutes until thick and creamy. Do not allow the yogurt to boil. Simply whisk the sauce briskly if the curry looks like it is curdling.

3 For the tempering, heat the oil in a small pan over a high heat and add the fenugreek seeds, cloves and peppercorns. When they start to sizzle, add the curry leaves (standing back from the pan, as they will splutter) and chillies and pour into the curry. Serve warm.

Paneer Jalfrezi

| PANEER WITH GREEN PEPPERS, ONIONS
AND TOMATOES |

This is a restaurant-style dish, made either in a tomato and onion curry sauce or as a semi-dry side dish like this recipe. It looks festive and colourful and is a good addition to a party meal when entertaining friends. Use shop-bought or dense homemade paneer for this, as it needs to hold its shape. *Serves 4* PREPARATION → *15 minutes* COOKING *25 minutes*

2 tablespoons vegetable oil
1 teaspoon cumin seeds
1 large onion, thinly sliced
1 tablespoon ginger-garlic paste *(page 45)*
1 teaspoon ground turmeric
½ teaspoon medium-hot red chilli powder
1 teaspoon ground coriander
2 peppers (one red and one green),
    deseeded and thinly sliced
250g paneer, cubed
1 tomato, sliced vertically
small handful of fresh coriander leaves, chopped, to garnish
salt and freshly ground black pepper
Rotis *(pages 108–109)* or Parathas *(pages 120–121)*, to serve

1 Heat the oil in a heavy-based saucepan over a high heat, add the cumin seeds and fry for 30 seconds until slightly dark. Add the onion and fry for 7–8 minutes until soft.

2 Add the ginger-garlic paste and fry for a few seconds until well blended, then sprinkle in the ground spices and season with salt and pepper. Cook over a low heat for a few seconds then add a couple of tablespoons of water. Continue cooking for a few minutes, stirring from time to time, until the oil begins to separate.

3 Add the peppers, stir and cook for about 8 minutes until they are softened but still hold their shape, then add the paneer and mix well. Add the sliced tomato, cover, and cook for a couple of minutes until soft but not mushy.

4 Remove from the heat, garnish with the fresh coriander, and serve hot with rotis or parathas.

Muttar Paneer

| INDIAN COTTAGE CHEESE WITH PEAS |

A classic north Indian dish, this tastes best when the paneer is lightly fried before adding it to the curry. You can use fresh or frozen peas (adjust the cooking times accordingly). *Serves 4* PREPARATION —➤ *5 minutes* COOKING *20 minutes*

2 tablespoons vegetable oil

150g paneer, cubed

1 teaspoon cumin seeds

½ teaspoon dried fenugreek leaves
    (kasoori methi – *page 393* – optional)

1 large fresh green chilli, slit lengthways

1 tablespoon tomato purée

½ teaspoon ground turmeric

1 teaspoon ground coriander

200g green garden peas (fresh or frozen)

pinch of caster sugar

a handful of chopped fresh coriander leaves,
    to garnish

salt

Rotis *(pages 108–109)*, to serve

1   Heat half the oil in a non-stick frying pan over a high heat, add the paneer and lightly fry for 1–2 minutes on each side. Transfer to kitchen paper and leave to drain.

2   Add the remaining oil to the pan, add the cumin seeds and fry until they darken slightly, then sprinkle in the fenugreek leaves (if using).

3   Tip in the chilli and tomato purée, sprinkle in the ground spices, stir a few times and pour in 100ml water. Bring to the boil then simmer for 4–5 minutes until the oil begins to separate.

4   Add the peas and cook for 6–7 minutes (longer if using fresh) until tender, adding more water if necessary to cook the peas. Season with salt and add the sugar.

5   Fold in the paneer and simmer for a couple of minutes, then remove from the heat and serve hot, sprinkled with the fresh coriander, with rotis alongside.

Palak Paneer

| SPINACH WITH PANEER |

This is called 'saag paneer' in north India and in many restaurants. You can use frozen spinach instead of fresh. Some cooks lightly fry the paneer before adding it but I prefer this version where the creaminess of the spinach matches the softness of the paneer. *Serves 4*

PREPARATION —➤ *10 minutes* COOKING *25 minutes*

450g fresh spinach, washed and drained (or frozen spinach)
2 tablespoons vegetable oil
½ teaspoon cumin seeds
large pinch of dried fenugreek leaves (kasoori methi –
     page 393 – optional)
1 large onion, finely chopped
1 tablespoon ginger-garlic paste *(page 45)*
2 large tomatoes, roughly chopped
½ teaspoon medium-hot red chilli powder
½ teaspoon garam masala *(page 64)*
225g paneer, cubed
salt
Rotis *(pages 108–109)* or boiled rice *(pages 78–79)* and
     Tarka Dal *(page 279)*, to serve

1 Put the spinach in a heavy-based pan over a high heat with 3 tablespoons of water and wilt for 5 minutes. Leave to cool slightly then blitz in a blender along with the cooking water to form a thick purée. Set aside.

2 Heat the oil in a heavy-based pan over a high heat, add the cumin seeds and fry until they turn slightly dark, then tip in the fenugreek leaves (if using). Add the onion and fry for 7–8 minutes until soft, then stir in the ginger-garlic paste and tomatoes and cook over a low heat for 5 minutes until soft. Stir in the spice powders and a couple of tablespoons of water and continue cooking for a few minutes until the oil begins to separate.

3 Pour in the spinach purée, season with salt, reduce the heat and gently add the cubed paneer. Simmer for 1 minute then remove from the heat. The paneer will soften in the heat. Serve hot with roti, or as an accompaniment to rice and Tarka Dal.

Paneer Ki Bhurji

| SPICY SCRAMBLED PANEER |

This is a quick, creamy dish that can add protein to a vegetarian meal. Make it as spicy as you wish, by increasing the number of chillies. This dish is from north India where paneer is an important part of the cuisine. The Punjabis consider milk to be energising and associate its products with good, healthy eating. Yogurt, lassi (made by thinning yogurt with a bit of water) and paneer are all eaten on a regular basis. *Serves 4* PREPARATION —➤ *10 minutes, plus chhena/ paneer making time (see page 252)* COOKING *15 minutes*

1 tablespoon vegetable oil
½ teaspoon cumin seeds
1 small onion, finely chopped
2 fresh green chillies, finely chopped
½ green pepper, deseeded and finely diced
2 tomatoes, chopped
1 teaspoon ground turmeric
200g freshly-made chhena or paneer *(pages 252–253)*
a few fresh coriander leaves, chopped
salt

1 Heat the oil in a saucepan over a high heat then add the cumin seeds and fry for a minute or so until they turn dark. Add the onion, chillies and green pepper and cook for 6–7 minutes until soft.

2 Stir in the tomatoes and turmeric and cook for about 3 minutes until well blended.

3 Add the chhena or paneer and cook over a low heat for a few minutes, scrambling it into the mixture until warmed through. Season, stir in the fresh coriander and serve hot.

Mor Kulambu

| YOGURT CURRY WITH OKRA |

This curry has different versions in different southern states such as Tamil Nadu and Andhra Pradesh. In Tamil Nadu, a native vegetable – 'sundaikkai' or pea aubergine – is sometimes added. This berry-like vegetable grows in clusters and looks like green peas. In Andhra Pradesh, local chillies are added to make a spicier curry. Sometimes vegetables like okra, aubergine or onion, or even fritters made of flour and onion, similar to an onion bhajia (page 350), are added to make it more substantial. *Serves 4* PREPARATION → *20 minutes, including soaking time* COOKING *35 minutes*

2 teaspoons coriander seeds
1 teaspoon split gram lentils (chana dal)
1 tablespoon coconut oil
1 teaspoon black or brown mustard seeds
large pinch of fresh curry leaves
250g okra, top and tailed and cut into 1cm pieces
1 teaspoon ground turmeric
2 fresh green chillies
100g grated fresh or frozen coconut
thumb-sized piece of fresh root ginger, scraped and chopped
250g natural yogurt
salt
boiled rice *(pages 78–79)*, to serve

1   Soak the coriander seeds and lentils in a little warm water.
2   Meanwhile, heat the oil in a saucepan over a high heat and add the mustard seeds. When they start to pop, add the curry leaves (standing back from the pan, as they will splutter) and the okra. Season with salt and stir over a medium heat without any water for 8–10 minutes until the okra is tender. Sprinkle in half the turmeric and cook for a further minute. You should be able to cut through a piece of okra with a spoon.
3   Drain the coriander seeds and lentils and put them in a blender along with the chillies, coconut and ginger. Add enough water to barely cover the mixture and blitz to a fine purée. Pour in the yogurt and stir in the remaining turmeric.
4   Heat the mixture in a pan over a medium heat until you see the first bubbles appear on the surface.
5   Remove from the heat and stir in the okra. Serve hot with rice.

Kalan

| YOGURT AND COCONUT CURRY |

This dish from Kerala is always included in a 'sadhya' or traditional feast that is served on a banana leaf, especially during the Hindu rice harvest festival of Onam. The best plantain to use is the Kerala Nendran, which is firm and does not squash down easily. It can be replaced with other firm plantains or yam – this will take longer to cook – or ripe mangoes (leave the skin on and cook for a couple of minutes over a high heat). *Serves 4* PREPARATION → *15 minutes (longer if you are grating the coconut from scratch)* COOKING *25 minutes*

2 plantain, peeled and thickly sliced
1 teaspoon ground turmeric
½ teaspoon medium-hot red chilli powder
150g freshly grated or frozen coconut
2 fresh green chillies (seeds and all)
1 teaspoon cumin seeds
7–8 fresh or 10 dried curry leaves
200g natural yogurt
2 tablespoons coconut oil
1 teaspoon black or brown mustard seeds
½ teaspoon fenugreek seeds
3 dried red chillies
salt
boiled rice *(pages 78–79)*, to serve (optional)

1   Put the plantain in a saucepan over a high heat with the turmeric, chilli powder, salt to season and just enough water to cover. Bring to the boil, reduce the heat and simmer for 7–8 minutes.
2   Put the coconut, green chillies, cumin seeds and half the curry leaves in a blender, add enough water to cover the mixture, and blitz until you have a very fine purée. Pour it into a bowl and stir in the yogurt.
3   Stir the coconut and yogurt mixture into the pan with the cooked plantain and cook over a medium heat until it begins to bubble. Season with salt.
4   Heat the oil in a small pan over a high heat and add the mustard seeds. When they begin to pop, tip in the fenugreek seeds, red chillies and remaining curry leaves (standing back from the pan if using fresh leaves, as they will splutter).
5   Pour this oil over the curry along with the spices. Serve hot with rice or as a side dish to a curry.

Shahi Paneer

| RICH CREAMY PANEER CURRY |

Shahi means 'royal' and this is essentially a north Indian restaurant or party dish due to its richness. It is mild and pale with the richness of nuts, cream, saffron and spices, all hallmark ingredients of Mughlai cooking which this dish forms a part of. *Serves 4* PREPARATION → *15 minutes* COOKING *40 minutes*

2 onions, thinly sliced
3 tablespoons unsalted cashew nuts
large pinch of saffron
100ml single cream
2 tablespoons vegetable oil or ghee
4 cloves
1 small cinnamon stick
2 bay leaves
3 green cardamom pods, seeds crushed and husks discarded
2 teaspoons ginger-garlic paste *(page 45)*
2 fresh green chillies, slit lengthways
350g paneer, cubed
1 teaspoon garam masala *(page 64)*
50g full-fat yogurt
salt
Naans *(pages 110–113)* or Pulao Rice *(page 82)*, to serve

1 Put the onions and cashew nuts in a saucepan with just enough water to cover. Bring to the boil then reduce the heat and simmer for 15 minutes until very soft. Cool slightly then blitz to a purée in a blender along with the cooking liquid until smooth: it will look creamy and pale.

2 Combine the saffron and cream in a small saucepan. Heat gently for a few minutes until the cream has turned pale orange, then remove from the heat.

3 Heat the oil or ghee in a saucepan over a high heat and add all the whole spices. When they start to sizzle, stir in the ginger-garlic paste and green chillies. Stir a couple of times and add the paneer. Fry until light golden.

4 After a minute, pour in the pale sauce from the blender and bring to the boil. Stir in the saffron cream and garam masala, and season with salt. Cook for a couple of minutes.

5 Add the yogurt, bring up to almost boiling point and remove from the heat.

6 Serve hot with naans or pulao rice.

Avial

| MIXED VEGETABLES IN COCONUT AND YOGURT |

This recipe is served as part of an Onam feast in Kerala. Onam usually falls around August/September. The recipe features local vegetables that can be found in south Indian shops around the world, including drumstick, which is a long bean-like vegetable that's cut into 4cm lengths and cooked and served in its skin. When eating it, you break the tender stick in half, scoop out the soft flesh from inside and discard the chewy skin. *Serves 4* PREPARATION → *25 minutes* COOKING *45 minutes*

300g mixed raw vegetables, such as carrots, green beans, raw banana, red pumpkin, yam, drumstick
1 teaspoon ground turmeric
100g grated fresh or frozen coconut
2 fresh green chillies
½ teaspoon cumin seeds
10 black peppercorns
150g natural yogurt, seasoned with salt
1 tablespoon coconut oil
10 fresh curry leaves
salt
boiled rice *(pages 78–79)*, to serve

1 Chop all the vegetables, except the beans and drumstick, into even-sized cubes so that they cook evenly together. Cut the drumstick or green beans in half. Put all the vegetables, except the beans and yam, in a pan with enough water to just cover them, then add the turmeric and season with salt. Bring to the boil, reduce the heat and simmer for 8–10 minutes. Add the beans and yam and continue cooking for 6–7 minutes until all the vegetables are almost done.

2 Meanwhile, blitz the coconut, chillies, cumin seeds and peppercorns to a purée in a blender with a little water.

3 When the vegetables are almost done, add this purée to the pan. Bring to the boil, then reduce the heat and pour in the seasoned yogurt. Simmer for a couple of minutes, add the coconut oil and curry leaves and stir. Remove from the heat and serve hot with rice.

LENTILS & BEANS

DAL IS THE STAPLE FOOD ALL OVER INDIA AND IS EATEN WITH RICE OR ROTIS.
THIS FAIRLY INEXPENSIVE COMBINATION OF DAL AND RICE CAN SUSTAIN A LARGE
VEGETARIAN POPULATION QUITE EASILY.

Lentils are ancient foods and were eaten in India in prehistoric times. 'Masura' or red lentils are mentioned in texts dating back to 800 BC. 'Mudga' or mung originated in India and is mentioned in the Yajurveda (c.1200–100 BCE) along with wheat, sesame, rice and barley.

Lentils are called 'dal' in many parts of India. The word denotes the raw product as well as cooked lentils. They are essentially carbohydrate and protein with no fat. India is one of the largest growers of lentils in the world because of ideal climatic conditions as well as the high demand for them. Indians consume them on a daily basis because they're so readily available, cheap and filling, and as they bulk up on cooking, a little goes a long way in feeding the whole family.

Dal is the staple food all over India and is eaten with rice or rotis. The amino acids cysteine and methionine missing in lentils are provided by grains, and the lysine that is limited in grains is supplied by lentils. Lycine is an amino acid that is essential in the bio synthesis of proteins. The human body cannot synthesise it so it must be acquired from the diet. Therefore, this fairly inexpensive combination of dal and rice forms a powerhouse of complete protein, that is an adequate proportion of all the nine essential amino acids needed by humans, and which can sustain a large vegetarian population quite easily.

The word 'dal' is quite confusing because it is loosely used for a large group of lentils, pulses and legumes, both cooked and uncooked. Lentils are legumes that are shaped like a convex lens, whereas beans are bigger. The term also includes beans like kidney beans, chickpeas or dried peas, all of which are grown and eaten in India. Every Indian food shop I have been to has quite a few shelves stacked with

legumes. Regional Indian cuisines reflect what is grown locally – so Kashmiri cooking uses red kidney beans that are grown in abundance there. 'Moth' beans are popular in Rajasthan, Gujarat and Maharashtra where they're grown. Some of the most popular lentils and beans are listed below.

Indian dals are available in three main forms:
Whole Pulse (Sabut Dal) → This is the whole bean, as in mung bean (green), urad/urid bean (black), masoor (brown lentils) so will be called, for example, 'sabut mung ki dal'.
Split Pulse (Chilka) → This is the split bean with the skin on, such as mung dal chilka.
Hulled Pulse (Dhuli Hui Dal) → This is the split, skinned bean such as mung dal (these are yellow when the green skin is stripped away), urad dal (when the black skin is removed, the lentil within is creamy white) or masoor dal (red lentils which are inside the brown skin).

Pulses are most often cooked into a stew-like preparation called dal but are also used to make desserts like 'puran poli' (see page 458) where cooked and sweetened lentils are layered between fine flour pancakes, or snacks such as 'dhokla', a spongy, savoury cake tempered with mustard and cumin.

They are used for batters as in 'dosa' or south Indian pancakes (see page 126) or to thicken curries as in 'kadhi', a yogurt and gram flour preparation.

The whole beans and the split ones are quite different and are not always interchangeable, so check what the recipe asks for before buying. You can store them in an airtight container for up to 6 months. Sometimes lentils can be interchangeable, as long as you keep to the same size.

RED/ORANGE LENTILS (MASOOR DAL)

Orange lentils are the seeds of a bushy plant and grow in long pods. When left whole the lentils are dark brown to greenish-black in colour, round and flattish. The fairly thick skin conceals a pinkish-orange centre. These lentils are delicate in flavour and have a nutty, fresh taste. The whole lentils are muskier, chewy and coarser.

YELLOW LENTILS

Mung Beans (Moong) → Mung beans, or green gram, are very versatile. 'Bean sprouts', commonly available everywhere, are actually sprouted mung beans.

Whole mung beans, or green gram, are small, oval and olive-green in colour. When split, they are small, flattish and yellow. Whole mung beans have a stronger flavour and texture than the split ones. They are rather chewy and musky. The yellow, split mung beans are extremely easy to cook, need no soaking and are easy to digest.

They are used for both sweet and savoury dishes and are easy to sprout at home (see page 277).

Pigeon Pea (Toor or Arhar Dal) → In some parts of India, yellow lentils are slightly oiled to increase their shelf life, more so when the lentils are exported, and therefore Indian shops outside India usually stock the oily variety of yellow lentils as well as non-oily.

These lentils are yellow and sold split into two round halves. The oily variety is sticky and glossy; the non-oily one is matte. They are very easy to digest and have a pleasant, nutty flavour. They take longer to cook than red lentils and can be soaked for an hour or so to hasten the cooking process.

If you buy oily yellow lentils, soak them in boiling hot water for a while and throw away the resulting cloudy, white liquid. Then wash the lentils several times to get rid of most of the oil.

Gram Lentils (Chana Dal) → Gram, or Bengal gram as it is also known, is the most widely grown lentil in India. They are husked and left whole, split or ground into a flour called besan. This flour is used to make batter (as in fritters), as a thickening agent in curries or is cooked with jaggery to make many different sweets.

Matte and yellow, gram lentils resemble yellow lentils but are slightly bigger and coarser. They are stronger in taste than most other lentils, with a nutty sweet aroma and flavour. Soaking them for 1 hour in hot water will reduce their cooking time.

URAD DAL

This is also known as black lentil or gram and is the same size and shape as the mung bean. It has been used in India since ancient times as is evident from texts where it is referred to as 'maasha'. It has an earthy flavour and when cooked develops a creamy, slippery texture that is prized in recipes such as the north Indian 'dal makhani' (page 280).

CHICKPEAS (CHANA)

There are two main varieties of chickpeas: white (kabuli chana) and brown (strangely called kala chana or black chickpeas).

These peas are small, hard and have a thick skin, which often comes away during soaking and cooking. On their own, chickpeas have little aroma or taste, but when cooked with flavourings and spices, they take on a nutty, creamy flavour.

Chickpeas are available dried or cooked and tinned in brine. Some cooks swear by soaking and cooking them at home, but I use canned chickpeas to save time. Dried chickpeas need to be soaked in water at room temperature for at least 8 hours, after which they nearly double in size.

The dark variety is dark brown, small and hard and has a strong, earthy aroma. They have a thick skin and a pleasant, nutty flavour and are also available tinned.

VAL

Tender val pods are eaten as a fresh vegetable. Dried val beans are creamy-white to light tan in colour. They have a thick, white ridge on one side. On cooking, val acquires a strong, nutty aroma and the taste becomes creamy with a slight, but not unpleasant, bitterness.

Val needs soaking in water overnight as it is quite hard. It is usually sprouted to enhance its flavour. The beans need to be peeled to remove the thick, chewy skin, then they are ready to be cooked.

MOATH (MATKI)

You will see these in Indian shops as 'moth' beans but the pronunciation is 'moat'. These are small, elongated beans with a brown skin and a brownish-yellow interior and they have a nutty, mildly bittersweet flavour and a strong, earthy smell. They are often sprouted to make a dry side dish or served on buttered toast for breakfast.

BUTTER BEANS (PAVTA)

Butter beans are large, creamy-white and flattish. They have a medium-thick skin. The name shows the bean's most obvious characteristic: a buttery, smooth taste. They have a pleasant, nutty aroma.

You can buy them dried or in cans. Cans are time-saving though the beans may be a bit soft and disintegrate on further cooking. Dried beans are better for intense Indian cooking techniques or if using canned ones, add them at the very last minute.

RED KIDNEY BEANS (RAJMA)

The Portuguese brought the red kidney bean to India along with other staples such as tomato and chilli.

At the temple dedicated to the goddess Vaishno Devi in Kashmir, a mosaic of roadside restaurants welcomes visitors with a traditional meal of kidney beans and rice.

You can buy bags of dried beans or the canned ones. If using dried beans, make sure to soak them in water for 8–10 hours, discard the soaking water and cook them very well as the raw beans are toxic. The recommended time for boiling them is 1 hour, or until they can be squashed between the thumb and a finger. Canned beans can be used straightaway but it is a good idea to rinse them first to get rid of the salt and thick liquid they are in. Indian kitchens have pressure cookers to cook lentils and beans.

OVERLEAF (PAGE 272): *1 Mutter; 2 Mung; 3 Matki; 4 Rajma; 5 Toor/Ahar Dal; 6 Val;* (PAGE 273): *7 Lobia; 8 Mung – hulled; 9 Urad Dal; 10 Chana Dal; 11 Masoor Dal; 12 Lobia Chawli; 13 Pavta.*

DRIED PEAS (MUTTER)

The pea plant is believed to have originated in western Asia and was later cultivated by the Greeks, Romans and Persians. The three commonly used varieties of pea – black, white and green – are small, round and smooth. Reconstituted peas (soaked and boiled) have an earthy smell and taste quite different from fresh ones.

Dried peas must be soaked in water for 8–12 hours before use.

BLACK-EYED BEANS (LOBIA/CHAWLI)

These large, oblong beans are creamy-white, with a black 'eye' on one side. The skin is quite thick. They have a subtle, nutty aroma and a rich, creamy taste that is slightly earthy.

Old beans sometimes get a rusty-brown tinge and become wrinkled, so choose those that are plump, even and unbroken. You can buy them canned but rinse them in a sieve before using them, to get rid of excess salt.

HOW TO COOK LENTILS

The three forms of lentils – whole beans, 'chilka', and skinless, split ones – all take different lengths of time to cook. The time will also depend on the heat source – whether you are using, for example, a gas hob, an electric cooker or induction heat. The shape and size of your pan will also make a difference – a wide, shallow pan will encourage faster evaporation, so you will need to add more liquid while cooking.

SOAKING

Whole beans, whether they are big like red kidney beans or small like mung, all benefit from soaking, as the cooking time reduces and they cook softer. Although many raw beans contain the toxin phytohaemagglutinin, a protein also known as kidney bean lectin, kidney beans contain the highest levels. Cooked beans also have it but in much lower and harmless levels. Soaking and cooking the beans fully ensures that no harmful side effects occur.

Using canned beans is a perfectly good alternative and a safe way to enjoy beans if you're not sure about cooking dried ones or want to save time.

Dried kidney beans, especially, must be soaked for a minimum of 6 hours. Other beans also cook better with long soaking times. Drain away the soaking water, rinse and then cook the beans.

Amongst the split lentils, I find that soaking chana dal and toor dal helps to cook them faster. Red lentils, mung dal and split urad dal do not need to be soaked.

RINSING

It's best to rinse and drain lentils before using, to remove some of the starch. Rinse under cold running water until the water turns from milky to almost clear.

COOKING

1 Start by adding double the amount of water by volume to the dal. You need not measure this; the water should be roughly a couple of centimetres over the lentils.

2 Bring the water to a rapid boil then reduce the heat to a gentle bubble and continue cooking. You can cover the pan to reduce the cooking time but leave it partially uncovered to stop the liquid from boiling over. You may find that, depending on the source of heat (gas/electric/big ring/small ring) as well as the pan, you need to add more water as the lentils cook. Remember to add only enough water to keep the lentils submerged. You can add hot water from a kettle or just pour in cold water and increase the heat to bring it to the boil. Reduce the heat again and continue simmering.

3 You'll find that a frothy scum rises to the top when lentils and beans are coming to a boil. You can skim this off with a slotted spoon. As soon as you have reduced the heat to a simmer, the scum formation reduces.

4 Lentils are 'done' when they have plumped up and disintegrated into a mush. Whole beans or pulses will not fall apart during cooking – they should soften just enough to fall apart on the merest touch, so that they can be eaten with rice or scooped up with a piece of roti.

I don't add salt or acidic foods like tomatoes or lemon juice to lentils when they are cooking as I find it makes the lentils take longer to cook. I season them when they are still warm, when I add the rest of the flavouring.

THE RIGHT CONSISTENCY

Various regional dal recipes have differing consistencies. A Punjabi 'Dal Makhani' (page 280) is quite thick, whereas a south Indian 'rasam' is soup-like. Dal is always eaten with a bread such as roti, or with rice. If eaten with a roti the consistency is thicker so that the dal can be scooped up, but with rice it's soupier to act as a sauce to bind the rice together. You can decide on the consistency; my everyday dal has a pouring consistency.

You will find that a dal will thicken as it sits after cooking, so if you are making it in advance, you can add a splash of water to bring it back to the correct consistency before serving. Make sure to check and adjust the seasoning depending on how much water you've added.

USING LENTILS

DIGESTIBILITY → For people new to beans and lentils, they can sometimes be difficult to digest or cause flatulence. Start by eating small amounts. Soaking all beans and lentils helps to make them more digestible and in India, most bean and dal recipes will have the addition of a wonderful, powerfully sulphuric-smelling spice called asafoetida. A pinch of this yellow powder, known as 'hing' in India, adds a curry-like flavour to the dish and greatly improves digestibility. Sprouting beans also help.

SPROUTING → The process of sprouting induces a riot of bio-chemical changes in which complex components break down into simpler substances that are easy to digest. Sprouted legumes have higher amounts of vitamin C, iron and calcium than those that are not sprouted.

Sprouted beans are an essential part of Indian vegetarian cookery. Cooks often have some beans soaking in a corner of the kitchen and these are eaten cooked with spices or lightly steamed.

Beans will take different amounts of time to sprout depending on a variety of factors, such as temperature, light, moisture and the container used. Start by soaking the beans in water at room temperature for at least 6 hours. Drain away the water then tie them in a muslin cloth or put them in a sprouting jar. I use a small stainless-steel box with holes in it – this is traditionally used in India to store herbs in the fridge. Put the beans in a dark place to sprout. You will have to rinse them every day, or a couple of times each day in very hot weather, and put them back in their draining position. In a couple of days they will begin to sprout. As soon as little white shoots appear, they are ready to be cooked.

MAKING A LENTIL BATTER → In some parts of India, lentils are made into a batter. First, the lentils are soaked for at least 6 hours to soften them, then they are blitzed with a little water in a blender until they turn into a purée. This is made into fritters called 'vadas' (see page 359), pancakes called 'dosas' (see page 126) or cakes called 'idlis'.

Tarka Dal

| LENTILS WITH ONIONS AND CORIANDER |

There are many versions of this north Indian recipe, as the name literally means spiced, flavoured lentils. I make my Tarka Dal as below because it's easy, unfussy and tastes light and delicious. The 'tadka' (see page 36), could include a variety of spices such as cloves, cinnamon, fenugreek seeds, curry leaves or herbs. *Serves 4*

PREPARATION ⟶ *15 minutes* COOKING *45 minutes*

200g red lentils, washed and drained
2 tablespoons vegetable oil
1 teaspoon cumin seeds
1 large onion, diced
2 garlic cloves, finely diced
1 tomato, finely chopped
2 fresh green chillies, slit lengthways
1 teaspoon ground turmeric
1 teaspoon garam masala *(page 64)*, plus extra to serve
a handful of fresh coriander leaves, chopped, to garnish
salt
Rotis *(pages 108–109)*, to serve

1 Put the lentils and double the volume of water in a heavy-based saucepan and bring to the boil, then reduce the heat and simmer for 30 minutes until soft and mushy, skimming the scum off the surface from time to time. You may need to add a splash of water if the dal becomes too dry.

2 Meanwhile, heat the oil in a frying pan over a high heat and add the cumin seeds. When they start to crackle, add the onion and stir for 7–8 minutes until golden. Stir in the garlic and cook for 2–3 minutes until brown.

3 Add the tomato, chillies, turmeric and garam masala to the pan, season with salt and cook for 3–4 minutes until soft. Carefully pour in the cooked lentils with the cooking liquid, stir and season to taste.

4 Serve hot, sprinkled with the coriander and garam masala, with rotis alongside.

Aamti

| MAHARASHTRIAN LENTILS WITH ASAFOETIDA |

I grew up eating this delicious dish with rice and ghee. It has no onion or garlic to overwhelm the clean taste of the toor dal, which are slightly sweet and earthy. The dal is flavoured with fresh coriander and 'goda masala', which is a dark, sweet spice blend made by toasting fragrant spices such as cinnamon, cloves and cardamom with desiccated coconut, then crushing everything to a fine powder (see page 65). You can leave this out for a lighter dish. *Serves 4*

PREPARATION ⟶ *10 minutes, plus 1 hour soaking time* COOKING *50 minutes*

150g toor dal, soaked in water at room temperature for 1 hour, then washed and drained
1 teaspoon vegetable oil
½ teaspoon mustard seeds
1 teaspoon cumin seeds
pinch of asafoetida
8 fresh or 12 dried curry leaves
2 fresh green chillies, slit lengthways
½ teaspoon ground turmeric
1 teaspoon goda masala *(page 65 – optional)*
1 large tomato, chopped
a small handful of fresh coriander leaves, finely chopped, to garnish
salt

1 Wash the lentils in several changes of water then place them in a heavy-based saucepan over a high heat with double the volume of water. Bring to the boil then reduce the heat and simmer for 40 minutes, adding more water as necessary, until soft and mushy, skimming the scum off the surface from time to time.

2 Heat the oil in small saucepan over a high heat and fry the mustard seeds until they start to pop, then add the cumin seeds, asafoetida, curry leaves (standing back from the pan if using fresh leaves, as they will splutter) and chillies and cook for 10–15 seconds.

3 Add the turmeric, goda masala (if using) and tomato. Cook for a couple of minutes until the tomato softens, then stir the mixture into the cooked lentils. Season with salt and add enough water to make a pouring consistency. Simmer for 1 minute and serve hot, sprinkled with the coriander.

DAL MAKHANI – Creamy, Buttery Black Dal

This rich and indulgent dal is a true north Indian restaurant-style dish, and is also called 'kali dal' or 'maa di dal'. Some restaurants cook it in the tandoor, which gives it a unique smoky flavour. The longer you cook the black beans, the creamier they become. 'Makhan' is butter and this dal can be flavoured with ghee or butter – the final consistency should be soft and buttery. *Serves 4* PREPARATION → *15 minutes, plus overnight soaking time* COOKING *1 hour 15 minutes*

YOU WILL NEED:

1 large onion, finely chopped

1 tablespoon ginger-garlic paste *(page 45)*

large pinch of asafoetida

1 teaspoon ground turmeric

1 teaspoon medium-hot red chilli powder

1 teaspoon garam masala *(page 64)*

150g whole urad beans, soaked in water overnight, rinsed and drained

2 tablespoons double cream

2 tablespoons finely chopped fresh coriander leaves

2 tablespoons ghee, butter or vegetable oil

2 garlic cloves, finely chopped

2 large tomatoes, chopped

salt

boiled rice *(pages 78–79)*, Parathas *(pages 120–121)* or Naans *(pages 110–113)*, to serve

1 Put all the ingredients from the onion to the beans in a heavy-based pan with enough water to cover the mixture by 2.5cm, and bring to the boil. Reduce the heat and simmer for 1 hour or more, until the beans are well cooked, creamy and almost dissolving, adding water as necessary, to keep the beans covered.

2 Remove from the heat, stir in salt to season, the cream and coriander leaves.

3 Heat the ghee, butter or oil in a frying pan over a high heat and fry the garlic for 1 minute until golden brown, then add the tomatoes and fry for a few minutes until soft. Stir this mixture into the lentils.

4 Serve hot with rice, parathas or naan.

Poondu Rasam

| LIGHT LENTIL SOUP WITH GARLIC |

Rasam is a close relative of sambhar but it is thinner and is therefore often served as a spicy soup. It is also eaten with boiled rice, as a second course after rice and sambhar. It is often made by adding extra water to the lentils when making sambhar, straining this, then frying spices in oil and pouring this into the lentils. *Serves 4* PREPARATION → *15 minutes, plus 15 minutes soaking time* COOKING *50 minutes*

4 tablespoons toor dal, soaked in water at room temperature for 15 minutes then washed and drained
3 teaspoons tamarind pulp *(page 418)* or shop-bought tamarind paste
2 tablespoons vegetable oil
½ teaspoon black mustard seeds
½ teaspoon cumin seeds
large pinch of asafoetida
10 fresh or 15 dried curry leaves
3 garlic cloves, peeled and bruised
1 teaspoon sambhar powder *(page 65)*
½ teaspoon crushed black peppercorns
1 teaspoon ground turmeric
2 tablespoons finely chopped fresh coriander leaves, to garnish
salt
boiled rice *(pages 78–79)*, to serve

1 Place the lentils in a heavy-based saucepan with 750ml water, bring to the boil, then reduce the heat and simmer for 45 minutes until mushy, skimming the scum off the surface from time to time. Season with salt and stir to dissolve. When the lentils are cooked, pass them through a sieve into a clean pan, reserving the liquid and discarding the contents of the sieve. Stir in the tamarind.
2 Heat the oil in a small pan over a high heat and add the mustard seeds. When they begin to crackle, add the cumin, asafoetida, curry leaves and garlic cloves. Fry for 1 minute, then stir in the sambhar powder, pepper and turmeric.
3 Pour the lentil liquid into the pan, bring to the boil then remove from the heat, sprinkle with the fresh coriander and serve hot with rice.

Poosanikai Sambhar

| SOUTH INDIAN LENTILS WITH PUMPKIN |

This is served with the first helping of rice in a south Indian meal. Three servings are traditional in every meal: the first with a thick sambhar, the second with a thin 'rasam' and the third with yogurt. You can add any firm vegetable – aubergine, gourds, carrots, beans and beetroot are typical. *Serves 4* PREPARATION → *15 minutes, plus 30 minutes soaking time* COOKING *1 hour 15 minutes*

200g toor dal, soaked in water at room temperature for 30 minutes then washed and drained
100g pumpkin, deseeded and cut into 2.5cm cubes (skin left on)
2 tablespoons vegetable oil
1 teaspoon black mustard seeds
1 teaspoon cumin seeds
12 fresh or 15 dried curry leaves
large pinch of asafoetida
3 tablespoons tamarind pulp *(page 418)* or shop-bought tamarind paste
1 teaspoon sambhar powder *(page 65)*
½ teaspoon ground turmeric
2 tablespoons finely chopped fresh coriander leaves, to garnish
salt
boiled rice *(pages 78–79)*, to serve

1 Put the lentils and double the volume of water in a heavy-based saucepan over a high heat and bring to the boil, then reduce the heat and simmer for 50 minutes, skimming off the scum that rises to the top and adding more water as necessary, to prevent the lentils from drying out. When almost completely soft, add the pumpkin and simmer for 15 minutes until cooked. The lentils can continue cooking with the pumpkin – they are meant to be mushy.
2 Season with salt, mix, remove from the heat and set aside.
3 Warm the oil in a large saucepan over a high heat and add the mustard seeds. When they start to crackle, add the cumin seeds, curry leaves and asafoetida. Add the tamarind pulp. Cook over a low heat for 4–5 minutes until thick and bubbly, adding a splash of water so that the mixture does not dry out.
4 Add the sambhar powder and turmeric and cook for 1 minute, then pour the lentils into the spice mixture and stir. Add a bit of water if necessary to get a pouring consistency. Sprinkle with the coriander and serve hot with rice.

Bengali Cholar Dal

| CHANA DAL WITH RAISINS |

This is a festive dal made at feasts or on special occasions such as the Hindu Pujo festival in Bengal when the Goddess Durga is honoured for 9 days and nights. The consistency should be fairly thick and it is eaten with fried pooris. *Serves 4* PREPARATION → *20 minutes, plus 1 hour soaking time* COOKING *1 hour*

200g split gram lentils (chana dal), soaked in water at
    room temperature for 1 hour then drained
1 teaspoon ground turmeric
3 tablespoons vegetable oil
2 tablespoons panch phoron *(page 66)*
4 dried red chillies, deseeded and crumbled
2 bay leaves
few slices of dried or fresh coconut
2 teaspoons raisins
salt
Pooris *(pages 114–115)*, to serve

1 Place the lentils in a heavy-based saucepan with about 450ml boiling hot water and simmer for 1 hour until soft and mushy, skimming the scum off the surface from time to time. Add more water as necessary, to get a thick consistency.
2 Add the turmeric, season with salt and mix well. Remove from the heat.
3 Heat the oil in a small frying pan over a high heat then add the panch phoron. When it crackles, add the red chillies, bay leaves, coconut and raisins. Reduce the heat and cook for a few seconds, then season to taste.
4 Pour the oil and the spices over the lentils, stir, bring to the boil once and serve hot with pooris.

Gujarati Dal

| SWEET AND SOUR LENTILS |

I love the depth of flavour in this tangy, sweet dal, which is eaten with plain rice. Sometimes vegetables such as yam are added but even on its own, it is a treat. Traditionally, toor dal will be used but you can use red or mung dal for a speedier version. *Serves 4* PREPARATION → *10 minutes, plus 30 minutes soaking time* COOKING *1 hour*

150g toor dal, soaked in hot water for 30 minutes,
    then washed and drained
½ teaspoon ground turmeric
4 kokum petals *(see page 417)* or 3 tablespoons tamarind pulp
    (page 418)
2 fresh green chillies, slit lengthways
2 tablespoons grated jaggery or soft brown sugar
2 tablespoons vegetable oil
1 teaspoon black mustard seeds
1 teaspoon cumin seeds
large pinch of asafoetida
½ teaspoon fenugreek seeds
pinch of fresh or dried curry leaves
a small sprig of fresh coriander leaves, finely chopped, to garnish
salt
boiled rice *(pages 78–79)*, to serve

1 Place the lentils in a heavy-based saucepan with double the volume of water and bring to the boil. Reduce the heat and simmer for at least 40 minutes until soft and mushy, skimming the scum off the surface from time to time.
2 Add the turmeric, kokum or tamarind pulp, green chillies, jaggery and salt to season. Simmer for a further 10 minutes or until the lentils are completely cooked. Remove from the heat.
3 Heat the oil in a small pan over a high heat, then tip in the mustard seeds. When they begin to crackle, add the cumin seeds, asafoetida, fenugreek seeds and curry leaves (standing back from the pan if using fresh leaves, as they will splutter). Cook for 1 minute, then remove from the heat and pour the oil and spices into the lentil mixture.
4 Stir well, season to taste, sprinkle with the fresh coriander and serve hot with rice.

Matkichi Usal

| STIR-FRIED MOTH SPROUTS |

Sprouted beans are a common addition to a Maharashtrian or Gujarati meal and are a must in a thali feast, where many small dishes from this region are served together. During the process of sprouting, proteins break down into separate amino acids and complex carbohydrates break down into simpler carbohydrates that are easier to digest (see page 277). The bean starts to produce nutrients such as B-group vitamins, vitamin C and iron in preparation for becoming a full plant, thus making sprouts a healthy addition to a main meal or a delicious breakfast with a slice of toast. *Serves 4* PREPARATION → *10 minutes, plus 5 hours soaking time and overnight sprouting time* COOKING *35 minutes*

150g dried moth beans, sprouted *(see page 277)*
1 tablespoon vegetable oil
½ teaspoon black mustard seeds
½ teaspoon cumin seeds
8 fresh or 10 dried curry leaves
1 small fresh green chilli, slit lengthways, seeds left in
1 medium onion, finely chopped
¼ teaspoon ground turmeric
2 tablespoons freshly grated coconut or desiccated coconut, to garnish
1 tablespoon chopped fresh coriander leaves, to garnish
1 tablespoon lemon juice
salt

1 Refresh the sprouted beans in cold water and set aside.
2 Heat the oil in a frying pan over a high heat and add the mustard seeds. When they start to pop, add the cumin seeds, curry leaves (standing back from the pan if using fresh leaves, as they will splutter) and the green chilli. When the seeds sizzle, add the onion and fry for 7–8 minutes until soft.
3 Tip in the sprouted beans, turmeric and salt to season. Add about 3 tablespoons of water and bring to the boil. Reduce the heat, cover and cook for about 25 minutes until the beans are soft but firm, adding more water if the pan dries out. The final dish should be dry. Season to taste and finish off by sprinkling coconut, coriander and lemon juice on top. Serve warm.

Bhuna Lobia

| STIR-FRIED BLACK-EYED BEANS |

Black-eyed beans work very well with tomatoes and onions, which seem to bring out their nutty sweetness as in this north Indian recipe. They are rich in soluble fibre, which helps eliminate cholesterol from the body. Black-eyed beans are eaten all over India – my Konkani relatives from Karnataka cook them with coconut into a creamy curry whereas in Maharashtra, they are stir-fried to make a semi-dry dish called 'usal'. *Serves 4* PREPARATION → *15 minutes, plus overnight soaking time (optional)* COOKING *1 hour 15 minutes, or 25 minutes if using canned beans*

2 tablespoons vegetable oil
1 teaspoon cumin seeds
large pinch of asafoetida
1 medium onion, thinly sliced
1 tablespoon ginger-garlic paste *(page 45)*
150g dried black-eyed beans, soaked in water overnight and drained or 1 x 400g can, drained and rinsed
½ teaspoon medium-hot red chilli powder
½ teaspoon ground turmeric
2 large ripe tomatoes, chopped
1 teaspoon garam masala *(page 64)*
½ teaspoon caster sugar
a small sprig of fresh coriander leaves, chopped, to garnish
salt

1 Heat the oil in a heavy-based saucepan over a high heat, then add the cumin seeds and fry until they darken. Add the asafoetida, fry for a few seconds then add the onion and stir-fry for 8–10 minutes until golden.
2 Add the ginger-garlic paste and mix well. Cook for 1–2 minutes, then tip in the beans (dried and soaked, or tinned), sprinkle in the chilli powder and turmeric and fry for 1 minute, then mix in the tomatoes, garam masala, sugar and salt to season. Add a little water, cover and bring to the boil. Reduce the heat and simmer for 1 hour until done (or just 3–4 minutes if using tinned beans). The beans should retain their shape. Mash a few to add thickness to the sauce and season to taste.
3 Serve hot, garnished with the coriander.

Valache Birde

| SWEET VAL BEANS |

These slightly bitter beans team up well with jaggery and mustard seeds. They can be served dry as a side dish or in a thin sauce to be eaten with rotis. The thick skins will peel away easily once the beans have been soaked. *Serves 4* PREPARATION →
20 minutes, plus 8 hours soaking and overnight sprouting time COOKING *35 minutes*

1 tablespoon vegetable oil
1 teaspoon black mustard seeds
1 teaspoon cumin seeds
large pinch of asafoetida
10 fresh or 15 dried curry leaves
200g val beans, soaked for 8 hours, sprouted overnight *(see page 277)* and skinned
1 teaspoon ground turmeric
½ teaspoon medium-hot red chilli powder
1 teaspoon ground coriander
2 tablespoons grated jaggery or soft brown sugar
4 kokum petals *(see page 417)* or 2 teaspoons lemon juice
2 tablespoons chopped fresh coriander leaves
salt

1 Heat the oil in a pan over a high heat and add the mustard seeds. When they begin to pop add the cumin seeds, asafoetida and curry leaves (standing back from the pan if using fresh leaves, as they will splutter). Tip in the skinned beans and the ground spices, then add the jaggery or sugar, salt to season and enough water to cover the mixture. Stir in the kokum or lemon juice.

2 Bring to the boil then reduce the heat, cover and simmer for 30 minutes until the beans are tender, adding more water as necessary to keep the beans submerged. If you want a dry dish, uncover the pan and boil off the liquid over a high heat. Season to taste, stir in the coriander leaves and serve hot.

Cholay

| CURRIED CHICKPEAS |

1 tablespoon strong tea leaves or a teabag
   of everyday or breakfast tea
2.5cm piece of cinnamon stick
4 green cardamom pods, bruised
2 black cardamom pods, bruised
5 cloves
2 x 400g cans of chickpeas, drained and rinsed
   or 150g dried chickpeas, soaked in
   water overnight
1 teaspoon ground turmeric
½ teaspoon medium-hot red chilli powder
1 teaspoon ground coriander
1 teaspoon anardana powder or
   2 tablespoons lemon juice
1 teaspoon amchoor (dried mango powder)
   or 1 tablespoon lemon juice
2 tablespoons vegetable oil
1 teaspoon cumin seeds
2 tablespoons ginger-garlic paste
   (page 45)
2 fresh green chillies, slit lengthways
a small handful of fresh coriander leaves,
   finely chopped, to garnish
salt

Punjabi cooking is known to be hearty and bold flavours abound. The state has had a largely agricultural population who have needed big breakfasts and meals to get through long days working on farms, especially through the cold winters. This is one of Punjab's favourite recipes, often eaten with fried bread called 'bhatura' (see page 124) at breakfast, or as a main meal, and each family has their own version. You can use dried chickpeas but you'll need to soak them overnight and cook them for a couple of hours until they are soft. The recipe uses dried, powdered pomegranate seeds (anardana powder) as a souring agent – if you can't find these use lemon juice instead. *Serves 4* PREPARATION → *15 minutes* COOKING *25 minutes*

1 Tie the tea leaves, cinnamon, both cardamoms and cloves in a piece of muslin to make a bouquet garni. Immerse it in a pan with 250ml water and bring to the boil. Reduce the heat and simmer for 7–8 minutes to extract the colour and flavour of the bouquet garni's contents. If using dried, soaked chickpeas, put them in enough water to cover them, along with the bouquet garni and cook for a couple of hours, adding more water as necessary to keep the chickpeas submerged until soft. If using canned chickpeas, place them in a pan, pour in the liquid from Step 1 (discarding the bouquet garni) and bring to the boil. Season with salt and sprinkle the ground spices on top.

2 Heat the oil in the pan over a high heat, add the cumin seeds and fry for 10 seconds until they darken, then add the ginger-garlic paste and chillies and fry for 30 seconds. Pour this spiced oil over the chickpeas. Reduce the heat and cook for 4–5 minutes, stirring, until the sauce is thick and dark.

3 Season to taste and serve hot, garnished with the coriander.

Rajma Tamater

| RED KIDNEY BEANS WITH TOMATOES |

Red kidney beans are popular in north India, especially in Jammu where some of the best varieties grow. Paired with plain rice, 'rajma' is a comfort meal and needs only a bowl of yogurt served on the side. If using dried kidney beans, soak and cook them, following the method on page 274.

Serves 4 PREPARATION —→ *10 minutes* COOKING *20 minutes*

3 tablespoons vegetable oil
2 medium onions, sliced
2 tablespoons ginger-garlic paste *(page 45)*
2 tablespoons tomato purée
1 teaspoon ground turmeric
½ teaspoon medium-hot red chilli powder
1 teaspoon ground coriander
1 x 400g can of red kidney beans, drained and rinsed or 150g
    dried kidney beans, soaked, drained and cooked *(see page 274)*
2 tablespoons chopped fresh coriander leaves, to garnish
salt
boiled rice *(pages 78–79)*, to serve

1 Heat half the oil in a heavy-based pan over a high heat, add the onions and fry for 7–8 minutes until soft.
2 Add the ginger-garlic paste and the tomato purée and fry for 2 minutes until mushy.
3 Remove from the heat and leave to cool slightly, then transfer the mixture to a blender, pour in enough water to just cover the mixture and blitz until smooth. Set aside. This is the curry paste.
4 Heat the remaining oil in the pan over a medium heat and add the ground spices. When they sizzle, add a splash of water and cook for 1–2 minutes until the water evaporates, leaving spiced oil in the pan. Stir in the beans.
5 Add the curry paste and salt to season and mix well. Pour about 150ml water into the blender, rinse it and pour this into the curry. Bring to the boil, reduce the heat, cover and cook for about 5 minutes until well blended.
6 Season to taste and serve hot, garnished with the coriander and rice to serve.

Chanyachi Amti

| COASTAL BLACK CHICKPEA CURRY |

This fragrant curry is made in Mumbai each year for the Hindu Ganesh festival around August/September. It is accompanied by fried rice-flour bread called vade but goes equally well with any bread or rice. *Serves 4* PREPARATION —→ *20 minutes, plus overnight soaking time (if using dried chickpeas)* COOKING *1 hour 30 minutes or 30 minutes if using canned chickpeas*

150g dried black chickpeas, soaked in water overnight or
    1 x 400g can of black or white chickpeas, drained and rinsed
1 teaspoon medium-hot red chilli powder
1 teaspoon ground turmeric
2 tomatoes, chopped
4 kokum petals *(see page 417)* or 2 teaspoons lemon juice
2 tablespoons vegetable oil
4 cloves
10 black peppercorns
1 teaspoon coriander seeds
4 tablespoons freshly grated or desiccated coconut
1 teaspoon black mustard seeds
1 teaspoon cumin seeds
salt
boiled rice *(pages 78–79)*, Pooris *(pages 114–115)* or poppadums,
    to serve

1 Drain the soaked chickpeas and boil them in double the volume of water for 1 hour or so until soft and you can squash one between your fingers. There should still be enough water to cover the chickpeas in the pan. Stir in the ground spices, salt to season, tomatoes and kokum or lemon juice and cook for a couple of minutes. If using canned chickpeas, bring them to the boil with some water and add these flavourings.
2 Meanwhile, make the curry paste. Heat half the oil in a pan over a high heat and add the cloves, peppercorns and coriander seeds. When they sizzle, add the coconut and fry for 4–5 minutes until brown. Transfer this mixture to a blender with enough water to just cover the mixture and blitz to a fine paste. Add the paste to the chickpeas, bring to the boil, then remove from the heat and season to taste.
3 Heat the remaining oil in a pan over a high heat and add the mustard seeds and cumin seeds. When they begin to pop, pour the oil and seeds over the curry and mix well. Serve hot with rice, pooris or poppadums.

Vellarikka Kootu

| CUCUMBER AND LENTIL STEW |

A 'kootu' is a south Indian vegetable and lentil combination dish with a consistency that is like a thick porridge. It is eaten with rice, and sometimes ghee is added into the mix for extra flavour. You can substitute the cucumber with any firm vegetable such as carrot, courgette or turnip. *Serves 4*

PREPARATION → *15 minutes* COOKING *1 hour*

200g split, skinned mung dal, washed and drained
1 teaspoon ground turmeric
1 teaspoon sambhar powder *(page 65)*
½ cucumber, peeled and cut into bite-sized chunks
1 tablespoon vegetable oil or ghee
1 teaspoon black or brown mustard seeds
pinch of fresh or dried curry leaves
1 small onion, finely diced
salt
boiled rice *(pages 78–79)*, to serve

1 Put the mung dal into a pan with double the volume of water and bring to the boil. Reduce the heat and simmer for 40 minutes, skimming the scum off the surface from time to time, until very soft.

2 Stir in the turmeric and sambhar powder then add the cucumber. Season with salt, and cook for a further 7–8 minutes to soften the cucumber.

3 Heat the oil or ghee in a small frying pan over a high heat, then add the mustard seeds. As soon as they begin to pop, sprinkle in the curry leaves (standing back from the pan if using fresh leaves, as they will splutter) and add the onion. Fry for 5–6 minutes until very soft, then stir this mixture into the lentils. Serve hot with rice.

Sabut Masoor Ki Dal

| SPICED BROWN LENTILS |

Sprouted or unsprouted brown lentils can be used for this dal. Red lentils, which are actually split brown lentils, can also be used, but whole lentils add a delicious chewiness to the dish. Make sure you cook the lentils until they are very soft but still hold their shape. They should break down enough to make a creamy homogenised dish rather than a watery soup with lentils sitting at the bottom! *Serves 4*

PREPARATION → *15 minutes, plus 2 hours soaking time* COOKING *1 hour 15 minutes*

200g brown lentils, soaked in water for 2 hours and drained
2 tablespoons vegetable oil
1 large red onion, thinly sliced
2 teaspoons ginger-garlic paste *(page 45)*
1 fresh green chilli, finely diced
2 fresh tomatoes, finely chopped
1 teaspoon ground turmeric
1 teaspoon garam masala *(page 64)*
2 tablespoons chopped fresh coriander leaves, to garnish
salt

1 Place the lentils in a pan with double the volume of water, bring to the boil and cook for 1 hour or until they are mushy, skimming the scum off the surface from time to time. Keep topping up the water if the lentils become too dry.

2 Heat the oil in a heavy-based saucepan over a high heat, add the onion and fry for 8–10 minutes until golden, then add the ginger-garlic paste and chilli to the pan and stir for a few seconds. Tip in the tomatoes and the ground spices and cook for 3–4 minutes until soft.

3 Season with salt and stir in the cooked lentils. Serve hot, sprinkled with the coriander.

Palak Dal

| LENTILS WITH SPINACH |

This simple fragrant dal is made all over India with a few variations. In Maharashtra it may have a few shavings of locally grown fresh coconut sprinkled on top, and in Karnataka it would have a few curry leaves added in. It can be eaten with rotis or rice as a light meal. You could use a variety of greens instead of spinach – try kale or chard.

Serves 4 PREPARATION → *10 minutes* COOKING *40 minutes*

200g split skinned mung dal, washed and drained
3 generous handfuls of fresh spinach, washed, drained
    and finely chopped
2 tablespoons vegetable oil
1 teaspoon black mustard seeds
1 teaspoon cumin seeds
1 teaspoon ginger-garlic paste *(page 45)*
2 fresh green chillies, finely chopped
1 teaspoon ground turmeric
½ teaspoon finely ground black pepper
juice of ½ lemon
salt
Rotis *(pages 108–109)* or boiled rice *(pages 78–79)*, to serve

1 Put the mung dal into a heavy-based saucepan with double the volume of water. Bring to the boil, reduce the heat and simmer for about 30 minutes until the lentils are mushy, skimming the scum off the surface from time to time.

2 Add the spinach to the lentils and let it wilt.

3 Heat the oil in a small saucepan over a high heat. Add the mustard seeds. When they start to pop, add the cumin seeds, then stir in the ginger-garlic paste and green chillies. Add the turmeric and pepper, stir this into the cooked lentils and simmer for a further minute. Remove from heat. Squeeze in the lemon juice, season with salt and serve hot with rotis or rice alongside.

Bootor Dali

| CHANA DAL WITH ONION AND SPICES |

I had this lovely dal at an Assamese friend's home. She had combined two lentils to get the right thick consistency that could be scooped up in a poori or fried bread. The dal will thicken as it cools after cooking so feel free to adjust the final consistency by adding as much – or no – water, as you prefer. *Serves 4* PREPARATION → *15 minutes, plus 1 hour soaking time* COOKING *1 hour*

2 tablespoons vegetable oil
1 teaspoon cumin seeds
2 bay leaves
1 onion, finely diced
2 fresh green chillies, slit lengthways
1 teaspoon ginger-garlic paste *(page 45)*
150g split gram lentils (chana dal), soaked in hot water
    for 1 hour then washed and drained
100g red lentils, washed and drained
1 teaspoon ground turmeric
1 teaspoon garam masala *(page 64)*
1 tablespoon grated jaggery or soft brown sugar
salt

1 Heat the oil in a saucepan over a high heat and add the cumin seeds and bay leaves. When they sizzle and change colour, add the onion and green chillies. Cook for 4–5 minutes until the onions begin to soften and change colour.

2 Stir in the ginger-garlic paste then add both the lentils. Fry for a couple of minutes, then sprinkle in the turmeric. Pour in water up to a couple of centimetres above the lentils and bring to the boil. Reduce the heat and simmer for 50 minutes or until the lentils have become soft and mushy, skimming the scum off the surface from time to time.

3 Mix in the garam masala and jaggery or sugar, season with salt and bring to the boil once more. Remove from the heat and serve hot.

Dalitoy

| LENTILS WITH ASAFOETIDA |

Growing up as a child in Bombay, this was one of the most comforting meals in my aunt's home. Served with plain rice and a papad (poppadum), it is something that I still long for when tired or hungry. This dal from the Konkani community has a powerful fragrance of asafoetida and curry leaves. *Serves 4* PREPARATION→ *15 minutes, plus 30 minutes soaking time* COOKING *1 hour*

200g toor dal, soaked in water at room temperature
    for 30 minutes, then washed and drained
1 fresh green chilli, slit lengthways
1 tablespoon coconut oil or vegetable oil
1 teaspoon black or brown mustard seeds
¼ teaspoon asafoetida
2 dried whole red chillies
large pinch of fresh or dried curry leaves
½ teaspoon ground turmeric
salt
boiled rice *(pages 78–79)* and papad, to serve

1 Put the toor dal and green chilli in a pan with double the volume of water. Bring to the boil then reduce the heat and simmer for 50 minutes, skimming the scum off the surface from time to time, until very soft. You can reduce the cooking time by soaking the lentils for longer, even overnight.
2 Heat the oil in a small frying pan over a high heat and add the mustard seeds. When they begin to pop, add the asafoetida, red chillies, curry leaves (standing back from the pan if using fresh leaves, as they will splutter) and turmeric.
3 When this mixture sizzles, stir it into the lentils. Season with salt and serve hot with rice and a papad.

Bhaja Muger Dal

| FRIED MUNG LENTILS |

A Bengali household is a fish- and meat-loving one but a couple of days each week, the menu becomes vegetarian, with not even onion or garlic added to the food, to give the digestion a rest from heavy and strongly flavoured foods. This dal with rice and a few vegetable fritters becomes a simple feast. The lentils are first fried, to give a nutty taste to the dal. *Serves 4* PREPARATION→ *10 minutes* COOKING *50 minutes*

200g split skinned mung dal
1 tablespoon vegetable oil
1 small cinnamon stick
3 green cardamom pods, seeds crushed and husks discarded
3 cloves
2 bay leaves
2 dried whole red chillies
1 teaspoon cumin seeds
2.5cm piece of fresh root ginger, scraped and grated
½ teaspoon ground turmeric
½ teaspoon caster sugar
1 tablespoon ghee, melted (optional)
salt

1 Heat a heavy-based saucepan over a high heat and dry-toast the mung dal for 7–8 minutes until they turn golden brown.
2 Pour in enough water to cover the lentils and bring to the boil. Reduce the heat and simmer for 30 minutes until they are soft, adding more water as necessary, to prevent them from drying out.
3 Heat the oil in a small frying pan over a high heat and add the cinnamon stick, crushed cardamom, cloves, bay leaves and chillies. Fry until the spices sizzle, change colour and become aromatic, then tip in the cumin seeds and after a few seconds, add the ginger and turmeric. Cook for a few seconds and stir the fried spices into the cooked lentils.
4 Season with salt, stir in the sugar, and pour the melted ghee over the top, if using.

Sindhi Dal
| TANGY LENTILS |

This is a popular Sindhi breakfast served with crisp bread called pakwan, although it is still as delicious with any bread. I first ate this as a child in Bombay, at a friend's eighth birthday party. It tasted wonderful and made a lovely change from the usual sandwiches and crisps!

Serves 4 PREPARATION → *15 minutes, plus 2 hours soaking time* COOKING *1 hour*

200g split gram lentils (chana dal), soaked in water for 2 hours, then washed and drained
½ teaspoon ground turmeric
1 tablespoon tamarind pulp *(page 418)* or shop-bought tamarind paste
1 tablespoon ghee or vegetable oil
1 teaspoon garam masala *(page 64)*
1 teaspoon medium-hot red chilli powder
1 teaspoon ground cumin
1 teaspoon amchoor (dried mango powder)
salt
bread, to serve

1 Put the lentils in a heavy-based saucepan with double the volume of water and bring to the boil. Stir in the turmeric, reduce the heat, partially cover the pan and simmer for 45 minutes, skimming the scum off the surface from time to time, until the lentils are very soft. You will need to keep topping up the water as the dal cooks and thickens. Stir in the tamarind pulp and season with salt.
2 Heat the ghee or oil in a small pan over a high heat. Add all the ground spices. When they begin to sizzle, add a splash of water to cook them without burning. When the water evaporates, pour the spices and oil over the cooked lentils, stir and serve hot with bread.

Panchmel Dal
| FIVE-LENTIL DAL |

'Panch' is 'five' in several Indian languages, 'mel' is a 'mix' and the dal is also called 'panchratna' or five-jewelled. It is sometimes eaten with a rich fried bread called 'bati' but goes well with rice or roti for a lighter meal. *Serves 4*
PREPARATION → *10 minutes, plus overnight soaking time* COOKING *1 hour*

200g mixed lentils, such as chana dal, toor dal, whole green mung beans, skinless urad dal, red lentils, soaked in water overnight at room temperature, then washed and drained
2 tablespoons vegetable oil or ghee
1 teaspoon cumin seeds
large pinch of asafoetida
2 dried whole red chillies
4 green cardamom pods, seeds crushed and husks discarded
1 small cinnamon stick
3 cloves
1 teaspoon grated fresh root ginger
1 teaspoon ground turmeric
1 teaspoon medium-hot red chilli powder
2 tomatoes, finely diced
a small handful of fresh coriander leaves, finely chopped, to garnish
salt
Rotis *(pages 108–109)* or boiled rice *(pages 78–79)*, to serve

1 Put the lentils in a saucepan along with double the volume of water. Bring to the boil, reduce the heat and simmer, partially covered, for about 50 minutes until soft and mushy, skimming the scum off the surface from time to time. Add water as necessary to keep the lentils submerged.
2 Heat the oil or ghee in a frying pan over a high heat and add the cumin seeds, asafoetida, dried chillies, cardamom seeds, cinnamon and cloves.
3 When the spices start to sizzle and change colour, stir in the ginger, turmeric and chilli powder. Cook for a few seconds, then mix in the tomatoes and season with salt. Add a splash of water and cook for 3–4 minutes until the oil begins to separate around the edges.
4 Pour the spice mix into the cooked lentils and heat through. Adjust the seasoning and consistency to taste. You should be able to pour the dal. Sprinkle with the fresh coriander and serve hot with rice or rotis.

VEGETABLES

A VEGETABLE MARKET IN INDIA IS A COLOURFUL, BUSTLING, BUSY PLACE.
THERE ARE FARMERS' MARKETS IN EVERY LOCALITY OF BIG CITIES AND IN TOWN OR VILLAGE SQUARES.
INDIANS EAT A LOT OF VEGETABLES ON A DAILY BASIS AND HAVE A HUGE VARIETY TO CHOOSE FROM.

Ancient Indian vegetables include lotus root and cucumber, both mentioned in the *Rigveda*, a religious text dating back to c.1500–1200 BC. It is often seen in Hindu texts that very esoteric concepts are explained through everyday objects or occurrences to make them easier to understand. A hymn to the god Shiva from this text is in use even today – it likens the liberation from death to the separation of the cucumber from the creeper.

After 1500 AD new vegetables came to India through foreign trade and conquest. The Portuguese brought potatoes, tomatoes, chillies, cashews, pumpkins and lychees whereas the British are credited with introducing India to cauliflowers and cabbages.

Native aubergines called brinjals probably spread to the Mediterranean through Arab traders. Although early aubergines were quite bitter, today's harvests are not, as the bitterness has been bred out.

A vegetable market in India is a colourful, bustling, busy place. There are farmers' markets in every locality of big cities and in town or village squares. Indians eat a lot of vegetables on a daily basis and have a huge variety to choose from, such as snake gourd and cluster beans. The repertoire of Indian vegetarian cooking is endless!

Whenever I am in Mumbai, I always make a point of wandering through my local farmers' markets – my favourite is the one at Grant Road where I have been shopping for so many years that I know several of the farmers personally. Some stalls are owned by people who buy vegetables such as potatoes, beans, carrots, gourds or cabbages from the farmers or from wholesale markets. Often the farmers themselves travel in from places such as Vasai, just outside Mumbai, with small stocks of unusual farm vegetables and one has to go to the market early to be able to find treasures such as breadfruit, jackfruit seeds, banana flower, wild fenugreek and colocasia leaves.

Breadfruit is a grapefruit-sized green vegetable with dense cream-coloured flesh that grows on large trees. It is peeled and diced to make curries and fritters in southern and coastal India where it grows. Similar in appearance but three times the size of a breadfruit is the strongly aromatic jackfruit, which when ripe is eaten as a fruit but when tender is used a vegetable. The large seeds are prized for their floury texture but also because they are a source of protein, fibre and vitamin B. Banana flowers are the edible blossoms of the banana tree. The dark purple outer husks are stripped away to reveal tender, yellow buds that are used for cooking. Wild fenugreek leaves are smaller than the bunches of fenugreek we see in Western shops. They are more powerful in aroma and slightly more bitter in taste, a quality for which they are prized. The colocasia plant is eaten from root to leaf. The tubers are starchy, like potatoes, and the large leaves are aromatic and stuffed with spiced gram flour to make a steamed snack called 'patrel'.

India still largely eats seasonally. People look forward to winter carrots and summer mangoes. It is a treat to eat a perfectly ripe Alphonso mango in May and enjoy a feast of Gujarati 'oondhiyoon' (see page 339) bursting with winter vegetables such as purple yam and carrots.

Chillies

Given that they are used in almost every savoury recipe from any part of the country, it is surprising that until a few hundred years ago, chillies were unknown in India. They were first introduced by the Portuguese at the end of the fifteenth century. Commercially, chillies, which are fruits of the capsicum species, are classified on their colour, shape and pungency, and over a hundred varieties are grown and eaten. Chillies have a strong, smarting aroma and their taste ranges from mild to dynamite. The level of heat is dependent on the amount of capsaicin present in the seeds, veins and skin of the chillies and is not diminished by cooking, storing or freezing. This is why, generally, the smaller the chilli, and the more concentrated the seeds and veins, the hotter it is.

Chillies bring heat as well as fragrance to a dish. Many of India's hottest places, such as Rajasthan and Andhra Pradesh, have a fiery cuisine because chillies actually cool down the body in hot weather. The capsaicin dilates blood vessels to increase circulation and encourage perspiration. However, if you ever bite into a chilli unexpectedly, don't reach for a jug of water – capsaicin is insoluble in water. Dairy products have the power to neutralise capsaicin so try yogurt or milk to calm the fire.

Chillies are available fresh, dried, powdered, flaked, in oil, in sauce, bottled and pickled.

How to buy chillies → When buying fresh chillies, look for crisp, unwrinkled ones that are glossy and green. Fresh red chillies (which are ripe green ones) are usually dried for better storage and to intensify their colour. Fresh green chillies are used when one wants a fresher 'green' chilli flavour and to supplement the green colour of a curry. Red chillies, dried as well as powdered, are used when one wants a red or brown colour in the sauce as well as a deeper, slightly smoky flavour.

The pungency can vary from the moderate Kashmir chilli and some dried south Indian varieties such as Tomato chillies and Byadagi chillies that give more colour than heat, to the fiery bird's-eye chillies from the north-east and the dried Guntur chillies which have a dark red, thick skin and incredible firepower. As with all ground spices, chilli powder loses its strength and sparkle after a few months. Whole dried chillies will keep for up to a year if stored in a dry, dark place.

How to prepare chillies → All chillies need to be treated with respect. The capsaicin in chillies is highly irritating to skin, so be careful when preparing them. Try to avoid contact with the inside of the fruit and wash hands with soap and water immediately after use.

1 To get more flavour than heat, hold a chilli at the stalk and run your knife down its length. Add the whole chilli to the pan. You can see the chilli and pull it out at any point during cooking.

2 For a hotter curry, finely chop the chilli and add the whole lot in, seeds and all. If you don't want too much heat but the recipe asks for diced chillies, for example in meatballs (see page 140), reduce the number of chillies used – one in place of two or half in place of one. I don't bother scraping the seeds out of chillies!

3 To make a quick chilli paste, roughly chop a chilli and crush it in a pestle and mortar with a tiny amount of salt.

4 To prepare dried chillies, remove the stems and shake out the seeds. They can be torn into bits, soaked in warm water or boiled in water for 5–6 minutes and ground to a paste for curries and sauces. The seeds are harder than in fresh chillies and can sometimes refuse to soften even on cooking. I like to shake out the seeds before puréeing them, but if they are going into the dish whole, more for flavour than for heat, leave the seeds in.

Indian Gourds

Gourds are fleshy fruit with a hard skin, although a few, such as the tindora or ivy gourd, have a thin, edible skin. They are grown all over India due to the warm, humid climate, which is ideal for these climbing plants. Many are neutral enough in taste to absorb the flavours of the spices they are cooked in. They grow easily in domestic gardens and keep well for long periods of time. I have seen an increasing number of gourds available in the West over the last few years, such as doodhi or bottle gourd and karela or bitter gourd. Gourds vary in size, shape and colour, but almost all have a distinctive skin and a multitude of seeds embedded in the inner flesh.

Some Indian gourds are 'turai' or ridged gourds, which have raised ridges along their length. The young fruits are cooked in stir-fries much like a courgette. Thinly peel the ridges before cooking (the remaining skin can be eaten). In south India, the discarded ridges are soaked in water and ground up into a delicious chutney with coconut and spices.

Karela or bitter gourds are popular in spite of their intense bitter flavour and are often combined with onions and tomatoes. Their skin is bright green and knobbly when fresh, and as they mature the skin turns yellow and the seeds start to turn orange. Karelas are prized in India as they contain active substances with anti-diabetic properties including charantin, which has a glucose-lowering effect and an insulin-like compound called polypeptide-p (see www.diabetes.co.uk). Western scientists are working on studies to prove this, but in India, people have eaten karela for a long time to help regulate blood sugar.

To prepare karela, slice it thinly and soak the slices in salted water for 15–20 minutes before cooking. This helps to draw out the juices and reduce the bitterness of the final dish slightly. After soaking, drain it and squeeze out the juices. It can be fried like chips or cooked with spices as in Karela Masala (page 322).

Lauki, dudhi or doodhi is also called bottle gourd. There are many varieties of shapes and sizes, such as the long, slim one or the round ball-like one commonly referred to as 'calabash gourd', and these grow on climbing frames in domestic gardens. The fruits have a smooth pale-green skin and the inner flesh is white, spongy and a bit like cucumber in taste. It is quite a bland watery vegetable but very versatile and can be made into curries, pancakes or sweets such as halwa.

Snake gourds are long and thin and can measure over 6 feet in length! They are plucked when very tender and flexible, and weights are often placed on them while growing to keep them straight. If left to grow naturally, they end up curling around themselves like huge green snakes.

Tindora, tendli or ivy gourds are slender oval fruits measuring only about 5cm in length. They taste crunchy and cucumber-like and are quite fresh and juicy. They are sliced lengthways or in small discs and are used in stir-fries or pickles. Overripe tindora are red on the inside and can be bitter, in which case they need to be discarded.

Tinda are smooth-skinned, lemon-sized round gourds that are cooked with garlic and tomatoes and are quite popular in north India where they are mostly grown.

Parwal or pointed gourds have a dark green striped skin and large seeds. The skin is quite coarse but edible.

Leafy Vegetables

These are eaten all over India, combined with lentils, meat, dairy or grains. Spinach, called 'palankya' in Sanskrit, is mentioned in the *Sushruta Samhita*, a sixth-century BC text about Ayurveda. Spinach is considered cooling and light to digest. It was widely used in ancient India and was known for its nutritional properties such as its iron content, which increased vitality.

Fenugreek or 'methi' is eaten fresh, combined with potatoes (see page 393). The slightly bitter, fragrant flavour plays an important role in vegetarian cookery and Ayurveda considers the seeds healing and anti-diabetic due to their ability to improve glucose tolerance. To prepare fresh methi, pluck the leaves off the thick stalks. The tender stems that grow towards the top of the plant can be eaten. In the West, bunches of fenugreek leaves are available at Indian grocers or in large stores in areas with a high Asian population.

Mustard greens or 'sarson' are a winter treat in Punjab. Ayurveda classifies them as warming and they are cooked with other vegetables and flour to make a green stew that is eaten with corn bread and butter. Mustard greens are available at Indian grocers in the West but if you can't find them, substitute them with kale.

Amaranth leaves are called 'maath', 'thotakura' or 'saga' and are available in green or red varieties, typically during the monsoon months from June to October. The leaves cook to a silky texture and are combined with onions and chillies. Spinach is an acceptable alternative.

Sorrel leaves called 'gongura' are a favourite vegetable in Andhra Pradesh, where they are even made into a tangy, spicy pickle. Again, available as red or green, it is a summer vegetable, which becomes more sour depending on how hot the growing conditions are. In the West, these can be substituted with spinach to which a bit of lemon juice has been added.

Colocasia, or 'arvi', 'eddoe' or 'taro', is eaten as leaves or roots all over the country. There are two varieties: one with a tender green stalk that is used for curries, the other with a purple stalk, used to make a side dish or snack called 'patra' or 'patrode'. However, colocasia leaves contain calcium oxalate in the form of microscopic needles that can irritate the throat and mouth. Therefore it has to be cooked with an acid such as tamarind, kokum or lemon before eating it. The roots do not have these needles and cook to a texture resembling a sticky potato. A suitable alternative in the West is spinach.

Root Vegetables

'Aloo', 'batata' or 'bangala dumpa', as potatoes are variously known, play a key role in Indian cooking. India is one of the world's largest producers, with romantic-sounding varieties such as Kufri Sindhuri, a waxy red potato and Kufri Himalini, a floury, mild variety suitable for growing on hillsides.

In the West, I tend to use whichever potato is in season, so at times I will have a floury one and at others, a waxy one. I quite enjoy the difference in textures and will happily swap a new potato for a King Edward.

Carrots are mostly a winter vegetable in India. The Eastern or Asiatic variety is darker orange in colour and slimmer than its Western counterpart. It is sought after for its colour and flavour in recipes such as Gajar ka Halwa (page 457), a jammy, fragrant mix of shredded carrots, sugar, nuts and cardamom.

Yams of different kinds are eaten in various parts of the country. 'Suran' or 'oal' is starchy elephant foot yam which is cooked with spices into a curry, mashed for chutneys or pickled in warming oil and spices. It is quite sticky once peeled so cooks oil their hands before handling it and use an acidic food in its cooking to make it more manageable. It's all well worth the effort because suran has a wonderful dry texture that is quite unlike other root vegetables. Purple yams called 'kand' are large, knarled tubers and again, mostly seen in markets in the winter months when they are made into a fabulous Gujarati mixed vegetable dish called 'oondhiyoon' (see page 457) or spiced and fried as chips. This can be substituted with sweet potato or potato in the West.

Sweet potatoes, commonly eaten in India, are not from the potato family at all. Potatoes belong to the nightshade family whereas sweet potatoes belong to the genus that has flowers, such as morning glory. They are sliced and fried like chips, cooked in curries with lentils or onions and tomatoes, or combined with spices to make stir-fried side dishes.

Aubergines

Indian vegetarian cooking would be sadly diminished without this popular vegetable known as brinjal or 'baingan'. Brinjals have been cultivated in India since prehistoric times. Large aubergines are fire-roasted and mashed into a dish called 'bharta' or 'bhareet'. Medium-sized, green, white or purple ones are cut open and stuffed with onions, coconut, tomatoes, flour and spices, and sometimes aubergines are diced and simply cooked with potatoes to make a stir-fried side dish called 'bhaji'.

Some aubergines have more seeds than others, but these are soft and edible. There is no need to salt and drain aubergines – modern varieties are not bitter. There are many varieties of Indian brinjals, such as the north Indian Pusa Kranti, with small oblong fruit that are stuffed with spices, or the Vaishali, a medium-sized, purple brinjal with white stripes, grown in Maharashtra, that is cooked with coconut to make curries.

Regional Vegetables

Home kitchens pride themselves on using local and seasonal produce found in farmers' markets. The southern states, such as Tamil Nadu, India's largest banana growing state, will have banana flowers, plantain and raw and ripe jackfruit, which needs a hot, humid climate to grow in. In the southern summer, jackfruit is chopped up into coconut curries or cooling salads.

In Maharashtra, small spiny gourds called 'kantola' and red sorrel leaves are found in monsoon markets around August. In the winter, vegetable markets in Delhi are full of mustard greens and bathua or pigweed, a leafy vegetable that is boiled to remove its bitterness and then added to curries, or to yogurt to make a raita. Turnips can be seen in Punjabi winter markets and these are made into a seasonal pickle to be eaten through the cold months. Markets around the country sell bamboo shoots, chillies, ginger, tomatoes, pumpkins, okra (ladies' fingers), raw mangoes and all kinds of stems, stalks, leaves, roots and fruit. These are rarely seen on restaurant menus but come into their full glory in festive seasonal menus.

HOW TO BREAK AND GRATE A COCONUT

Coconuts are important not just in Indian cooking but also in Hindu rituals and celebrations. In Sanskrit, the coconut is called 'shrifal' or fruit of auspiciousness. It grows on coastal shores, taking in salty water, and yet creates sweet water and flesh, a quality that, according to Hindu philosophy, should be emulated. Coconuts are placed on a brass pot decorated with mango leaves during the Hindu marriage ceremony to signify a future life of plenty. Kerala, which means 'Land of Coconuts', is the state with the ideal climate, that grows the highest number of coconuts in India.

The origin of the coconut tree is vague but the fruit, being water resistant and able to float, certainly spread to various lands via the oceans and sprouted on coasts far and wide. In India, coconuts grow all over the southern peninsula and in Bengal and Assam. These cuisines use coconut in the form of milk, water or the flesh itself.

HOW TO BUY A COCONUT

Coconuts are sold in many forms – as jelly nuts, tender green coconuts or the hard brown ones. Green coconuts are prized for the nourishing, sweet water they contain – one of nature's finest drinks. The brown coconut, on the other hand, is a cooking fruit and forms the base of a lot of south Indian and Bengali cooking. When buying a brown coconut, look for a hard, unbroken shell. If there is a crack the inner flesh will be dry or mouldy. Then lift the coconut and shake it close to your ear. You should hear the water inside which means that it is fresh.

HOW TO BREAK AND GRATE A COCONUT

A brown coconut is naturally fibrous. Pull off the fibres and discard. You will find three 'eyes' on one of the tapered ends of the coconut. They look like three large, black dots. Hold the coconut over a bowl. Using a screwdriver or corkscrew, pierce these eyes and drain the water into the bowl. This should be clear and sweet smelling. If it is cloudy, slimy or foul smelling, the coconut is either not fresh or has gone off. Clear coconut water is sweet and can be drunk strained into a cup.

Next, use a hammer or blunt end of a large knife and smack the coconut sharply but gently along the 'equator'. Do this until you see a crack forming, then hit a little harder to break it into two pieces.

Using a sharp knife, prise away the flesh from the shell in large chunks. The brown skin can be easily peeled away using a vegetable peeler, leaving you with pieces of bright white coconut flesh. It can then be grated in a food processor or on a grater or thinly sliced.

In India, a coconut is typically cracked open by banging it on the ground if one has an outdoor space or as above, using a curved kitchen instrument called a 'koyta'. The two halves are then grated on a coconut scraper. This is a flat, wooden base to which a sickle-shaped blade is attached. It has a serrated fan at the end, which is used to scrape out the white flesh from the coconut shell. The blade is also used to chop meat and vegetables. This whole device is placed on the floor and one has to sit on the plinth to use it.

Frozen, grated coconut is available in the freezer section of Indian shops as well as some supermarkets.

DESICCATED COCONUT

Some Indian recipes, such as dry chutneys, specifically require desiccated coconut, which is called 'kopra' in India. Unsweetened desiccated coconut can be used instead of fresh coconut but the taste will differ a bit. If substituting fresh with desiccated, soak the dried coconut in some warm water for 30 minutes. Drain the coconut before use.

MASTERCLASS

COCONUT MILK

Making coconut milk is not
difficult but it is slightly time
consuming. *Makes 400ml thick milk and
10mml thin milk* PREPARATION → *5 minutes*

YOU WILL NEED:
fresh coconut, shredded
– warm water
– jug blender
– sieve
– bowl

1 Once the coconut has been cracked open, peeled and
shredded (see page 310), soak the flesh in warm water
(enough to cover the coconut) for a few minutes.

2 Put the coconut and water in a blender and blitz until
coarse. Pour into a sieve placed over a bowl and press and
squeeze the coconut to extract the thick white milk. In
Indian kitchens, this process is repeated to extract 'thin'
coconut milk after the first 'thick' pressing. Recipes will
often ask you to cook the curry in the 'thin' milk and finish
it with the 'thick' milk at the end. This is because rich
coconut milk may split on prolonged cooking.

STORE CUPBOARD VARIATIONS

Canned coconut milk You can also buy cans of coconut
milk, but make sure to check the ingredients on the label
for unwanted thickeners such as guar or xanthan gums.
Partly used cans of milk can be decanted into tubs and
frozen for later use. To make 'thin' milk from a can, dilute
half the can with an equal amount of water. The remainder
can be used as 'thick' milk.

Coconut powder or creamed coconut If you require a small
amount of coconut milk, make this with coconut powder
or creamed coconut.

2 tablespoons coconut powder or creamed coconut
    (or more, depending on how thick you want the milk to be)
200ml warm water
sieve
bowl

1 Combine the powder or creamed coconut with the warm
water and whisk until smooth. Strain through a sieve into
a bowl.

Aloo Gobi

| NORTH INDIAN SPICED POTATO
WITH CAULIFLOWER |

This much-loved dish has been made even more popular
by north Indian restaurants in the West. Cauliflowers
grow in abundance in the north Indian winter and are a
popular vegetable dish there. They, along with potatoes,
are available all year round in Western countries and are
therefore a restaurant staple. This tastes divine when the
vegetables are almost fried rather than stewed, so my
recipe has a bit more oil than I'd normally use. Typically a
dry side dish, it goes well with rotis, pooris, parathas or rice
dishes. *Serves 4* PREPARATION → *10 minutes* COOKING *40 minutes*

3 tablespoons vegetable oil
1 teaspoon cumin seeds
1 medium onion, finely diced
½ teaspoon ginger-garlic paste *(page 45)*
2 fresh green chillies, finely chopped
2 potatoes, peeled and cut into 2cm dice
2 fresh tomatoes, finely diced
½ head of cauliflower, cut into florets
1 teaspoon ground turmeric
1 teaspoon amchoor (dried mango powder) or lemon juice
1 teaspoon garam masala *(page 64)*
a small handful of fresh coriander leaves, chopped, to garnish
salt
Rotis *(pages 108–109)*, to serve

1 Heat the oil in a heavy-based pan over a high heat and add
the cumin seeds. As soon as they darken, add the onion and
fry for about 6 minutes until soft. Add the ginger-garlic paste
and chillies and fry for a few seconds.
2 Tip in the potatoes. Fry for a couple of minutes, stirring
frequently to prevent the mixture from sticking to the bottom
of the pan, then add the tomatoes and allow to soften. Cook
for a couple of minutes, then tip in the cauliflower florets,
turmeric and amchoor powder (if using) and season with salt.
Mix well, reduce the heat and cook for 30 minutes, sprinkling
in a couple of handfuls of water if it begins to stick to the pan.
3 When the vegetables are completely done, remove from
the heat, sprinkle with the garam masala, add lemon juice
(if using instead of amchoor), season to taste and serve hot
sprinkled with the coriander and rotis alongside.

Palak Ki Subzi

| SPINACH AND DILL MEDLEY |

I find the combination of spinach with other greens such
kale, chard or collard greens irresistible for its taste and
texture. Greens are often combined in Indian cooking for
this reason. The dill brings a freshness to this recipe, which
is a powerhouse of nutrients such as vitamins A and C.
Serves 4 PREPARATION → *10 minutes* COOKING *30 minutes*

2 tablespoons vegetable oil
1 teaspoon cumin seeds
1 large onion, finely chopped
1 teaspoon dried fenugreek leaves (kasoori methi – *page 393*)
    or a good handful of fresh fenugreek leaves,
washed, drained and finely chopped
1 teaspoon ginger-garlic paste *(page 45)*
1 fresh green chilli, finely chopped
300g fresh spinach, washed, drained and chopped
150g fresh dill, washed, drained and chopped
salt
Rotis *(pages 108–109)*, to serve (optional)

1 Heat the oil in a heavy-based pan over a high heat and add
the cumin seeds. Fry for about 1 minute until they darken,
then add the onion and fry for about 5 minutes until soft.
Add the kasoori methi, if using. Stir in the ginger-garlic paste
and the chilli.
2 Tip in the chopped spinach and dill along with the
fenugreek leaves, if using, season with salt and stir well. Keep
stirring for 8–10 minutes until the leaves are well blended
and cooked through. Serve hot with rotis or to accompany a
chicken curry and rice.

MASTERCLASS

BAINGAN BHARTA – Fire-roasted Aubergine with Spices

This very popular north Indian dish is simple to prepare but might seem a bit scary at first! The aubergine can be cooked in several ways: directly on a gas hob without oil, on a barbecue, or grilled or baked in an oven after brushing with oil. I prefer to cook it on the hob – it takes only 7–8 minutes and achieves the smokiest flavour. *Serves 4* PREPARATION →

10 minutes COOKING *40 minutes*

1 Place the aubergine directly on a lit gas hob without brushing with oil. Cook for 7–8 minutes, turning it from time to time with a pair of tongs, until you can pierce the thickest part easily with a knife. By this time the skin will look crinkly and crisp. Leave to cool, then peel off the skin with a small knife or with your fingers.

2 Discard the stalk and mash the flesh of the aubergine in a bowl with a fork. Set aside.

YOU WILL NEED:

1 large aubergine
2 tablespoons vegetable oil
½ teaspoon cumin seeds
1 medium onion, finely chopped
1 teaspoon ginger-garlic paste *(page 45)*
1 fresh green chilli, chopped
2 tablespoons tomato purée or 2 fresh tomatoes,
    finely chopped, seeds and all
1 teaspoon ground turmeric
1 teaspoon ground coriander
3 tablespoons green garden peas (fresh or frozen)
a small sprig of fresh coriander leaves, chopped, to garnish
salt
Rotis *(pages 108–109)* or Naans *(pages 110–113)*, to serve

3 Heat the oil in a saucepan over a high heat, add the cumin seeds and fry for 30 seconds until they darken. Add the onion and fry for 7–8 minutes until soft, then add the ginger-garlic paste and the green chilli and fry for 1 minute. Add the tomato purée and the spices and cook for 4–5 minutes until well blended, adding a tablespoon of water to stop the purée from sticking to the bottom of the pan. If using fresh tomatoes, you will not need to add water.

4 Tip in the peas, season with salt and cook for 7–8 minutes over a medium heat until they are tender.

5 Stir in the aubergine. Season to taste and serve hot, sprinkled with the coriander. Enjoy with a rotis or naan.

Bhindi Ki Subzi

| SPICED STIR-FRIED OKRA |

This straightforward stir-fry has many regional variations.
These are based on locally-grown ingredients such as
coconut, which is sprinkled on top in the south, or on
cooking styles such as the north Indian 'tadka', where
onions, ginger, garlic and tomatoes are stir-fried at the
beginning to create a base for the dish. You'll find that at
the end of cooking, the bottom of the pan appears black –
this is the sliminess that has cooked off and does not mean
that the okra has burnt. *Serves 4* PREPARATION → *10 minutes, plus
overnight drying time* COOKING *25 minutes*

2 tablespoons vegetable oil
1 teaspoon black mustard seeds
½ teaspoon cumin seeds
1 medium onion, thinly sliced
300g okra, washed and dried overnight *(see page 235)*, tops
    and tails removed, cut into 2cm dice
1 teaspoon ground turmeric
½ teaspoon medium-hot red chilli powder
1 tablespoon lemon juice
salt
Rotis *(pages 108–109)*, to serve

1 Heat the oil in a heavy-based saucepan over a high heat
and add the mustard seeds. When they begin to pop, add
the cumin seeds. As they darken, add the onion and fry for
4–5 minutes until soft.
2 Tip in the okra and stir well. Season with salt. Cook over
a medium heat for 12–15 minutes, stirring from time to time,
until the okra softens. The vegetable will change from being
firm to soft – you can test this by cutting through a piece with
your ladle. The stickiness should disappear by now. The
colour will have also changed from a bright to a dull green.
3 Stir in the ground spices and lemon juice, cook for a couple
of minutes and serve hot with rotis.

Bhindi Kurkure

| CRISP, TANGY, SPICY OKRA |

Okra is a well-loved vegetable throughout India, but only
when it's not gloopy. The sticky sap is cooked off by the
addition of some acid such as amchoor (see page 61) or
kokum (see page 417) and no water is added while making
a dry okra dish. When adding it to a curry, there will always
be an acidic base that cuts through the sliminess.

Serves 4 PREPARATION → *15 minutes, plus overnight drying time*
COOKING *15 minutes*

1 teaspoon medium-hot red chilli powder
1 teaspoon ground turmeric
1 teaspoon amchoor (dried mango powder)
2 tablespoons gram flour
vegetable oil, for deep-frying
300g okra, washed and dried overnight *(see page 235)*, tops
    and tails removed, and cut diagonally into thick slices
salt
small pinch of caster sugar, to serve

1 Mix the chilli powder, turmeric, amchoor, salt to season
and gram flour in a bowl together with a little bit of water to
make a thick batter.
2 Heat enough oil in a frying pan to hold a single layer of
okra. Dip the okra in the batter, let any excess batter drip off
before frying and fry them in batches for 4–5 minutes until
crisp and golden. You may need to separate the frying okra
with a fork, as the flour can make them clump together.
3 Remove from the oil with a slotted spoon, drain on kitchen
paper and serve hot with a sprinkling of caster sugar.

Gucchi Korma

| MUSHROOM AND PEA KORMA |

Mushrooms have been cultivated in India only for the past 40 years or so. Earlier, foragers used to gather small quantities for home use but they were never considered a mainstream vegetable. Ayurveda classifies them as 'tamasic' or unpalatable, promoting laziness and pessimism. With the increase in farmed closed-cup mushrooms, one sees them in Indian markets and on restaurant menus but some people still avoid them because of Ayurvedic thinking. *Serves 4*

PREPARATION —➔ *15 minutes* COOKING *40 minutes*

1 large onion, sliced
1 fresh green chilli, chopped
50g unsalted cashew nuts
2 tablespoons vegetable oil
2 teaspoons ginger-garlic paste *(page 45)*
200g closed cup mushrooms, sliced
100g frozen green peas
1 teaspoon ground coriander
1 teaspoon ground cumin
1 teaspoon garam masala *(page 64)*, plus extra to serve
1 teaspoon ground turmeric
1 tablespoon single cream (optional)
salt
Pooris *(pages 114–115)*, Rotis *(pages 108–109)* or
    boiled rice *(pages 78–79)*, to serve

1 Put the onion, chilli and cashew nuts in a pan with just enough water to cover them and bring to the boil. Simmer for about 10 minutes, until the onion is very soft, then transfer to a blender and blitz to a smooth paste. Set aside.
2 Heat the oil in a heavy-based saucepan over a high heat. Add the ginger-garlic paste, cook for 30 seconds, then add the mushrooms and peas to the pan. Season with salt and stir in the ground spices. Cook for a few minutes, until the mushrooms release their juices and the spices cook, then add the onion and cashew paste.
3 Cook for 7–8 minutes until the peas are done. Stir in the cream, if using. Season to taste, heat through, sprinkle with a pinch of garam masala and serve hot with pooris, rotis or rice.

Banarasi Aloo

| POTATOES WITH TAMARIND AND CREAM |

The addition of cream makes this lovely recipe rich enough to be served at parties. Banaras, Varanasi or Kashi, as it is variously known, is situated on the banks of the river Ganga in Uttar Pradesh and is one of the holiest cities for a Hindu because of its ancient Shiva temple. The cuisine is a mix of various styles but vegetarian cookery is especially popular for religious reasons. This recipe demonstrates how rich ingredients are added to humble vegetables such as the potato to make a rather festive dish. *Serves 4*

PREPARATION —➔ *55 minutes* COOKING *40 minutes*

200g potatoes
2 tablespoons vegetable oil
1 teaspoon fennel seeds
1 teaspoon medium-hot red chilli powder, mixed with
    2 tablespoons of water
2 teaspoons tamarind pulp *(page 418)* or shop-bought
    tamarind paste
2 tablespoons tomato purée
2 tablespoons single cream
salt
1 teaspoon garam masala *(page 64)*, to serve

1 Boil the potatoes in their skins, then peel and cut into 2cm cubes.
2 Heat the oil in a saucepan over a high heat, then add the fennel seeds. When they darken, add the chilli water. Cook for 1 minute, until the water evaporates, then add the tamarind and tomato purée. Cook for a few seconds. Fold in the cooked potatoes, season with salt and pour in the cream. Heat through, adding a little water to make a thick sauce.
3 Sprinkle with the garam masala and serve hot.

Doodhi Chana

| BOTTLE GOURD WITH CHANA DAL |

Bottle gourd, 'doodhi', 'dudhi' or 'lauki', is a watery but nutritious vegetable that can take on the flavour of the spices it is cooked in. You can swap the chana dal for a tin of chickpeas for a speedier version. This recipe is made all over the central, western and northern parts of India.

Serves 4 PREPARATION → *10 minutes, plus 30 minutes soaking time* COOKING *30 minutes*

2 tablespoons vegetable oil
1 teaspoon cumin seeds
1 teaspoon ginger-garlic paste *(page 45)*
1 teaspoon ground turmeric
3 tablespoons split gram lentils (chana dal), soaked in
    warm water for 30 minutes and drained
1 medium doodhi (bottle gourd), peeled and cut into 2cm cubes
1 teaspoon ground coriander
1 fresh tomato, chopped
a handful of fresh coriander leaves, chopped
salt
Roti *(pages 108–109)* or boiled rice *(pages 78–79)*, to serve

1 Heat the oil in a heavy-based saucepan over a high heat, add the cumin seeds and fry until they darken, then add the ginger-garlic paste and turmeric. Stir for a few seconds, then add the lentils and pour in 150ml water. Bring to the boil, reduce the heat and simmer for about 10 minutes, adding more water if it dries out.

2 Tip in the doodhi, then add the ground coriander, tomato and season with salt. Mix well, add a splash of water and bring to the boil. The doodhi will release its juices due to the added salt. Reduce the heat, cover and simmer for 10 minutes.

3 Remove from the heat, season to taste, stir in the coriander and serve hot with rotis or rice.

Karela Masala

| SPICED BITTER GOURD |

The bitterness of these gourds is an acquired taste, but being a natural blood sugar stabiliser, they are eaten frequently in Indian homes. Many Indians are prone to Type 2 diabetes. A World Health Organization study from 2004 has suggested that by 2030, 80 million people in India will have the disease, partly because of increased prosperity leading to an increase in caloric intake.

Gourds are soaked in salted water and drained to remove some of the bitterness but some people actually drink this water as well, because of its blood-sugar-stabilising properties. Look for bright green, firm fruits. Discard the inner seeds if they are hard (the soft ones can be eaten). *Serves 4* PREPARATION → *10 minutes, plus 20 minutes soaking time* COOKING *35 minutes*

2 tablespoons vegetable oil
1 teaspoon cumin seeds
1 large onion, finely diced
300g karela (bitter gourd), washed, thinly sliced and soaked
    in salted water for 20 minutes
1 teaspoon ground turmeric
½ teaspoon medium-hot red chilli powder
salt
Rotis *(pages 108–109)*, Parathas *(page 120–121)* or
    Naans *(page 110–111)*, to serve

1 Heat the oil in a heavy-based saucepan over a high heat, then add the cumin seeds. Fry until they darken, then add the onion and fry for 7–8 minutes until soft.

2 Squeeze out the excess water from the karela and add it to the onions. Reduce the heat to medium and cook for 12–15 minutes, until they begin to change colour and soften. Continue cooking until you can cut through a piece with a spoon.

3 Add the ground spices, season with salt and mix well. Continue to cook over a low heat, stirring frequently to prevent it from sticking to the bottom of the pan, for a further couple of minutes. The karela should be dry, well browned and slightly crisp. Serve hot with rotis, parathas or naans.

Bagare Baingan

| AUBERGINES IN A SESAME AND PEANUT SAUCE |

There are several versions of this very famous Hyderabadi dish, depending on what variety of aubergine is available or based on family preferences, but all contain sesame and nuts. *Serves 4* PREPARATION ➔ *15 minutes* COOKING *40 minutes*

2 tablespoons vegetable oil
4 dried red chillies, halved and seeds shaken out
2 tablespoons unsalted peanuts
1 tablespoon coriander seeds
1 medium onion, sliced
2 tablespoons freshly grated or desiccated coconut
1 tablespoon white sesame seeds
1 tablespoon ginger-garlic paste *(page 45)*
1 teaspoon ground turmeric
250g whole small aubergines or 1 large aubergine, diced
2 teaspoons tamarind pulp *(page 418)* or shop-bought
    tamarind paste
1 tablespoon jaggery or soft brown sugar
a small handful of fresh coriander leaves, chopped, to garnish
salt

1 Heat half the oil in a heavy-based saucepan over a high heat and add the chillies, peanuts and coriander seeds. Fry until they turn dark, then add the onion. Continue frying, stirring from time to time, and when the onion turns golden brown, add the coconut and sesame seeds. As the coconut starts to brown, add the ginger-garlic paste and mix well. Remove from the heat, leave to cool slightly then transfer to a blender, add enough water to cover and blitz to make a fine paste. Season with salt, stir in the turmeric and set aside.
2 Keeping the stem intact, slit the aubergines twice in a cross nearly all the way to the stem. Stuff each aubergine with the curry paste. If there is some left over, reserve this for the sauce. If using diced aubergine, proceed to the next step.
3 Heat the remaining oil in a heavy-based saucepan over a high heat. Put the stuffed aubergines in the pan and fry for a couple of minutes. Add the remaining curry paste (or all of it if using diced aubergine). Pour in the tamarind pulp, sprinkle in the jaggery and bring to the boil. Reduce the heat and simmer, adding more water as required, for 25–30 minutes until the aubergines are cooked through.
4 Season to taste and serve hot, sprinkled with the coriander.

Bharela Ringan Nu Shak

| STUFFED BABY AUBERGINES |

Many Indian regions have a recipe for stuffed aubergines – this one is from Gujarat and uses peanuts and gram flour to thicken and flavour the sauce. In Maharashtra cooks use local coconut and in the north, the stuffing might have onions and tomatoes. I have chosen this one for its nutty fragrance. If you can't find the small variety of aubergines, this recipe can still be made with large aubergines cut into a dice and cooked in the sauce rather than being stuffed with it. *Serves 4* PREPARATION ➔ *15 minutes* COOKING *45 minutes*

2 tablespoons gram flour
1 x 400g can of chopped tomatoes
2 teaspoons unsalted peanuts, crushed
1 tablespoon ginger-garlic paste *(page 45)*
a handful of fresh coriander leaves, chopped
½ teaspoon ground turmeric
½ teaspoon medium-hot red chilli powder
300g small aubergines, slit lengthways but stalks left on
2 tablespoons vegetable oil
½ teaspoon black mustard seeds
salt
Rotis *(pages 108–109)* or Gujarati Dal *(page 284)* and boiled rice
    (pages 78–79), to serve

1 Combine the gram flour, tomatoes, peanuts, ginger-garlic paste, coriander leaves, ground spices and salt in a mixing bowl. Stuff the aubergines with this mixture, saving any that is left over for the curry.
2 Heat the oil in a heavy-based saucepan over a high heat. Add the mustard seeds and fry until they begin to pop, then gently place the stuffed aubergines in the pan and pour in any leftover spice mixture. Pour in a few tablespoons of water and cover the pan. Bring to the boil, reduce the heat and simmer for 25 minutes or until the aubergines are cooked. Keep adding water as necessary to prevent the mixture from sticking. Season to taste and serve hot – the sauce should be quite thick – with rotis or Gujarati dal and rice.

Aloo Methi

| FENUGREEK LEAVES WITH POTATO |

Fresh fenugreek (methi) is sold in bunches with the roots still intact. The leaves are plucked off and the large stems and roots are discarded. If you can't find fresh fenugreek, substitute it with dried fenugreek, called 'kasoori methi', which is sold in Indian grocery or spice shops. Cutting the potatoes into small chunks means they cook faster and absorb the flavours better. *Serves 4* PREPARATION → *15 minutes* COOKING *35 minutes*

1 tablespoon vegetable oil
1 teaspoon cumin seeds
2 onions, finely diced
1 fresh green chilli, finely diced
2 large potatoes, peeled and cut into 2cm cubes
½ teaspoon ground turmeric
1 teaspoon ground coriander
1 bunch fresh fenugreek (methi), leaves picked, washed
    and finely chopped or 2 tablespoons dried fenugreek leaves
    (kasoori methi – *page 393*)
salt
Rotis *(pages 108–109)* or boiled rice *(pages 78–79)* and lentils
    (try Aamti – *page 279*), to serve

1 Heat the oil in a heavy-based pan over a high heat, add the cumin seeds and fry for 20 seconds until they darken, then add the onions and chilli and cook for 5–6 minutes until soft.
2 Tip in the potatoes and fry well for a few minutes, until starting to brown. Add the ground spices and cook for a few seconds, then stir in the fenugreek leaves and season with salt. Cover and cook over a low heat for 25 minutes, until the potatoes are tender and you can pierce them easily with a knife. To prevent the potatoes from sticking to the bottom of the pan, place a convex lid on the pan and fill it with a few tablespoons of cold water. As the vegetables heat up, steam that hits the inside of the lid condenses and falls back into the pan, providing a bit of moisture.
3 Season to taste and serve hot with rotis or with rice and a lentil dish such as Aamti.

Muttakos Thoran

| CABBAGE WITH COCONUT |

This simple, dry side dish is a Kerala speciality and is often served on a banana leaf as part of a traditional meal such as a wedding feast. You can replace the cabbage with other firm vegetables such as carrots, parsnips or broccoli.
Serves 4 PREPARATION → *15 minutes* COOKING *30 minutes*

2 tablespoons coconut or vegetable oil
1 teaspoon black or brown mustard seeds
10 fresh or 15 dried curry leaves
2 fresh green chillies, slit lengthways
large pinch of asafoetida
1 teaspoon ground turmeric
200g white cabbage, finely shredded
1 tablespoon fresh or frozen grated coconut
salt

1 Heat the oil in a heavy-based frying pan over a high heat and add the mustard seeds. When they begin to pop add the curry leaves (standing back from the pan if using fresh leaves, as they will splutter) and chillies. Sprinkle in the asafoetida, stir in the turmeric and add the cabbage. Season with salt, cover and cook over a medium heat for 20–25 minutes, stirring occasionally, until tender. The salt will draw out the water from the cabbage.
2 Remove from the heat, stir in the coconut, season to taste and serve hot.

Vange Fry

| FRIED SPICED AUBERGINE |

This recipe from Maharashtra is simple and makes a great side dish with rice and dal. The crisp crust is a delicious contrast to the soft centre. You'll need a large aubergine for this and the slices should be about a centimetre thick to hold their shape when cooking. *Serves 4*
PREPARATION → *15 minutes* COOKING *15 minutes*

1 teaspoon ground turmeric
1 teaspoon medium-hot red chilli powder
1 teaspoon ground cumin
1 large aubergine, thickly sliced
vegetable oil, for shallow-frying
3 tablespoons rice flour
salt

1 Mix the spices and salt to season. Rub the aubergine slices with this spice mixture and set aside for 10 minutes.
2 Heat enough oil to cover the base of a frying pan over a high heat. Test the temperature of the oil by dipping a slice of aubergine into it. If it sizzles, the oil is ready. Dip each slice of aubergine in the rice flour to coat it on both sides and place in the oil. Fry the slices in batches, for 3–4 minutes on each side, until crisp and golden. You may need to drizzle a bit more oil if the pan gets too dry.
3 Remove with a slotted spoon, drain on kitchen paper and serve at once.

Navratan Korma

| NINE-JEWELLED CURRY |

This rich, slightly sweet, north Indian vegetable curry has its origins in Mughlai cooking, which is a blend of Indian and Persian styles where you find fruit added to curries, unlike in other styles around India. *Serves 4* PREPARATION → *15 minutes*
COOKING *50 minutes*

2 tablespoons vegetable oil
1 small cinnamon stick
½ teaspoon crushed black peppercorns
3 green cardamom pods, seeds crushed and husks discarded
2 onions, grated
1 tablespoon ginger-garlic paste *(page 45)*
2 tablespoons tomato purée
3 fresh green chillies, slit lengthways
200g mixed raw vegetables, such as peas, cauliflower, carrots, beans and potatoes, peeled and diced into bite-sized pieces (except the peas)
1 teaspoon ground turmeric
1 teaspoon garam masala *(page 64)*, plus extra to serve
2 tablespoons unsalted cashew nuts
2 tablespoons canned pineapple chunks, chopped, plus 3 tablespoons of the juice
100ml single cream
small sprig of fresh coriander leaves, to garnish
salt
boiled rice *(pages 78–79)* and poppadums, to serve

1 Heat the oil in a saucepan over a high heat, add the cinnamon stick, pepper and cardamom and fry for 1 minute until they sizzle, then add the onions, reduce the heat to medium and fry for 7–8 minutes until they begin to change colour. Keep stirring to prevent them from sticking. Stir in the ginger-garlic paste, tomato purée and chillies and cook for 2–3 minutes until the oil separates, adding a couple of tablespoons of water to hasten the process.
2 Increase the heat and tip in the vegetables, turmeric, garam masala and salt to season. Mix gently, just cover with water and bring to the boil. Reduce the heat and simmer for 35 minutes until the vegetables are tender.
3 Fold in the cashew nuts and pineapple and pour in the pineapple juice with the cream. Warm through, season to taste and serve hot, sprinkled with garam masala and the coriander leaves.

Kumra Charchari

| PUMPKIN WITH MUSTARD SEED PASTE |

This is a dry Bengali dish served with rice and dal. The pumpkin can be swapped for potatoes, aubergines or carrots but cooking times will increase for potatoes and carrots. The sweetness of pumpkin or 'kumro' goes well with the slight sharpness of mustard. Shop-bought mustard pastes are not suitable as they often have additional ingredients such as wine, vinegar or wheat flour.

Serves 4 PREPARATION → *15 minutes* COOKING *40 minutes*

1 teaspoon black or brown mustard seeds
1 fresh green chilli
1 tablespoon mustard or vegetable oil
1 teaspoon nigella (kalonji) or cumin seeds
300g pumpkin, cut into bite-sized pieces (skin left on)
salt
Pooris *(pages 114–115)* or boiled rice *(pages 78–79)* and dal, to serve

1 Crush the mustard seeds and chilli in a pestle and mortar or grind in a spice mill to make a paste.

2 Heat the mustard oil in a non-stick pan to smoking point then reduce the heat and add the nigella or cumin seeds. If using vegetable oil, warm it before adding the seeds. Tip in the pumpkin, season with salt and fold in the mustard and chilli paste. Pour in enough water to cover the base of the pan and bring to the boil.

3 Reduce the heat, cover and simmer for 8–10 minutes, until the pumpkin is tender. Remove from the heat, season to taste and serve hot with pooris or rice and dal.

Kanda Mirchi Cha Zunka

| SPRING ONIONS AND PEPPERS
WITH GRAM FLOUR |

A Maharashtrian side dish, this is traditionally eaten with millet bread called 'bhakri' (see page 117). It can be made dry, or slightly runny with the addition of more water at the end. I prefer mine to be soft and squidgy as in this recipe. *Serves 4* PREPARATION → *20 minutes* COOKING *20 minutes*

3 tablespoons gram flour
2 tablespoons vegetable oil
1 teaspoon black mustard seeds
½ teaspoon cumin seeds
large pinch of asafoetida
10 fresh or 15 dried curry leaves
3 spring onions, finely chopped
1 green pepper, deseeded and finely diced
1 teaspoon ground turmeric
1 teaspoon ground coriander
½ teaspoon medium-hot red chilli powder
salt
Bhakri *(page 117)* or Rotis *(pages 108–109)*, to serve

1 Heat a heavy-based pan over a medium heat, add the gram flour and dry-toast it for 2–3 minutes, stirring constantly to prevent it from scorching. Reduce the heat and toast it for 6–7 minutes, until it darkens and becomes fragrant. Remove from the heat, tip into a bowl and set aside.

2 Wipe the pan, add the oil and place it over a high heat. Add the mustard seeds and when they begin to crackle, add the cumin, asafoetida and curry leaves (standing back from the pan if using fresh leaves, as they will splutter). Fry for 1 minute, then add the spring onions, diced pepper, ground spices, salt to season and mix well. Reduce the heat and stir-fry for 5 minutes until the vegetables are soft.

3 Add the toasted gram flour and stir well. It will absorb any liquid and oil to form clumps. Break up the clumps to cook them, sprinkling in a couple of handfuls of water to hasten the process. The flour takes only 3–4 minutes to cook.

4 Remove from the heat when the flour has absorbed all the liquid and has turned golden brown and moist.

5 Season to taste and serve hot with bhakri or rotis.

Gode Batate

| SPICED POTATO CURRY |

This is a speciality of the Maharashtrian Pathare Prabhu community and uses their special curry powder called 'Parbhi sambhar' (see page 65). It is made without onions or garlic so is considered suitable for calm, fasting days when abstinence from these invigorating foods is encouraged. Being quite thin in consistency, it is eaten with pooris (page 114) or other bread. *Serves 4*
PREPARATION → *15 minutes* COOKING *40 minutes*

2 tablespoons vegetable oil
3 cloves
1 small cinnamon stick
pinch of asafoetida
1 teaspoon grated fresh root ginger
3 potatoes, peeled and cubed
1 teaspoon ground turmeric
½ teaspoon medium-hot red chilli powder
1 teaspoon parbhi sambhar or sambhar powder *(page 65)*
salt
Pooris *(pages 114–115)*, to serve

1 Heat the oil in a saucepan over a high heat and add the cloves and cinnamon stick. When they start to sizzle, tip in the asafoetida and ginger. Cook for a few seconds, then stir in the potatoes, turmeric, chilli powder and parbhi sambhar. Season with salt and pour in enough water to barely cover the potatoes. Bring to the boil then reduce the heat, cover and simmer for 30 minutes until the potatoes are tender. The gravy should be quite watery with oil floating on top.
2 Season to taste and serve hot with pooris.

Batatya Talasani

| POTATO BATONS WITH CHILLI AND GARLIC |

This recipe is made by the Konkani community, a sect of Brahmins from Karnataka both inland as well as coastal, to which most of my family belong. As a child, it was comforting to have this on a Sunday night with plain dal, rice and a yogurt raita. The potatoes are always cut in a distinctive baton shape like chips, with edges that catch the flavour of garlic and chilli. *Serves 4* PREPARATION → *15 minutes*
COOKING *30 minutes*

2 tablespoons vegetable oil
½ teaspoon black mustard seeds
½ teaspoon cumin seeds
3 dried red chillies, split and seeds shaken out
pinch of asafoetida
3 garlic cloves, lightly crushed and left in the skin
2 large potatoes, peeled and cut into thick batons
salt

1 Heat the oil in a shallow non-stick frying pan over a high heat, add the mustard seeds and fry until they begin to pop. Add the cumin seeds, then – almost immediately – add the chillies and asafoetida.
2 Add the garlic and fry for 1 minute until it turns golden, then add the potatoes. Season with salt, reduce the heat and fry for 15–20 minutes until the potatoes are tender (this will depend on the variety of potato used).

Sindhi Kadhi

| VEGETABLES IN A GRAM FLOUR SAUCE |

I grew up in Mumbai with lots of Sindhi friends and this dish was always a treat when I was invited to eat at their homes. You can use a mix of the vegetables mentioned in the recipe or whichever firm vegetable you have available, such as sweet potatoes, green beans or butternut squash (all cut into bite-sized pieces). Drumstick is a long, thin green vegetable that has a chewy inedible skin but tender, buttery flesh. *Serves 4* PREPARATION → *15 minutes* COOKING *40 minutes*

2 tablespoons gram flour
½ x 400g can of chopped tomatoes
2 tablespoons vegetable oil
½ teaspoon fenugreek seeds
10 fresh or 15 dried curry leaves
1 teaspoon grated fresh root ginger
300g mixed raw vegetables, such as cluster beans, carrots,
    potatoes, aubergines, drumstick, peeled and cubed
1 teaspoon ground turmeric
1 teaspoon medium-hot red chilli powder
3 tablespoons tamarind pulp *(page 418)* or shop-bought
    tamarind paste
salt
boiled rice *(pages 78–79)*, to serve

1 Place the flour in a small dry pan over a medium heat and toast for 7–8 minutes, stirring frequently, to toast it evenly, until it begins to change colour and becomes fragrant. Mix the gram flour with the tomatoes and blitz to a purée in a blender. Pour in 300ml cold water and blitz again to blend.
2 Heat the oil in a saucepan over a high heat and add the fenugreek seeds and curry leaves (standing back from the pan if using fresh leaves, as they will splutter). When they darken slightly, add the ginger and stir. Add the vegetables, turmeric and chilli powder, then tip in the tamarind and cook for a few seconds. Add the tomato and flour mixture and season with salt.
3 Bring to the boil, reduce the heat, cover and cook, stirring frequently, for 30 minutes until the vegetables are tender. Season to taste and serve hot with rice.

Beans Poriyal

| GREEN BEANS WITH COCONUT |

A poriyal is a southern Indian dry, sautéed vegetable dish usually served on the side with rice or roti. You can make a poriyal with any number of 'dry' vegetables – cabbage, cauliflower and other beans are favourites. This is not a spicy dish – the chillies are there more for flavour than for heat. *Serves 4* PREPARATION → *10 minutes* COOKING *15 minutes*

2 tablespoons vegetable oil
1 teaspoon black or brown mustard seeds
large pinch of asafoetida
1 teaspoon white urad dal, washed and drained
2 dried whole red chillies
300g green beans, topped, tailed and finely diced
1 tablespoon freshly grated or desiccated coconut
salt
Rotis *(pages 108–109)* or boiled rice *(pages 78–79)*, to serve

1 Heat the oil in a non-stick pan over a high heat and add the mustard seeds. When they begin to pop, add the asafoetida, urad dal and red chillies. When the lentils begin to darken, tip in the green beans and stir.
2 Pour in a couple of teaspoons of water, season with salt and cook, uncovered, for 12–15 minutes until the beans are soft.
3 Remove from the heat, stir in the coconut, season to taste and serve hot with rotis or rice.

Vegetable Saagu

| MIXED VEGETABLE CURRY WITH COCONUT |

This creamy curry is from the southern state of Karnataka and is eaten for breakfast with Dosas (page 126) or as a main meal with rice. There are several versions – I have tasted some with onions or mint and know that some cooks add poppy seed paste (see page 337) for thickness. I have chosen this recipe for its simple flavours. Try to use fresh coconut for this (see page 310 for how to prepare coconut). *Serves 4* PREPARATION → *25 minutes* COOKING *45 minutes*

1 teaspoon black or brown mustard seeds
large pinch of fresh or dried curry leaves
200g mixed raw vegetables, such as carrots, beans, peas,
     cauliflower, cut into bite-sized pieces (except peas)
salt
For the curry paste
2 tablespoons split gram lentils (chana dal)
2 tablespoons coconut or vegetable oil
1 tablespoon coriander seeds
1 small cinnamon stick
4 cloves
½ teaspoon freshly ground black pepper
1 tablespoon ginger-garlic paste *(page 45)*
2 fresh green chillies
3 tablespoons freshly grated or frozen coconut

1 Heat a frying pan over a high heat, add the lentils and dry-toast them for a few minutes until they begin to change colour. Add half the oil to the pan and add the coriander seeds, cinnamon, cloves and pepper. Once the spices are sizzling, stir in the ginger-garlic paste. Remove from the heat and transfer to a blender along with the green chillies and coconut. Pour in enough water to cover and blitz to a fine purée.
2 Heat the remaining oil in a pan over a high heat and add the mustard seeds. As they begin to pop, tip in the curry leaves (standing back from the pan if using fresh leaves, as they will splutter) and then the vegetables. Season with salt and pour in enough water to just cover the vegetables. Bring to the boil then reduce the heat and simmer for 25–30 minutes until the vegetables are tender but still have some bite.
3 Stir in the coconut and spice paste from the blender, season to taste, heat through and serve hot.

Makkai Simla Mirch Ki Subji

| SWEETCORN AND MIXED PEPPER CURRY |

Cobs of corn are sold as street food in many parts of India and the kernels are sold in markets to be used in curries. They are combined with coconut in the south, onions in the north or yogurt in the west. This is a north Indian recipe.

Serves 4 PREPARATION → *15 minutes* COOKING *30 minutes*

2 tablespoons vegetable oil
1 large onion, finely diced
1 teaspoon ginger-garlic paste *(page 45)*
2 fresh green chillies, finely diced
1 teaspoon ground cumin
1 teaspoon ground coriander
1 teaspoon ground turmeric
2 medium tomatoes, chopped
100g frozen or tinned sweetcorn kernels
1 small green pepper, deseeded and diced
1 small red, yellow or orange pepper, deseeded and diced
a small handful of finely chopped fresh coriander leaves,
     to garnish
salt

1 Heat the oil in a heavy-based pan over a high heat, add the onion and fry for 7–8 minutes until soft. Add the ginger-garlic paste and the diced green chillies. Cook for a minute or so then add the ground spices, cook for a few seconds, then tip in the chopped tomatoes and season with salt. Cook for 2–3 minutes until the tomatoes soften.
2 Mix in the corn and diced peppers, add about 150ml water and stir well. Bring to the boil, reduce the heat, cover and cook for 10–12 minutes until the peppers are soft. Check and adjust the seasoning if necessary.
3 Serve hot, sprinkled with the coriander leaves.

Flowercha Rassa

| CAULIFLOWER WITH COCONUT AND PEPPER |

In this coastal Maharashtrian recipe, the coconut brings a sweetness that contrasts with the slight bitterness of the cauliflower. I use the tender green stalks as well – in my home these are the most coveted part of this dish! *Serves 4*

PREPARATION → *15 minutes* COOKING *40 minutes*

2 tablespoons vegetable oil
10 black peppercorns
5 cloves
1 tablespoon coriander seeds
2 onions, finely chopped
3 tablespoons freshly grated coconut
    or desiccated coconut
½ large head of cauliflower, cut into florets
1 teaspoon ground turmeric
1 teaspoon medium-hot red chilli powder
2 large tomatoes, finely chopped
salt
boiled rice *(pages 78–79)* and a lentil dish,
    such as Tarka Dal *(page 279)*,
    or Pooris *(pages 114–115)*, to serve

1 Heat half the oil in a heavy-based frying pan over a high heat, add the peppercorns, cloves and coriander seeds and fry until they sizzle. Add the onions and fry until they start to brown, then reduce the heat and continue cooking for 8–10 minutes until they are very soft. Stir in the coconut and continue to brown for 2–3 minutes.

2 Remove from the heat, leave to cool slightly then transfer to a blender with a little water and blitz to a fine paste. Set aside.

3 Heat the remaining oil in a large frying pan over a high heat, add the cauliflower and stir-fry for a couple of minutes. Add the ground spices, tomatoes and salt and cook for a further 5 minutes.

4 Add the reserved coconut paste, pour in 150ml water and bring to the boil. Reduce the heat and simmer for 10–12 minutes, until the cauliflower is cooked but firm.

5 Season to taste and serve hot with rice and a lentil dish like Tarka Dal or with pooris.

Kobi Vatana Nu Shak

| GUJARATI-STYLE CABBAGE AND
PEAS STIR-FRY |

Gujarati vegetarian cooking is very delicate as the flavours of the vegetables are highlighted with just a few herbs and spices, such as green chilli and ginger, and are not usually cooked in a heavy curry base as with a lot of north Indian cooking. This recipe works well if the cabbage is very finely shredded. It should look translucent and shiny when cooked. You can use red cabbage here and swap the peas for tinned black chickpeas if you wish. *Serves 4*
PREPARATION → *10 minutes* COOKING *45 minutes*

2 fresh green chillies, finely chopped
1 teaspoon grated fresh root ginger
2 tablespoons vegetable oil
1 teaspoon black mustard seeds
½ teaspoon cumin seeds
large pinch of asafoetida
1 teaspoon ground turmeric
½ small white cabbage, shredded
150g green garden peas (fresh or frozen)
2 tablespoons freshly grated coconut or desiccated coconut,
   to garnish
salt

1   Crush the chillies and ginger to a paste in a pestle and mortar or spice mill.
2   Heat the oil in a heavy-based or non-stick saucepan and add the mustard seeds. As they begin to pop, add the cumin seeds and asafoetida and cook for 10 seconds, then stir in the chilli-ginger paste. Sprinkle in the turmeric and add the cabbage and peas at once. Season with salt and stir for 4–5 minutes until the vegetables start to turn translucent. Cover the pan and cook over a low–medium heat for 20 minutes. The salt will draw out enough moisture from the cabbage to cook it.
3   Serve hot, sprinkled with the coconut.

Aloo Posto

| POTATOES COOKED WITH POPPY SEEDS |

White poppy seeds or 'posto' are popular in Bengali cookery for their ability to thicken and flavour a dish. Poppy seed paste is a base for several vegetable curries in Bengal.
Serves 4 PREPARATION → *15 minutes* COOKING *40 minutes*

3 tablespoons white poppy seeds
2 tablespoons mustard or vegetable oil
1 teaspoon nigella seeds (kalonji)
2 fresh green chillies, finely diced
2 large potatoes, peeled and cubed
1 teaspoon ground turmeric
salt

1   Make a poppy seed paste. You can do this in several ways – by crushing the seeds with some water in a pestle and mortar, which can be a bit time consuming, by blitzing the seeds with some water in a spice or coffee mill or by grinding the seeds to a powder in a spice mill, then mixing them with water.
2   Heat the mustard oil in a frying pan over a high heat to smoking point, then reduce the heat and add the nigella seeds and chillies. If using vegetable oil, warm it before adding the seeds. Fry for a few seconds then tip in the potatoes.
3   Increase the heat, add the turmeric, season with salt and fry the potatoes for a couple of minutes, then stir in the poppy seed paste and add enough water to barely cover the potatoes. Bring to the boil, reduce the heat and simmer for 30–35 minutes until the potatoes are tender.
4   Remove from the heat and season to taste. You can serve this dish dry or with a bit of sauce (which is how I prefer it), depending on your preference.

Saag Aloo

| SPINACH WITH POTATOES |

Potatoes are often added to vegetable dishes for bulk and texture. This north Indian dish is popular in Indian homes as well as in restaurants because of its striking colour, creamy taste and the wide availability of spinach. If making this in advance, add the spinach at the last minute when you reheat the curry. *Serves 4* PREPARATION → *10 minutes* COOKING *35 minutes*

2 tablespoons vegetable oil
½ teaspoon cumin seeds
1 onion, finely chopped
1 fresh green chilli, diced
1 teaspoon ginger-garlic paste *(page 45)*
1 tomato, finely chopped
1 teaspoon garam masala *(page 64)*
2 potatoes, peeled and cubed
450g fresh spinach, washed, drained and finely chopped
salt

1 Heat the oil in a heavy-based pan over a high heat, add the cumin seeds and fry for 10 seconds until they darken. Add the onion and chilli and fry for 5–6 minutes until soft.
2 Stir in the ginger-garlic paste and tomato and cook over a low heat for 2–3 minutes, until mushy.
3 Add the garam masala and the potatoes and season with salt. Add enough water to barely cover the potatoes and bring to the boil. Reduce the heat and simmer for 25 minutes until the potatoes are soft. Add the spinach, season to taste, heat through and serve.

Oondhiyoon

| MIXED VEGETABLES WITH AJOWAN AND COCONUT |

This Gujarati delicacy makes the most of vegetables such as aubergines, peas and sweet potatoes, which are at their freshest in the Indian winter. I chop a whole banana in its skin and place it on top of the curry while it's cooking to give the dish a distinctive sweet fragrance. Cut the vegetables into equal-sized pieces for even cooking. *Serves 4* PREPARATION → *1 hour* COOKING *1 hour*

2 tablespoons vegetable oil
1 teaspoon cumin seeds
1 teaspoon ajowan seeds
4 small aubergines, quartered
3 small potatoes, peeled and quartered
1 large sweet potato, peeled and roughly chopped
90g green garden peas (fresh or frozen)
1 carrot, peeled and chopped
2 teaspoons ginger-garlic paste *(page 45)*
2 fresh green chillies, minced
a large handful of fresh coriander leaves, finely chopped
a large handful of fresh fenugreek leaves (methi), washed and finely chopped
a large handful of freshly grated or desiccated coconut
1 teaspoon ground turmeric
1 teaspoon caster sugar
1 ripe banana, cut into quarters (skin left on)
salt
Rotis *(pages 108–109)* or Pooris *(pages 114–115)*, to serve

1 Heat the oil in a large pan over a high heat and add the cumin and ajowan seeds. When they darken, add all the vegetables. Mix well and stir-fry for 5–6 minutes.
2 Add the remaining ingredients one after the other, season with salt and mix. Place the chopped banana on top. Pour in a little water, cover and cook over a low heat for 45–50 minutes, stirring occasionally, until the vegetables are tender. Season to taste and serve hot with rotis or pooris.

SNACKS, SIDES & STREET FOOD

EACH REGION IN INDIA HAS ITS OWN SPECIAL STREET FOOD BASED ON WHAT GROWS LOCALLY AND THE FOOD PREFERENCES AND RELIGIOUS RULES OF THE POPULATION.

In India, sharing one's food is almost as important as eating it oneself. Indians seem to think of food all the time. They might eat breakfast before leaving home but buy a nibble on their way to work, then await a tiffin from home at lunchtime. They would probably stop at a street food cart on the way home, have a snack before dinner and then sit down to a family meal. It is possibly one of the top three topics of conversation at this very moment in many parts of the country! This happens all over India, both in rural and urban areas.

Snacks, sides and street food have many things in common. They are served in small portions, they tend to surprise and excite the palate with their vibrant flavours and textures and they can often double up as a main meal. So, for instance, baby samosas, which are triangular pastries stuffed with spiced potatoes, vegetables, paneer or meat, may be served as a crisp side in a lavish feast, a larger samosa could be eaten at teatime with a dip and a street cart might be frying these at the last minute to tempt passers-by with their fragrance. Roaming street vendors carry baskets of samosas to sell.

These finger foods are often fried to a succulent crispness and served with hot, tangy or sweet chutneys. Each region in India is famous for a particular snack and the locals are understandably proud of it. Spiced flaked rice called 'poha' is served with sweet fried 'jalebis' in Indore in central India. 'Bhelpuri', a delightful mix of puffed rice, gram flour straws, savoury biscuits, potatoes, tangy, sweet tamarind chutney and a hot chilli and coriander chutney is eaten everywhere. Hollow puris filled with sprouts and tamarind water are called 'pani-puri', 'puchka', 'gol-guppa', 'gup-chup' or 'pani ke bataashe'.

Although a side is not served with every Indian meal, it is one way of making it a bit more special, if one is entertaining or for special feasts. Sides such as vegetable fritters and rice cakes are popular in Gujarat, where they are called 'farsan'. These are so tempting that people often eat them on their own as a light meal.

India is one of the largest tea producers in the world and it is one of the country's most popular drinks. Tea in Hindi is 'chai', so when Western restaurants serve chai tea, they are actually selling tea tea! When spices are added to tea, it is called 'masala chai'. Every street corner in India will have a tea stall with a young employee ever ready to deliver room service to nearby businesses.

MASTERCLASS

HOW TO MAKE CHAAT MASALA

YOU WILL NEED:

1 teaspoon cumin seeds

1 teaspoon coriander seeds

1 teaspoon amchoor (dried mango powder)

1 teaspoon powdered black salt
   (kala namak)

1 teaspoon ground black pepper

½ teaspoon medium-hot red chilli powder

– a small frying pan

– a spice mill or pestle and mortar

– 30ml clean jar to store the spice blend

Chaats are savoury foods, made with a variety of ingredients, that are high on taste and a mix of textures. Chaat can also denote a salad but is most commonly associated with street food. They will always be drizzled with an assortment of highly flavoured chutneys, fresh coriander and crisp bits of some kind. They are finished with 'chaat masala' which is a distinctive, sour, salty, dry spice mix. It always contains black salt or 'kala namak', a unique rock salt that has a strong sulphuric smell, along with chilli, cumin and amchoor (dried mango powder), although different cooks may vary the proportions in keeping with personal preferences. Kala namak is quite different to the white salt used in cooking and cannot be substituted. It is used as a finishing salt in chaats and yogurt raitas, and is available as large crystals which look almost black or as a fine pink powder. Chaat masala is available commercially in packs. These are very good and most people in India would buy them for convenience rather than making the mix at home.

Makes small batch of about 25g

1 Heat the frying pan over a high heat, add the cumin and coriander seeds and dry-toast for a few seconds.

2 When they darken, tip them into a spice mill or mortar, cool for a minute then crush them to a fine powder.

3 Add the remaining ingredients and mix well. Transfer to a clean jar and store in a cool, dark, dry place. Use within 2 months.

Bombay Frankie
| SPICY WRAPS |

A popular street food snack in Mumbai, this is sold from trailers in some parts of the city. The distinctive chaat masala mix sprinkled over at the end gives it a savoury, tangy taste. *Makes 8 wraps* PREPARATION → *15 minutes* COOKING *30 minutes*

For the stuffing
3 tablespoons white wine vinegar
4 fresh green or red chillies, finely chopped (2 for the vinegar dip and 2 for the mince)
2 tablespoons vegetable oil
2 onions, finely diced
1 teaspoon ginger-garlic paste *(page 45)*
1 teaspoon ground turmeric
1 teaspoon garam masala *(page 64)*
500g lamb mince
large pinch of chaat masala *(see opposite)*
salt
For the wraps
vegetable oil, for shallow-frying
8 Rotis *(pages 108–109)*
2 free-range eggs, beaten and seasoned with salt and pepper

1 Combine the vinegar and 2 chillies in a small glass bowl and set aside.

2 Heat the oil in a saucepan over a high heat, add half the onions and fry for 7–8 minutes until soft. Reserve the remaining onions for the garnish.

3 Add the ginger-garlic paste, the remaining chillies, turmeric and garam masala. Mix well. Stir in the mince and season with salt. Cook for 10–12 minutes, breaking up the mince with a wooden spoon, until done.

4 To finish the rotis, heat a tablespoon of oil in a shallow frying pan over a high heat. Dip each roti into the beaten egg and fry on both sides for 2–3 minutes until golden brown. Remove and set aside to drain on kitchen paper.

5 To assemble, place one of the rotis on a serving plate. Arrange some of the mince down the centre. Drizzle with some of the reserved chilli-vinegar mixture, including a few chopped chillies. Sprinkle some of the reserved, chopped raw onion and chaat masala on top and fold the wrap into a roll. Make the remaining wraps up in a similar way and serve.

Puris

| FLAT, CRISP BISCUITS |

These puris or pooris are eaten as part of other snacks, as in Sev Puri (page 349) or on their own. They are sometimes flavoured with spices such as cumin or ajowan. Typically they are about 3.5cm in diameter so can be eaten in a single mouthful. Slightly larger ones are called 'mathris'.

Makes 40–50 puris PREPARATION → *15 minutes, plus 30 minutes resting time* COOKING *30 minutes*

250g plain flour, plus extra for dusting (if necessary)
90g fine semolina
pinch of ajowan or cumin seeds
1 teaspoon salt
4 tablespoons vegetable oil, plus extra for deep-frying
150–180ml tepid water, as needed

1 Combine the flour, semolina, seeds and salt in a bowl. Pour in the oil and mix with your fingers.
2 Pour in the tepid water, a little at a time, until you have a firm yet springy dough. Knead well for a few minutes, then place back in the bowl, cover the dough with a clean, damp tea towel and leave to rest at room temperature for 30 minutes.
3 Divide the dough into 40–50 small balls, each the size of a cherry. Roll these out into small discs (on a floured surface if the dough is sticky) and set to one side on a sheet of greaseproof paper. Prick each puri several times with a fork. This ensures that they do not puff up when cooked.
4 Heat enough oil in a deep frying pan to fry the puris in a single layer. To check if the oil is hot enough, drop a small piece of the dough in. It should rise up to the surface within a couple of seconds. If it rises up immediately, the oil is too hot. Reduce the heat and wait for a few seconds.
5 Reduce the heat to medium and fry a batch of puris for 4–5 minutes until they are golden brown. Remove with a slotted spoon and drain on kitchen paper.
6 You will need to regulate the heat, increasing the temperature of the oil every time you put in a fresh batch of puris and reducing the heat when they begin to change colour.
7 You can store these puris in an airtight container for up to 2 months.

Sev

| CRISP GRAM FLOUR STRAWS |

Sev comes in many thicknesses, the finest one is called 'nylon sev'. Usually the thinner ones are used to top street food snacks and the thicker variety, sometimes called 'ganthia', is eaten on its own. The thickness depends on the size of the holes in the equipment used. Traditionally a 'sev maker' is used but this can be substituted with a potato ricer. *Serves 4* PREPARATION → *20 minutes* COOKING *15 minutes*

150g gram flour
1 teaspoon ground turmeric
1 tablespoon hot vegetable oil, plus extra for deep-frying
salt and freshly ground black pepper

1 Season the flour with salt and pepper and combine with the turmeric and the hot oil in a bowl. Mix well, then pour in 70–80ml cold water, a little at a time, to make a very firm dough. Grease your palms with a little oil and knead the dough for 4–5 minutes until smooth.
2 Grease the inside of a sev maker or potato ricer and put the dough in. Line a plate with greaseproof paper or foil. Press the dough into short strands onto the lined plate.
3 Heat enough oil in a deep frying pan to come 6cm up the sides of the pan over a high heat. Test the temperature of the oil (see left, Step 4).
4 Lift the nest of sev strands and lower them gently into the hot oil. The sev will sizzle in the oil and this sizzling will stop after 15–20 seconds when the sev is cooked. It should be light golden in colour so flip the nest over and cook for a few seconds before lifting out onto a plate lined with kitchen paper.
5 When cool, crush lightly with your hands to make short lengths (about 1cm each). You can store the sev in an airtight container for up to 1 month.

Sev Puri

| CRISP FLAT PURIS WITH SPICED POTATOES, DRIZZLED WITH SWEET, HOT, SOUR CHUTNEYS |

A portion of sev puri normally has 6 puris. The level of heat and sweetness can be personalised by adding more or less of the coriander and mint chutney and the sweet tamarind chutney. If you add a dollop of yogurt on each puri before finishing the dish with 'sev', it is called 'dahi batata puri'. *Makes 24 sev puris* PREPARATION ➔ *20 minutes* COOKING *15 minutes*

24 Puris *(page 346)*
2 potatoes, boiled, peeled and roughly mashed, seasoned with
    salt, pepper and lemon juice
100g Sweet Tamarind Chutney *(page 422)*
100g Coriander and Mint Chutney *(page 427)*
yogurt (optional)
pinch of chaat masala *(page 344)*
80g Gram Flour Straws (Sev – *page 346*)
a few fresh coriander leaves, chopped, to serve

1 Assemble the puris on a plate.
2 Place a bit of the cooled potato mixture on top and drizzle a teaspoonful of each chutney over the potato. (If making dahi batata puri, add a spoonful of yogurt here.)
3 Sprinkle with chaat masala and sev, and serve topped with the coriander.
4 Each puri is to be eaten in a single mouthful to enjoy the complete range of flavours, textures and aromas.

Vegetable Pakora

| VEGETABLE FRITTERS |

These deep-fried fritters are also known as 'bajji' in south India. A variety of vegetables can be used, either singly or in a combination (as in this recipe). The consistency of the batter is key in getting this recipe right – it should be thick enough to hold the vegetables together or coat a piece of vegetable. I would describe the consistency as that of a thick custard – it should fall off a spoon easily. *Serves 4* PREPARATION ➔ *15 minutes* COOKING *25 minutes*

½ teaspoon medium-hot red chilli powder
pinch of ajowan seeds
5 tablespoons gram flour
a handful of fresh spinach leaves, finely chopped
1 carrot, peeled and grated
couple of cauliflower florets, grated
2 tablespoons grated white cabbage
vegetable oil, for deep-frying
salt
Coriander and Peanut Chutney *(page 421)* or Sweet Tamarind
    Chutney *(page 422)*, to serve

1 Combine the chilli powder, salt to season, ajowan seeds and gram flour in a bowl, adding 180–200ml cold water to make a thick batter.
2 Fold in the vegetables, evenly coating them with the spice and salt mixture.
3 Heat enough oil in a deep frying pan over a high heat so that the fritters will be submerged when you cook them.
4 Fry the mixture in batches, dropping in as many dessertspoonfuls as the pan will hold, with enough room to flip the fritters over. Fry for 3–4 minutes until golden, then flip over and cook for a further couple of minutes to cook them evenly. Transfer to kitchen paper to drain. Serve immediately, with Coriander and Peanut Chutney or Sweet Tamarind Chutney alongside.

ONION BHAJIAS – Onion Fritters

YOU WILL NEED:

½ teaspoon medium-hot red chilli powder

pinch of ajowan seeds

100g gram flour

2 medium onions, thinly sliced

vegetable oil, for deep-frying

salt

Coriander and Peanut Chutney *(page 421)* or
    Sweet Tamarind Chutney *(page 422)*, to serve

Often called onion bhaji outside India, this is a very popular Indian snack all over the world. However, the round, stodgy balls sold commercially in the West are a world apart from the delicate, crisp, irregularly shaped ones made at home. Homemade bhajias are fritters of sweet, cooked onions held together by a salty, spiced batter unlike the ones you buy in a Western takeaway, which taste mostly of flour. In India, an onion 'bhaji' would mean a stir-fry of onions rather than the fritter! Fried snacks are often flavoured with a digestive spice called ajowan. It has the scent of oregano and is sharp in taste. If you can't find it, substitute it with cumin seeds which are also known for their digestive properties. *Serves 4*

PREPARATION ⟶ *15 minutes* COOKING *25 minutes*

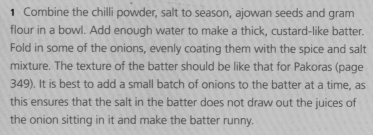

1 Combine the chilli powder, salt to season, ajowan seeds and gram flour in a bowl. Add enough water to make a thick, custard-like batter. Fold in some of the onions, evenly coating them with the spice and salt mixture. The texture of the batter should be like that for Pakoras (page 349). It is best to add a small batch of onions to the batter at a time, as this ensures that the salt in the batter does not draw out the juices of the onion sitting in it and make the batter runny.

2 Heat enough oil in a deep frying pan to hold a single layer of fritters over a high heat. Test the temperature of the oil by dropping in a slice of onion – the oil should sizzle. Fry the mixture in batches, dropping in as many dessertspoonfuls as the pan will hold, with enough room to flip the fritters over. Fry for 3–4 minutes until golden, flip them over and cook for a further couple of minutes to cook them evenly. Transfer to kitchen paper to drain. Serve immediately with Coriander and Peanut Chutney or Sweet Tamarind Chutney.

VEGETABLE SAMOSAS – Triangular Vegetable Parcels

These are the most common form of samosa and come from northern India. The most traditional filling used is made with spiced potatoes. Peas are added when in season, in the Indian winter.

Makes 16 samosas PREPARATION → *15 minutes*
COOKING *40 minutes*

YOU WILL NEED:

vegetable oil, for deep-frying

For the pastry

300g plain flour, plus extra for dusting

½ teaspoon salt

½ teaspoon ajowan seeds (optional)

2 tablespoons vegetable oil or ghee

For the filling

1 teaspoon cumin seeds

2 tablespoons vegetable oil

2 fresh green chillies, finely diced (seeds and all)

1 teaspoon grated fresh root ginger

2 large potatoes, boiled, peeled and finely cubed

1 teaspoon amchoor (dried mango powder)
    or 1 tablespoon lemon juice

salt

Press down the moist side to seal. Fill it with one part of the potato mix. Fold over the open edge and press together to seal. Make 16 samosas similarly (one round disc will make two).

5 Heat enough oil in a deep frying pan to completely submerge the samosas, without letting them sit on the bottom of the pan. When very hot, reduce the heat to medium and deep-fry the samosas, a couple at a time, for 5–6 minutes. Flip halfway through cooking, to fry evenly, until they turn golden brown, then remove with a slotted spoon and transfer to kitchen paper to drain.

1 To make the pastry, combine the flour, salt and ajowan seeds in a bowl. Heat the oil or melt the ghee in a small saucepan over a high heat and pour this into the flour. Carefully fold in the oil or ghee, then pour in 3–4 tablespoons of cold water and mix well until it resembles breadcrumbs. Carefully add 90–100ml more water, as necessary, until you have a springy but firm dough. Knead well for 3–4 minutes then set aside to rest while you make the filling.

2 Heat a frying pan over a high heat and add the cumin seeds. Dry-toast until they darken, then tip them into a mortar or spice mill and crush or blend to a fine powder.

3 Add the oil to the same pan and fry the chillies and ginger for 1 minute, then tip in the potato and amchoor. Season with salt, tip in the toasted cumin and mix thoroughly. Divide this into 16 equal parts.

4 Divide the dough into 8 equal parts and form into balls. Flatten one of the balls and roll out on a floured surface into a flat disc about 15cm in diameter. Cut the disc in half. Moisten the side that's a straight line with water. Fold the half into a cone and pinch the tip to seal it.

Chicken Samosas

| TRIANGULAR CHICKEN PARCELS |

1 skinless chicken breast
1 tablespoon vegetable oil,
    plus extra for brushing
¼ white cabbage, finely shredded
2 spring onions, finely chopped
1 carrot, peeled and grated
1 teaspoon ground turmeric
1 teaspoon medium-hot red chilli powder
1 teaspoon freshly ground black pepper
a small handful of fresh coriander leaves,
    finely chopped
2 teaspoons plain flour
8 sheets of filo pastry
salt
Mint and Coriander Chutney (*page 427*),
    to serve

The origins of the samosa are probably Middle Eastern but today it is one of India's best-known snacks. The *Ain-i-Akbari*, a sixteenth-century Mughal document, lists the recipe for 'Qutab', which the people of Hindustan call 'sanbusa'. Interestingly, it goes on to say that the mix of meat, flour, ghee and spices can be cooked in twenty different ways. In India there are two kinds of samosas called, for ease, the Gujarati samosa and the Punjabi samosa. The first one has a thinner crust and is made with pastry sheets as in this recipe. The Punjabi samosa has a thicker crust made by rolling out dough as in the Vegetable Samosas recipe (page 352). In the West, where historically most migrants from the Indian subcontinent are from the north, the Punjabi samosa is more widely seen. Traditionally, samosas would be deep-fried in hot oil but I prefer to bake these. *Makes 8 samosas*

PREPARATION ⟶ *20 minutes* COOKING *50 minutes*

1 Put the chicken breast in a pan, cover with lightly salted water and bring to the boil. Reduce the heat and simmer for 20 minutes until it is cooked through. Drain, cool and shred.

2 Preheat the oven to 180°C/gas mark 4 and line a baking tray with greaseproof paper.

3 Heat the oil in a frying pan over a high heat and add the cabbage, spring onions and carrot. Stir-fry for 7–8 minutes until soft.

4 Add the turmeric, chilli powder, salt to season, pepper and coriander. Cook for a couple of minutes, then stir in the shredded chicken and remove from the heat.

5 Mix the flour with a little water to make a runny paste. Lay out the filo pastry sheets and cut each sheet in half lengthways. Brush one strip with oil and stack it over the other strip, making a total of 8 double-layer strips.

6 Spoon an eighth of the chicken mixture towards the left corner end of one double-layer strip. Brush the water and flour mixture along all the edges of the pastry, then fold the pastry to make a triangle: lift the top left corner and fold it over the filling to be in line with the bottom edge, making a triangle shape. Now lift the right bottom corner over to the top and then the top left down again. Carry on until you have a triangular parcel. Make sure that the edges are well sealed by pressing them together. Brush with oil on all sides and place on the lined baking tray. Repeat for the remaining and pastry sheets.

7 Bake for 15–20 minutes, turning them over once halfway through to cook them evenly, until golden and crisp. Serve hot with Mint and Coriander Chutney for dipping alongside.

Kothimbir Vadi

| HERBY CORIANDER FRITTERS |

This Maharashtrian recipe is made in several ways. Some like to add a few more vegetables like carrots, or add spices such as crushed coriander seeds to the mix. I have found this a good way to use up big bunches of coriander, and serve it as a side to a main meal. *Serves 4*

PREPARATION → *10 minutes* COOKING *40 minutes*

1 teaspoon white sesame seeds
150g gram flour
2 tablespoons rice flour
1 teaspoon ginger-garlic paste *(page 45)*
1 fresh green chilli, finely minced
1 teaspoon ground turmeric
a large handful of fresh coriander leaves, finely chopped
1 tablespoon lemon juice
vegetable oil, for shallow-frying and greasing
large pinch of bicarbonate of soda
salt

1 Heat a small frying pan over a high heat, add the sesame seeds and dry-toast until golden, then tip them into a bowl. Add the gram and rice flours and 250–280ml cold water to the bowl make a thick batter, then whisk well to remove any lumps.

2 Stir in the ginger-garlic paste, chilli, turmeric, coriander leaves, lemon juice, 1 tablespoon of oil and season with salt. Gently stir in the bicarbonate of soda.

3 Grease a heatproof dish that will fit into a steamer with oil. Pour the mixture in – the batter should be 2cm thick so you may have to do this in batches. Steam it for 15 minutes or until a knife inserted into the centre comes out clean. Leave to cool completely then cut it into bite-sized pieces.

4 Heat enough oil to cover the base of a frying pan over a high heat. Shallow-fry the pieces for 3–4 minutes until they are golden all over, and serve warm.

Aloo Bonda

| CRISP POTATO AND GARLIC BALLS |

These are eaten as a snack in southern India, but baby versions are also served in a thali meal alongside main curries and vegetable side dishes. The thin batter should have a pouring consistency, so that it just about coats the potato balls. *Makes 8 small balls* PREPARATION → *10 minutes* COOKING *40 minutes*

2 large potatoes, boiled, peeled and mashed
1 teaspoon ground turmeric
2 tablespoons finely chopped fresh coriander leaves
2 fresh green chillies, finely chopped (seeds and all)
2 garlic cloves, finely chopped
1 tablespoon vegetable oil, plus extra for deep-frying
1 teaspoon black mustard seeds
large pinch of asafoetida
1 teaspoon cumin seeds
salt
White Coconut Chutney *(pages 424–425)*, to serve
For the batter
150g gram flour
½ teaspoon ground turmeric

1 Combine the mashed potatoes, turmeric, coriander leaves, green chillies and garlic in a bowl and season with salt.

2 Heat the tablespoon of oil in a small pan over a high heat and add the mustard seeds. When they start to crackle add the asafoetida and cumin seeds. Fry for a few seconds, then pour this into the potato mixture and mix well. Divide the potato mixture into 8 small balls and set aside.

3 Place the gram flour, turmeric and salt to season in a bowl, and whisk in 200–225ml cold water to make a batter of pouring consistency. Whisk well to remove any lumps.

4 Heat enough oil to submerge the balls in a deep frying pan over a high heat. When it is nearly smoking, dip each potato ball in the batter and deep-fry, a few balls at a time, for 5–6 minutes until golden. Reduce the heat to prevent the ball from browning too quickly. When the balls are golden, remove them with a slotted spoon and transfer to kitchen paper to drain.

5 Serve hot with Thengai Chutney.

Masala Cutlets

| SPICY VEGETABLE CUTLETS |

In Indian cooking, a cutlet is a batter-fried cake made of minced meat or vegetables. The vegetarian version is more popular because it keeps better if carried to work or school, and because it has more appeal in a country with so many vegetarians. These are great at teatime or in a lunchbox as they taste good hot or cold. *Makes 8 cutlets*

PREPARATION → *15 minutes* COOKING *45 minutes*

2 large potatoes, boiled, peeled, mashed and cooled
1 carrot, peeled and grated
a handful of green beans, washed and finely diced
a handful of finely chopped fresh coriander leaves
a handful of finely chopped dill
2 fresh green chillies, finely diced (seeds and all)
1 teaspoon ground turmeric
1 teaspoon ground coriander
1 teaspoon ground cumin
1 teaspoon amchoor (dried mango powder) or
    1 tablespoon lemon juice
vegetable oil, for shallow-frying
150g breadcrumbs
salt
Mint and Coriander Chutney *(page 427)*, to serve

1 Mix all the ingredients except the breadcrumbs and oil together in a bowl.
2 Heat enough oil to liberally cover the base of a frying pan over a high heat. Shape the mixture into 8 round, flat cakes, dip in the breadcrumbs to coat all over and shallow-fry, a couple at a time, for 4–5 minutes until golden brown on each side. Remove and drain on kitchen paper.
3 Serve hot with Mint and Coriander Chutney.

Vatane Pohe

| FLAKED RICE WITH PEAS |

Rice that is cooked, drained, flattened and dried is called 'poha' ('pohe' is the plural). This is available in different thicknesses: fine, which is fried to make a crisp snack that will keep for a few days, medium or thick, both used for dishes such as this one, depending on personal preference. I like using the medium variety, as it has a less starchy feel. Fine poha will not work for this recipe as it tends to get mushy when washed. As it is pre-cooked, poha only needs a few minutes of soaking before one can briefly cook it with spices. When soaked, the flakes swell up into a mass that can be easily separated with a fork. *Serves 4*

PREPARATION → *20 minutes* COOKING *20 minutes*

200g Indian rice flakes (poha)
1 teaspoon ground turmeric
1 teaspoon caster sugar
1 tablespoon vegetable oil
1 teaspoon black mustard seeds
½ teaspoon cumin seeds
large pinch of asafoetida
2 fresh green chillies, slit lengthways
10 fresh or 15 dried curry leaves
100g green garden peas (fresh or frozen)
2 teaspoons lemon juice
a few fresh coriander leaves, chopped, to garnish
salt

1 Rinse the rice flakes in a colander under cold running water and drain. Sprinkle them with the turmeric, sugar and salt to season.
2 Heat the oil in a frying pan over a high heat and add the mustard seeds. When they start to crackle, add the cumin seeds, asafoetida, chillies and curry leaves (standing back from the pan if using fresh curry leaves, as they will splutter). Fry for a minute, then stir in the peas. Reduce the heat to low and cook for 6–7 minutes until the peas are tender. Add the flaked rice, increase the heat to high and mix well. Cook for 2–3 minutes then reduce the heat, sprinkle in about 4 tablespoons of water, cover and cook for 7–8 minutes. Drizzle in the lemon juice and remove from the heat.
3 Serve hot, garnished with the coriander.

Dahi Vada

| LENTIL FRITTERS IN YOGURT |

These are called 'dahi bhalla' in Punjabi and 'thayir vadai' in Tamil and are popular all over India. The fritters or 'vadas' are crisp when fried, but after they've been soaked in the yogurt for an hour or so, they become wonderfully soft and squidgy. *Serves 4* PREPARATION → *20 minutes, plus 2 hours soaking time* COOKING *25 minutes*

150g split white urad lentils, washed and drained
1 fresh green chilli, minced
vegetable oil, for deep-frying
300g natural yogurt
2 teaspoons caster sugar
1 teaspoon cumin seeds
½ teaspoon medium-hot red chilli powder
a few sprigs of fresh coriander leaves, finely chopped
salt

1   Soak the lentils in plenty of water for at least 2 hours. Drain off the water and blitz the lentils in a blender with enough fresh water to just cover them, until you have a smooth grain-free paste, the consistency of thick custard. Season with salt, stir in the chilli and set aside.

2   Heat the oil in a deep frying pan over a high heat. To test the temperature, drop in a tiny ball of the lentil batter. It should rise to the top in a couple of seconds. Gently drop a few separate tablespoons of the batter into the oil. Fry for 3–4 minutes, turning them over a few times to brown them evenly. When done, remove the fritters with a slotted spoon and drain them on kitchen paper. Cook the remaining fritters in the same way.

3   In another bowl, whisk together the yogurt, salt to season and the sugar.

4   Heat a small frying pan over a high heat, add the cumin seeds and dry-toast until they darken, then tip them into a pestle and mortar or spice mill and crush or blend to a fine powder. Stir half of this into the yogurt along with some of the chilli powder.

5   Just before serving, soak the fritters in the yogurt. To do this, dip them in water, squeeze them out, then add them to the yogurt. Serve cool, sprinkled with the remaining cumin and chilli powder and coriander leaves.

Pav Bhaji

| CRUSHED VEGETABLE CURRY WITH BUTTERED ROLLS |

A quick street meal, restaurant versions of this tangy, wholesome curry come with a dollop of butter and diced onions on top. *Serves 4* PREPARATION → *20 minutes* COOKING *40 minutes*

2 tablespoons vegetable oil
2 medium onions, finely diced
1 tablespoon ginger-garlic paste *(page 45)*
2 small fresh green chillies, finely chopped
3 large tomatoes, finely diced
1 teaspoon ground turmeric
1 teaspoon ground coriander
1 x 400g can of chickpeas, drained and rinsed
200g mixed raw vegetables, such carrots and beans
     (both finely diced) and peas
2 tablespoons finely chopped fresh coriander leaves
salt
bread rolls and butter, to serve

1   Heat the oil in a heavy-based frying pan, add the onions and fry for 7–8 minutes until soft.

2   Add the ginger-garlic paste and chillies and fry for a few seconds, then stir in the tomatoes and fry for 5–6 minutes until very soft.

3   Add the ground spices then add the chickpeas and the vegetables. Season with salt.

4   Pour in enough water to just cover the vegetables and bring to the boil. Reduce the heat, cover and cook for 25–30 minutes until the vegetables are very soft. Roughly mash the mixture with a potato masher. Sprinkle over the coriander leaves.

5   Butter the rolls and place buttered side down on a hot frying pan. Fry for a minute until golden and serve alongside the curry.

KHANDVI – Soft Gram Flour Rolls

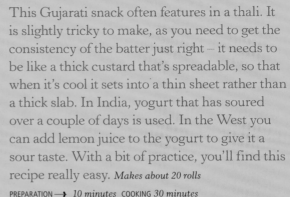

This Gujarati snack often features in a thali. It is slightly tricky to make, as you need to get the consistency of the batter just right – it needs to be like a thick custard that's spreadable, so that when it's cool it sets into a thin sheet rather than a thick slab. In India, yogurt that has soured over a couple of days is used. In the West you can add lemon juice to the yogurt to give it a sour taste. With a bit of practice, you'll find this recipe really easy. *Makes about 20 rolls*

PREPARATION ⟶ *10 minutes* COOKING *30 minutes*

YOU WILL NEED:

200g gram flour

200g natural yogurt

2½ tablespoons lemon juice

1 teaspoon ground turmeric

2cm piece of fresh root ginger, scraped and finely grated

1 fresh green chilli, finely minced

1 tablespoon vegetable oil, plus extra for brushing

1 teaspoon black or brown mustard seeds

pinch of asafoetida

a few sprigs of fresh coriander leaves, chopped, to garnish

1 tablespoon fresh or frozen grated coconut, to garnish

salt

1 Sift the gram flour into a bowl. Combine the yogurt and 1½ tablespoons of the lemon juice with 200ml cold water and whisk to a smooth consistency.

2 Combine the flour, yogurt mixture, turmeric, ginger and chilli, season with salt and whisk well so that there are no lumps and you get a pouring consistency.

3 Brush a metal tray with some oil.

4 Put the flour mixture into a heavy-based saucepan and cook over a low heat for 18–20 minutes, stirring constantly to prevent the mixture from sticking to the bottom of the pan, until it is thick. Be patient – it will take a bit of time.

5 Once the mixture has thickened enough to coat the back of a ladle completely, taste it and check if the flour is cooked; it should taste smooth and mellow. You can also brush a little on the oiled metal tray, wait a few seconds and check whether it lifts off easily. Remove from the heat and quickly spread the mixture thinly onto the oiled tray while it is still very hot. Leave it cool for 5–10 minutes.

6 When it has cooled, cut the mixture into long strips, about 5cm wide, and roll each one up tightly. Arrange on a serving plate.

7 Heat the tablespoon of oil in a frying pan over a high heat and add the mustard seeds. When they begin to pop, tip in the asafoetida. Pour this mixture over the rolls.

8 Serve cold, garnished with the coriander, coconut and a drizzle of lemon juice.

Sabudana Vada

| SAVOURY SAGO AND POTATO CAKES |

Sago is manufactured from tapioca root or cassava, mainly in the state of Tamil Nadu. However, local consumption is very low due to the belief that it is only suitable as a pudding. Much of the sago produced is exported to other regions such as Maharashtra, Gujarat and Madhya Pradesh where cooks have developed a variety of recipes such as this one. Here, these sago cakes are a favourite teatime snack or fasting food. Sago contains complex carbohydrates that digest slowly, giving a feeling of fullness. Their crisp texture goes well with Coriander Chutney (page 421). *Serves 4 (Makes 10 small cakes)*
PREPARATION —→ *15 minutes, plus 2 hours soaking time* COOKING *45 minutes*

100g pearl sago
2 medium potatoes
2 tablespoons roasted unsalted peanuts, finely crushed
2 fresh green chillies, minced (seeds and all)
few sprigs of fresh coriander leaves, finely chopped
1 tablespoon rice flour
vegetable oil, for deep-frying
salt

1 Wash the sago well, then soak it in enough water to cover it by 2.5cm. Leave for 2 hours, then drain through a sieve, spread out on a clean, dry tea towel and leave on the kitchen counter to soften until the potatoes are cooked. You should be able to squash a sago pearl easily between the thumb and index finger when it's ready to cook.
2 Meanwhile, boil the potatoes in their skins until you can pierce one easily with a knife. Cooking them in their skins will help them absorb less water as they cook.
3 Peel and mash the potatoes. In a bowl, combine the drained sago, potatoes, peanuts, chillies, coriander, rice flour and salt to season. Knead well for a few minutes, then shape into 10 equal lime-sized balls. Flatten each one.
4 Heat enough oil for deep frying in a large frying pan over a high heat. When almost smoking, reduce the heat and deep-fry the patties in batches for 5–6 minutes. If they begin to break up, dust them with rice flour before frying them. Serve hot.

Sabudana Khichdi

| SPICED PEARL SAGO |

Sago is made from tapioca starch and is sold as tiny 'pearls'. You can buy them in two sizes: the small ones are used in puddings and some savoury dishes that make the most of their starchy texture. I use large sago pearls for this recipe as they fluff up into separate grains. *Serves 4*
PREPARATION —→ *10 minutes, plus 1 hour soaking time and 3 hours draining time* COOKING *20 minutes*

150g pearl sago
80g roasted unsalted peanuts, roughly crushed
pinch of caster sugar
2 tablespoons vegetable oil
1 teaspoon cumin seeds
2 fresh green chillies, slit lengthways
10 fresh or 15 dried curry leaves
1 potato, peeled and cut into small dice
2 tablespoons freshly grated or desiccated coconut (soaked in
    warm water for 30 minutes and drained, if using desiccated)
a small handful of fresh coriander leaves, chopped, to garnish
2 teaspoons lemon juice
salt

1 Wash the sago well then soak it in enough water to cover it by 2.5cm. Leave for 1 hour, then drain through a sieve, spread out on a clean, dry tea towel and leave on the kitchen counter to soften. After 3 hours, the water should be completely absorbed. The draining time can vary depending on the quality of the sago – a sago pearl should squash easily between the thumb and index finger when it is ready to be cooked.
2 Mix the crushed peanuts, salt to season and sugar into the sago. Set aside.
3 Heat the oil in a frying pan over a high heat and add the cumin seeds. Fry until they darken, then add the chillies and curry leaves (standing back from the pan if using fresh leaves, as they will splutter). Add the potato, season with salt and fry for 4–5 minutes until golden. Reduce the heat and cook for 8–10 minutes until the potatoes are tender.
4 Add the sago. Cook over a very low heat, stirring, for 5–6 minutes until the sago is soft all the way through.
5 Sprinkle over the coconut, coriander leaves and lemon juice and serve hot.

Upma

| SAVOURY SEMOLINA |

This south Indian breakfast food can also be eaten at teatime. Its soft squidgy texture and savoury, slightly sweet taste goes well with Coriander and Peanut Chutney (page 421). It can be made with either fine or coarse semolina but I prefer the coarse one for its sandy, grainy texture. *Serves 4* PREPARATION→ *10 minutes* COOKING *25 minutes*

200g coarse or fine semolina
2 tablespoons vegetable oil
1 teaspoon black mustard seeds
½ teaspoon cumin seeds
2 small fresh green chillies, slit lengthways
10 fresh or 15 dried curry leaves
1 tablespoon unsalted cashew nuts
large pinch of asafoetida
4 tablespoons frozen green peas
1 teaspoon caster sugar
a small handful of fresh coriander leaves, chopped, to garnish
1 tablespoon lemon juice
salt

1 Heat a frying pan over a medium heat, add the semolina and dry-toast for 4–5 minutes until it starts to turn brown. Tip into a bowl and set aside.

2 Heat the oil in a heavy-based saucepan over a high heat then add the mustard seeds. As soon as they start to pop, add the cumin seeds and fry for a few seconds until slightly dark, then add the chillies, curry leaves (standing back from the pan if using fresh leaves, as they will splutter), cashew nuts and asafoetida. Cook for a few seconds until the cashews start to turn golden.

3 Tip in the peas, add the toasted semolina, sugar and season with salt. Standing away from the pan, pour in 400ml boiling-hot water and bring to the boil. The hot water will make the semolina splutter so be careful.

4 Reduce the heat and simmer for 6–7 minutes, stirring, until all the water has been absorbed and the semolina leaves the sides of the pan.

5 Loosen with a fork and serve hot, sprinkled with the coriander and drizzled with lemon juice.

Aloo Tikki

| POTATO CAKES |

These are very popular all over north and central India as a teatime or street snack, although patties made with mashed potato are eaten all over India. In the south, they are flavoured with mustard seeds and curry leaves and are called 'bondas', whereas on the streets of Mumbai, they are served with a chickpea curry and called 'pattice'. They can be flavoured or plain, served with a chickpea curry such as Cholay (page 289), or simply with some sweet or hot chutney and plain yogurt. *Makes 8 potato cakes*
PREPARATION → *20 minutes* COOKING *35 minutes*

2 large potatoes, boiled, peeled and mashed
1 teaspoon ground turmeric
a few sprigs of fresh coriander leaves, finely chopped
1 fresh green chilli, finely diced (seeds and all)
2 slices of white bread, soaked in water and squeezed
    to remove all water
vegetable oil, for shallow-frying
2 tablespoons plain flour
salt

1 Combine the mashed potato in a bowl with the turmeric, coriander, chilli and bread, season with salt and knead together. Shape into 8 thick, flat rounds.
2 Heat enough oil to liberally cover the base of a frying pan over a high heat, dip each potato cake in the flour and shallow-fry the cakes a couple at a time for 5–6 minutes, turning them over until both sides are golden. Remove and drain on kitchen paper.
3 Serve hot with curry, or chutney and plain yogurt.

Murgh Pankhi Masala

| MASALA CHICKEN WINGS |

In India, this easy recipe is eaten as a snack at home or at small, roadside restaurants called 'dhabas' which are found on highways and act as truck stops. As most long-distance truck drivers are of Punjabi descent, these eateries serve north Indian food which is wholesome and tastes homemade. The 'dhabas' are earthy restaurants, often open air with wooden tables and benches where people stop for a quick meal. City folk will sometimes drive out to a dhaba for the delicious, fresh food on offer. You can swap the wings for cubed chicken breast if you want a boneless version. *Serves 4* PREPARATION → *10 minutes, plus 30 minutes marinating time (or ideally overnight)* COOKING *15 minutes*

1 teaspoon ginger-garlic paste *(page 45)*
1 teaspoon medium-hot red chilli powder
1 tablespoon ground cumin
400g chicken wings, skinned
vegetable oil, for deep-frying
3 tablespoons cornflour
salt

1 Combine the ginger-garlic paste, chilli powder, cumin and salt to season in a bowl. Tip in the wings, coat them in the marinade, cover and marinate for at least 30 minutes or overnight in the fridge if possible.
2 Heat enough oil for deep-frying in a deep frying pan. Once the oil is very hot, dip each wing in the cornflour so that it is evenly coated and deep-fry them in batches for 6–7 minutes. Make sure that they are cooked through by cutting one open to check the flesh is white all the way to the bone. Remove with a slotted spoon and drain on kitchen paper. Serve hot.

Macchi Ke Cutlet

| INDIAN FISHCAKES |

Here the fish is spiced and flavoured to take away the smell that some Indians find distasteful. I have used tinned tuna but you could cook and flake any fish such as cod, coley or even frozen salmon. In India, cooks would use local fish such as 'rohu' in Bengal or 'surmai' in Mumbai for this recipe. *Makes 8 fishcakes* PREPARATION → *15 minutes, plus 30 minutes soaking time* COOKING *20 minutes*

2 x 120g tins of tuna in brine, well drained
juice of 1 lemon
½ teaspoon cumin seeds
1 fresh green chilli, minced
½ teaspoon garam masala *(page 64)*
2 slices of white bread, soaked in water and squeezed
    to remove all water
a handful of fresh coriander leaves, finely chopped
a few sprigs of dill, finely chopped
vegetable oil, for shallow-frying
2 tablespoons plain flour
salt
Mint and Coriander Chutney *(page 427)*, to serve

1 Squeeze out all the water from the tuna and combine the tuna with the lemon juice in a mixing bowl. Set aside for 30 minutes.

2 Heat a small frying pan over a high heat, add the cumin seeds and dry-toast for 30 seconds until they darken. Tip them into a pestle and mortar or spice mill and crush or blend to a fine powder.

3 Add the crushed cumin, chilli and garam masala to the tuna and season with salt.

4 Crumble the bread into the bowl. Mix in the coriander and dill. Shape the mixture into 8 equal-sized balls and flatten.

5 Heat enough oil to cover the base of a frying pan over a high heat. Dip each fish patty in flour, shake off the excess and shallow-fry for 4–5 minutes on each side until golden brown.

6 Drain on kitchen paper and serve warm with Mint and Coriander Chutney.

Mutton Ke Kofte

| MINI LAMB KOFTAS |

These are so simple to prepare and so delicious that you will find yourself making them quite often once you've tasted them! In India they are served as a teatime or party snack, or sometimes folded into spicy curries to be eaten with a roti. *Serves 4* PREPARATION → *15 minutes* COOKING *10 minutes*

150g lean lamb mince
1 teaspoon ginger-garlic paste *(page 45)*
1 fresh green chilli, minced
a few sprigs of fresh coriander leaves, finely chopped
½ teaspoon garam masala *(page 64)*
salt
Mint and Coriander Chutney *(page 427)*, to serve

1 Preheat the oven to 200°C/gas mark 6 and line a baking tray with greaseproof paper.

2 Combine the mince with the ginger-garlic paste, chilli, coriander and garam masala, season with salt and knead well.

3 Shape into little balls the size of a cherry and place on the baking tray. Bake for 10 minutes.

4 Serve hot with Mint and Coriander Chutney.

GRILLED FOODS

A tandoor is a cylindrical, clay, wood or coal-fired oven in which meats or breads are cooked. Its origins are said to be in the Middle East although many historians have recorded findings of small mud-plastered ovens in the Indus Valley civilisation, dated 3300–1700 BC.

Contrary to what most people outside of India believe, not all of India uses tandoor ovens. These large ovens are confined to north India and Punjab in particular. In many Punjabi villages, the tandoor was a communal oven where women would take their dough to be cooked into rotis.

The Moti Mahal restaurant in New Delhi claims that they made the communal tandoor a household name through their offering of tandoori foods. Famous patrons loved this cuisine so much that it came to be a part of state banquets and royal feasts. Today, most north Indian restaurants have a tandoor and it is almost confined to the restaurant business. Being a 'tandoori chef' is no easy thing – you have to be adept at putting your hand in an oven that is blazing at up to 450°C and pulling out a naan or kebab at the exact moment it is cooked.

Indian cooking does not require any oven baking and most Indian homes are not fitted with Western-style ovens. Considering this, most grilled foods, such as kebabs or tandoori chicken, are considered 'restaurant' food in India. Of course these grilled foods are occasionally made in north Indian homes, on a griddle, but most people would agree that the slightly charred, smoky flavour of tandoor-cooked food is incomparable.

Grilled foods are served with a highly flavoured or creamy dip, sliced fresh onions and wedges of lemon or lime.

In this chapter, I have recreated some popular kebabs using a conventional Western-style gas oven. The cooking time in a perfectly heated tandoor is much less than in a conventional oven as the temperature is much higher and the thick clay walls seal the heat in. A whole chicken weighing 1.5kg could cook in 30 minutes in a tandoor whereas it would take much longer in a gas or electric oven. Also, cooking in a tandoor gives that lovely charred, smoky flavour which never really tastes burnt. It is difficult to achieve that in the oven, even under a grill. The high temperature in a tandoor ensures that the meat is cooked and juicy on the inside and slightly crusty on the outside, with the marinade cooking into crisp bits that cling to it. Once the outer layer of meat has been sealed by the heat, the juices are sealed in whereas in a conventional oven, the juices drip into the tray, partially cooking the meat in steam. The times and temperatures may vary slightly depending on what sort of oven you are using. For example, a whole chicken will take 25 minutes per 500g at 200°C (plus 25 minutes), or 180°C in a fan-assisted oven.

TIPS FOR SUCCESSFUL GRILLING:

1 Marinate your meat, chicken or fish at least for 1 hour or overnight if possible, so that the flavours of the spices are absorbed. For more on marinades see page 137.

2 Make sure that your oven is hot so that the food gets slightly charred.

3 You can also cook the recipes in this chapter on a barbecue – make sure your food is cooked through.

4 Grilled foods in some restaurants have a bright red colour. This comes from edible food colouring. You can add this to the recipe or leave it out. Omitting it won't change the flavour of the dish. Most good restaurants will not use food colouring, as it is considered unnecessary. Ready-made 'tandoori masala', available in Indian shops, has red food colouring. I prefer not to use food colouring as I think it makes food look unnatural.

Chicken Tikka

| CUBED SPICED CHICKEN |

The word 'tikka', often misunderstood as a 'sauce' or a 'tandoori-cooked food', is actually a dice-cut of chicken breast, usually an inch in size. The word is largely used in restaurants in north India where chicken tikka has been popularised as morsels of highly spiced, marinated chicken that are cooked in a tandoor or clay oven. These can be served a canapé or as a light meal with a salad.

Serves 4 PREPARATION → *15 minutes, plus 1 hour marinating or overnight if possible)* COOKING *15 minutes*

1 tablespoon ginger-garlic paste *(page 45)*
½ teaspoon medium-hot red chilli powder
½ teaspoon ground turmeric
½ teaspoon ground cumin
½ teaspoon ground coriander
1 teaspoon garam masala *(page 64)*
4 green cardamom pods, seeds crushed and husks discarded
2 tablespoons full-fat yogurt
juice of ½ lime
400g skinless chicken breast, cubed
salt
fresh onion rings and wedges of lemon or lime, to serve

1 Combine the ginger-garlic paste, ground spices, yogurt, lime juice and salt to season in a large mixing bowl. Add the cubed chicken, stir to coat, cover and refrigerate for 1 hour or overnight if possible.

2 Preheat the oven to 200°C/gas mark 6 and line a baking tray with foil.

3 Place the marinated chicken on the lined baking tray and bake for 15 minutes. Make sure it is cooked right through by cutting open a piece and checking that it is completely white inside.

4 Remove from the oven and serve at once, with fresh onion rings and wedges of lemon or lime.

Seekh Kebabs

| MINCED LAMB KEBABS |

'Seekh' means skewers, so the meat in this dish, either minced beef or lamb, is wrapped around skewers in sausage shapes. Kebabs originated in Turkey/Persia and came to India through the Mughals. Seekh kebabs are popular in the north where Mughlai cooking has great influence, and they are also sold as street food as they are quick and easy to cook on small roadside coal barbecues.

Serves 4 PREPARATION → *10 minutes, plus 1 hour marinating time or overnight if possible* COOKING *15–20 minutes*

1 small onion, finely diced
2 fresh green chillies, finely minced
1 tablespoon garam masala *(page 64)*
1 teaspoon freshly ground black pepper
2 teaspoons ginger-garlic paste *(page 45)*
2 teaspoons natural yogurt
500g minced lamb
a small handful of finely chopped fresh coriander leaves
a small handful of finely chopped fresh mint leaves
salt
Mint and Coriander Chutney *(page 427)*, to serve

1 Combine the onion, chillies, garam masala, pepper, ginger-garlic paste, salt to season and yogurt in a large mixing bowl. Mix well, then stir in the lamb, break up the mince, cover and leave it to marinate in the fridge for at least 1 hour or overnight if possible.

2 Preheat the oven to 200°C/gas mark 6 and line a baking tray with foil.

3 Soak 12 bamboo skewers in warm water for 30 minutes, and mix the chopped herbs into the marinated lamb mince.

4 Shape the meat around the soaked skewers, place them on the foil-lined baking tray and cook for 15–20 minutes, turning them over to cook evenly on all sides.

5 Remove from the oven and serve hot with Mint and Coriander Chutney.

PANEER KE SULEY – Skewered Paneer and Vegetables

You can use ready-bought paneer or make your own (see page 252). I have used the dhungar method, popular in the north Indian Awadhi style of cooking to smoke the paneer. The Awadhi style is inspired by Mughal cooking; and 'dhungar' is when a small piece of coal is lit and placed in a small metal bowl inside the pan of food to impart a smokiness to the food (see page 39). You can leave this part of the recipe out if you wish.

Serves 4 PREPARATION → *20 minutes, plus 30 minutes marinating and soaking time* COOKING *20 minutes*

YOU WILL NEED:

300g paneer, cut into 2cm cubes

1 red pepper, deseeded and cut into 3cm cubes

1 green pepper, deseeded and cut into 3cm cubes

1 small onion, cut into 3cm cubes

1 tablespoon vegetable oil

small piece of coal (optional)

2 cloves

1 teaspoon melted ghee or vegetable oil

Mint and Coriander Chutney *(page 427)*, to serve

For the marinade

50g natural yogurt

½ teaspoon ajowan seeds

1 teaspoon Kashmiri red chilli powder

1 tablespoon ginger-garlic paste *(page 45)*

2 tablespoons lemon juice

1 teaspoon garam masala *(page 64)*

½ teaspoon dried fenugreek leaves (kasoori methi – *page 393*)

salt

1 Mix all the ingredients for the marinade together in a large bowl and stir in the cubed paneer and vegetables. Set aside to marinate for 30 minutes.

2 Preheat the oven to 200°C/gas mark 6, line a baking tray with foil and if using bamboo skewers, soak 6 skewers in warm water for 30 minutes.

3 Skewer the marinated paneer and vegetables in an attractive fashion: I alternate the paneer, peppers and onions so that each skewer is colourful and has some of each. Drizzle with the vegetable oil. Place on the lined baking tray and bake for 15 minutes.

4 Remove the tray from the oven and place the skewers in a deep, lidded frying pan. Place the small metal bowl in the centre of the frying pan. Light the coal and when the initial thick smoke has died away, place it in the bowl.

5 Add the cloves to the bowl and pour the ghee or oil over the top. Cover the pan with a tight-fitting lid and seal for 2–3 minutes.

6 Remove the lid and serve the skewers immediately, with Mint and Coriander Chutney.

Tandoori Gobhi

| GRILLED SPICED CAULIFLOWER STEAKS |

1 large cauliflower, leaves removed

1 teaspoon cumin seeds

1 small onion, chopped

1 teaspoon ginger-garlic paste *(page 45)*

2 fresh green chillies, chopped

1 teaspoon ground turmeric

½ teaspoon amchoor (dried mango powder)
or 2 teaspoons lemon juice

½ teaspoon chaat masala *(page 344)*

vegetable oil, for drizzling

salt

Mint and Coriander Chutney *(page 427)*,
to serve

I love the dramatic appeal of this recipe. The cauliflower must be cooked until just tender to make the most of its crunch and juiciness. This dish is served in north Indian restaurants which have tandoors. It is a fairly new addition to the tandoori repertoire as traditional kebabs were non-vegetarian and modern-day restaurants are catering to vegetarians as well.

Serves 4 PREPARATION → *15 minutes, plus 30 minutes marinating time* COOKING *30 minutes*

1 Cut the cauliflower into large steaks about 5mm thick. Rub them with salt on both sides, to season, and set aside for 30 minutes.

2 Heat a frying pan over a high heat, add the cumin seeds and dry-toast until they begin to darken and develop an aroma. Remove from the heat and crush to a powder in a pestle and mortar.

3 Put the onion, ginger-garlic paste and chillies into a small blender or pestle and mortar and crush to a purée.

4 Preheat the oven to 200°C/gas mark 6 and line a baking tray with foil.

5 Stir the ground spices into the chilli purée and brush the mixture onto both sides of the cauliflower steaks. Drizzle over a couple of teaspoons of oil. Place on the foil-lined baking tray and bake for 30 minutes or until tender and golden around the edges.

6 Remove from the oven and serve hot with Mint and Coriander Chutney.

Murgh Malai Tikka

| CREAMY CHICKEN TIKKA |

This is a popular restaurant kebab and combines Western-style Cheddar cheese with Indian spices to achieve a subtle, creamy flavour. It was created by tandoori chefs in fine dining restaurants located in five-star hotels, but the exact origin is unclear. They can be finished with a light sprinkling of chaat masala, a tangy hot spice mix, for extra flavour. *Serves 4* PREPARATION → *15 minutes, plus 1 hour marinating time* COOKING *21 minutes*

1 egg
20g mild Cheddar cheese, grated
2 fresh green chillies, finely diced
1 teaspoon freshly ground black pepper
½ teaspoon grated nutmeg
2 tablespoons double cream
1 tablespoon cornflour
300g skinless chicken breast, cut into 2cm cubes
salt
pinch of chaat masala *(page 344)*, to serve (optional)
Mint and Coriander Chutney *(page 427)* and Naans
    (pages 110–113), to serve

1 Combine the egg, cheese, chillies, pepper, nutmeg, cream, salt to season and cornflour in a bowl. Add the chicken to this mixture, stir to coat, cover and transfer to the fridge to marinate for 1 hour.

2 Preheat the oven to 200°C/gas mark 6 and line a baking tray with foil or greaseproof paper.

3 Transfer the marinated chicken to the lined baking tray and bake for 20 minutes, then place under a hot grill for 1 minute or so to get a slightly charred effect.

4 Serve hot, sprinkled with chaat masala, if you like, alongside naans and Mint and Coriander Chutney.

Lal Masalyatli Macchi

| RED CHILLI FISH |

You can make the marinade for this dish as spicy or mild as you wish, by increasing or reducing the amount of chilli powder in the marinade. The flavour of the chilli is more important than the heat! Choose a firm fish such as kingfish, mackerel, bream, trout or salmon so it holds its shape when cooking. Traditionally cooks in coastal Maharashtra and Goa, where this recipe comes from, would use local sea fish such as pomfret or mackerel. You could also use the marinade for prawns. *Serves 4* PREPARATION → *10 minutes, plus 1 hour marinating time or overnight, if possible* COOKING *20 minutes*

1 teaspoon Kashmiri red chilli powder
1 teaspoon ground coriander
1 teaspoon ground cumin
2 tablespoons lemon juice
1 teaspoon crushed garlic
4 x 200g fish steaks, such as kingfish, mackerel, bream, trout
    or salmon
2 tablespoons vegetable oil
salt
fresh onion rings and wedges of lemon or lime, to serve

1 Combine the spices in a bowl with the lemon juice, garlic and salt to season.

2 Rub the spice mix onto the fish steaks, cover and refrigerate for at least 1 hour (or overnight if possible).

3 Preheat the oven to 200°C/gas mark 6 and line a baking tray with foil.

4 Place the marinated fish steaks on the lined baking tray, drizzle with the oil and bake for 15–20 minutes, depending on the thickness of the steaks. Gently pierce a knife into a steak, push open and check that it is opaque all the way through.

5 Serve hot with slices of fresh onion and wedges of lemon or lime.

Jhinga Hariyali

| PRAWNS WITH GREEN HERBS |

Use the best prawns you can buy for this dish. Again, this is a restaurant-style dish from north India where they are cooked on skewers in the tandoor. You can use the marinade with other seafood such as squid, or any firm fish such as cod or haddock. Serve the skewers with Green Apple Chutney and some of the marinade used for flavouring the prawns. *Serves 5* PREPARATION → *15 minutes, plus 30 minutes marinating time* COOKING *4–6 minutes*

a large handful of fresh coriander leaves
a large handful of fresh mint leaves
2 fresh green chillies
1 teaspoon ginger-garlic paste *(page 45)*
½ teaspoon ground turmeric
1 tablespoon lemon juice
20 large raw prawns, shelled and deveined
   (leave the tails on if you wish)
salt
Green Apple Chutney *(page 429)*, to serve

1 Blitz all the ingredients apart from the prawns in a blender, season with salt and add a little water to make a smooth purée.
2 Marinate the prawns for 30 minutes in half of the purée, setting the remainder aside to serve with the skewers as a dip. If using bamboo skewers, soak 5 skewers in warm water while the prawns are marinating.
3 Preheat the grill to high and line a baking tray with foil.
4 Thread the marinated prawns onto the skewers, place the skewers on the foil-lined baking tray and grill for 2–3 minutes. As soon as the prawns change colour, remove the tray out from the oven, flip the skewers over and cook the prawns on the other side for a further 2–3 minutes. Serve with Green Apple Chutney.

Tandoori Murgh

| TANDOORI-STYLE CHICKEN |

Popularly known as tandoori chicken, this dish originated from the Mughlai style of cooking in clay ovens, and was popularised by the Punjabis. Today, it is considered a readily available restaurant treat. *Serves 4* PREPARATION → *15 minutes, plus 1 hour marinating time or overnight if possible* COOKING *50 minutes*

4 cloves
3 green cardamom pods, seeds removed and husks discarded
½ teaspoon fenugreek seeds
1 teaspoon cumin seeds
1 tablespoon ginger-garlic paste *(page 45)*
½ teaspoon medium-hot red chilli powder
½ teaspoon ground turmeric
1 teaspoon ground coriander
2 tablespoons lemon juice
8 chicken drumsticks, skinned and pricked
2 tablespoons vegetable oil
salt
fresh onion rings, wedges of lemon or lime and Naans
   (pages 110–113), to serve

1 Heat a small frying pan over a high heat, add the cloves, cardamom seeds, fenugreek and cumin seeds and dry-toast until they darken and become fragrant. Tip them into a pestle and mortar or spice mill and crush or blend to a fine powder.
2 Combine the ginger-garlic paste, ground spices, chilli powder, turmeric, ground coriander, lemon juice and salt to season in a large mixing bowl. Add the chicken drumsticks, coat them in the marinade, cover and refrigerate for at least 1 hour or overnight if possible.
3 Preheat the oven to 220°C/gas mark 6 or heat the barbecue and line a baking tray with foil.
4 Rub the marinated drumsticks with the vegetable oil.
5 Put the chicken on the hot barbecue grill or in the oven on the lined baking tray and cook for 45 minutes (25–30 minutes on a barbecue), turning them halfway through cooking, until tender and cooked through to the bone. Cut open a drumstick to check that the flesh is white. If you're cooking the chicken in the oven, finish by placing the drumsticks under a hot grill for 4–5 minutes to get a slightly charred effect.
6 Serve hot with fresh onion rings, lemon or lime and naans.

Murgh Tikka Achari

| CHICKEN IN PICKLING SPICES |

Pickling spices vary from region to region. In the south fenugreek, chilli and asafoetida are commonly used in a base of sesame oil, whereas in Gujarat, fennel and cumin are combined with jaggery and chilli to form a hot, sweet base. Most pickles all over India contain a mix of mustard seeds and chilli. *Serves 4* PREPARATION ➞ *20 minutes, plus 1 hour marinating time* COOKING *20 minutes*

1 teaspoon aniseed
½ teaspoon fenugreek seeds
½ teaspoon nigella seeds (kalonji)
½ teaspoon freshly ground black pepper
1 tablespoon ginger-garlic paste *(page 45)*
½ teaspoon medium-hot red chilli powder
2 tablespoons lemon juice
3 tablespoons full-fat yogurt
400g skinless chicken breast, cut into 2cm cubes
salt
Mint and Coriander Chutney *(page 427)* and Naans
    (pages 110–113), to serve

1 Heat a small frying pan over a high heat, add the aniseed, fenugreek, nigella seeds and pepper and dry-toast for a minute or so until the mix darkens and becomes fragrant. Tip the toasted spices into a pestle and mortar or spice mill and crush or blend to a fine powder.
2 Put the ginger-garlic paste, chilli powder, ground spices from the mortar or spice mill, lemon juice and yogurt in a bowl and mix well. Season with salt and taste to check. Stir in the chicken to coat it in the marinade, then cover and refrigerate for 1 hour.
3 Meanwhile, soak 10 bamboo skewers in warm water for at least 30 minutes and preheat the grill to high.
4 Thread the marinated chicken onto the soaked skewers, putting a few pieces on each one. Place under a hot grill and cook for 3–4 minutes. Flip over and cook for a further 3–4 minutes until the chicken is cooked all the way through.
5 Serve hot with Mint and Coriander Chutney and naan.

Tandoori Macchli

| WHOLE SPICED FISH |

This easy recipe can be made with any firm fish – I like mackerel or trout as they are easily available, the right size to fit into my oven and are wonderfully firm when cooked whole.

    Punjab, which means 'the land of the five rivers' is where this recipe comes from, so freshwater fish such as carp, rohu and tilapia found in the Beas, Jhelum, Ravi, Sutlej and Chenab rivers are used in that region. *Serves 4* PREPARATION ➞ *15 minutes, plus 30 minutes marinating time* COOKING *25 minutes*

1½ teaspoons garam masala *(page 64)*
1 teaspoon medium-hot red chilli powder
1 teaspoon ground turmeric
2 teaspoons ginger-garlic paste *(page 45)*
1 egg, beaten
1 tablespoon gram flour
2 tablespoons lemon juice
2 x 400g whole firm fish, such as rainbow trout or mackerel,
    gutted, scaled and well cleaned
1 tablespoon vegetable oil
salt
fresh onion rings and wedges of lemon and lime, to serve

1 Combine the ground spices, ginger-garlic paste, egg, gram flour, lemon juice and salt to season in a small bowl.
2 Smear the spice mixture over the fish, making sure that it is evenly coated inside and out. Leave the fish to marinate in the fridge, covered, for at least 30 minutes.
3 Preheat the oven to 200°C/gas mark 6 and line a baking tray with foil.
4 Place the marinated fish on the lined baking tray, drizzle with the oil and cook for 25 minutes or until the fish is cooked through. Gently insert a sharp knife into the thickest part. The flesh should slightly resist but still look firm. (It will continue to cook for a few more minutes after it's removed from the oven.)
5 Serve hot with fresh onion rings and wedges of lemon and lime.

SALADS & RAITAS

ALMOST EVERY INDIAN MEAL IS ACCOMPANIED BY A SALAD OR RAITA, WHICH IS GENERALLY
A COMBINATION OF VEGETABLES AND HERBS WITH YOGURT. THIS PROVIDES AN INTERESTING
CONTRAST OF TEXTURES AND TEMPERATURES.

Almost every Indian meal is accompanied by a salad or raita, which is generally a combination of vegetables and herbs with yogurt. Each region has its own repertoire. In the north and central parts of the country, raitas are sprinkled with toasted ground cumin and red chilli powder. In the south, they are called 'pachadi', a term that loosely means raw or green ('pacha') vegetables, that are coarsely crushed or beaten ('adi'). Pachadi also refers to the innumerable pickles and relishes, such as the tender mango one, made in southern India. A pachadi is highly flavoured with salt and spices such as chilli and mustard and therefore it is to be eaten in smaller quantities than a main dish. It may also include locally grown coconut. Some raitas such as Cucumber and Mint Raita (page 394) have been made famous by Indian restaurants the world over. Western versions are very much like those you would find in India – one reason for its popularity is the ease of finding both cucumber and yogurt in shops around the world.

Both raitas and pachadis can be made with vegetables, pulses or fruit. Local ingredients are key, so in the north, one would see winter carrots or summer cucumbers. Gram flour is fried into little pearls called 'boondi' that are added to yogurt. North-growing fruit such as pomegranate makes a bejewelled raita in combination with yogurt.

In the south, ridge gourd, with its tough peel, may be used along with amla (Indian gooseberry), tomatoes and sorrel or 'gongura' leaves. Being close to the Equator, temperatures can soar in the summer and chillies, with their ability to make us perspire by way of the capsaicin they contain, are included in fiery pachadis. Seasonal mangoes and pineapple are combined with coconut and chilli to make sweet, hot and tangy raitas called 'sasam'. Pachadis are often finished with a tempering of spice seeds (see page 425) such as mustard and cumin.

A salad not only adds essential fibre to a meal, but also interesting textures and vibrancy of colour. A raita will certainly cool down the palate but also provide the excitement of a new temperature layer in a mostly hot meal.

Salads and raitas make the most of seasonal produce and clever cooks will find interesting ways to include market vegetables into daily meals. Raitas can be sweet, tangy or savoury and include ingredients such as cucumber, tomato, aubergine, mango, carrot, spinach, banana stem or bananas. They are served plain or flavoured with spices such as cumin and chilli as well as herbs such as coriander, mint and dill.

Most salads and raitas are served at room temperature or marginally cool. Indians do not like their main meals to be cold and certainly never ice-cold! Ayurveda suggests that very cold foods help to extinguish 'agni' or the digestive fire in the stomach, making the system sluggish and weak.

HERBS

CORIANDER → This is the most commonly used herb in India. Variously called 'dhania', 'kothmir' or 'kothimbir', it is puréed for curries or sprinkled on as a garnish. It looks similar to parsley so when buying, sniff the roots or stalks for that distinctive powerful fragrance that only coriander has. Some people describe this as soapy but I think it is more a combination of citrus and ginger. People seem to love or hate coriander leaves; if you are catering for someone who does not appreciate its fine flavour, leave it out.

How to use and store coriander — Indian cooking uses the leaves and tender stems of the plant as a herb. The seeds are the spice. Wash the plants and snip off the lower stems and roots. Chop gently but finely, making sure not to bruise the leaves too much.

To keep coriander fresh for longer, line a plastic box with a few sheets of dry kitchen paper and put the bunch of coriander in. If the bunch is tied with a rubber band or string, discard this. Seal the box with a lid. Don't wash the coriander before storing it. The paper absorbs the trapped moisture from the herb which can cause it to wilt and become mouldy. Change the kitchen paper every couple of days. The coriander will keep well for up to 10 days.

MINT → Most Indians associate mint with chutney and snacks such as crisp samosas, bhajias and street food, such as bhelpuri, which are served with it. Mint is used more in north India than in the south as it was probably introduced into Indian cookery by the Muslim rulers of Delhi. They used mint to perfume their meats and, after settling down in the fertile rice-rich land of India, developed their cuisine to include many mint-flavoured biryanis and pulaos.

How to buy and store mint — Mint is sold fresh and is also available dried and crushed to a fine olive-green powder. Fresh mint should be selected on the basis of its vitality and colour. Avoid bruised, blackened or wilted leaves. Fresh mint keeps well for a week or longer in the fridge – follow the same storage method as for fresh coriander (see above). Dried mint has a subtle fragrance but loses its flavour after 3–4 months. I am not fond of freezing mint or coriander as I think they lose their colour, flavour and vitality.

CURRY LEAF → Few south Indian savouries are complete without this herb. The ancient Hindu practice of Ayurvedic medicine relies heavily on curry leaves for many of its cures. It lends its lingering aroma to a dish but can be too chewy to actually eat.

Curry leaves grow on medium-sized trees and are different to the curry plant. The tree is native to India and Sri Lanka and thrives in tropical climates. In India, the plant is grown on kitchen windowsills so that a few leaves can easily be plucked when needed. As the plant is so widely grown, the herb is cheap and some vegetable sellers in India often toss a few fresh sprigs into your shopping basket free of charge as a little extra.

The whole plant, including the stems, has a strong curry-like odour. The taste is slightly bitter but pleasant and aromatic.

How to buy and store curry leaves — Curry leaves are available fresh, frozen or dried. Fresh leaves have a beautiful fragrance that is partially lost on drying or freezing. If you have a bunch of fresh curry leaves, these can be home dried for later use: spread the bunch out on a tray, stalks and all, and dry for 2–3 days at room temperature. Discard the stalks and store the leaves in a plastic container in the fridge for up to 6 months. I find this a better way to retain their flavour than freezing them. Dried ones are also available commercially.

DILL → Indian dill or 'suva' is used practically all over India. Dill has an aroma that is slightly reminiscent of caraway – warm, aromatic and tingly. The fresh fronds are used to flavour dals or added to vegetable side dishes such as Palak Ki Subzi (page 315).

How to buy and store dill — Dill is available in bunches – choose fresh, green, firm fronds. Over time, dill starts to turn yellow and dry – avoid these bunches. Store dill in the same way as fresh coriander (see page 389).

HOW TO BUY AND STORE FENUGREEK

Fenugreek is eaten fresh as a vegetable, the leaves are dried and sold as a herb called 'kasoori methi' and the seeds are used as a spice. Fenugreek has a bitter and lingering taste but a wonderful sweet, curry-like aroma.

Fenugreek seeds are available whole, crushed or ground. The fresh stalks with leaves are sold in every Indian food shop and 'kasoori methi' is sold in packs. Kasoori methi is used in small amounts so buy small packs and store them away from moisture and light. It can be added to warm oil at the beginning of cooking a curry or as a finishing herb at the end. If you cannot find kasoori methi, here's how to make it.

YOU WILL NEED:
a bunch of fresh fenugreek
    leaves
– a tray
– a clean tea towel
– a large baking tray lined with
    foil or greaseproof paper
– a clean 250ml (no need to
    sterilise) jar to store
    the dried herb

1 Pluck the fenugreek leaves off the stems, wash, pat them gently to get rid of excess moisture, spread them out on a tray and leave to dry for a few hours until there is no moisture left.

2 Preheat the oven to 80°C/gas mark ½. Once the leaves are completely dry, spread them out on a baking tray and put in the centre of the oven, leaving the door slightly open so that there is some circulation of air. If this is not done, the methi will bake rather than dry.

3 Depending on your oven and the amount of air circulating, it should take 45–50 minutes to completely dry the methi. Check halfway through cooking and, if necessary, shake the tray to separate the leaves a bit.

4 To check if they are done, crush a few leaves between your fingers. They should crumble easily. Remove the tray from the oven and cool completely. Store the leaves in a clean, dry jar for up to a year.

Kheere Pudine Ka Raita

| CUCUMBER AND MINT SALAD |

This north Indian raita goes well with rich meat or fragrant rice dishes such as Biryani (page 90) or Rogan Josh (page 147), as it provides a fresh, light balance. You can add a chopped fresh tomato for a slight tang and colour. *Serves 4*

PREPARATION —➤ *10 minutes*

½ cucumber, coarsely grated, skin on
¼ teaspoon cumin seeds
8 tablespoons natural yogurt
few sprigs of fresh mint, leaves finely chopped
salt

1 Put the grated cucumber in a sieve over a bowl and squeeze out most of the juice. This juice can be added to curries or dals.
2 Dry-toast the cumin seeds and crush with a pestle and mortar.
3 Combine the cucumber in a bowl with the remaining ingredients, season with salt and serve immediately.

Khamang Kakdi

| FRAGRANT CUCUMBER AND PEANUT SALAD |

This festive Maharashtrian salad makes the most of locally grown peanuts and is served at celebrations and weddings. The fragrance of peanuts and coconut along with curry leaves and mustard elevates the simple flavour of cucumber, making it a perfect accompaniment to the many vegetables, rice and dal preparations that make up a Hindu vegetarian feast. The coconut is optional in the interior regions of Maharashtra, away from the coast where it grows, so leave it out if you prefer. *Serves 4*

PREPARATION —➤ *10 minutes* COOKING *2 minutes*

½ cucumber, very finely chopped, skin on
2 tablespoons toasted peanuts, coarsely crushed
2 tablespoons finely chopped coriander leaves
1 tablespoon freshly grated or desiccated coconut
1 teaspoon vegetable oil
1 teaspoon black mustard seeds
6 fresh or 10 dried curry leaves
salt

1 Combine the cucumber, peanuts, coriander and coconut together in a bowl.
2 Heat the oil in a small frying pan over a high heat and add the mustard seeds. When they begin to pop, add the curry leaves (standing back from the pan if using fresh leaves, as they will splutter) then pour the oil over the cucumber mixture. Add salt to season just before serving.

Kachumber

| ONION AND TOMATO SALAD WITH DILL, CORIANDER AND LIME |

A kachumber is variously called a 'kachoomer' or 'koshimbir' and is made of finely diced, raw vegetables such as radish and carrot. Common combinations include onion, tomato and cucumber, as these are available all over the country (in Hindi, 'kacha' is raw). *Serves 4*

PREPARATION → *10 minutes*

1 red onion, finely chopped
2 tomatoes, finely chopped
a handful of fresh dill fronds, finely chopped
a handful of fresh coriander leaves, finely chopped
pinch of caster sugar
big squeeze of lime
salt and freshly ground black pepper

1   Mix all the ingredients together in a bowl, season with salt and pepper, and serve at once.

Dahi Kachumber

| ONION AND CORIANDER RAITA |

This simple raita goes well with rich, spicy meat dishes such as Saag Gosht (page 143) and Dal Gosht (page 138), and is often served in restaurants serving north Indian Mughlai food. *Serves 4* PREPARATION → *10 minutes, plus 10 minutes chilling*

1 large onion, finely diced
100ml natural yogurt
few sprigs of fresh coriander leaves, finely chopped
1 teaspoon cumin seeds, dry toasted and crushed *(see page 56)*
salt

1   Combine all the ingredients in a bowl, chill for 10 minutes and serve. If making it in advance, remove it from the fridge 30 minutes before serving and season with salt at the last minute. Adding salt in advance will draw out the juices from the onion making the raita watery.

Beetroot Raitha

| BEETROOT AND YOGURT RAITA WITH MUSTARD AND CURRY LEAVES |

This is a south Indian recipe but a north Indian version that accompanies heavy sauce-based curries such as a korma can also be made by simply combining cooked, grated beetroot with yogurt, salt and crushed, toasted cumin. This southern version makes the most of locally grown coconut and curry leaves. *Serves 4* PREPARATION → *10 minutes*

COOKING *2 minutes*

150g natural yogurt
pinch of caster sugar
1 tablespoon sunflower or coconut oil
1 teaspoon black or brown mustard seeds
small pinch of fresh curry leaves
½ teaspoon finely grated fresh root ginger
2 cooked beetroot, coarsely grated
1 tablespoon freshly grated or desiccated coconut
salt and pepper

1   Combine the yogurt, salt to season, a large pinch of pepper and sugar in a bowl.
2   Heat the oil in a small frying pan over a high heat and add the mustard seeds. When they begin to pop, add the curry leaves and ginger. Reduce the heat to medium and cook for a few seconds, then pour into the yogurt and stir in the beetroot and coconut. Serve cold.

Palak Ka Raita

| SPICED SPINACH RAITA |

You can use fresh or frozen spinach for this recipe from north India. It helps add a fresh green colour to a meal that may have a brown curry and white rice, and provides a vegetable side dish to this simple meal. In the south, this combination of spinach and yogurt would be tempered with spices such as black mustard seeds, dried red chillies and asafoetida. *Serves 4* PREPARATION →* 10 minutes* COOKING *5 minutes*

3 good handfuls of spinach, washed, drained and chopped
150g natural yogurt
1 tablespoon vegetable oil
½ teaspoon cumin seeds
salt and freshly ground black pepper

1 Place the spinach in a pan and cook over a high heat for 3–4 minutes. As soon as it has wilted, remove from the heat and drain.
2 Season the yogurt with salt and pepper and stir in the spinach.
3 Heat the oil in a small frying pan over a high heat, add the cumin seeds and fry for a few seconds. When they darken, pour them into the raita and stir in. Serve cold.

Vellarika Pachadi

| CUCUMBER AND COCONUT RAITA |

Served at celebratory feasts at weddings and festivals like Onam, this side dish from Kerala often forms a part of 'sadhya'. This meal can consist of up to twenty dishes all served on a banana leaf. The sheer number of dishes that complement each other in flavour, temperature, colour and texture makes a 'sadhya' meal very special. Meals for large numbers of people are served on banana leaves in southern India as they form a biodegradable plate that can be discarded without wasting resources on washing up. *Serves 4* PREPARATION →* 10 minutes* COOKING *10 minutes*

½ cucumber, peeled, seeds scraped out and flesh
    cut into bite-sized pieces
150g full-fat yogurt
2 tablespoons freshly grated or frozen coconut
1 fresh green chilli
1 tablespoon coconut oil
1 teaspoon black or brown mustard seeds
small pinch of fresh curry leaves
2 dried red chillies
salt and freshly ground black pepper

1 Put the cucumber in a saucepan with enough water to barely cover it, season with salt and bring to the boil. Reduce the heat and simmer for 4–5 minutes to just soften it, then drain and set aside, saving the liquid for blending.
2 Meanwhile, combine the yogurt with salt to season and a large pinch of pepper in a bowl.
3 Put the coconut and green chilli, along with some of cucumber cooking liquid from Step 1, into a blender and blitz to a fine purée. Add this to the yogurt, along with the cooked cucumber.
4 Heat the oil in a small frying pan over a high heat, add the mustard seeds and fry until they begin to pop. Tip in the curry leaves and red chillies then pour into the raita. Stir in and serve cold.

BOONDI RAITA – Tiny Gram Flour Drops in Yogurt

YOU WILL NEED:

½ teaspoon cumin seeds

150g natural yogurt

pinch of caster sugar

salt

For the boondi

100g gram (besan) flour

1 tablespoon fine semolina

½ teaspoon salt

vegetable oil, for deep-frying

'Boond' in Hindi means 'drop' and this is one of the most popular raitas made in north Indian homes. It is quick to prepare when using shop-bought boondi and the squidgy texture seems to complement the richness of north Indian cooking. Although ready-made boondi or flour balls are widely available in many places in India, in the West you can find them in Indian grocery shops. However, Boondi are also easy to prepare at home. *Serves 4*

PREPARATION → *15 minutes, plus chilling time*

COOKING *25 minutes*

1 Combine the flour, semolina and salt in a mixing bowl and add enough cold water (roughly 150–180ml) to make a thick batter. Whisk together to remove any lumps.

2 Heat the oil in a deep frying pan over a high heat. When it reaches smoking point, reduce the heat. Hold a perforated spoon about 10cm above the pan and pour some batter onto it. It should drip in droplets into the oil.

3 The drops of batter will float up to the surface of the oil quite quickly. Fry for a minute or so once they've risen to the surface of the oil, remove with a slotted spoon and drain on kitchen paper. Repeat with the remaining batter. The boondis can be stored in an airtight container in the kitchen cupboard for a couple of months.

4 Heat a frying pan over a high heat, add the cumin seeds and dry-toast until they begin to darken and develop an aroma. Remove from the heat and crush to a powder in a pestle and mortar.

5 To make the raita, combine the yogurt, salt to season, sugar and cumin in a serving bowl.

6 Stir in a third of the boondis to make a semi-liquid raita. Chill for an hour so that the boondis have time to soak up the moisture and soften, then bring back to room temperature and serve. Store the remaining boondis in an airtight container for up to 3 months.

Sweetcorn Sundal

| SWEETCORN SALAD WITH SPICES AND COCONUT |

Sundal is a festive, dry side dish from south India and is typically prepared on certain religious days as blessed food. Foods that can be prepared quickly are favoured so that the day can be spent in meditation and reflection rather than in doing household chores. On such days, one can expect to have visitors who will need to be catered for by way of a small but filling snack such as this one, which is also sometimes made with chickpeas. *Serves 4*

PREPARATION → *15 minutes* COOKING *2 minutes*

1 x 200g can of sweetcorn, drained
2 tablespoons freshly grated coconut or desiccated coconut
    (soaked in warm water for 15 minutes and drained)
1 tablespoon sunflower or coconut oil
1 teaspoon brown or black mustard seeds
pinch of asafoetida
½ teaspoon white urad dal
1 dried red chilli
small pinch of fresh curry leaves
salt and freshly ground black pepper

1 Combine the sweetcorn, coconut and salt to season in a mixing bowl.

2 Heat the oil in a small frying pan over a high heat and add the mustard seeds. When they begin to pop, add the asafoetida and urad dal. Cook for a few seconds and as soon as they start to turn golden, tip in the chilli and curry leaves. Pour this over the corn, mix well and serve at room temperature.

Cheenikayi Raitha

| PUMPKIN RAITA |

A simple side dish from Karnataka, this recipe combines the creamy flavour of pumpkin with the sweetness of coconut. It is served with a roti or with a curry such as Egg and Ridge gourd Curry (page 229). You can use any variety of pumpkin or butternut squash. *Serves 4*

PREPARATION → *15 minutes* COOKING *10 minutes*

200g red pumpkin, peeled, deseeded and grated
2 fresh green chillies
2 tablespoons grated fresh or frozen coconut
small sprig of fresh coriander leaves, chopped
4 tablespoons natural yogurt
¾ teaspoon caster sugar
2 teaspoons vegetable oil
1 teaspoon black mustard seeds
½ teaspoon white urad dal, washed and drained
pinch of asafoetida
salt

1 Put the pumpkin in a saucepan with enough boiling water to cover it and bring to the boil. Reduce the heat and simmer for 5 minutes until soft. Drain and set aside.

2 Blitz the chillies, coconut, coriander leaves and yogurt in a blender to make a fine purée (you may need to add a little water to turn the blades). Pour it into a bowl, season with salt then add the sugar and the cooked, drained pumpkin.

3 Heat the oil in a small frying pan over a high heat. Add the mustard seeds. As they begin to pop, add the dal and asafoetida. As soon as the dal begin to change colour, pour the oil over the pumpkin and yogurt mix. Serve cool.

Fruit Sasam

| SPICED FRUIT SALAD |

In the mango season, around April–May each year, Konkani households in western India look forward to eating this fabulous fruit salad. As someone who belongs to this food-loving clan, one of the most fabulous childhood memories I have is of eating this mixed into steaming rice! *Serves 4* PREPARATION → *15 minutes*

150g fresh, grated coconut, or desiccated, soaked in
    warm water for 30 minutes and drained
¼ teaspoon medium red chilli powder
1 teaspoon black or brown mustard seeds
2 tablespoons soft dark brown sugar or crumbled
    or grated jaggery
1 ripe mango, peeled, stoned and cut into 2cm cubes
small handful of red or green grapes, halved
7–8 small cubes of fresh pineapple
salt

1 Put the coconut, chilli powder, mustard seeds and enough water to just cover the mixture in a blender and blitz to a fine purée.
2 Season with salt and stir in the sugar or jaggery. Mix well until it melts.
3 Tip in the fruit, mix gently and serve cold.

Ananas Aur Anar Ka Raita

| PINEAPPLE AND POMEGRANATE
IN SPICED YOGURT |

You can add a small cubed, cooked potato to this raita for added creaminess. Fruit is not often found as part of a main meal in India as it's expensive – this is an exception. The raita should have sweet, salty, tangy flavours. *Serves 4* PREPARATION → *15 minutes*

½ teaspoon cumin seeds
200g full-fat yogurt
large pinch of freshly ground black pepper
1½ teaspoons caster sugar (or more or less to taste)
¼ teaspoon medium red chilli powder
a large handful of fresh, cubed pineapple
2 tablespoons pomegranate seeds
few sprigs of fresh coriander leaves, finely chopped
salt

1 Heat a frying pan over a high heat, add the cumin seeds and dry-toast until they begin to darken and develop an aroma. Remove from the heat and crush to a powder in a pestle and mortar.
2 Combine the yogurt with the pepper, sugar, chilli powder and ground cumin in a bowl and season with salt.
3 Stir in the pineapple. Pour into a serving bowl.
4 Halve the pomegranate, hold the cut side over a bowl and tap the skin firmly to dislodge the seeds.
5 Sprinkle with the pomegranate seeds and fresh coriander. Serve cold.

Gajar No Sambharo

| WARM CARROT SALAD |

This delightful Gujarati side dish is served with main meals. Here it's made with carrot, but it can also be made with finely shredded cabbage or raw papaya. It is sometimes served as an accompaniment to crisp, savoury and sweet Sunday breakfast snacks such as 'ganthiya', which are crisp wafers made with gram flour and spices, and 'jalebi', a rich sweet made with flour, deep-fried and soaked in sticky sugar syrup. *Serves 4* PREPARATION → *10 minutes* COOKING *10 minutes*

1 teaspoon vegetable oil
½ teaspoon black mustard seeds
½ teaspoon cumin seeds
pinch of asafoetida
½ teaspoon white sesame seeds
2 large carrots, peeled and finely grated
pinch of caster sugar
2 tablespoons fresh coriander leaves, finely chopped
salt

1 Heat the oil in a small saucepan over a high heat and add the mustard seeds. When they begin to pop, add the cumin seeds, asafoetida and sesame seeds. Fry for a few seconds.
2 Tip in the grated carrots, season with salt, add the sugar and cook, stirring, over a medium heat for 5–6 minutes. Remove from the heat.
3 Stir in the coriander and serve warm.

Chawli Rajma Ka Salaad

| BEAN SALAD |

I use tinned beans for this recipe to save time and because it is easier – you can swap the ones I've used in the recipe below for any firm beans you like. If cooking your own beans, make sure that they are soaked overnight and cooked until very tender. *Serves 4* PREPARATION → *10 minutes*

½ teaspoon cumin seeds
½ x 400g can of black-eyed beans, drained and rinsed
½ x 400g can of red kidney beans, drained and rinsed
½ teaspoon caster sugar
2 spring onions, finely diced
3–4 fronds of fresh dill, finely chopped
1 teaspoon lemon juice
small sprig of fresh coriander leaves, finely chopped
salt and freshly ground black pepper

1 Heat a frying pan over a high heat, add the cumin seeds and dry-toast until they begin to darken and develop an aroma. Remove from the heat and crush to a powder in a pestle and mortar.
2 Mix all the ingredients together in a bowl, season with salt and pepper and serve at once.

Tikhat Keli

| SWEET AND SPICY BANANA SALAD |

This is a good way to use up ripe bananas as they add
a lovely flavour and creaminess to a spicy meal. *Serves 4*
PREPARATION → *5 minutes* COOKING *5 minutes*

½ teaspoon cumin seeds
2 teaspoons vegetable oil
¼ teaspoon medium red chilli powder
2 ripe bananas, peeled and thickly sliced
1 tablespoon lemon juice, to serve
salt and freshly ground black pepper

1 Heat a frying pan over a high heat, add the cumin seeds
and dry-toast until they begin to darken and develop an
aroma. Remove from the heat and crush to a powder in a
pestle and mortar.
2 Heat the oil in a frying pan over a high heat and add the
ground spices. When they begin to sizzle, add 3 tablespoons
of water and season with salt and pepper.
3 When the water has evaporated and the spices have
cooked, fold in the bananas and cook them for a couple of
minutes. Serve warm or cold, drizzled with the lemon juice.

Fruit Chaat

| FRUIT SALAD WITH TANGY SPICES |

This is eaten as a snack, sold as street food and sometimes
accompanies a main meal. The fruit varies seasonally
as well as regionally. In summer, mangoes are added in
growing regions such as Maharashtra, Gujarat and Uttar
Pradesh. In the north, pears from Himachal Pradesh and
Uttar Pradesh are used. *Serves 4* PREPARATION → *15 minutes*

200g mixed, fresh firm fruit, such as mango, apple, pear, whole
    grapes, banana, papaya or melon, diced as you wish
¼ teaspoon medium red chilli powder
pinch of chaat masala *(page 344)*
1 teaspoon lemon juice

1 Put all the ingredients in a bowl, mix together lightly and
serve at once.

Vangyache Bhareet

| ROASTED AUBERGINE WITH YOGURT |

This Maharashtrian side dish has some variations,
depending on personal preference, such as one where
the onion is stirred in raw or another where a tempering
of mustard seeds is added on top. I like the sweetness of
cooked red onion combined with the tang of tomato in
this recipe. *Serves 4* PREPARATION → *10 minutes, plus chilling time*
COOKING *20 minutes*

1 large aubergine
1 tablespoon vegetable oil
1 medium red onion, finely chopped
1 medium fresh green chilli, finely chopped
1 tablespoon chopped fresh coriander leaves
1 tomato, finely chopped
150g natural yogurt
salt

1 Place the aubergine on a gas hob without brushing with
oil. Turn from time to time (for roughly 7–8 minutes) with
a pair of tongs until you can pierce the thickest part easily
with a knife. By this time the skin will look crinkly and crisp.
Leave to cool then peel off skin with a small knife or with
your fingers.
2 Discard the stalk and mash the flesh of the aubergine in a
bowl with a fork. Set aside.
3 Heat the oil in a frying pan over a high heat, add the onion
and fry for 7–8 minutes until soft. Add the chilli, coriander,
tomato and salt to season, then add the mixture to the mashed
aubergine. Mix in the yogurt and chill before serving.

Bengali Tomato Raita

Kalonji is variously known as onion seed, black cumin or black caraway but actually, it is none of these. In the West it is known as nigella and is a small black seed with the flavour of onion and pepper. *Serves 4* PREPARATION→ *10 minutes*

150g full-fat yogurt
2 tomatoes, finely diced
1 tablespoon mustard or vegetable oil
½ teaspoon cumin seeds
½ teaspoon nigella seeds (kalonji)
salt and freshly ground black pepper

1 Combine the yogurt and tomatoes in a bowl and season with salt and pepper.
2 Heat the mustard oil to almost smoking point in a small frying pan. Remove from the heat and leave to cool slightly, then add the cumin and nigella seeds. As soon as they start to sizzle and develop an aroma, pour them into the bowl. Stir and serve. If using vegetable oil, simply heat the oil in a small frying pan and add the seeds. Serve cold.

Mung Chaat
| SPROUTED MUNG BEANS SALAD |

Sprouts are very popular in Indian cooking because the availability of so many beans and a largely warm climate allows home cooks to use the technique of sprouting fairly regularly (see page 277). Also, sprouting makes beans easier to digest as the complex carbohydrates break down into simpler carbohydrates. *Serves 4* PREPARATION→ *15 minutes, plus soaking and sprouting time* COOKING *10 minutes*

½ teaspoon cumin seeds
80g mung beans, sprouted *(see page 277)*
⅓ cucumber, finely diced, skin on
1 tomato, finely diced
1 red onion, finely diced
juice of ½ lemon
a large handful of fresh coriander leaves, finely chopped
salt and freshly ground black pepper

1 Heat a frying pan over a high heat, add the cumin seeds and dry-toast until they begin to darken and develop an aroma. Remove from the heat and crush to a powder in a pestle and mortar.
2 Steam the mung bean sprouts for 5–6 minutes until just tender, then set aside to cool.
3 Combine the cucumber, tomato, onion and cumin in a bowl. Season with salt and pepper and drizzle in the lemon juice.
4 Gently stir in the steamed sprouts, add the coriander and toss the salad. Serve at once.

CHUTNEYS, PICKLES & RELISHES

INDIANS LOVE 'ACHAAR' OR PICKLES AND A VAST NUMBER ARE COMMERCIALLY AVAILABLE
OR MADE AT HOME WITH SEASONAL VEGETABLES AND FRUIT TO BE CONSUMED WITH MAIN MEALS
OR SNACKS THROUGHOUT THE YEAR.

Every Indian kitchen has an assortment of chutneys, pickles and relishes that are placed
on the table along with a meal. Chutney comes from the Hindi 'chatna' or 'to lick'. It is an
accompaniment made of fruit, vegetables or lentils and spices that is highly flavoured and served
in small quantities with a meal to add a little top note of concentrated flavour – usually salty, sour,
hot, sweet (or a combination).

Chutneys can be wet or powdery dry and they can be made with fresh ingredients such as
coriander leaves, ginger and green chillies or with storecupboard ingredients such as desiccated
coconut and dried red chillies. Chutneys made with fresh ingredients have to be eaten within
a couple of days whereas dry ones or those with a lot of sugar (such as mango chutney) can
be stored.

Chutneys serve to personalise a meal – one member of the family may enjoy spicier food
than the rest and will serve themselves a portion of hot mango or chilli pickle to increase the level
of heat. It is only in Indian restaurants that you will find a plate of poppadums being served with
chutneys and relishes at the start of a meal.

Each family has a selection of their favourite pickles or 'achaar', and these recipes are passed
down the generations. Each region and community also has their own special ones – the Gajar
Gobi Shalgam Ka Achaar (page 430) is one of north India's favourite pickles, whereas the tender
mango pickle 'avakkai' is preferred in south India and is relished with a mixture of plain yogurt
with rice.

Pickles are made with seasonal ingredients – some are made to be eaten within a few days
whereas others are cooked in sugar or spices and can be eaten over a year. Many of these are
sun-dried and it is common to see jars of pickles maturing on sunny terraces during the summer.
Sun-drying matures them and increases their shelf life. In any case, all pickles have to be treated
with care if they are to last – never use a wet spoon and make sure to seal your jars as tightly as you
can to keep air and moisture out.

Relishes are made from highly flavoured, seasonal vegetables served to add a burst of
flavour to a meal. Some relishes are made in particular seasons to boost immunity, such as a fresh
Indian gooseberry (amla) one, which is eaten in the winter because of its very high vitamin C
content, which ranges between 400–600mg per 100g of fruit.

SOURING AGENTS

Different regions in India use a variety of souring agents in different ways. Lemon and lime are used all over the country.

TAMARIND → Many Indian people remember eating tamarind pulp as children, with friends, hidden away from disapproving adults, on hot, lazy afternoons. Its sour sweetness is all the more tasty with a sprinkling of coarse salt. Children mercilessly stone the tree to get the fruit. In the hot summer months, balls of tamarind are laid out to dry in the sun, especially in central and southern India. They are then stored in earthen jars and bits are broken off as and when required to use throughout the year. To make tamarind pulp, see page 418.

KOKUM → The kokum fruit is native to India and is used in the regional cookery of Gujarat, Maharashtra and a few southern states, where big glasses of kokum sherbet are drunk throughout the parched summer months. The fruit is round and about 2.5cm in diameter. It is deep purple when ripe and contains 5–8 large seeds. The fruits are picked when ripe then the rind is removed, soaked repeatedly in the juice of the pulp and sun-dried. The rind is used as a souring agent.

Sun-dried kokum petals are dark purple to black and rather sticky with curled edges. Sometimes the entire fruit is halved and dried, so that the dried seeds are visible in their chambers, like a halved orange. When added to food, it imparts a beautiful pinkish-purple colour.

VINEGAR → In India, the inclusion of vinegar in cookery is limited to a few communities. Of these, the Parsees and the Goans have been most influenced by international cuisines and use many 'Western' ingredients like pasta, marzipan and vinegar. The most commonly used vinegars are malt and white. In the north, vinegar or 'sirka' is made by fermenting sugarcane juice. In Goa, it is made from coconut sap. Coconut vinegar is slightly cloudy and yeasty.

A traditional way of using vinegar in curries is to grind the curry spices with it. Gourmets claim that the best flavour is achieved when this is done on a rough grinding stone. The resulting paste is used as a marinade or fried in hot oil before adding meat or fish. Alternatively, vinegar can be added to the dish during cooking. Vinegar is also used for pickling vegetables as in the Punjabi Gajar Gobi Shalgam Ka Achaar (page 430). In Goa, 'tendli' or baby ivy gourds as well as aubergines, called brinjals locally, are pickled in vinegar.

HOW TO MAKE TAMARIND PULP

YOU WILL NEED:
¼ block (about 100g) wet tamarind
warm water, to cover the tamarind
– sieve
– bowl

Tamarind is a sausage-shaped fruit that grows on large trees (see page 417). The pods ripen in the summer and the shell becomes brittle. The fruit inside is pulpy and is held together by a fibrous husk. Within this pulp are square-ish, dark brown, shiny seeds. It is the pulp that is used for its sweet, sour, fruity aroma and taste.

It is available as a pressed, fibrous slab, or as a jam-like bottled concentrate. As slabs, you can buy 'wet' or 'dry' tamarind. The wet one is softer to squash and easier to use whereas the dry one is more difficult to break down.

1 Soak the block of tamarind in warm water for about 15 minutes. Once it softens, squash it into a paste with your fingers and pass it through a sieve. The fine pulp and juice will go through, leaving behind the fibrous husk.

2 Put some more water in the sieve and do a second pressing. You should be able to see the seeds and fibres. Discard these. You should have 5–6 tablespoons of pulp. The pulp will keep well in the fridge, in an airtight container, for up to 3 weeks.

TIP If all this seems too time consuming, you can buy a jar of tamarind pulp or paste. This is different from and much better than jars of tamarind concentrate, which I find too dark and gooey.

DHANIYE KI CHUTNEY – Coriander and Peanut Chutney

Green coriander chutney is the ubiquitous dipping sauce in India. As it made mostly of herbs, some thickening needs to be added. In Gujarat and Maharashtra, this may be locally grown coconut or peanuts, whereas in the north it could be an inexpensive onion or more expensive nuts such as almonds, which are an influence from Mughal cookery. *Makes about 200g* PREPARATION → *10 minutes*

YOU WILL NEED:

2 good handfuls of fresh coriander, stalks and leaves, washed and roughly chopped

1.25cm piece of fresh root ginger, scraped and chopped

2 fresh green chillies, roughly chopped

2 tablespoons roasted unsalted peanuts or freshly grated coconut or both

1 tablespoon caster sugar

a good squeeze of lemon juice

salt

1 Put the coriander in a blender with the ginger, chillies and peanuts or coconut or both. Blitz to a fine paste with 3–4 tablespoons of cold water then add the sugar.

2 Season with salt, add the lemon juice and mix well. The final texture should be thick and creamy. Store in an airtight container in the fridge for up to 3 days.

Lasnachi Chutney

| DRY COCONUT AND GARLIC
FIREBALL CHUTNEY |

This storable chutney from Maharashtra is a wonderful combination of flavour, heat and texture. It is used as an accompaniment to snacks or dosas (see page 126) or sprinkled into sandwiches, thickly spread with butter and filled with cucumber and tomato. It is also associated with a Mumbai street food called 'vada pav' where an Aloo Bonda (page 356) is stuffed into a bread roll and sprinkled with this chutney. As this is a dry chutney, no water is added while blitzing it to a powder and the amchoor cannot be substituted with a 'wet' souring agent like lemon juice. If you can't find amchoor, you can squeeze in a little lemon juice when serving the chutney. You may find that you have to use the pulse mode on your machine as the coconut can become claggy with prolonged blitzing. *Makes about 200g* PREPARATION → *10 minutes* COOKING *6 minutes*

1 teaspoon white sesame seeds
100g desiccated coconut
2 tablespoons roasted unsalted peanuts
4 large garlic cloves, chopped
2 tablespoons medium-hot red chilli powder
    (or less if you want a mild chutney)
1 teaspoon caster sugar
1 teaspoon amchoor (dried mango powder)
salt

1 Heat a small frying pan over a high heat, add the sesame seeds and coconut and dry-toast for 5–6 minutes until they begin to turn golden. Remove from the heat, transfer to a blender or coffee mill and blitz, along with the peanuts and garlic, to make a coarse powder. Don't add any water to the blender as this is a dry chutney.

2 Tip the chutney into a bowl and add the chilli powder, salt to season, sugar and amchoor.

3 Store in a clean, sterilised glass jar in the fridge for up to 4 months.

Imli Ki Chutney

| SWEET TAMARIND CHUTNEY |

Another classic dipping sauce, which is an essential part of street food, this tamarind chutney is served with foods such as Onion Bhajias (page 350) or Sev Puri (page 346), made by topping crisp puris with mashed potatoes or chickpeas and drizzling with a spicy mint chutney and this sweet chutney. *Makes about 250g* PREPARATION → *10 minutes* COOKING *10 minutes*

1 teaspoon cumin seeds
4 tablespoons grated jaggery or soft brown sugar
4 tablespoons tamarind pulp *(page 418)*
    or shop-bought tamarind paste
a large pinch of medium-hot red chilli powder
salt

1 Heat a frying pan over a high heat, add the cumin seeds and dry-toast until they begin to darken and develop an aroma. Remove from the heat and crush to a powder in a pestle and mortar.

2 Put the jaggery or sugar and tamarind in a pan, bring to the boil, reduce the heat to low and simmer for 4–5 minutes until the mixture turns shiny and the jaggery has completely dissolved. If the mixture starts to get too dry and sticky, add a couple of tablespoons of water.

3 Add the ground toasted cumin and chilli, season with salt, then simmer for a further couple of minutes.

4 Remove from the heat, leave to cool and serve at room temperature. Store in an airtight container in the fridge for up to 4 weeks.

THENGAI CHUTNEY – White Coconut Chutney

This creamy chutney is made regularly in Tamil households and is served with breakfast foods such as dosas (see page 126). Desiccated coconut does not work well here as it is too dry and does not have the level of creaminess this chutney needs. You can reduce or increase the number of chillies as per your taste. *Makes about 200g* PREPARATION → *20 minutes* COOKING *7–8 minutes*

1 Heat a small frying pan over a high heat, add the chana dal and dry-toast until it begins to darken. Tip it into a blender, add the coconut, green chillies, salt to season and a few tablespoons of water and blitz to a fine purée. Pour the purée into a serving bowl.

YOU WILL NEED:

1 tablespoon split gram lentils
    (chana dal)
a large handful of freshly
    grated coconut
2 fresh green chillies, chopped
1 tablespoon coconut or vegetable oil
1 teaspoon black or brown
    mustard seeds
½ teaspoon white urad dal
a large pinch of fresh curry leaves
salt

2 Heat the oil in a small pan over a high heat and add the mustard seeds. As soon as they begin to pop, add the urad dal and fry for a few seconds until it starts to turn golden, then add the curry leaves (standing back from the pan as the leaves will splutter) and stir this mixture into the chutney.

3 Store in an airtight container in the fridge for up to 3 days.

Thakkali Pachadi
| TOMATO AND COCONUT CHUTNEY |

South Indian restaurants often serve two kinds of chutneys and sambhar (see page 65) with their dosas. One is White Coconut Chutney (see opposite) and the other is this red version, which is hotter and tangier. *Makes about 200g*

PREPARATION → *20 minutes, plus 10 minutes soaking time*

COOKING *10 minutes*

2 tablespoons coconut or vegetable oil
1 tablespoon split gram lentils (chana dal)
1 onion, diced
2 dried red chillies, cut open, deseeded and soaked
   in warm water for 10 minutes
2 ripe tomatoes, chopped
1.25cm piece of fresh root ginger
4 tablespoons coconut milk
1 teaspoon black or brown mustard seeds
a pinch of fresh curry leaves
a pinch of asafoetida
salt

1 Heat half the oil in a frying pan over a high heat, add the chana dal and fry until it begins to darken. Add the onion and fry over a medium heat for 7–8 minutes until very soft.

2 Drain the chillies and add them to the pan. Cook for a couple of minutes then mix in the tomatoes and ginger. Cook for 5–6 minutes until the tomatoes have softened.

3 Transfer this mixture to a blender, add the coconut milk and blitz to a fine purée.

4 Pour the purée into a serving bowl and season with salt.

5 Heat the remaining oil in a small frying pan over a high heat, add the mustard seeds and fry until they begin to pop, then add the curry leaves (standing back from the pan as the leaves will splutter) and asafoetida and remove from the heat. Stir this into the chutney. Store in an airtight container in the fridge for up to 3 days.

Brinjal Chutney

| SOUR AND HOT AUBERGINE CHUTNEY |

Aubergines have a meaty texture and preserve well. To prepare the aubergine here, you can also dice it and deep-fry it in very hot oil. I have roasted it as on page 316 for a healthier option. This south Indian recipe can be enjoyed with a main meal or breakfast foods such as idlis and dosas (see page 126). *Makes about 250g* PREPARATION → *10 minutes* COOKING *25 minutes*

1 large aubergine
2 tablespoons sunflower or coconut oil
1 tablespoon unsalted cashew nuts
2 fresh green chillies, diced
3 garlic cloves, peeled and diced
2.5cm piece of fresh root ginger, scraped and diced
1 tablespoon tamarind pulp *(page 418)*
    or shop-bought tamarind paste
2 tomatoes, diced
1 teaspoon black or brown mustard seeds
1 teaspoon cumin seeds
a large pinch of fresh curry leaves
salt

1 Roast the aubergine under a grill or over a gas flame until cooked (see page 316). Peel and roughly chop the flesh.
2 Heat half the oil in a frying pan over a high heat, add the cashew nuts and fry for 2–3 minutes until they start to darken. Add the chillies, garlic and ginger and fry over a medium heat for a couple of minutes.
3 Stir in the tamarind pulp and diced tomatoes and cook for 4–5 minutes until soft, adding a pinch of salt to hasten the cooking process.
4 Remove from the heat and mix in the cooked, peeled and chopped aubergine. Transfer to a blender and blitz to a purée, then transfer to a bowl.
5 Heat the remaining oil in a small frying pan over a high heat, add the mustard seeds and fry until they begin to pop, then tip in the cumin seeds and curry leaves (standing back from the pan as the leaves will splutter).
6 Pour this tempering over the chutney, then season with salt, stir and serve at room temperature. Any leftover chutney can be stored in an airtight container in the fridge for a couple of days.

Inchi Pachadi

| FRESH GINGER RAITA |

In Kerala, this chutney is served with rice or dosas (see page 126) and idlis. *Makes about 175g* PREPARATION → *15 minutes*

3 tablespoons freshly grated coconut
2.5cm piece of fresh root ginger, scraped and chopped
1 fresh green chilli
½ teaspoon cumin seeds
100g natural yogurt
1 teaspoon caster sugar
salt

1 Put the coconut, ginger, chilli and cumin seeds in a blender, along with barely enough water to cover the mixture, and blitz until very fine.
2 Pour into a small serving bowl and stir in the yogurt. Season with salt, add the sugar and mix well. Store in an airtight container in the fridge for up to 2 days.

Pudine Ki Chutney

| MINT AND CORIANDER CHUTNEY |

Served with all kinds of kebabs and snacks, such as samosas or bhajias, this also makes a great sandwich spread with a filling of thinly sliced tomato and cucumber. *Makes about 200g* PREPARATION → *10 minutes*

2 good handfuls of fresh coriander (leaves and stalks), chopped
2 garlic cloves, chopped
1.25cm piece of fresh root ginger, scraped and chopped
2 fresh green chillies, roughly chopped
a handful of fresh mint leaves, chopped
1 small onion
a good squeeze of lemon juice
salt

1 Put the coriander in a blender, add the garlic, ginger, chillies, mint and onion and blitz to a fine paste, adding a little bit of cold water to turn the blades.
2 Season with salt, add the lemon juice and mix well. Store in an airtight container in the fridge for up to 3 days.

Green Mango Pachadi
| MANGO AND COCONUT CHUTNEY |

South India is famous for chutneys that are eaten with every meal from breakfast to dinner. You can substitute the green mango with an equal quantity of a cooking apple such as Bramley. *Makes about 150g* PREPARATION → *5 minutes* COOKING *10 minutes*

2 tablespoons vegetable oil
1 fresh green chilli, chopped
1 dried red chilli, split and seeds shaken out
1 teaspoon white urad dal, washed
1 onion, diced
2 cheeks of green mango, peeled and diced
2 tablespoons freshly grated coconut or
    3 tablespoons coconut milk
pinch of caster sugar
½ teaspoon black or brown mustard seeds
½ teaspoon cumin seeds
a pinch of fresh curry leaves
salt

1 Heat half the oil in a frying pan over a high heat and add the chillies and urad dal. Cook for 1–2 minutes until the dal becomes golden then add the onion and stir-fry for 7–8 minutes until very soft.

2 Add the mango and season with salt. When the mango softens, stir in the grated coconut or coconut milk, transfer the mixture to a blender and blitz until smooth, adding a little water to turn the blades if using fresh coconut. Pour the chutney into a serving bowl and stir in the sugar.

3 Heat the remaining oil in a frying pan over a high heat. Add the mustard seeds and fry until they begin to pop, then add the cumin seeds and curry leaves (standing back from the pan as the leaves will splutter). When everything sizzles, stir this into the chutney. Store in an airtight container in the fridge for up to 2 days.

Aam Ka Chhunda
| SWEET MANGO CHUTNEY |

During the mango season in India, raw mangoes are made into sweet or savoury preserves. This recipe is from Rajasthan and is eaten as a snack with savoury biscuits called 'puris' (see page 346) or with main meals. Traditionally, jars of mango and sugar are placed in the blazing summer sun for the sugar to dissolve but this stovetop version is equally delicious. *Makes about 1.1kg* PREPARATION → *30 minutes, plus 4 hours steeping time* COOKING *40 minutes*

500g peeled and grated raw green mango
500g caster sugar
5 cloves
1 teaspoon medium-hot red chilli powder
1 tablespoon salt

1 Combine all the ingredients in a saucepan, cover and set aside for 4 hours to steep.

2 Place over a medium heat and cook for 40 minutes until the mixture has thickened, stirring frequently to prevent it from sticking to the bottom of the pan.

3 Cool completely, transfer to a sterilised glass jar (or jars) and store in the fridge for up to 2 months.

Seb Ki Chutney
| GREEN APPLE CHUTNEY |

My apple tree produces a fabulous crop of cooking apples every year. I have made several versions of this chutney over the years, some sweet and others more savoury and hot. The tartness of the apples here is like that of raw green mangoes, which are frequently used in Indian preserves, along with other seasonal sour fruit such as apples, gooseberries and berries. *Makes about 350g*
PREPARATION → *25 minutes* COOKING *15 minutes*

½ teaspoon cumin seeds
½ teaspoon fennel seeds
1 tablespoon vegetable oil
½ teaspoon crushed black pepper
½ teaspoon medium-hot red chilli powder
2 cooking apples, peeled and roughly chopped
1 teaspoon grated fresh root ginger
1 tablespoon caster sugar
1 tablespoon distilled white vinegar
salt

1 Heat a small frying pan over a high heat, add the cumin and fennel seeds and dry-toast until they darken, then tip them into a pestle and mortar or spice mill and crush or blend to a fine powder.
2 Heat the oil in a heavy saucepan over a high heat and add the pepper and chilli powder. When they start to sizzle, add the apples and ginger. Season with salt and stir in the sugar. Sprinkle in the powdered spices from the mortar or spice mill.
3 Cook over a medium heat for 8–10 minutes until the apples are very soft, then mix in the vinegar. Remove from the heat, leave to cool and store in a sterilised airtight jar in the fridge for up to 2 weeks.

Khajur Aur Dhaniye Ki Chutney
| DATE AND CORIANDER CHUTNEY |

In western and northern India, this sweet, spicy, tangy chutney is served with fried snacks such as bhajia and pakoras (see page 349). Dates bring a fruity sweetness, the coriander a herby freshness and the tamarind, a wonderful tang. *Makes about 200g* PREPARATION → *15 minutes*
COOKING *20 minutes*

150g stoned dates
3 tablespoons tamarind pulp *(page 418)* or shop-bought
    tamarind paste
½ teaspoon medium-hot red chilli powder
½ teaspoon cumin seeds
1.25cm piece of fresh root ginger, scraped
a large handful of fresh coriander leaves, chopped
salt

1 Put the dates in a saucepan with just enough water to cover them. Bring to the boil and add the tamarind pulp, then reduce the heat to medium and simmer for 7–8 minutes to soften the dates.
2 Remove from the heat and leave to cool slightly then transfer to a blender along with the chilli powder, cumin seeds, ginger and coriander, season with salt and blitz until smooth.
3 Store in an airtight container in the fridge for up to 3 days.

Nimbu Ka Meetha Achaar

| SWEET LIME PICKLE |

Traditionally, Indian lemons would be used for this recipe – these are the size of limes found in the West, yellow, thin-skinned and juicy. You could use Western lemons but as they have a thicker skin and rind, and less juice than limes, the texture of the pickle will be different and you will also need the juice of a couple more lemons. This quick and easy pickle can be stored for up to a month in the fridge.

Makes about 500g PREPARATION → *10 minutes* COOKING *40 minutes*

5 limes, plus the juice of 2 limes
2 teaspoons salt
1 teaspoon medium-hot red chilli powder
200g caster sugar
2 cinnamon sticks

1 Put the 5 whole limes into a pan with enough water to cover them and bring to the boil. Reduce the heat and simmer for 35 minutes until they are very soft. Drain and leave to cool. Dry each lime completely with a clean tea towel.
2 In a bowl, cut the cooked limes into 8 pieces each, allowing the juice to fall back into the bowl. Add the juice of the 2 extra limes, the salt and chilli powder and mix well.
3 Start mixing in the sugar, a little at a time, until it dissolves. Once all the sugar is mixed in, transfer the pickle to a clean, sterilised glass jar. Add the cinnamon, seal and leave it to stand for 3–4 days at room temperature in a cool, dark place, shaking the jar from time to time. In a day or so, the sugar will form a syrup. The skins of the limes may taste bitter at first but this subdues as the pickle matures. Store in an a sterilised, airtight jar in the fridge for up to a month.

Gajar Gobi Shalgam Ka Achaar

| CARROT, CAULIFLOWER AND TURNIP PICKLE |

A popular sweet, sour and spicy Punjabi pickle, this is made in the winter to be stored and eaten through the year with Rotis (page 108) and Parathas (page 122). *Makes about 1.5kg*
PREPARATION → *30 minutes* COOKING *40 minutes*

200g grated jaggery or soft brown sugar
150ml distilled white vinegar
250g carrots, peeled and cut into long thick strips
250g cauliflower, cut into small florets
250g turnip, peeled and cut into long thin strips
200ml mustard oil
2 tablespoons ginger-garlic paste *(page 45)*
2 tablespoons black or brown mustard seeds, crushed coarsely in a pestle and mortar
2 teaspoons medium-hot red chilli powder
1 teaspoon ground turmeric
2 teaspoons garam masala *(page 64)*
6 teaspoons salt, plus extra for seasoning the cooking water

1 Put the jaggery or sugar and vinegar in a small saucepan and bring to the boil. Reduce the heat and simmer for 7–8 minutes until the jaggery or sugar has dissolved. Continue cooking until the mixture thickens slightly.
2 Bring a pan of water to the boil, add a little salt and blanch the vegetables for 3–4 minutes.
3 Drain the vegetables, then spread them out on a clean tea towel to dry completely. There should be no moisture or the pickle will spoil. If you want to be sure, you can finish drying the vegetables on a tray in the oven at 40°C/gas mark ¼ for 30 minutes.
4 Heat the mustard oil in a large frying pan until it is almost smoking. Reduce the heat to leave it to cool down slightly then add the ginger-garlic paste. Fry for a few seconds, then add the dry vegetables, mustard seeds, chilli powder, turmeric, garam masala and salt.
5 Mix well and add the vinegar and jaggery mixture. Stir and simmer for 6–8 minutes.
6 Remove from the heat and leave to cool completely, then transfer to a sterilised glass jar and store in the fridge for up to 4 months.

PRAWN BALCHAO – Spicy Goan Prawn Pickle

You will find jars of this hot, tangy, slightly sweet pickle being sold in many shops in Goa, and it is delicious, but it tastes even better homemade because of the better-quality ingredients one can choose to use. *Makes about 600g*

PREPARATION → *40 minutes*   COOKING *45 minutes*

YOU WILL NEED:

250ml vegetable oil (more or less depending on your storage jar)

400g raw prawns, shelled and deveined

a large pinch of fresh curry leaves

2.5cm piece of fresh root ginger, scraped and shredded

4 garlic cloves, minced

3 onions, thinly sliced

2 teaspoons salt

2 tablespoons grated jaggery or soft brown sugar

For the spice paste

20 dried red Kashmiri chillies (shake the seeds out if you want a milder flavour)

2.5cm piece of fresh root ginger, scraped and chopped

2 garlic cloves

2 teaspoons cumin seeds

4 tablespoons tamarind pulp *(page 418)* or shop-bought tamarind paste

200ml coconut vinegar or other vinegar

1 Put all the ingredients for the spice paste in a blender and blitz to a very fine purée.

2 Heat a couple of tablespoons of vegetable oil in a large frying pan over a high heat, add the prawns and fry for 7–8 minutes until they are opaque all the way through. Transfer to kitchen paper to drain and leave to cool.

3 Add a further 2 tablespoons of oil to the pan and fry the curry leaves for a few seconds (standing back from the pan as the leaves will splutter), then reduce the heat to medium, tip in the ginger and garlic and cook for a few minutes to soften, taking care not to burn the garlic. Add the onions and cook for 8–10 minutes until very soft and golden.

4 Add the spice paste to the pan and continue cooking for 4–5 minutes until the oil starts to separate around the edges. Season with the salt and add the jaggery or sugar. Stir until it has dissolved.

5 Chop the prawns roughly and add these to the pan. Cook for 4–5 minutes to blend the flavours.

6 Remove from the heat and leave to cool completely then spoon into a clean, sterilised glass jar. Top with oil, making sure that the pickle is completely submerged and therefore sealed from moisture and air. Seal, store in the fridge and consume within 1 week.

Kaju Chutney

| CASHEW NUT CHUTNEY |

Cashew nuts grow in peninsular India and are used in everyday cooking in some regions such as Karnataka and Maharashtra. This chutney is mild and creamy and goes well with fried foods such as Bhajias (page 350) and Aloo Bonda (page 356) as a dip. You can buy broken or split cashew nuts for this as they are cheaper than the whole ones. You can also add a tablespoon of skinned roasted peanuts for a different flavour. *Makes about 200g*

PREPARATION ➔ *10 minutes* COOKING *10 minutes*

2 teaspoons vegetable oil
100g unsalted cashew nuts
1 fresh green chilli, chopped
1.25cm piece of fresh root ginger, scraped and chopped
a large squeeze of lemon juice
½ teaspoon black or brown mustard seeds
a small pinch of fresh curry leaves
salt

1 Heat half the oil in a frying pan over a high heat, add the cashew nuts and fry for 4–5 minutes until slightly golden brown.

2 Drain and put them into a blender along with the chilli, ginger and enough water to barely cover the mixture. Blitz to a fine purée. The chutney should be of pouring consistency. Tip it into a serving bowl, squeeze in the lemon juice and season with salt.

3 Heat the remaining oil in a small frying pan over a high heat and fry the mustard seeds. As they begin to pop, add the curry leaves (standing back from the pan as the leaves will splutter) then stir this into the chutney.

4 Store in an airtight container in the fridge for up to 3 days.

Dhaarun Ji Chutney

| SINDHI POMEGRANATE CHUTNEY |

The Sindhi community has its roots in Sind, now in Pakistan. The cuisine includes ingredients from that region such as pomegranates, lotus stems and lotus seeds. Black salt tastes sulphuric and is sold as 'kala namak' in Indian grocery shops. *Makes 200g* PREPARATION ➔ *15 minutes*

1 teaspoon cumin seeds
a large handful of fresh pomegranate seeds
a large handful of fresh coriander leaves
a large handful of fresh mint leaves
1.25cm piece of fresh root ginger, scraped and chopped
½ teaspoon crushed black peppercorns
juice of ½ lime
¼ teaspoon powdered black salt (kala namak)
salt (optional)

1 Heat a frying pan over a high heat, add the cumin seeds and dry-toast until they begin to darken and develop an aroma. Remove from the heat and crush to a powder in a pestle and mortar.

2 Put the pomegranate seeds, coriander, mint leaves and ginger along with a little water into a blender and blitz to a fine purée. It should be slightly but not too runny. Pour into a serving bowl.

3 Add the ground toasted cumin, pepper, lime juice and black salt and mix well. Taste before adding more salt as the black salt may be enough. Store in an airtight container in the fridge for up to 3 days.

Kacha Amer Achaar

| QUICK BENGALI GREEN MANGO PICKLE |

The use of the unique Bengali five-spice mix called 'panch phoron' with tender mangoes makes this a fragrant, tangy pickle. Panch phoron consists of equal parts of mustard, cumin, fenugreek, fennel and nigella seeds. As it is 'cooked' rather than 'matured' in the sun, it needs to be consumed within a month or so. Such quick pickles are often made in bulk and small quantities distributed to friends. *Makes about 600g* PREPARATION —➔ *30 minutes* COOKING *30 minutes*

2 teaspoons panch phoron *(page 66)*
200ml distilled white vinegar
200ml mustard oil
5 garlic cloves, minced
500g raw green mango, washed, completely dried
     and cut into bite-sized pieces, skin on
1 teaspoon medium-hot red chilli powder
1 teaspoon ground turmeric
1 teaspoon ground cumin
2 teaspoons salt

1 Heat a small frying pan over a high heat, add the panch phoron and dry-toast until fragrant, then grind to a fine powder in a spice mill or pestle and mortar. Mix this with a couple of tablespoons of the vinegar.

2 Heat the oil in a pan over a high heat until it is almost smoking, then remove from the heat and leave to cool slightly.

3 Scoop 2 tablespoons of this oil into a frying pan and add the minced garlic. Leave the remaining oil to cool completely. Fry the garlic over a high heat for 2–3 minutes until golden, then add the mango. Stir-fry for 2–3 minutes, then stir in the chilli powder, turmeric, cumin, salt and the panch phoron paste. Pour in the remaining vinegar.

4 Cook over a high heat for 6–7 minutes until the mixture sizzles, then cover the pan and cook over a low heat for 10–15 minutes until the mango softens.

5 Remove from the heat and leave to cool completely, then transfer it to a sterilised, airtight glass jar and pour in the now cooled mustard oil so that the pickle is completely submerged. Seal the jar, store in the fridge and consume within 1 month.

Haldi Ka Achar

| FRESH TURMERIC ROOT RELISH |

Turmeric is one of the healthiest spices used in Indian cooking. The active compound curcumin is considered anti-inflammatory and an anti-oxidant, which means that it can help inhibit cell damage. The spice has been popular in Indian medicine such as Ayurveda for centuries. The fresh root looks like ginger and can be found in some Asian food shops. You may also find 'amb halad', a ginger-like root that smells of raw mangoes. You can use a mix of both varieties in equal quantities in this recipe. Wear gloves if you don't want your hands stained! *Makes about 100g* PREPARATION —➔ *10 minutes*

4 teaspoons fresh turmeric root, scraped and finely chopped
     or a mix of amb halad
1 teaspoon finely chopped fresh root ginger
1 small fresh green chilli, minced
lemon juice, to cover the mixture
salt

1 Mix the turmeric root, ginger and chilli together, then pour in the lemon juice and season with salt. Transfer to a sterilised, airtight container, seal tightly and shake well to blend. The relish will keep well for up to 1 week in the fridge.

Kothimeera Podi

| SPICY CORIANDER POWDER CHUTNEY |

South India, with its tropical heat, is fond of 'podis' or spiced powders that are eaten with breakfast foods or mixed into rice at main meals. Typically made with lentils, chillies and spices, these spicy powders help to cool the body by way of the capsaicin in the chillies but they are also often made into a cream by mixing them with a spoonful of ghee that helps to cool the digestive system. This recipe from Andhra Pradesh is only one of the several podis made in this state. *Makes about 100g*

PREPARATION → *15 minutes* COOKING *15 minutes*

2 large handfuls of fresh coriander leaves
1 tablespoon split gram lentils (chana dal)
½ teaspoon asafoetida
3 tablespoons vegetable oil
10 dried red Kashmiri chillies, deseeded
4 tablespoons desiccated coconut
1 teaspoon black or brown mustard seeds
salt

1 Wash the coriander leaves, pat them dry and spread them out on a clean tea towel to dry.

2 Heat a small frying pan over a high heat, add the lentils and dry-toast them until they turn golden brown, then tip them out into a bowl and dry-toast the asafoetida for a few seconds. Tip this into the lentils.

3 Chop the coriander.

4 Heat a tablespoon of the oil in a frying pan over a high heat, add the chillies and fry for 2–3 minutes until they darken. Drain them and add them to the lentils. Add another tablespoon of oil to the pan and add the chopped coriander. Cook for 1 minute.

5 Put the chillies, coconut, lentils, coriander and asafoetida into a spice mill and blend to a fine powder. This won't work in a blender as the blades will not turn without water. Tip into a bowl and season with salt.

6 Heat the remaining oil in a frying pan over a high heat and fry the mustard seeds until they begin to pop. Pour this into the powdered chutney and cool completely.

7 Store in a sterilised airtight container in the fridge for up to a month.

Bilahir Tok

| ASSAMESE SWEET AND SOUR TOMATO CHUTNEY |

This popular chutney is served with soft rice called khichdi (see page 88) or fried Pooris (pages 114–115) to add a burst of tangy, sweet flavours to the meal. 'Tok' means sour in the local Assamese language, and the tartness of tomatoes is tempered down by the addition of jaggery. Pas phuron is the same mix of five spices as the Bengali panch phoron. *Makes 200g* PREPARATION → *10 minutes* COOKING *20 minutes*

2 tablespoons mustard oil
1 teaspoon pas phuron *(see Panch Phoron on page 66)*
2 bay leaves
3 dried red chillies
3 large tomatoes, diced
2 teaspoons grated jaggery or soft brown sugar
salt

1 Heat the oil to smoking point in a frying pan then remove and leave to cool slightly. Add the pas phuron and as soon as it crackles, add the bay leaves and red chillies. Cook for a few seconds over a medium heat then add the tomatoes.

2 Season with salt and add the jaggery or sugar. Bring to the boil, then reduce the heat and simmer for 10 minutes or so until the tomatoes are completely soft and jammy. Remove from the heat and leave to cool.

3 Transfer to an airtight container and store in the fridge for up to 3 days.

DESSERTS

INDIA'S VAST RANGE OF SWEET, FRAGRANT FRUIT PROVIDES INSPIRATION
FOR AN ENDLESS ARRAY OF SWEETS, PUDDINGS AND DESSERTS THAT ARE CONSUMED ON FESTIVE DAYS
AND HAPPY OCCASIONS, SUCH AS BIRTHDAYS OR EVEN ON THE RECEIPT OF EXCELLENT EXAM RESULTS.

India could very well be called a sweet-toothed nation given the number of desserts, sweets and confectionery that is consumed every day. Honey, sugar, jaggery or fruit are cooked along with various flours, seeds, nuts, vegetables and milk to create a fantastic variety of delicacies variously called 'meetha' (sweet in Hindi) or 'mishti'. The term 'mithai' is generally used to describe the vast repertoire of dense, set sweet confections – those that can be cut with a knife – and these include such delicacies as burfies, halwas, jalebis, gulab jamuns, rasmalai and rossogullas (see pages 469, 446, 466 and 454). Burfies are usually set in thick squares and have the sticky texture of fudge. Halwas are slightly softer and can be scooped up with a spoon. Jalebis are extremely sweet confections made by piping nests of a flour and yogurt batter into hot oil, frying them, then immersing them in a sticky sugar syrup. They are then drained and eaten warm or cold. Gulab jamuns, rasmalai and rossogullas are all made by forming dumplings of thickened or split milk which are then poached (rasmalai, rossogulla) or fried (gulab jamun). Some of these sweets are soaked in sugar syrup, others in sweetened milk. They all have a soft texture like that of a moist cake.

Many other desserts are simply called sweet dishes – so 'kheer' is a milky pudding thickened with rice, wheat flakes, sago or fruit. Shrikhand, a dense, strained yogurt dessert, is flavoured with saffron and cardamom.

Sweets have been made and eaten in India since ancient times. Early literature talks about the use of honey and even after the production of sugar, forest honey was still a preferred sweetener. Sugar, from the Sanskrit word 'sharkara', was made from sugarcane juice around 500 BC and introduced to Europe from India by Alexander the Great's returning troops around 300 BC. The Greeks were astonished by reeds that produced honey without bees, obviously referring to the sugarcane that grew in northern India. Around the fifth century AD, sugar crystallisation began and, being easy to transport, became one of India's largest exports. Today, India is a leading producer of sugarcane and the highest growing states are Uttar Pradesh, Maharashtra and Tamil Nadu. Sugar is exported by India to countries such as Sudan and the UAE.

In an Indian thali, the sweet is served with the rest of the courses and is sometimes eaten with fried pooris. This blurring of courses is common at wedding feasts.

JAGGERY

Apart from white sugar, which is used in everyday cookery as well as for making sweets, jaggery is used in many parts of India.

JAGGERY → Sugarcane grows in abundance in the north, west and south of India. Freshly pressed sugarcane juice is sold in street stalls, often with a dash of lime and ginger juice.

During the manufacture of sugar from sugarcane juice, several products are formed: molasses, alcohol and jaggery. Jaggery is reduced or cooked-down sugarcane juice that forms soft but solid blocks and is mostly produced by small cultivators in huge crushers run by bullocks. The jaggery is not purified and therefore has all the quality of the juice itself. Jaggery is as important as sugar in Indian cookery. It has a heavy, caramel-like aroma and tastes very sweet and musky. It cannot really be substituted for by sugar, although brown or demerara sugar is the closest equivalent. Jaggery is considered healthier than sugar as it contains more complex carbohydrates that release energy slowly rather than in simple sugars which get absorbed into the blood stream quickly. As sugarcane juice is cooked in large iron vessels, the jaggery absorbs some of this mineral. Also, jaggery is a rich source of phenolic acids and flavonoids, which are considered anti-inflammatory. It has held a special place in Hindu ritual as an auspicious food because of its health benefits and sweet taste.

Jaggery ranges from mustard yellow to deep amber in colour, depending on the quality of the sugarcane juice. It is sticky but can be crumbled, grated or cut easily. It is made up of big lumps, which melt to form a thick, gooey paste.

Different varieties of jaggery are available and although the one made from sugarcane juice is most widely available, Bengal produces jaggery that is especially prized, from the sap of the locally grown date palm. Bengalis have a special emotional response to this 'Nolen Gur' which, though available throughout the year, is freshest for a short time in the winter. The sap of the palm is collected in earthen pots to be drunk as toddy or to be cooked in huge metal pots to form a syrupy jaggery which, when solidified to a dense cake, is known as 'patali'. Nolen Gur is not seen much outside of the region where it is produced. It is relished scooped up with a roti then stirred into yogurt, or cooked with milk to make winter sweets.

The variety that is most exported is Kolhapur jaggery. Kolhapur is a town in Maharashtra, which produces the largest amount of jaggery in India. Buy a small amount to try first. You will find that the jaggery is moulded in various sizes and wrapped in plastic or jute cloth. To store, use a dry container and keep in a cool, dark place. Most jaggery lasts for up to a year.

HONEY

Honey or 'madhu' is considered a sacred ingredient in India and is mentioned as a health food in ancient Hindu texts such as the Vedas from about 4,000 years ago. It is said to be one of the five elixirs including milk, ghee, yogurt and sugar that are combined to make 'panchamrita', a food that is considered by Ayurveda to be strengthening and cleansing. It is therefore used in Hindu rituals to symbolise purity and wellbeing. In Hindu literature it is called the nectar of immortality and is valued for its healing properties. Ayurveda considers it sweet and astringent, with antibacterial properties that can heal cuts and wounds. According to the Ashtanga Hridayasamhita, a text written by Vagbhata, one of the most influential writers of Ayurveda, around the sixth century, 'honey is good for the eyes and eyesight, it quenches thirst and heals wounds'. Honey is also referred to as 'yogavahi' in Ayurveda, which means that it can penetrate the deepest tissues of the body. It is therefore mixed with medicinal herbs whose efficacy it can carry to these deeper tissues. For it to be healing, Ayurveda suggests that honey should not be heated, a precaution not always followed in Indian cooking that has been influenced by foreign cultures such as in Mughal cookery.

WHY ARE INDIAN DESSERTS SO SWEET?

There is a distinct difference between commercially made sweets and homemade desserts. Due to the intense tropical heat and the short shelf life of ingredients such as fruit, vegetables or milk, plenty of sugar needs to be added to be able to store sweets for longer. This is especially true of commercial sweets that are sold over a few days. Home-cooked desserts that are to be consumed within a day or two of preparation are therefore less sweet.

Most Indian sweets are flavoured with 'sweet' spices such as cardamom and saffron. They do not usually have a 'sour' note such as lemon or a 'bitter' one as in chocolate that many Western desserts have. The idea is to taste the main ingredient – wonderful delights such as dates, figs, clotted milk, almonds and pistachios that are held together in a sugar syrup and butter or ghee. Without the right quantity of sugar, the sweet will fall apart.

When are they eaten? → Most Indians do not eat sweets every day. Fruit is plentiful and people who need a dessert will choose a small banana or a seasonal mango. However, sweets come into their own at festive and celebratory times. All religious festivals in India are linked to sweets and people make some at home as well as buy boxes of assorted 'mithai' to give as gifts. It's very much like in the West where one would possibly make a pudding at home but buy a box of assorted chocolates.

Diwali, the Hindu festival of light, is especially associated with 'mithai', as sweet foods are considered treats in many ancient cultures. People make some sweets and snacks at home, weeks in advance, so that there is always something special to offer the countless visitors that arrive. Burfies, which are dense fudges, laddoos or round balls made of flour and held together by a sugar syrup, halwas or soft puddings and milky sweets are all popular at this time.

Each Hindu festival is also linked to a particular sweet so people look forward to enjoying it at that time of year. 'Modaks', rice flour dumplings filled with coconut and jaggery, are made for the Ganesh festival in honour of the elephant-headed god. Holi, the festival of colour, brings 'puran poli' or jaggery- and lentil-stuffed pancakes, and the birth of Krishna is celebrated with milky sweets and desserts such as 'kheer'.

The Muslim population makes 'sheer kurma' and other vermicelli preparations for Eid and the Christians bake plum cakes and coconut puddings called 'bebinca' for Christmas. I remember, as a child, eagerly receiving small bags of marzipan and small, hand-shaped fancies of flour and butter called 'kulkuls' from our Christian friends.

FLAVOURINGS FOR DESSERTS

The main flavourings are green cardamom and saffron, which you will find in the spices chapter (see page 61).

Rose and screw pine water → These floral essences used in north Indian cooking were probably brought to India by the Mughals. Flowers are steeped and the aromatic oils are distilled and mixed in small parts into water. Desserts such as 'gulab jamun', balls of thickened milk that are deep fried, ('gulab' means rose in Hindi) (see page 466) are steeped in a rose water syrup.

Camphor → In south India, desserts are flavoured with edible camphor or 'karpoora', a product found in the bark of the camphor laurel tree. Only a very small amount is used as its strong, menthol-like flavour can overpower the dish.

Edible silver and gold foil (Varq) → Added as a garnish over sweets or rich dishes such as biryanis, edible silver or gold foil can be seen shimmering in the glass cases of any sweetmeat shop. Tiny balls of gold or silver are placed between sheets of tissue paper and laid flat in a leather pouch. This is beaten repeatedly but carefully with a heavy, metal hammer flattening the balls into sheets a few micro millimetres thick.

Varq has been certified as safe to eat by agencies all over the world but it is not very easily available to retail buyers. Where available, it is sold between sheets of tissue paper usually in boxes. Each sheet contains such a tiny amount of silver that it is not prohibitively expensive and has a shelf life of many years.

To use, carefully lift off a sheet of silver foil along with its lower sheet of tissue paper. Then turn it over on top of the prepared dish so that the foil sticks to the food. Bits will remain on the paper, which can be pressed on the food similarly. It is nearly impossible to stick on a uniform coating of silver foil!

MASTERCLASS

SOOJI KA HALWA – Semolina and Saffron Pudding

There are several regional names for this dish, such as 'rava kesari' in the south and 'sheera' in Maharashtra, although the basic recipe remains the same. This saffron-scented sweet is considered food for the gods in Hinduism and is often made on festive days. It is sometimes flavoured with tiny bits of pineapple or banana and a selection of nuts. *Serves 4*

PREPARATION ⟶ *10 minutes* COOKING *20 minutes*

YOU WILL NEED:

150g coarse semolina

120g caster sugar

large pinch of saffron

5 green cardamom pods, seeds crushed and
  husks discarded

2 teaspoons raisins

150ml melted ghee or unsalted butter

2 tablespoons unsalted cashew nuts

1 Heat a frying pan over a medium heat, add the semolina and toast it for 8–10 minutes until it begins to change colour. Keep stirring, to prevent it burning on the bottom of the pan. When slightly golden, remove from the heat and tip into a bowl.

2 Meanwhile, combine the sugar, 250ml water, saffron, cardamom seeds and raisins in a saucepan. Bring to the boil, then remove from the heat and stir to dissolve the sugar.

3 Heat the ghee in a heavy-based saucepan over a high heat and add the cashew nuts. When they start to turn golden, tip in the toasted semolina. Fry for 5 minutes, then pour in the sugar and spice water, standing back as it will splutter. Stir rapidly to avoid lumps from forming.

4 Reduce the heat and cook for about 5 minutes, until the mixture comes away from the sides of the pan as you stir. Remove from the heat and cover the pan. Leave for 5–6 minutes then serve warm.

Mung Dal Halwa

| NORTH INDIAN LENTIL AND
SUGAR PUDDING |

This rich dessert takes time and effort to prepare and is therefore served for special occasions or at north Indian and Rajasthani weddings. It is the ghee that makes it creamy and aromatic so don't be tempted to reduce the amount. *Serves 4* PREPARATION → *10 minutes, plus 2 hours soaking time* COOKING *1 hour*

100g split yellow lentils (mung dal), soaked in cold water
    for 2 hours
150g ghee
100g caster sugar
10 almonds, thinly sliced, to decorate
10 pistachios, thinly sliced, to decorate

1 Drain the mung dal, place in a blender and blitz to make a smooth purée, adding a little water to help turn the blades.
2 Heat the ghee in a non-stick pan over a high heat and add the blended dal. Reduce the heat to low and fry, stirring frequently, for 10–12 minutes, until it turns golden brown. It will turn from being a paste to looking grainy, and the aroma will change from raw to cooked.
3 Meanwhile, heat 200ml water in a saucepan, add the sugar and boil the mixture for 4–5 minutes until sugar dissolves.
4 Put the dal mixture in the sugar syrup and cook over a low heat for 40 minutes, until the liquid has evaporated and the halwa is glossy but firm.
5 Transfer from the pan to a heatproof dish and serve warm, decorated with the sliced nuts.

Shrikhand

| CONDENSED YOGURT AND
CARDAMOM CREAM |

This gorgeous dessert is served at Maharashtrian or Gujarati feasts such as weddings, and when families and friends gather to celebrate Hindu festivals like Diwali. You can add a couple of tablespoons of tinned or fresh Indian mango purée (when in season) to make a variation called 'aamrakhand'. *Serves 4* PREPARATION → *15 minutes, plus 8 hours draining time*

900g full-fat yogurt
about 6 tablespoons caster sugar or to taste
6 green cardamom pods, seeds crushed and husks discarded
large pinch of saffron, soaked in 1 teaspoon warm milk
    for 10 minutes
2 tablespoons pistachio nuts, crushed

1 Tie the yogurt in a clean piece of muslin and hang it up over the kitchen sink or a bucket for about 8 hours to drain off the whey.
2 When the yogurt is semi-dry, scoop it out of the cloth and place in a bowl. Beat well with a wooden spoon or whisk, adding the caster sugar a little at a time.
3 When the yogurt is light and fluffy in texture, stir in the cardamom, saffron (along with the milk it has been soaking in) and half of the crushed nuts. Chill and serve sprinkled with the remaining pistachio nuts.

Qubani Ka Meetha

| STEWED DRIED APRICOTS WITH CARDAMOM |

200g Indian Hunza apricots or
    organic dried apricots
80g caster sugar
4 tablespoons double cream
1 tablespoon flaked almonds, to garnish
1 tablespoon pistachios, crushed, to garnish
4 green cardamom pods, seeds crushed
    and husks discarded, to garnish

This is believed to have been the favourite of the erstwhile ruler of Hyderabad, the Nizam Osman Ali Khan (1886–1967), who was considered the wealthiest man on Earth during his time. Hunza apricots are smaller, denser and sweeter than Western ones and they have a hard seed in the centre. *Serves 4* PREPARATION —→ *10 minutes* COOKING *35 minutes*

1 Put the apricots and sugar, along with enough water to just cover them, in a heavy-based saucepan over a high heat and cook for 30 minutes until tender and pulpy. If they dry out, add a splash of water. Remove from the heat and stone the fruit (if using Hunza apricots), discarding the seeds.
2 Put half the apricots in a blender and blitz a couple of times until they resemble a jam.
3 Spoon some of the whole apricots and some of the jam into four stemmed serving glasses. Leave to cool. Drizzle with the cream, sprinkle the almonds, pistachios and cardamom on top and serve chilled.

Chaaval Ki Kheer

| SPICED INDIAN RICE PUDDING |

Kheer is a generic term given to puddings that resemble creams. They can be made with wheat, rice, nuts or fruit such as mango, jackfruit or banana and always have a milk component. Rice kheer is made all over India; this is the northern version which is often made at religious feasts. I use any cheap basmati (including broken rice) for this recipe as it gives a better, stickier texture to the pudding.

Serves 4 PREPARATION→ *30 minutes, plus 30 minutes soaking time* COOKING *1 hour*

150g cheap basmati rice, soaked in plenty of cold water
    for at least 30 minutes
500ml full-fat milk
caster sugar to taste (at least 4 tablespoons or more)
2 tablespoons pistachio nuts and almonds, roughly chopped
a few strands of saffron
6 green cardamom pods, seeds crushed and husks discarded

1 Drain the rice and place it in a heavy-based pan with the milk and bring to the boil, then leave to simmer for 1 hour, or until mushy. Mash the rice roughly with a whisk while it's still over the heat.

2 Add the sugar, pistachios, almonds and saffron and sprinkle in the crushed cardamom. Stir for a couple of minutes until thick and creamy.

3 Serve chilled or warm.

Shahi Tukde

| RICH BREAD PUDDING |

This Mughlai dessert is reserved for very special events such as Eid or Diwali as it is so rich. Traditionally, the 'tukde' (bits of bread) are deep-fried in ghee, but I have used oil for a lighter dish. The 'rabdi' (see page 452) or milk sauce that is poured over is made by cooking milk for about 1 hour until it thickens. To save time, I have used evaporated milk here that is already quite thick. *Serves 4*

PREPARATION→ *15 minutes* COOKING *25 minutes, plus cooling time*

vegetable oil, for deep-frying
3 thick slices of white bread, each cut into bite-sized squares
300ml evaporated milk
120ml sweetened condensed milk (or to taste)
a generous pinch of saffron
3 green cardamom pods, seeds crushed and husks discarded
2 tablespoons crushed pistachios

1 Heat enough oil in a frying pan to be able to submerge a single layer of the squares of bread, over a high heat, and fry the squares of bread for 3–4 minutes, flipping them over until golden all over. Remove and drain on kitchen paper.

2 Mix both the milks, saffron and crushed cardamom in a saucepan and bring to the boil. Simmer for 4–5 minutes then remove from the heat and leave to cool for 30 minutes or so.

3 To serve, arrange the fried bread squares on a serving platter. Pour the milk over and sprinkle the pistachios on top. Refrigerate for 1 hour, so that some of the sauce is absorbed by the bread, producing a texture that is varyingly crunchy and soft.

Sevian Kheer

| FINE VERMICELLI PUDDING |

Fine vermicelli is available in Indian shops in toasted or untoasted forms. You can use either – roasted vermicelli is browner and has a slightly more intense flavour. Both need to be fried as in this recipe. Vermicelli takes just moments to cook so make sure you have all your ingredients ready before you begin. *Serves 4* PREPARATION → *15 minutes* COOKING *20 minutes*

2 tablespoons vegetable oil or ghee
2 teaspoons unsalted cashew nuts
2 teaspoons raisins
2 good handfuls of vermicelli, roughly crushed by hand into small bits
400ml full-fat milk
5 tablespoons caster sugar, or to taste
a few strands of saffron
5 green cardamom pods, seeds crushed and husks discarded

1 Heat the oil or ghee in a saucepan over a high heat, add the cashew nuts and raisins and fry for 1 minute until golden. Drain and set aside, and return the pan to the heat.
2 Add the crushed vermicelli to the pan and fry for a couple of minutes until golden, stirring and taking care not to over-brown them.
3 Add the milk and bring to the boil, scraping down the sides of the pan and stirring continuously. Add some water if the mixture thickens too much.
4 Simmer for a couple of minutes until the vermicelli is soft, then add the sugar. Stir well and remove from the heat. Stir in the saffron and the cardamom.
5 This pudding can be served warm or cold, garnished with the fried nuts and raisins. If you are cooking it in advance and it thickens up, add a few tablespoons of milk to loosen it. It should have a thick pouring consistency.

Rabdi

| CLOTTED SWEET MILK |

Many north Indian cities and towns have a 'milk shop' where you can buy milk and various products such as yogurt and paneer made from it. Some sell this dessert as well, as it can take a long time to make at home. Both the homemade as well as the commercially available ones are rich and delicious! *Serves 4* PREPARATION → *10 minutes* COOKING *1 hour 20 minutes*

2 litres full-fat milk
3 tablespoons caster sugar
4 green cardamom pods, seeds finely crushed and husks discarded
a pinch of saffron
1 tablespoon crushed pistachios
1 teaspoon rose water

1 Put the milk in a heavy-based saucepan and bring to the boil. Reduce the heat to medium or until you see a steady bubbling simmer. Stir from time to time.
2 As the milk forms a skin on top, stir this back in and scrape the thickened milk from the edges back into the pan. Stir to make sure that the milk is not browning at the bottom of the pan.
3 After about 30 minutes of simmering, the milk will have begun to evaporate and clot into creamy, soft bits. Add the sugar, cardamom, saffron and pistachios. Continue cooking for a further 30 minutes, or until the mixture looks almost like creamy cottage cheese.
4 Remove from the heat, stir in the rose water and leave to cool. Serve cold – it will thicken further on cooling.

MASTERCLASS

RASMALAI – Creamy Cottage Cheese in Spiced Milk

'Ras' means juice or ambrosia and 'malai' is cream in Hindi. This dessert is delicate and fragrant, with dumplings of fresh cottage cheese steeped in a thick, sweetened, spiced nutty milk. Once made, the cheese is often washed to remove traces of lemon but I tend to leave it for extra flavour. *Serves 4*

PREPARATION → *10 minutes, plus 3 hours draining time* COOKING *45 minutes*

YOU WILL NEED:

900ml full-fat milk

a few drops of lemon juice

1 x 410g can of evaporated milk

120g caster sugar

6 green cardamom pods, seeds crushed
    and husks discarded

a pinch of saffron

2 teaspoons sliced almonds and pistachios

1 Put a large square of muslin over a clean, tall pan or bucket.

2 Put the milk in a pan and bring to the boil, the add the lemon juice and let the milk curdle. Remove from the heat and scoop out the curdled solids with a slotted spoon. Put them into the muslin hanging over the pan or bucket, then tie the muslin into a bundle and put a wooden spoon through the knot. Hang this over the pan or bucket, leaving the whey to drain off for about 3 hours.

3 Meanwhile, in a separate pan, heat the evaporated milk and most of the sugar over a high heat (reserving 3 tablespoons of sugar to make the sugar syrup later on). Add the crushed cardamom, saffron and nuts. Leave to cool then refrigerate.

4 When the cheese has drained, bring 500ml of water to the boil in a large, shallow saucepan and add the reserved 3 tablespoons of sugar to it.

5 Remove the cheese from the muslin and knead it lightly for about 1 minute. Shape it tightly into small balls each the size of a cherry. You should get about 16 balls.

6 Reduce the heat under the boiling water and gently slip the balls in. Cook them for 10 minutes, then remove from the pan. Drain the balls well and add them to the cold, spiced milk from Step 2. Serve cold.

Besan Ke Laddoo

| GRAM FLOUR SWEETS |

A festive sweet that can be made and stored for up to two weeks in an airtight container, this is often served at teatime or eaten as a snack. When the flour and ghee is cooked it will be quite runny. It becomes firm as it cools and easier to shape. You have to do this while it is still warm though because if it cools completely, it is very difficult to shape it into balls. *Makes 12–16 balls*
PREPARATION → *5 minutes* COOKING *30 minutes, plus cooling time*

200g gram flour
3 tablespoons fine semolina
70ml melted ghee
100g caster sugar
8 almonds, sliced
6 green cardamom pods, seeds finely crushed
    and husks discarded
a few raisins, to decorate

1 Put the gram flour and semolina in a heavy-based saucepan and dry-toast over a medium heat for about 10 minutes, stirring continuously, until an aroma develops and the flour turns slightly golden. Make sure to keep the heat down and keep stirring so that the gram flour toasts right through.
2 Pour in the ghee and continue frying over a medium heat for a further 20 minutes, until the mixture becomes slightly runny and develops a nutty aroma.
3 Remove from the heat and cool until just warm. Stir in the sugar, almonds and cardamom.
4 Take a small fistful of the flour mixture and press into a ball or 'laddoo', the size of a large plum – you'll have enough mixture for 12–16 balls. Press a raisin into each one to decorate. Cool completely to set the laddoos, then serve.

Gajar Ka Halwa

| INDIAN CARROT PUDDING |

This is a winter dessert when Indian carrots, usually darker in colour, are in season. You can use any variety, though – the results will be just as delicious. It is best eaten warm and is served with a scoop of vanilla ice cream at Indian weddings in central and northern India, where these carrots grow. *Serves 4* PREPARATION → *20 minutes* COOKING *1 hour 20 minutes*

100g caster sugar
2 tablespoons ghee or butter
300g carrots, peeled or scraped, and grated
200ml full-fat milk
4 green cardamom pods, seeds crushed and husks discarded
1 tablespoon unsalted cashew nuts, roughly broken, to decorate

1 Place the sugar in a heavy-based saucepan with double the volume of water and bring to the boil. Stir until all the sugar has dissolved, then reduce the heat and cook the syrup for a few minutes, remove from the heat and set aside.
2 Meanwhile, heat the ghee or butter in a heavy-based pan over a high heat, add the carrots and fry, stirring occasionally, for 5–6 minutes.
3 Pour in the sugar syrup and the milk, reduce the heat and cook for 1 hour, until the carrots are mushy and all the liquid has evaporated.
4 Remove from the heat, mix in the cardamom and serve warm, decorated with the nuts.

Puran Poli

| SWEET LENTIL-AND JAGGERY-STUFFED FLATBREAD |

For the stuffing

200g split gram lentils (chana dal), soaked
    in warm water for 1 hour then washed and
    drained

200g jaggery, grated

8 green cardamom pods, seeds finely crushed
    and husks discarded

1 teaspoon ground nutmeg

For the flatbread (makes 8)

250g stoneground wholewheat flour (atta),
    plus extra for dusting

150g plain flour

2 tablespoons melted ghee

a pinch of salt

a pinch of ground turmeric

200–220ml warm water, as needed

vegetable oil, to cook the flatbread

This delicious dessert from Maharashtra and Gujarat is almost always made for the Hindu springtime festival of Holi. It is slightly tedious to prepare but the results are very worth it! Eat it warm dunked in melted ghee, butter or a cup of warm milk. *Makes 8* PREPARATION → *20 minutes, plus 1 hour soaking time* COOKING *2 hours*

1 Put the dal in a pan with double the volume of water and bring to the boil. Reduce the heat and simmer for 1 hour, until you can easily squash a lentil between your fingers.

2 Meanwhile, combine both the flours in a large bowl and make a well in the centre. Add the ghee, salt and turmeric and begin to mix with your fingers. Start pouring in the warm water, a little at a time, until you have a soft but firm dough. Knead the dough until smooth then place back in the bowl and leave to rest, covered with a clean, damp tea towel, while you make the stuffing.

3 Drain the cooked chana dal and put it in a heavy-based pan with the jaggery. Cook over a medium heat for 10–15 minutes until the jaggery has melted. Tip in the ground cardamom and nutmeg. Stir continuously for 8–10 minutes until the mixture thickens, then mash with a potato masher until you have a smooth paste (this paste is called 'puran').

4 Remove the dough from the bowl and knead it on a floured surface, then divide it into 8 equal-sized balls.

5 Dust a dough ball with flour and roll it into a disc or 'poli' about 10cm in diameter. Place a small ball of stuffing in the centre and gather the edges of the dough around it to seal the stuffing in and make a parcel.

6 Dust the parcel with flour and gently roll it out into a poli about 15cm in diameter.

7 Heat a frying pan over a high heat and dot with oil. Place the poli in the hot pan and as soon as bubbles appear on the surface, flip it over. Cook for 1–2 minutes on each side until they are opaque and brown spots appear. Lift onto a plate and keep warm in foil or a clean tea towel, while you roll, stuff and cook the remaining polis.

Phirni

| SET RICE PUDDING |

Phirni and kheer are both rice puddings, though the first is made with ground rice and the latter with rice grains. I have eaten this in north India, where it is traditionally set in small earthenware cups called 'kulhad' or 'shikora'. These are biodegradable, never re-used and impart an earthy smell to the food they contain. They are also used to serve tea at Indian railway stations. *Serves 4* PREPARATION → *10 minutes, plus 1 hour soaking time* COOKING *15 minutes, plus 1 hour setting time*

50g cheap basmati rice, soaked in water for 1 hour then drained
250ml full-fat milk
a pinch of saffron
2 tablespoons caster sugar (or to taste)
8 almonds, finely sliced or 2 teaspoons flaked almonds,
    plus extra for garnishing
a few drops of rose essence or 2 teaspoons rose water

1 Dry the rice on a clean tea towel then blitz it in a coffee grinder or spice mill to make a coarse powder.
2 Heat the milk in a saucepan with the saffron and sugar over a high heat. When it comes to the boil, reduce the heat to medium and tip in the ground rice, stirring constantly. Add the almonds.
3 Continue cooking, stirring constantly, for 10 minutes until the milk begins to thicken. Bear in mind that the pudding will set when it is completely cold.
4 Remove from the heat and stir in the rose essence or rose water. Pour into individual heatproof serving bowls and chill to set. Serve cold, decorated with a few sliced almonds.

Gujiya

| KHOYA-FILLED PASTRIES |

This is a north Indian recipe, however many regional versions exist. In Goa, these pastries are called 'neoreo' and are stuffed with locally grown coconut and sugar, whereas in Maharashtra, the 'karanji' has coconut sweetened with locally produced jaggery. In Bihar, they are called 'padaukiya' and are sometimes stuffed with sweet, roasted semolina. The Gujarati version is 'ghugra' and has coconut with nuts and poppy seeds. They all look like moon-shaped samosas. *Makes 8* PREPARATION → *20 minutes* COOKING *1 hour*

250g plain flour, plus extra for dusting
3 tablespoons melted ghee
a pinch of salt
2 tablespoons chopped almonds and pistachios
200g Khoya *(pages 254–255)*
80g caster sugar
3 green cardamom pods, seeds crushed and husks discarded
vegetable oil, for deep-frying

1 Mix the flour, ghee and salt in a large bowl. Add 125–150ml cold water, a little at a time, until you have a firm dough. Knead for 5–6 minutes to soften, then put it back in the bowl and set aside covered with a clean, damp tea towel.
2 To make the filling, heat a tablespoon of the oil in a frying pan over a high heat, add the nuts and fry for 2–3 minutes until they sizzle. Stir in the khoya, sugar and cardamom and cook for 8–10 minutes until the mixture leaves the sides of the pan and forms a ball. Remove from the heat.
3 Divide the dough into 8 small equal-sized balls and roll each one out on a floured work surface into a thin disc roughly 10cm in diameter. Shake off any excess flour.
4 Put a spoonful of the filling down the middle of one half of each circle, leaving the edges bare. Wet the edges and press down firmly to form a half-moon shape. Trim edges with a serrated cutter or knife, making sure that the edges are sealed.
5 Heat enough oil in a deep frying pan to fry the pastries in a single layer. When nearly smoking hot, reduce the heat and deep-fry the pastries in batches for 3–4 minutes until golden, then drain and set aside. Serve cold or warm.

Kelya Muluk
| BANANA FRITTERS |

This sweet from the Konkani community, a sect of Hindu Brahmins from Karnataka, makes good use of overripe bananas that no one wants to eat. The recipe is quite similar to the 'unniappam' of Kerala but has added semolina and can be made without the traditional 'appam chatty', a dish with depressions to hold the batter and stop it from spreading when the fritters are frying. *Makes about 20 fritters* PREPARATION → *15 minutes, plus 30 minutes resting time* COOKING *20 minutes*

2 very ripe bananas, peeled and thickly sliced
3 tablespoons grated jaggery or soft brown sugar
2 tablespoons freshly grated coconut or desiccated coconut soaked in water for 15 minutes then drained
a pinch of salt
5 green cardamom pods, seeds finely crushed and husks discarded
150g rice flour, sifted
125g fine semolina
vegetable oil, for deep-frying

1 Mash the bananas in a bowl and add the jaggery, coconut and salt. Mix well, stirring until the jaggery melts and the mixture becomes runny. Tip in the cardamom.
2 Mix the rice flour and semolina together in a small bowl. Add this, a little at a time, to the banana mix and break up any lumps as you go. You should have a smooth, thick batter, almost the consistency of a soft dough. Cover and leave to rest at room temperature for 30 minutes.
3 Break off bits of the mixture and form into about 20 balls, each the size of a large cherry or small lime. Place them on a tray.
4 Heat the oil in a deep frying pan over a high heat, then test it's hot enough by putting in a bit of the dough – it should rise to the top in a few seconds. Carefully add the dough balls to the hot oil in batches. Reduce the heat to medium and fry for 3–4 minutes, until golden brown and the centre of each fritter is cooked.
5 Remove with a slotted spoon and drain on kitchen paper. Fry the remaining balls of batter similarly. Serve warm.

Saffron and Pistachio Ice Cream

Ice cream in all forms – as plain vanilla or the rich, spiced kulfi – are popular in India. My grandfather had an ice-cream machine at home and he made quite an occasion of it, hand-churning various flavours for the family on hot summer days. *Serves 4* PREPARATION → *30 minutes, plus overnight freezing time*

1 x 397g can of condensed milk
600ml double cream
8 green cardamom pods, seeds finely crushed and husks discarded
a pinch of saffron strands, soaked in 1 tablespoon hot milk
3 tablespoons crushed pistachios

1 Put the condensed milk, cream, cardamom and saffron milk along with the strands into a large bowl. Whisk for about 10 minutes until you get a thick dropping consistency.
2 Pour the mixture into a lidded plastic tub and freeze for 1 hour 30 minutes.
3 Remove the tub from the freezer, decant back into the bowl and fold in the crushed pistachios. Put back into the tub and freeze overnight.

Zarda

| SWEET RICE WITH NUTS |

The word 'zard' means yellow in Persian, suggesting that this dish was popularised in north India by the Mughals, who ruled there from 1526 to 1858. North Indian culture is influenced by the Mughals in terms of language, architecture, food and dress. Urdu, a language with Persian roots, was spoken by elite members of the Mughal Empire and it has become a part of the native Hindi spoken in north India. The *Ain-i-Akbari,* Emperor Akbar's chronicles, explain the recipe for 'zard birinj' made with rice, sugar candy, nuts, spices such as saffron and cinnamon along with fresh ginger. *Serves 4* PREPARATION → *20 minutes* COOKING *40 minutes*

200g basmati rice, washed and drained
2 large pinches of saffron
80g ghee or unsalted butter
1 tablespoon pistachios, chopped
1 tablespoon almonds, chopped
2 tablespoons fresh or dried coconut shavings
150g caster sugar
5 green cardamom pods, seeds crushed and husks discarded

1   Put the rice in a heavy-based saucepan with double the volume of water and the saffron. Bring to the boil, then reduce the heat to low, cover and simmer for 10 minutes. Remove from the heat and leave covered for 5 minutes.
2   Heat the ghee or butter in a frying pan over a high heat, add the nuts and coconut and fry for 3–4 minutes. When they begin to darken, fold in the cooked rice.
3   Tip in the sugar and cardamom and mix gently. Cover tightly and cook for 5 minutes over a low heat.
4   Remove from the heat, remove the lid and serve warm.

Kada Parshad

| WHOLEWHEAT PUDDING |

Every Sikh gurudwara (temple) serves this sweet to devotees. Prayers are chanted as it is being prepared, which people say makes it taste even more delicious! It is simple to make and the soft, creamy texture melts in the mouth. *Serves 4* PREPARATION → *5 minutes* COOKING *15 minutes*

100g ghee
100g stoneground wholewheat flour (atta)
100g caster sugar

1   Heat the ghee in a heavy-based frying pan over a medium heat then add the flour. Stir constantly for about 10 minutes until the flour turns golden brown.
2   Meanwhile, combine the sugar and 250ml water in a saucepan and bring to the boil. Remove from the heat and stir to dissolve the sugar.
3   When the flour is well browned and aromatic, reduce the heat to low and pour in half the sugar water. Stir continuously to break up any lumps and to cook the flour evenly. Pour in the remaining water.
4   In a few minutes, the water will evaporate and the pudding will come away from the sides of the pan. Remove from the heat and serve warm.

Aamras

| MANGO SMOOTHIE |

The month of May, mango season in India, is also an auspicious month for Hindu weddings when aamras is served with pooris (see page 114) at Maharashtrian and Gujarati feasts. It is important to use sweet, non-fibrous Indian mangoes such as Alfonso or Kesar for the best flavour and consistency. *Serves 4* PREPARATION → *20 minutes*

4 ripe mangoes, peeled, stoned, sliced and chopped
2–3 teaspoons caster sugar, if required
4 green cardamom pods, seeds finely crushed
   and husks discarded

1 Blitz the chopped mangoes to a smooth purée in a blender, adding the tiniest amount of water to help turn the blades. You want to make a thick purée rather than a mango drink.
2 Taste the purée and add sugar if necessary. Stir in the cardamom and serve chilled.

Mango Seekarane

| MANGOES IN COCONUT MILK |

This easy recipe from Karnataka was a childhood favourite of mine because it was so seasonal. Made within minutes, it is proof that the fragrance and sweetness of Indian mangoes needs minimum fuss and bother to shine. This is also known as 'rasayana' or 'hashaley'. *Serves 4*
PREPARATION → *10 minutes, plus chilling time*

1 x 400ml can of coconut milk
4 green cardamom pods, seeds crushed and husks discarded
2 tablespoons grated jaggery or soft dark brown sugar
2 ripe Indian mangoes (Alphonso or Kesar), peeled and diced

1 Combine the coconut milk and crushed cardamom. Stir in the jaggery or sugar until dissolved.
2 Spoon a few tablespoons of the coconut milk into a bowl and roughly mash 3–4 cubes of mango into it. Pour it back into the remaining coconut milk, stir in the remaining cubed mango and chill for an hour or so. Serve chilled.

Masala Chai Kulfi

| SPICED TEA ICE CREAM |

Kulfi is denser than popular ice cream as it is not aerated or whipped. It is traditionally made by boiling full-fat milk until it has reduced by two thirds but this is an easy, time-saving version. *Serves 4* PREPARATION → *10 minutes, plus 2–3 hours freezing time* COOKING *10 minutes*

1 x 410g can of evaporated milk
½ x 397g can of condensed milk
2.5cm piece of fresh root ginger, grated to extract juice
   and the fibrous part discarded
3 teabags or 2 teaspoons strong tea leaves
   (I use English Breakfast tea)

1 Combine all the ingredients in a heavy-based saucepan over a medium heat. Cook until the milk is almost boiling, then remove from the heat and pass through a sieve into a heatproof jug. Pour into small moulds or a plastic tub. I use small silicone moulds 4cm in diameter as they can be easily turned inside out to unmold the kulfi. Traditional kulfi moulds are conical.
2 Freeze overnight until set.

Mango Kulfi

I only make this during the Indian mango season in May because it works best with the fragrant Alphonso or Kesar varieties. You can use other seasonal fruit such as strawberries, raspberries or blueberries. *Serves 4*
PREPARATION → *5 minutes, plus 2 hours freezing time* COOKING *10 minutes*

1 x 410g can of evaporated milk
100g caster sugar
100g Indian mango pulp *(see Aamras above left)*

1 Heat the evaporated milk and sugar in a saucepan over a high heat for 10 minutes, until the sugar dissolves.
2 Remove from the heat and leave to cool, then stir in the mango pulp. Put into an 800ml plastic tub and freeze overnight.

GULAB JAMUN – Milk Dumplings in Rose-flavoured Syrup

Gulab is rose in Hindi and jamun are Indian berries. These dumplings are fried to resemble jamun and soaked in rose syrup. There are many recipes for this: some more 'instant' recipes use milk powder, but I have made these using khoya (milk that is cooked down to its solid form, see page 245), as I think it tastes better. *Serves 4* PREPARATION → *15 minutes* COOKING *30 minutes, plus 1 hour soaking time*

YOU WILL NEED:

250g Khoya *(pages 254–255)*

2 tablespoons plain flour

½ teaspoon bicarbonate of soda

vegetable oil, for deep-frying

For the syrup

200g caster sugar

2 teaspoons rose water or
    1 teaspoon rose extract

1 tablespoon crushed pistachios

5 Remove the syrup from the heat. Stir in the rose water (or extract) and pistachios.

6 Heat enough oil to fry the dough balls in a frying pan over a high heat and test it by putting in a bit of the dough. It should rise to the top in a few seconds. Reduce the heat to medium and carefully lower the dough balls into the oil in batches. Fry for 5–6 minutes until evenly golden brown all over.

7 Remove them with a slotted spoon and transfer them directly into the warm sugar syrup.

8 Leave the jamuns to soak up the syrup for at least 1 hour. Serve warm – they should be warm from the syrup. If making in advance, they can be gently heated for 7–8 minutes in the syrup.

1 Knead the khoya lightly until it is smooth and starts to become oily with the heat of your hands. Add the flour and bicarbonate of soda and knead again to make a soft dough.

2 Shape the dough into 16 cherry-sized balls that are smooth and have no cracks (or else they will absorb too much oil). Cover with a clean tea towel.

3 Combine the sugar and 200ml water in a heavy-based saucepan and cook over a high heat for 5–6 minutes until almost boiling, stirring to dissolve the sugar.

4 Reduce the heat and continue cooking for 10–15 minutes until it forms a single string consistency. Test this by putting a drop on a cold plate, waiting for it to cool and then dipping your index finger into it. The syrup should form a single string when your thumb and finger pull apart slowly. Alternatively, if you have a sugar thermometer, place it in the syrup: the thermometer should read 108–118°C.

Kaju Burfie

| CASHEW AND MILK FUDGE |

Burfies, which are like a dense fudge, are made from a wide range of ingredients from chocolate to figs. They can be picked up with one's fingers and the texture varies from being soft and moist to quite dense and dry. As they are quite sweet, they keep well for 3–4 days at room temperature and for up to a week in the fridge. They are often decorated with edible silver or gold foil called 'varq', which can be bought from some Indian shops.

Makes 12 squares PREPARATION ➝ *10 minutes* COOKING *30 minutes, plus 2–3 hours setting time*

1 x 400g can of condensed milk
30g unsalted butter, plus 1 teaspoon for greasing the dish
4 tablespoons unsalted cashew nuts, finely crushed
4 green cardamom pods, seeds finely crushed
    and husks discarded
edible silver foil, to decorate (optional)

1 Put the condensed milk in a heavy-based saucepan over a low heat and cook for 10–15 minutes, stirring constantly, until the mixture thickens and comes away from the sides of the pan. Stir in the butter, cashew nuts and cardamom, then remove from the heat. You should be able to move the mixture easily with the back of a wooden spoon.
2 Grease a flat dish with the extra butter. Pour the burfie mixture in and smooth the surface with a spatula.
3 Leave to cool and set for 2–3 hours, then cut into about twelve 2.5cm squares or diamonds and decorate with more crushed nuts and edible silver foil (if using).

Parsi Sev

| SWEET VERMICELLI PUDDING |

I have eaten this fragrant dessert at my Parsi friends' homes on festive days, such as Jamshed Navroz or Parsi New Year's Day, with sugar-sweetened yogurt or 'mithoo dahi'. I was told that the symbolic significance of the dish was at the heart of Parsi life. The fineness of the vermicelli indicated the hard work that had gone into making it. The sugar encouraged people to be sweet natured and the yogurt served with it reminded us of the animal kingdom that needs to be cherished. The Parsis and Maharashtrians use charoli nuts to garnish their desserts. This is a small almond-flavoured, flat nut the size of a lentil. *Serves 4*

PREPARATION ➝ *15 minutes* COOKING *20 minutes*

80g caster sugar
2 tablespoons ghee
2 tablespoons raisins
2 tablespoons flaked almonds
1 tablespoon charoli nuts or flaked almonds
100g fine vermicelli, crushed by hand into short lengths
½ teaspoon ground nutmeg
½ teaspoon vanilla or rose extract
yogurt sweetened with sugar, to serve (optional)

1 Combine the sugar and 80ml water in a saucepan over a high heat and bring to the boil. Remove from the heat, stir to dissolve the sugar and set aside.
2 Heat the ghee in a frying pan over a high heat, add the raisins, almonds and the charoli nuts and fry for 1 minute until golden. Remove with a slotted spoon and set aside.
3 In the same ghee, fry the vermicelli for 3–4 minutes until golden, without allowing it to turn too brown.
4 Pour in the sugar water, a little at a time, until the vermicelli softens completely but does not turn to a mush. Remove from the heat and sprinkle in the nutmeg and vanilla or rose extract. Stir gently with a fork, separating the strands of vermicelli.
5 Serve warm, garnished with the fried raisins, almonds and charoli nuts and a spoonful of yogurt sweetened with sugar on the side, if desired.

Mung Dal Payasam

| SOUTH INDIAN LENTIL AND MILK PUDDING |

This is a traditional pudding from south India, which uses lentils in countless ways to make dals, to add texture to vegetable dishes and even in desserts. In a hot climate, lentils provide protein in a meal that would become too heavy if it had meat or poultry. Also, there are a large number of vegetarians in south India and lentils form an essential part of their diet. Lentil-based desserts are usually milky and fragrant with cardamom. *Serves 4*

PREPARATION —➔ *10 minutes* COOKING *45 minutes*

3 tablespoons broken basmati rice
    or any sticky rice
4 tablespoons split yellow lentils (mung dal),
    washed and drained
4 tablespoons unsalted cashew nuts
5–6 green cardamom pods, seeds crushed
    and husks discarded
200ml coconut milk
2 tablespoons grated jaggery
    or soft dark brown sugar

1 Soak the rice in water while you prepare the remaining ingredients.

2 Heat a heavy saucepan over a high heat, add the lentils and dry-toast for 3–4 minutes until they start to darken.

3 Pour in 150ml water and bring to the boil. Reduce the heat and simmer for 25 minutes until the lentils are soft, then add the cashew nuts to the pan.

4 Meanwhile, drain the rice and blitz it in a blender with a few tablespoons of water until you have a gritty paste.

5 Add this rice paste to the cooked lentils then add the cardamom and coconut milk. Add the jaggery or sugar. Bring to the boil then cook over a medium heat for 12–15 minutes.

6 The final dish should be creamy and of pouring consistency, so you may need to add a bit of water if it is too thick. Serve warm.

DRINKS

LIGHTLY SPICED FRUIT OR VEGETABLE JUICES ARE AVAILABLE AS STREET FOOD
OR SERVED AS WELCOME DRINKS IN MANY INDIAN HOMES, ESPECIALLY DURING
THE BLAZING HOT SUMMER MONTHS.

People at my classes often ask me what Indians drink with their meal. The answer is simple – water. In an Indian home, water is the preferred beverage as it interferes neither with the taste of the food nor its digestion, when drunk in moderation. Ayurvedic nutrition advises us not to drink too much water through a meal as it dilutes digestive juices and delays effective digestion.

The tropical, seasonal heat over most of India means that drinks of various kinds are popular but these are often drunk through the day rather than with a meal. Fruit juices such as orange, lime, sugarcane or pineapple are sold at 'juice centres' and in coastal towns; fresh coconut water is the preferred thirst quencher. If you go to someone's home, you may be offered a 'sharbat' – a sweet drink with sugar, essence and colour that is diluted with water. Popular flavours are rose, 'khus' or vetiver and sandalwood. Fresh lemonade, sweetened, spiced and iced is popular.

Tea and coffee are drunk all over the country. Indian tea is stewed rather than brewed and is thicker and stronger than the tea served in Europe. Coffee comes from the south where it is served filtered and strong, in small steel cups.

Drinks are also a part of the Indian healing system. I grew up drinking many kinds of 'coolers' in the scorching summers, or spiced, herbal teas when I felt poorly. My grandmother always made me a warm tea with flax seeds to counteract the discomfort of an allergic cold. This may have worked because of the high selenium content in the seeds which is said to reduce symptoms. I loved the turmeric milk that I was given as a child every time I had a sore throat.

Turmeric is believed to be anti-inflammatory and antiseptic. The healing antioxidant curcumin which is present is considered to become more available when combined with good fats such as those in milk and ghee.

Alcohol is not a part of daily life in India. In the cities and towns, people may throw cocktail parties where whisky, vodka, rum and beer are also served but these do not often accompany the meal that follows. Beer is seen as a daytime drink, to be had with Sunday lunch. Wine is growing in popularity and India produces some very good wines, but these are still mainly only drunk in large cities and at restaurants. Women often do not drink so it's not uncommon for them to be offered a 'soft drink' rather than a glass of wine or whisky. Young people in large cities drink alcohol in bars and restaurants but in many families, this is considered taboo. In traditional families, drinking with your elders is considered a mark of disrespect.

Religious rules also dictate whether someone will drink alcohol or not. As a general rule, the Muslims do not and neither do the Jains, Buddhists or initiated Sikhs. Strict Hindus also refrain from alcohol for the sake of pleasure, although Ayurveda prescribes wines as medicine in the form of fermented juices called 'asavas' and 'arishtas'.

Regional alcoholic drinks are made using local ingredients. 'Feni' is made in Goa from coconut, rice beer called 'Chaang' or 'Kosna' is drunk in north-eastern states, and mahua flowers are made into a liquor in the tribal regions of Chhattisgarh state. Toddy, made from palm trees, is popular in Kerala which has well-known 'toddy shops'.

Namkeen Lassi

| SALTED LASSI |

Popular during north Indian summers, this drink is served in large jugs throughout the day. I use full-fat or Greek yogurt for this, to make it thick and creamy, but you can use low-fat yogurt if you wish. *Serves 4* PREPARATION → *10 minutes*

1 teaspoon cumin seeds
300ml cold water
300g natural full-fat or Greek yogurt
a few turns of a peppermill
salt

1 Heat a frying pan over a high heat, add the cumin seeds and dry-toast until they begin to darken and develop an aroma. Remove from the heat and crush to a powder in a pestle and mortar.
2 Combine all the ingredients, season with salt, whisk well and serve chilled.

Aam Ki Lassi

| MANGO LASSI |

This is a seasonal drink because you need the a certain type of Indian mangoes such as Alphonso or Kesar to achieve the right flavour. These are sweet, smooth and very fragrant. Out of season, you can use sweetened purée from a can. *Serves 5* PREPARATION → *15 minutes*

2 ripe Indian mangoes (such as Alphonso or Kesar), peeled,
    stoned and chopped or 150g mango purée from a can
300g natural yogurt
100ml cold water
3 green cardamom pods, seeds crushed and husks discarded
caster sugar, to taste (optional)

1 Blitz the chopped mango in a blender to make a smooth purée. Tip the yogurt into the blender and pour in the water. Blitz again until smooth.
2 Mix in the cardamom and sugar, if using, and serve chilled.

SOLKADI – Tangy Coconut Milk

Kokum is a tangy, purple fruit of the mangosteen family that grows mainly in Gujarat, Maharashtra and Goa (see page 417). This Maharashtrian drink is served cold and is often eaten mixed with rice and a piece of spicy fried fish, or served on its own. Kokum is known for its cooling properties; in the sweltering heat of the summer, it is made into a cordial to be diluted with water, called 'amrut kokum'. The active ingredient garcinol, which has anti-inflammatory properties, helps to prevent sunstroke and cool the digestive system.

Serves 4 PREPARATION→ *40 minutes*

YOU WILL NEED:
400ml coconut milk
8 kokum petals *(page 417)*, washed
    and soaked in 2 tablespoons
    of warm water for 10 minutes
pinch of caster sugar
2 garlic cloves, crushed
2 tablespoons finely chopped
    fresh coriander leaves
salt

1 Add all the ingredients to the coconut milk, mix well and leave to stand for 20 minutes. Strain.

2 Squeeze the juice from the kokum into the drink and discard the petals when the drink is pink and fairly sour. If it is not, leave the kokum in for longer. Serve at room temperature.

Kashaya

| HERBAL TEA |

Whenever I had a cold, cough or a temperature as a child, my grandmother would make me this lovely tea. It is called 'kadha' in many Indian languages and has its roots in Ayurvedic healing. There are several versions of this drink, depending on personal preference and the malady. Fennel is used for digestive upsets, cardamom for digestion, ginger helps with congestion, and cloves, which are heating, open up the channels (called 'srotas' in Ayurveda: these include the lymphatic and digestive systems). Even without an illness, it makes a wonderful winter warmer.

Serves 4 PREPARATION → *2 minutes* COOKING *10 minutes*

1 teaspoon cumin seeds
3 black peppercorns
3 green cardamom pods
1 cinnamon stick
3 cloves
a small knob of fresh root ginger
honey, to taste

1 Put the cumin seeds, peppercorns, cardamom, cinnamon, cloves and ginger in a mortar and crush roughly with a pestle to bruise.

2 Combine the contents of the mortar with 500ml water in a saucepan and bring to the boil. Reduce the heat and simmer for 5–6 minutes.

3 Strain and add honey to taste. Serve hot.

Masala Chai

| SPICED INDIAN TEA |

There are so many different recipes for this, depending on personal preference – you can also use spices such as cinnamon, pepper and cloves. You must boil everything together to extract all the flavour from the ingredients.

Serves 4 PREPARATION → *5 minutes* COOKING *15 minutes*

1 teaspoon fennel seeds
1.25cm piece of fresh root ginger
3 green cardamom pods, bruised
250ml boiling hot water
250ml full-fat or semi-skimmed milk (depending on preference)
3 teabags or 2 teaspoons strong loose-leaf tea
caster sugar, to taste (optional)

1 Crush the fennel seeds, ginger and cardamom in a mortar with a pestle. Put the spices in a heavy-based pan and pour in the water and milk. Bring to the boil, then add the teabags or tea.

2 Reduce the heat and simmer for 5 minutes, until a colour develops.

3 Remove from the heat, strain through a fine sieve into a heatproof jug and discard the spices and teabags. Serve hot, sweetened with sugar if desired.

Aam Ka Panna

| GREEN MANGO CORDIAL |

During the hot summer months when mangoes are in season, this refreshing drink is made in homes all over the country. It is a concentrate that can be stored in the fridge for up to a fortnight and to which water is added to dilute it. You can use other fruit as well – plums and pineapples work really well. *Serves 4* PREPARATION → *10 minutes*
COOKING *30 minutes*

1 large, raw green mango, peeled and roughly chopped
100g caster sugar or more to taste (the cordial should be quite
   sweet as it will be diluted later on)
a pinch of salt
a few strands of saffron
a couple of turns of the peppermill
3 green cardamom pods, seeds crushed and husks discarded

1   Place the mango in a pan with 300ml water and bring to the boil. I always boil the mango stone as well, to get its flavour into the drink. Reduce the heat and simmer for 15 minutes until the mango is pulpy.
2   Remove from the heat, leave to cool and discard the stone. Transfer to a blender and blitz until smooth. If the pulp is stringy, strain it through a fine sieve.
3   Add the remaining ingredients and return to the heat. Cook over a high heat for a few minutes until the sugar has dissolved completely.
4   Cool and store in the fridge. To make a glassful, add 3–4 tablespoons of this concentrate and top with chilled water.

Shikanjvi

| SUMMER LEMONADE |

Also known as 'nimbu pani' or 'shikanji', this is made with water or sparkling soda. You can flavour it with cooling ingredients such as rose water or saffron. *Serves 4*
PREPARATION → *5 minutes*

juice of 2 lemons or more for a tangy taste
salt, to taste
caster sugar, to taste
2.5cm piece of fresh root ginger, peeled and grated
a pinch of freshly ground black pepper

1   Mix the lemon juice with salt and sugar to taste, until well blended.
2   Squeeze the ginger juice out from the grated ginger and add this to the mix.
3   Add the pepper and 600ml cold water and serve chilled.

Narial Ka Sharbat

| ROSE-FLAVOURED COCONUT WATER |

Many years ago in Mumbai, before coconut water was widely available in packs, we would buy tender coconuts from the 'nariyal wallah' and crack them open at home. We would chill the water with cooling flavours such as rose water or 'khus', known in other parts of the world as vetiver. Khus is a fragrant grass that grows in northern and western India. It is commercially made into a bright green syrup with strong woody overtones that is diluted before being drunk to beat the scorching summer heat.

Serves 4 PREPARATION → *5 minutes*

1 litre coconut water
2 teaspoons rose water

1   Combine the ingredients and serve chilled.

Haldi Ki Chai

| TURMERIC TEA |

I have been drinking this tea, once a day, for a while now and have experienced its good effects, such as a higher resistance to colds and coughs and increased immunity to seasonal maladies such as the flu. I suggest it to everyone that attends my classes and often demonstrate how it easy it is to make! It has no taste and the turmeric does not make it spicy. You can add honey or sugar to sweeten it, if you prefer. *Serves 4* PREPARATION—➔ *5 minutes*

a pinch of ground turmeric
sugar or honey (optional)

1 Boil 800ml water in a kettle.
2 Put a pinch of turmeric in 4 mugs and pour the boiling water over the top. The turmeric will change in colour and turn slightly orange. Drink hot. You can sweeten it with sugar or honey if you wish.

Rasam

| LENTIL SOUP WITH TAMARIND |

Rasam is eaten with rice in south India but its soupy consistency also makes it a warming drink. You can make it when cooking dal by adding extra water that is drained off to use as stock in this recipe. *Serves 4* PREPARATION—➔ *15 minutes, plus 15 minutes soaking* COOKING *50 minutes*

4 tablespoons toor dal, soaked in water at room temperature for 15 minutes, then drained
1 teaspoon grated jaggery or soft light brown sugar
2 tablespoons vegetable oil
½ teaspoon black mustard seeds
½ teaspoon cumin seeds
large pinch of asafoetida
10 fresh curry leaves
1 teaspoon tamarind pulp *(page 418)* or shop-bought tamarind paste
1 teaspoon sambhar powder *(page 65)*
1 teaspoon ground turmeric
salt
2 tablespoons chopped fresh coriander leaves, to serve

1 Place the toor dal in a pan with 600ml water, bring to the boil then reduce the heat and simmer for 40 minutes until mushy, skimming the scum off the surface from time to time. When the lentils are cooked, strain them through a sieve over a heatproof bowl, reserving the liquid stock (discard the lentils). Add the jaggery or sugar to the stock and season it with salt, stirring until they dissolve.
2 Heat the oil in a frying pan over a high heat and add the mustard seeds. When they begin to crackle, add the cumin, asafoetida and curry leaves (standing back from the pan as the leaves will splutter!). Fry for a few seconds then add the tamarind and cook for 3–4 minutes until it becomes thick and bubbly. Stir in the ground spices.
3 Pour the stock into the tamarind mixture, bring to the boil and remove from the heat. Serve hot with fresh coriander.

PICTURE CREDITS

FURTHER INFORMATION

Books

Illustrated Foods of India
by K. T. Achaya (Oxford University Press India, 2009)
Royal Life in Manasollasa
by P. Arundhati (Sundeep Prakashan, 1994)
Vegetable Crops
by T. R. Gopalakrishnan (New India, New Delhi, 2007)
Kanvasatapathabrahmanam
*published by the Indira Gandhi National Centre for the
Arts in association with Motilal Banarasidass Publishers
Pvt Ltd.*
Ain-i-Akbari
*by Abu'l-Fazl ibn Mubarak, translated by Heinrich
Blochmann and Henry Sullivan Jarrett (Georgias Press,
2010) or https://archive.org*
Recent Advances in Indo-Pacific Prehistory,
*edited by Virendra N. Misra and Peter Bellwood (Oxford
and IBH Publishing Co., 1985)*
Charaka Samhita
https://archive.org
The Rigveda
*translated by Ralph Griffin (CreateSpace Independent
Publishing Platform, 2015)*

Ingredients

For online spices and ingredients try:
www.seasonedpioneers.com
www.redrickshaw.com

ACKNOWLEDGEMENTS

A big thank you to Kyle Cathie for offering
me this book – it was a project I so wanted
to do! Also to my editor, Vicky Orchard,
for her meticulous and persistent attention
to detail; to Gareth Morgans, for the
scrumptious photography and a jolly laugh
(or many) along with Sunil Vijayakar whose
styling makes the book almost edible! Polly
Webb-Wilson did a marvellous job with
props and Jenny and Rosie were delightful to
work with in the studio.

Thank you also to my children Arrush
and India for being willing 'testers' as I
created countless recipes in my kitchen and
for going with me on all those food trips
around India – may we do many more!!